ORDINARY SAINTS

MCGILL-QUEEN'S STUDIES IN THE HISTORY OF RELIGION
Volumes in this series have been supported by the Jackman Foundation of Toronto.

SERIES ONE: G.A. RAWLYK, EDITOR

1 Small Differences
Irish Catholics and Irish Protestants, 1815–1922
An International Perspective
Donald Harman Akenson

2 Two Worlds
The Protestant Culture of Nineteenth-Century Ontario
William Westfall

3 An Evangelical Mind
Nathanael Burwash and the Methodist Tradition in Canada, 1839–1918
Marguerite Van Die

4 The Dévotes
Women and Church in Seventeenth-Century France
Elizabeth Rapley

5 The Evangelical Century
College and Creed in English Canada from the Great Revival to the Great Depression
Michael Gauvreau

6 The German Peasants' War and Anabaptist Community of Goods
James M. Stayer

7 A World Mission
Canadian Protestantism and the Quest for a New International Order, 1918–1939
Robert Wright

8 Serving the Present Age
Revivalism, Progressivism, and the Methodist Tradition in Canada
Phyllis D. Airhart

9 A Sensitive Independence
Canadian Methodist Women Missionaries in Canada and the Orient, 1881–1925
Rosemary R. Gagan

10 God's Peoples
Covenant and Land in South Africa, Israel, and Ulster
Donald Harman Akenson

11 Creed and Culture
The Place of English-Speaking Catholics in Canadian Society, 1750–1930
Edited by Terrence Murphy and Gerald Stortz

12 Piety and Nationalism
Lay Voluntary Associations and the Creation of an Irish-Catholic Community in Toronto, 1850–1895
Brian P. Clarke

13 Amazing Grace
Studies in Evangelicalism in Australia, Britain, Canada, and the United States
Edited by George Rawlyk and Mark A. Noll

14 Children of Peace
W. John McIntyre

15 A Solitary Pillar
Montreal's Anglican Church and the Quiet Revolution
Joan Marshall

16 Padres in No Man's Land
Canadian Chaplains and the Great War
Duff Crerar

17 Christian Ethics and Political Economy in North America
A Critical Analysis
P. Travis Kroeker

18 Pilgrims in Lotus Land
Conservative Protestantism in British Columbia, 1917–1981
Robert K. Burkinshaw

19 Through Sunshine and Shadow
The Woman's Christian Temperance Union, Evangelicalism, and Reform in Ontario, 1874–1930
Sharon Cook

20 Church, College, and Clergy
A History of Theological Education at Knox College, Toronto, 1844–1994
Brian J. Fraser

21 The Lord's Dominion
The History of Canadian Methodism
Neil Semple

22 A Full-Orbed Christianity
The Protestant Churches and Social Welfare in Canada, 1900–1940
Nancy Christie and Michael Gauvreau

23 Evangelism and Apostasy
The Evolution and Impact of Evangelicals in Modern Mexico
Kurt Bowen

24 The Chignecto Covenanters
A Regional History of Reformed Presbyterianism in New Brunswick and Nova Scotia, 1827– 1905
Eldon Hay

25 Methodists and Women's Education in Ontario, 1836–1925
Johanne Selles

26 Puritanism and Historical Controversy
William Lamont

SERIES TWO IN MEMORY OF GEORGE RAWLYK
DONALD HARMAN AKENSON, EDITOR

1 Marguerite Bourgeoys and Montreal, 1640–1665
Patricia Simpson

2 Aspects of the Canadian Evangelical Experience
Edited by G.A. Rawlyk

3 Infinity, Faith, and Time
Christian Humanism and Renaissance Literature
John Spencer Hill

4 The Contribution of Presbyterianism to the Maritime Provinces of Canada
Edited by Charles H.H. Scobie and G.A. Rawlyk

5 Labour, Love, and Prayer
Female Piety in Ulster Religious Literature, 1850–1914
Andrea Ebel Brozyna

6 The Waning of the Green
Catholics, the Irish, and Identity in Toronto, 1887–1922
Mark G. McGowan

7 Religion and Nationality in Western Ukraine
The Greek Catholic Church and the Ruthenian National Movement in Galicia, 1867–1900
John-Paul Himka

8 Good Citizens
British Missionaries and Imperial States, 1870–1918
James G. Greenlee and Charles M. Johnston

9 The Theology of the Oral Torah
Revealing the Justice of God
Jacob Neusner

10 Gentle Eminence
A Life of Cardinal Flahiff
P. Wallace Platt

11 Culture, Religion, and Demographic Behaviour
Catholics and Lutherans in Alsace, 1750–1870
Kevin McQuillan

12 Between Damnation and Starvation
Priests and Merchants in Newfoundland Politics, 1745–1855
John P. Greene

13 Martin Luther, German Saviour
German Evangelical Theological Factions and the Interpretation of Luther, 1917–1933
James M. Stayer

14 Modernity and the Dilemma of North American Anglican Identities, 1880–1950
William H. Katerberg

15 The Methodist Church on the Prairies, 1896–1914
George Emery

16 Christian Attitudes towards the State of Israel
Paul Charles Merkley

17 A Social History of the Cloister
Daily Life in the Teaching Monasteries of the Old Regime
Elizabeth Rapley

18 Households of Faith
Family, Gender, and Community in Canada, 1760–1969
Edited by Nancy Christie

19 Blood Ground
Colonialism, Missions, and the Contest for Christianity in the Cape Colony and Britain, 1799–1853
Elizabeth Elbourne

20 A History of Canadian Catholics
Gallicanism, Romanism, and Canadianism
Terence J. Fay

21 The View from Rome
Archbishop Stagni's 1915 Reports on the Ontario Bilingual Schools Question
Edited and translated by John Zucchi

22 The Founding Moment
Church, Society, and the Construction of Trinity College
William Westfall

23 The Holocaust, Israel, and Canadian Protestant Churches
Haim Genizi

24 Governing Charities
Church and State in Toronto's Catholic Archdiocese, 1850–1950
Paula Maurutto

25 Anglicans and the Atlantic World
High Churchmen, Evangelicals, and the Quebec Connection
Richard W. Vaudry

26 Evangelicals and the Continental Divide
The Conservative Protestant Subculture in Canada and the United States
Sam Reimer

27 Christians in a Secular World
The Canadian Experience
Kurt Bowen

28 Anatomy of a Seance
A History of Spirit Communication in Central Canada
Stan McMullin

29 With Skilful Hand
The Story of King David
David T. Barnard

30 Faithful Intellect
Samuel S. Nelles and Victoria University
Neil Semple

31 W. Stanford Reid
An Evangelical Calvinist in the Academy
Donald MacLeod

32 A Long Eclipse
The Liberal Protestant Establishment and the Canadian University, 1920–1970
Catherine Gidney

33 Forkhill Protestants and Forkhill Catholics, 1787–1858
Kyla Madden

34 For Canada's Sake
Public Religion, Centennial Celebrations, and the Re-making of Canada in the 1960s
Gary R. Miedema

35 Revival in the City
The Impact of American Evangelists in Canada, 1884–1914
Eric R. Crouse

36 The Lord for the Body
Religion, Medicine, and Protestant Faith Healing in Canada, 1880–1930
James Opp

37 Six Hundred Years of Reform
Bishops and the French Church, 1190–1789
J. Michael Hayden and Malcolm R. Greenshields

38 The Missionary Oblate Sisters
Vision and Mission
Rosa Bruno-Jofré

39 Religion, Family, and Community in Victorian Canada
The Colbys of Carrollcroft
Marguerite Van Die

40 Michael Power
The Struggle to Build the Catholic Church on the Canadian Frontier
Mark G. McGowan

41 The Catholic Origins of Quebec's Quiet Revolution, 1931–1970
Michael Gauvreau

42 Marguerite Bourgeoys and the Congregation of Notre Dame, 1665–1700
Patricia Simpson

43 To Heal a Fractured World
The Ethics of Responsibility
Jonathan Sacks

44 Revivalists
Marketing the Gospel in English Canada, 1884–1957
Kevin Kee

45 The Churches and Social Order in Nineteenth- and Twentieth-Century Canada
Edited by Michael Gauvreau and Ollivier Hubert

46 Political Ecumenism
Catholics, Jews, and Protestants in De Gaulle's Free France, 1940–1945
Geoffrey Adams

47 From Quaker to Upper Canadian
Faith and Community among Yonge Street Friends, 1801–1850
Robynne Rogers Healey

48 The Congrégation de Notre-Dame, Superiors, and the Paradox of Power, 1693–1796
Colleen Gray

49 Canadian Pentecostalism
Transition and Transformation
Edited by Michael Wilkinson

50 A War with a Silver Lining
Canadian Protestant Churches and the South African War, 1899–1902
Gordon L. Heath

51 In the Aftermath of Catastrophe
Founding Judaism, 70 to 640
Jacob Neusner

52 Imagining Holiness
Classic Hasidic Tales in Modern Times
Justin Jaron Lewis

53 Shouting, Embracing, and Dancing with Ecstasy
The Growth of Methodism in Newfoundland, 1774–1874
Calvin Hollett

54 Into Deep Waters
Evangelical Spirituality and Maritime Calvinist Baptist Ministers, 1790–1855
Daniel C. Goodwin

55 Vanguard of the New Age
The Toronto Theosophical Society, 1891–1945
Gillian McCann

56 A Commerce of Taste
Church Architecture in Canada, 1867–1914
Barry Magrill

57 The Big Picture
The Antigonish Movement of Eastern Nova Scotia
Santo Dodaro and Leonard Pluta

58 My Heart's Best Wishes for You
A Biography of Archbishop John Walsh
John P. Comiskey

59 The Covenanters in Canada
Reformed Presbyterianism from 1820 to 2012
Eldon Hay

60 The Guardianship of Best Interests
Institutional Care for the Children of the Poor in Halifax, 1850–1960
Renée N. Lafferty

61 In Defence of the Faith
Joaquim Marques de Araújo, a Comissário in the Age of Inquisitional Decline
James E. Wadsworth

62 Contesting the Moral High Ground
Popular Moralists in Mid-Twentieth-Century Britain
Paul T. Phillips

63 The Catholicisms of Coutances
Varieties of Religion in Early Modern France, 1350–1789
J. Michael Hayden

64 After Evangelicalism
The Sixties and the United Church of Canada
Kevin N. Flatt

65 The Return of Ancestral Gods
Modern Ukrainian Paganism as an Alternative Vision for a Nation
Mariya Lesiv

66 Transatlantic Methodists
British Wesleyanism and the Formation of an Evangelical Culture in Nineteenth-Century Ontario and Quebec
Todd Webb

67 A Church with the Soul of a Nation
Making and Remaking the United Church of Canada
Phyllis D. Airhart

68 Fighting over God
A Legal and Political History of Religious Freedom in Canada
Janet Epp Buckingham

69 From India to Israel
Identity, Immigration, and the Struggle for Religious Equality
Joseph Hodes

70 Becoming Holy in Early Canada
Timothy Pearson

71 The Cistercian Arts
From the 12th to the 21st Century
Edited by Terryl N. Kinder and Roberto Cassanelli

72 The Canny Scot
Archbishop James Morrison of Antigonish
Peter Ludlow

73 Religion and Greater Ireland
Christianity and Irish Global Networks, 1750–1950
Edited by Colin Barr and Hilary M. Carey

74 The Invisible Irish
Finding Protestants in the Nineteenth-Century Migrations to America
Rankin Sherling

75 Beating against the Wind
Popular Opposition to Bishop Feild and Tractarianism in Newfoundland and Labrador, 1844–1876
Calvin Hollett

76 The Body or the Soul?
Religion and Culture in a Quebec Parish, 1736–1901
Frank A. Abbott

77 Saving Germany
North American Protestants and Christian Mission to West Germany, 1945–1974
James C. Enns

78 The Imperial Irish
Canada's Irish Catholics Fight the Great War, 1914–1918
Mark G. McGowan

79 Into Silence and Servitude
How American Girls Became Nuns, 1945–1965
Brian Titley

80 Boundless Dominion
Providence, Politics, and the Early Canadian Presbyterian Worldview
Denis McKim

81 Faithful Encounters
Authorities and American Missionaries in the Ottoman Empire
Emrah Şahin

82 Beyond the Noise of Solemn Assemblies
The Protestant Ethic and the Quest for Social Justice in Canada
Richard Allen

83 Not Quite Us
Anti-Catholic Thought in English Canada since 1900
Kevin P. Anderson

84 Scandal in the Parish
Priests and Parishioners Behaving Badly in Eighteenth-Century France
Karen E. Carter

85 Ordinary Saints
Women, Work, and Faith in Newfoundland
Bonnie Morgan

ORDINARY SAINTS

Women, Work, and Faith in Newfoundland

Bonnie Morgan

McGill-Queen's University Press
Montreal & Kingston • London • Chicago

ISBN 978-0-7735-5890-8 (cloth)
ISBN 978-0-7735-5891-5 (paper)
ISBN 978-0-2280-0027-3 (ePDF)
ISBN 978-0-2280-0028-0 (ePUB)

Legal deposit fourth quarter 2019
Bibliothèque nationale du Québec

Printed in Canada on acid-free paper that is 100% ancient forest free (100% post-consumer recycled), processed chlorine free

This book has been published with the help of a grant from the Canadian Federation for the Humanities and Social Sciences, through the Awards to Scholarly Publications Program, using funds provided by the Social Sciences and Humanities Research Council of Canada.

Funded by the Government of Canada | Financé par le gouvernement du Canada | Canada

Canada Council for the Arts | Conseil des arts du Canada

We acknowledge the support of the Canada Council for the Arts.

Nous remercions le Conseil des arts du Canada de son soutien.

Library and Archives Canada Cataloguing in Publication

Title: Ordinary saints : women, work, and faith in Newfoundland / Bonnie Morgan.

Names: Morgan, Bonnie, 1969- author.

Series: McGill-Queen's studies in the history of religion. Series two ; 85.

Description: Series statement: McGill-Queen's studies in the history of religion. Series two ; 85 | Includes bibliographical references and index.

Identifiers: Canadiana (print) 20190165863 | Canadiana (ebook) 20190165995 | ISBN 9780773558915 (softcover) | ISBN 9780773558908 (hardcover) | ISBN 9780228000273 (PDF) | ISBN 9780228000280 (EPUB)

Subjects: LCSH: Women and religion–Newfoundland and Labrador–History–20th century. | LCSH: Women–Religious life–Newfoundland and Labrador–History–20th century. | LCSH: Work–Religious aspects–Christianity. | LCSH: Christian women–Newfoundland and Labrador–History–20th century.

Classification: LCC BV639.W7 M67 2019 | DDC 270.082/09718–dc23

This book was designed and typeset by Peggy & Co. Design Inc. in 10.5/14 Sabon.

Contents

Tables and Figures

Tables

Figures

Acknowledgments

The successful completion of this work owes much to the support, stories, advice, goodwill, and encouragement of others.

I want to thank all the women who shared their time, knowledge and experience with me as I completed the research that informs this work. Our conversations were a pleasure and the cups of tea delightful! Their kindness and assistance and that of so many others made this work possible. Thank you especially to: Trudy Morgan-Andrews; Doris Bishop; Charles Conway; Dr Linda Cullum, honorary research professor, Memorial University; Aubrey Dawe; Cynthia Dawe; Judy Dawe; Marge Dawe; Larry Dohey, The Rooms; John Griffin, Newfoundland and Labrador Public Libraries; Edna Haines; Enid Haines; Reta Hill; Joan Jefford; Dr Linda Kealey, professor emeritus in history, University of New Brunswick; Dr Lynne Marks, Department of History, University of Victoria; Beulah Morgan; Eileen Morgan; Gordon Morgan; Joyce Morgan; Roy Morgan; Reg Morgan; Dr Sasha Mullally, Department of History, University of New Brunswick; Dr Nancy Nason-Clark, Department of Sociology, University of New Brunswick; Dr William Parenteau, Department of History, University of New Brunswick; Mary Porter; Mildred Porter; Terry Quinlan, Newfoundland and Labrador Statistics Agency; Colleen Reid; Myra Rideout; Prudence Rideout; Calvin Taylor; Barbara Tilley; Sandra Tilley; Dr Diane Tye, Department of Folklore, Memorial University; Edna Warford; Emma Warford; Violet Warford; and Pat Woolgar.

Thank you to the helpful staff at the Memorial University Folklore and Language Archive (MUNFLA) and the Centre for Newfoundland

Studies, Memorial University, as well as staff and clergy of the Parishes of All Saints and St Peter's, Conception Bay South, Diocese of Eastern Newfoundland and Labrador. A special thank you to the members of St Peter's and All Saints Anglican Church Women for permission to access their records.

Thank you to the amazing staff of McGill-Queen's University Press for their exemplary editorial work, advice, and support, especially Kathleen Fraser, Kyla Madden, copyeditor extraordinaire Carolyn Yates, and Dr Don Akenson, series editor of McGill-Queen's Studies in the History of Religion. Thank you to the talented design team for turning a photo from my late aunt's album into an amazing book cover. I acknowledge with gratitude the two anonymous readers of the manuscript.

I gratefully acknowledge funding for my doctoral studies provided by the Social Sciences and Humanities Research Council of Canada (Bombardier CGS grant) and the University of New Brunswick (Hugh John Flemming Maritime Provincial History Award). This support made possible the completion of the original research and writing.

Thank you to my family, Dr Sean Cadigan, associate vice-president (academic), Memorial University, who supported my interest in history and encouraged me to seek publication of the manuscript, as well as our children, Elizabeth Cadigan and Margaret Cadigan. Thank you especially to my mother, Marjorie Morgan, who taught me to worship and to work. I carry her eternal love in my heart and dedicate this book to her.

Preface

Today I remember a garden party. This event in support of St Peter's Anglican Church in Upper Gullies was held each year in the summer months, with games of chance on the church grounds (usually run by men) and a supper put on by women in the little Lodge next door. Coming from an activist church family, I understood how much work was involved in putting on these events. We had been hearing about preparations for weeks from my mother, paternal grandmother, and unmarried aunt, all volunteers with the local Anglican Church Women. My grandmother, somewhat famously, was president of the Seal Cove branch for over thirty years, starting in the 1940s when it was still the Church of England Women's Association (CEWA).

My memories come from the mid-1970s, when I was a little girl and very impressionable. Inside the Lodge, a game of bingo occupied a line of tables which would soon be set out with cloths, cutlery, and desserts – confections much fancier than the ordinary home-baked goodies we were used to, for everyone knew that any food prepared "for the church" would be extra special. I vividly recall going one year into the Lodge kitchen, which was crowded with women. Despite the brisk sea air outside (I do not recall the weather ever being overly warm at a garden party), the kitchen was steamy with tea kettles and dishwater, which had to be heated on the stove. There was a distinctive smell: potato salads, fragrant with diced onion and apple or else beautifully coloured with squares of beetroot or spoonfuls of mustard. This mingled with the odors of Sunlight soap, turkey dressing laced with savoury, and armpits dusted with talcum powder. I recall being asked "are you looking for a job?" and nodding, eager to be part of work I knew was important because I had already learned, at the age of seven or eight, that the church was important. When I set a table or dried dishes under the watchful eye of one of my mother's or grandmother's association friends, I didn't have to be told to be careful. I would be careful because I knew, almost innately, that the work I was doing was for God, the same God I was taught to pray to each night and, as the youngest in the family, before our meals. This was the same God who lived, mysteriously, in the big black family Bible along with snips of our baby hair and pressed flowers taken from long-withered funeral arrangements, wedding bouquets, and graduation corsages. This was the God I believed was with me at all times, who watched over me, and who loved me as he loved the little sparrow that fell.

The women in the Lodge kitchen that day were of different generations, yet they worked together. My mother and her friends, women in their mid-thirties or early forties, were dressed in pretty bib-less tea aprons over blouses and coordinating A-line skirts. The blouses were store-bought, but the skirts were often home-sewed. They had used curling irons on their hair; they wore modest jewels in their ears. My grandmother's generation, in their mid-sixties or early seventies, wore full-coverage aprons over homemade dresses. They were dressed in no-nonsense short sleeves that exposed strong forearms, as well as hair nets and lace-up shoes. Their smiles, directed at me as I ran a damp dishtowel over china plates or fastidiously set knives and forks on the supper table, were beautiful. For me, it seemed that God, through them, was smiling on my work, too.

In the pages that follow you will meet some of the women who worked in that Lodge kitchen over forty years ago, plus many more who worked in other kitchens at other times in support of their church, their families, and each other. You will hear their voices tell a twentieth-century story of lived religion among rural women, especially the ways in which religious belief and practice was linked to household labour. While previous histories of rural women have demonstrated the importance and extent of female labour in support of family economies and communities, this volume explores how that work was linked to the development and expression of women's religious beliefs. The example of Anglican women in Conception Bay shows how Christian practices, and the construction of female theological culture, was informed by the work that women did.

Growing up Anglican in Conception Bay during the 1970s and 1980s helped me to appreciate how complex lived religiosity could be, with official church teachings and liturgy, community activism, folk traditions, and family ritual forming a patchwork of Christian belief, practices, and meaning that informed our understanding of what was divine and our personal relationship with that divinity. I use the term "patchwork" deliberately. As anyone who has put together a myriad assembly of fabric pieces to form a quilt can testify, the work often combines creativity and pleasure with frustration and ingenuity. There are always imperfections despite the underlying goal to create something permanent – something made to last – that would bring physical comfort and aesthetic pleasure to those who used it. The same can be said for the way Conception Bay women conceived of Christianity in the middle decades of the twentieth century as they brought together bits and pieces from their own experiences to understand who or what God was and how best to be in relationship with that God. The Christianity they conceived of, and delivered in their day-to-day words and actions, was understood to be not only eternal in nature but all-encompassing in scope. It informed all aspects of their lives – lives that were largely defined by labour – and was an essential source of comfort and permanency at times of loss or change.

The women in this volume took pieces and transformed them into something whole as a part of their daily work. They made flour, yeast, and water into bread; turned a cow trotter and root vegetables into soup; transformed two contrasting balls of yarn into double-knit mitts; wove children in their bellies; and joined themselves into association. It is not surprising that they likewise constructed their religiosity from a variety of influences. To understand this complexity, and to explore the many different influences on local female theological culture, the research for this volume cast a wide methodological net. I have employed documentary sources, oral history, and material culture in order to "fully appreciate the local, denominational and class-specific forms that religion took."[1] My choice to use a microhistory approach, focused on deep exploration of a particular community, provides "opportunity for a truly bottom-up social history."[2] It also, as recent work on lived religion in a Quebec parish demonstrates, helps us to better understand the relationship between official churches and "the ordinary faithful."[3] There is attention to the "detail and nuance" of women's religious beliefs and practices, which one scholar describes as "the essence of local studies."[4]

Historical evidence of women's religious experience can be found in documents such as private diaries and correspondence, public census and church records, published journals, newspapers, and literary works. The official Diocese of Newfoundland periodical, *Diocesan Magazine*, provided local parish news as well as largely clerical and male perspectives on Anglican theology and practice.[5] It is worth noting that *Diocesan Magazine* lost its gender-neutral title in 1959, and became instead the *Newfoundland Churchman*. This change, seemingly small, is symbolic of the growing understanding among Anglican leadership of the gendered nature of church participation in post-confederation Newfoundland and Labrador. As I explore especially in chapter 10 and discuss in the conclusion, this changed perspective, coupled with a changing local economy, impacted women's theological culture in the 1960s. At a time associated with the second-wave feminist movement in North America and elsewhere, the Anglican women of Conception Bay became, if anything, less liberated within their church communities.

Sources for this study included minute and account books of CEWA branches operating in the Conception Bay communities of Seal Cove, Kelligrews, Foxtrap, and Long Pond, which were vital for hearing the voices of ordinary Anglican women no longer living. I discovered these books in steamer trunks at local church halls, placed there by activist women decades ago and nestled among fabric samples, gavels, Bibles and Books of Common Prayer, framed photographs, and playing cards.[6] Cross-referencing members' names with census records from 1921, 1935, and 1945 helped make real women who otherwise would have been just names in CEWA records, disconnected from the particular familial and material circumstances of their individual lives. Scholars of Newfoundland and Labrador are privileged in the availability of nominal census data for the mid-1900s, which are unusual for many jurisdictions including most of mainland Canada. This data made possible analysis of the religious composition of households and patterns of religious change and experimentation.[7]

Rural women, generally, produce few written records.[8] A focus on domestic practices, coupled with the often-undocumented nature of spirituality, means oral history methodology was centrally important to my research. Twenty-two local Anglican women, identified through

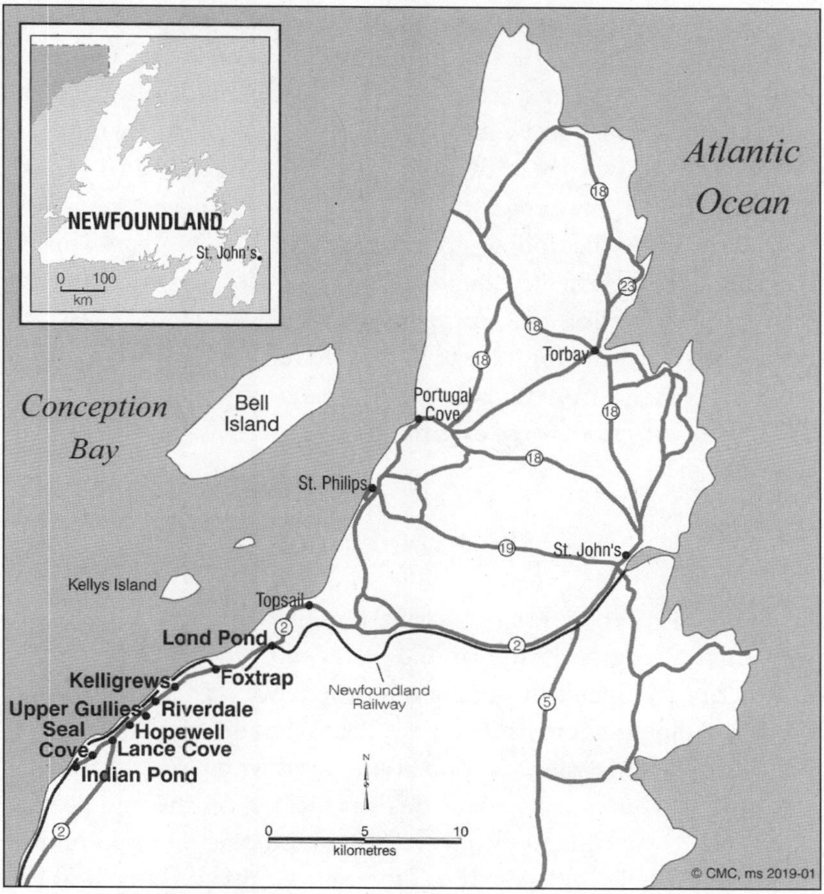

The south side of Conception Bay, showing communities which made up the Anglican Parish of Foxtrap and Hopewell in the mid-twentieth century.

personal contacts and referrals, generously agreed to be interviewed by me about their experience of religion. I feature their voices prominently throughout the work that follows.[9] I found the voices of other Anglicans and residents of Conception Bay South in interviews preserved in Memorial University's Folklore and Language Archive.[10] In addition, I use material culture evidence of Christian belief and practice within the study area to better understand patterns of belief. This includes religious prints and objects in the homes of the women I interviewed, as well as mid-1900s headstone inscriptions in local Anglican cemeteries with special attention to epitaphs selected by, and for, women.

This project benefitted from my connection to the local community, especially the local Anglican community. My relative ease in finding volunteers for interviews, access to CEWA records, and the relaxed and open conversations I had with participants were all partially rooted in my personal knowledge of the study area, its families, and its cultural practices. Readers may notice that many of the people whose voices we hear in the pages that follow share my family name, Morgan. This is a very common name in Newfoundland and Labrador, and in Conception Bay especially. While a few informants were relatives of mine, most were not.[11] Even so, researching close to home calls for special efforts to distinguish the personal from the cultural, to separate my own constructions and impressions from those of participants, especially those personally closest to me.[12]

Scholarly Influences

Since the 1980s, there has been considerable work on the history of women and religion in the United States, with increasing attention to American women's lived religious experience.[13] This is less true in Canada, although there has been excellent work on women's growing gender consciousness and assertion of autonomy within male-dominated institutional churches. Much of this has focused on the middle-class experience.[14] Lynne Marks's work on Salvationism, and the opportunities for official female leaders within nineteenth-century evangelical and Holiness movements, was ground-breaking in its focus on the working-class religious experience.[15] There has been important work on religion, gender, and family life, and, using the Newfoundland example, how women's social status within communities could be enhanced through the interplay of official religion and vernacular spirituality.[16]

In this volume, I consider the religious experiences, beliefs, and practices of Conception Bay women in light of growing literature on religion and feminism, including studies of feminist theology and feminist ritual. As Ann Braude recognizes, women's religious belief or church-based activism should no longer be considered antithetical to the development of feminist consciousness, as historians influenced by personal secular perspectives have sometimes treated it.[17] Historians of women and religion are now considering how "regional and denominational cultures could shape women's propensity to become feminists," suggesting that "carefully calibrated local studies that look deeply into regional variations" are one of the better means to explore this topic.[18]

Studies of women's church-based and Christian organizations have considered how women used prescribed gender expectations and domestic roles (such as "pious mother") as a respectable conduit into public political roles, especially within moral and social reform movements.[19] Canadian histories of women and religion have especially highlighted the place of Christian-inspired activism in nineteenth-century women's growing gender awareness and feminist consciousness.[20] In addition, rural women engaged in the family labour system could express "feminist consciousness" through gender relations (especially resistance to patriarchal authority within families and communities), mutuality, and the negotiation of gender divisions, rather than through formal activism.[21] Just as Anglican women of Conception Bay lived religion, they also lived feminism, and showed a commitment to women's rights and equality expressed in ordinary lives rather than in formal political declaration or organized activism.

Increasingly, scholars consider women's religious lives outside institutions, including questions of women's religious authority and how women expressed religiosity in their daily domestic lives.[22] This has influenced the work which follows, as has scholarship on female theological cultures which explores how women both "create" and "inherit" belief systems and practices. The latter especially has demonstrated how religious doctrine was not something passively received by women but was "constantly reinterpreted ... and invested with new meanings" in keeping with the gendered experiences of particular places, times, and identities.[23]

Many historians of Christianity are shifting their attention away from clerical elites and broad institutional trends to look at religion "from the bottom up," focusing on the experience of "ordinary" believers.[24] Studies of lived religion consider how identity shapes the practice of religion and the often-complex relationship between popular religious beliefs and practices and the doctrine, dogma, and discipline of the official churches. In the United States, Robert Orsi is a leading voice on lived religion; in Canada, Lynne Marks was one of the earliest proponents of what is becoming an increasingly important approach to the study of religion.[25]

By highlighting the relationship between religion, class, and labour, as well as the influence of gender, ethnicity, and socioeconomic setting on religious experience, Orsi's approach to lived religion deeply inspired my work on Conception Bay Anglicans. He considers the place of religion in people's daily lives, embraces the personal, and "pays close attention to the ways that social location and material setting have shaped the religious lives of individuals and communities."[26] Especially influential is his expansion of the concept of social relations to include relations that historical agents believe that they have with spiritual or divine figures, and how a sense of sacred presence impacts social relations, material decisions, and actions.[27]

Given the diversity of lived religious belief and practice among the women of Conception Bay, in this volume I draw on a variety of literatures related to embodied religious practice, material Christianity, and visual and sensory piety.[28] I likewise draw on insights from feminist theology, which "takes seriously the idea that women *as* women – whether as a result of biology or gendered experience – have distinctive insights into the divine to contribute to thinking about God and God's relation to the world."[29] By treating popular devotions within traditions as liturgy, and understanding ordinary women's thinking about the divine and their relationship with the sacred as theology, this volume joins recent efforts to break down binaries of sacred/profane, spiritual/material, and official/popular within the study of religion and to recognize the "fluidity of spirituality."[30] As Sarah Williams states in her work on British working-class religion, "Belief is a dynamic process which draws on folklore, superstition, formal belief and occasional or conditional conformity to institutions. The secular/popular and spiritual/official languages of belief were not mutually exclusive but inextricable parts of a web of broader cultural meaning."[31] In order to recover the complexity of ordinary people's religious lives, I likewise trace the circle wide when considering Conception Bay women's Christianity.

Roadmap for Reading

There are ten chapters in this volume, organized to establish context and to demonstrate change over time. In chapter 1, I provide background on women's work in rural Newfoundland households, the mid-twentieth-century transition from a family- to a wage-based economy within the parish of Foxtrap and Hopewell, and, in terms of population, the largely Anglican character of the south shore of Conception Bay. I discuss developments in institutional Anglicanism within the Diocese of Newfoundland, especially in relation to official understandings of women's roles within the church and home. I also explain the CEWA's origins, organization, and rituals.

The next chapters focus on domestic religion, including the dynamic of gender relations within households expressed through women's recollection of gendered participation in family devotions and rituals. In chapter 2, I explore everyday religion, including family and personal prayer, visual practice, Bible reading, and hymn singing. In chapter 3, I consider the observance of Christian holy days, especially Sundays and the season of Lent. I discuss food-based ritual and rest from labour (a key aspect of holy day observance) and compare official Anglican discourse with popular practices.

While household ritual reveals a mix of women's and men's religious authority, the perceived influence of women's spirituality on Conception Bay families is clearest at times of religious change and disruption. In chapter 4, I explore the way women's religious identities informed those of other family members and how women's acts of conversion and religious experimentation could both disturb and preserve households. Newfoundland is often associated with sectarianism, and I include discussion of Anglican discourse and action in relation to other Christian traditions, including how gender roles and expectations helped to shape those responses.

In chapters 5, 6, and 7, I explore the religious beliefs and practices that women developed and expressed through the work they performed in relation to the cycles of birth and death, especially in the decades before professional medical and mortuary services became pervasive within rural Conception Bay. In chapter 5, I consider rituals around childbirth, including popular practices that accompanied participation in the official Anglican rites of baptism and churching. I discuss the special spiritual status and personal religious experiences that accompanied women's work as midwives. In chapter 6, I focus on death rituals, including practices around dressing the dead, wakes, and funerals. I consider women-led public ritual at wakes in light of women's theological cultures and their expression of spiritual authority. In chapter 7, I employ written CEWA records as well as evidence from headstones in local Anglican cemeteries to investigate gendered aspects of Christian consolation, including how activist women cared for each other at times of bereavement, women's conception of eternity, and the place of domesticated heaven ideology in local theological culture.

In chapters 8, 9, and 10, I focus on three specific examples of women's household labour (caring for the sick, textile production, and food preparation) and how women practised their Christianity through that work, both at home and within the community. I demonstrate how women sanctified and transformed ordinary household tasks into public expressions of faithfulness through CEWA participation. I explore women's resistance to clerical authority and how women used their CEWA work to support each other materially and spiritually, in contrast to the growing belief among clergy and other church leaders that their household skills, especially food preparation and service, best expressed Christianity when they were used to financially support the church.

Women's traditional role in caring for the sick and the relationship to Christian cultures of suffering are my focus in chapter 8. Women's caregiving within families extended to caregiving in community, expressed through acts of benevolent mutuality and mercy informed by both Christian belief and resistance to patriarchal authority. In chapter 9, I consider textile production as a devotional sensory practice when performed in a Christian context. As with caregiving, women transformed the meaning of textile work through their Christian beliefs, which also sometimes brought them into direct conflict with official Anglican doctrine and authority.

In chapter 10, I explore women's use of food production and service as a means to express faithfulness, and how this practice was affected by the changing gender expectations of the 1950s and 1960s. Women's household work changed as the family-based economy transformed into a wage-based economy in post-confederation Newfoundland. The close ties between women's work and religious expression meant female theological culture changed, too. The 1960s saw the Diocese of Newfoundland's decision to dissolve the CEWA, with its culture of women's autonomy and resistance, and replace it with the Anglican Church Woman's Association, later the Anglican Church Women. I conclude this volume with a reflection on post-1970 female theological culture, the CEWA's lasting legacy, and the continuing relationship between work and Christian practice for the Anglican women of Conception Bay.

ORDINARY SAINTS

CHAPTER ONE

"They Worked Harder Than the Men": The Context of Anglican Women's Lives in Mid-1900s Conception Bay

The women whose religious beliefs and practices are at the heart of this volume lived and worked in the settlements which made up the Anglican parish of Foxtrap and Hopewell, in the Diocese of Newfoundland, in the middle decades of the twentieth century.[1] The parish, located on the island's Avalon Peninsula, was made up of coastal communities which stretched along the south side of Conception Bay. The easternmost settlement in the parish, Long Pond, was approximately twenty-five kilometres west of the Newfoundland capital, St John's; the westernmost settlement, Indian Pond, was a further twenty kilometres away. During the mid-1900s, there were numerous small settlements within the parish, and several of these later merged into larger communities. Indian Pond combined with Seal Cove; Lance Cove and Hopewell united with Upper Gullies; Lower Gullies, Riverdale, and Middle Bight became Kelligrews neighbourhoods; and Greeleytown and Peachytown joined with Foxtrap. In 1971, most of the communities in the parish of Foxtrap and Hopewell joined with Manuels, Chamberlains, and Topsail to form the new municipality of Conception Bay South. Residents of Foxtrap and Seal Cove initially rejected amalgamation, only joining Conception Bay South in 1986.[2]

Like much of the rest of Newfoundland, the communities of what would become Conception Bay South felt the effects of the long economic depression that stretched from the 1894 bank crash until the Second World War. By the 1930s, Newfoundlanders also faced political upheaval associated with suspension of responsible government and the imposition of a British Commission of Government in 1934. Tensions

Table 1.1 Study area population by census year and community, 1921–45

Community	*1921*	*1935*	*1945*
Foxtrap	271	382	378
Greeleytown	98	114	146
Hopewell	110	102	92
Indian Pond	91	91	82
Kelligrews	294	346	462
Lance Cove	33	32	27
Long Pond	632	615	852
Middle Bight	260	256	282
Peachytown	97	100	126
Riverdale	134	148	69
Seal Cove	148	152	211
Upper Gullies	171	158	254
TOTAL	2,339	2,496	2,981

associated with economic hardship could be seen in St John's, where unemployed persons rioted at the Colonial Building in 1932, and in outlying areas such as Battle Harbour, Labrador, where hungry inhabitants broke the law to stave off starvation.[3] Official fear of civil unrest was widespread. Arch Morgan of Seal Cove recalled being offered relief road work at Holyrood in 1932, although warned by a Department of Highways superintendent that "you might get an hour, you might get all day, but there's nothing only riots and strife and if you loses that job well don't blame me for it."[4] In agricultural south side of Conception Bay, Clarence Morgan recalled that people were not as badly off during the depression years as they were in other parts of Newfoundland. "There was nothing in the stores," Clarence remembered, but since most families grew vegetables, kept hens, and had a cow for milk, few went hungry. Being relatively close to the capital helped: he described how people, if necessary, "could go to St John's with a load of birch brooms and sell 'em to get a barrel of flour."[5] Other political changes came in the twentieth century. Newfoundland women won recognition of the right to vote in 1925 after a long campaign headed by middle- and upper-class women of St John's. In 1949, after a sometimes-bitter campaign, Newfoundlanders voted to enter the confederation and became Canada's tenth province.[6]

Figure 1.1 The agricultural landscape of Conception Bay south in the 1950s, with gardens and pastures laid out against a backdrop of the northern Atlantic Ocean, shows the determination of local families to survive in the face of declining nineteenth-century fish stocks.

Long Pond was the largest settlement within the parish of Foxtrap and Hopewell. In 1921, 632 persons lived there; the population dipped to 615 in 1935, and grew significantly to 852 by 1945. The smallest settlement, Lance Cove, had a population that hovered around thirty through each of these census years. Table 1.1 summarizes the population figures for the twelve communities that made up the parish geographically, showing a general trend of increasing population over time.[7] While Riverdale numbers indicate a significant population drop between 1935 and 1945, this may reflect changed boundaries rather than loss of residents.

In the early twentieth century, most families on the south shore of Conception Bay made their living through a combination of agricultural activities, growing vegetables, stock raising, dairying, and butchering, with some men engaged in trades such as carpentry and blacksmithing.[8] Farming had expanded considerably during the late nineteenth century, with dramatic increases in land under cultivation, animal husbandry (especially cattle and fowl), and crop production. Though it was a coastal area, declining fish stocks in Conception Bay meant that the people "increasingly turned away from the sea and toward the land to secure a livelihood," despite the "considerable effort" it took for families "to transform scrubby barrens into agricultural land."[9]

The resulting pastoral landscape, combined with ready access to sweeping pebbled beaches, made the area between Upper Gullies and Kelligrews an attractive destination for excursions, with residents recalling the special train that ran out from St John's on Sunday afternoon between mid-June and late August in the early 1900s.[10] While agriculture continued to be important through the 1950s, 1945 census data hint at transition to a more wage-based economy.[11] In that year, 37 per cent of households (301 of 817) named farming and stock raising, or farm labour, as the primary source of income, the highest proportion of all "gainful employment" in the area. Yet increasing numbers of families were supported by wage income, including 19.5 per cent supported by nonagricultural labour (160 of 817). It is likely many of these labourers were younger sons from agricultural households, for whom land was not available or who had voluntarily chosen the alternative of wage income.[12]

Wage earning was made easier by changes in transportation technology and infrastructure. The Commission of Government used road-building as a primary source of relief work. By 1945, only six blacksmiths remained active between Indian Pond and Long Pond, compared to seventeen mechanics, seventeen bus drivers, and eighty truck drivers. The transition from traditional to mechanized transportation was a source of humour for some residents and pathos for others. Clarence recalled laughingly of the 1940s how Americans from the base in Argentia were unable to clear snow from the Conception Bay highway "with all their machinery" while he travelled easily into St John's "every day" to deliver meat with a horse and slide.[13] In contrast, Ron Walsh of Kelligrews recalled witnessing a different intersection of old and new:

> One evening this farmer was passing down our house with a tray car and a load of potatoes, coming from his farm and he was walking behind his tray car and a motor car came down and ran right square into the back of him. He killed the man and drove the horse down in the drain the horse broke his neck. There was potatoes and everything strew over the road and I think that was the most pitiful sight I have ever seen.[14]

Despite such accidents, through the 1950s demand for private automobiles increased. Arch Morgan started a business refurbishing and selling used cars from his barn in the mid-1940s, and expanded to open a garage and gas bar by 1949. His son, Reginald, began to operate a used car lot at Seal Cove in 1964 and catered to the local need for automobiles as commuting to St John's and elsewhere for wage work increased.[15]

More changes came to the south side of Conception Bay after the Second World War, especially with construction of the American Naval base in Argentia.[16] Clarence Morgan described "around fifty butchers on the shore between Seal Cove and Long Pond bringing meat into St John's to sell" in the 1930s, with agricultural activity likewise reflected in his comment that "everyone" produced their own vegetables, milk and cream, eggs, ducks, and hens. "Even the poorest old widow on the Southern Shore," he mused, "had five or six heads of cattle." Clarence stated that up to the 1940s any Conception Bay family with land, cattle, and goats was considered well-off while anyone who worked for wages "under a master" was looked down upon and pitied. This changed "after the war," he said, when men who got work on the base in Argentia gave up farming and fishing and could not get back to it after the "ready money" of wage employment.[17] Selina Dawe Porter of Long Pond (born 1898) likewise recalled how during her childhood most men fished and farmed and sold what vegetables they did not need for household use.[18] After confederation with Canada in 1949, Selina noted, there was more variety in the work available, but "under responsible government" families had to do what they could to make a living. She listed fishing, farming, berry picking, hay making, spinning, knitting, and hooking mats as ways to make some cash, especially when families brought these items into St John's to sell.[19]

Despite regretting the change to a "modern" wage-based economy, Clarence recalled hard times before the Second World War, especially after 1931 "when the fishery failed" and some families "on the shore," while able to survive on eggs, milk, and vegetables produced in the household, were nevertheless desperate for money. He described relief work provided by the Commission of Government in the 1930s, especially "work on highroads" where men "with their horses and box cars" would be hired to haul loads of rock to a mechanical crusher that prepared materials for road construction. While the system was organized to provide men with two-week "turns" at this work, making twenty-five cents for a ten-hour day, concerns about fair distribution of this relief led to a women-led riot. Clarence described how "a hundred women" stopped a government-owned Highways truck on the Conception Bay highway near Cluney's Road in Kelligrews and demanded that their husbands get equal access to road work. Together, the women tipped the single-axle dump truck loaded with rock into a ditch, determined to secure their families' welfare.[20] Fifty years before, women also played a leading role in the famous Battle of Foxtrap, when local residents protested against railway construction by stopping a surveying team from working in the area in 1880.[21] Called by some a "noisy mob," this protest included women, their "aprons filled with stones,"[22] who were determined to make a stand:

> A crowd of over 500 irate residents (mostly women) armed with pitchforks, splitting knives, and rocks refused to let the surveyors pass. Indeed, at least some of those in the crowd made plain that if the surveyors pushed on with their work, the consequences might be dire. As the *Morning Chronicle* later reported, one woman, "arms bared and hair streaming behind her," vowed to "let daylight into the stomach of the invaders" should they persist.[23]

For the most part, the *Chronicle*'s coverage of Conception Bay women's activism in this instance was patronizing and used language like "native Amazonian troops" and twittering suggestions to form an "order of the broomstick" to downplay women's interest in protecting the land on which their labour and livelihood depended.[24]

Women and the Family Economy

Like others in rural North America, Conception Bay women contributed to the family household economy with various "indoor" and "outdoor" labour: gardening, animal husbandry, berry picking, cooking and serving, textile production, child care, laundry, and housekeeping. Women were responsible for clothing their families. In many parts of Newfoundland, they participated in the fishery through the "shore work" of cleaning and curing salt fish, which led to women's enhanced social status, especially in more well-to-do, property-owning households.[25] On the south side of Conception Bay, women were especially active in agricultural work. At the end of April 1942, members of the Long Pond Church of England Women's Association (CEWA) planned their closing meeting as "the busy times were drawing near." Similarly, members of Seal Cove

Figure 1.2. and Figure 1.3 Both men and women participated in agricultural work as part of the family economy of mid-1900s Conception Bay. In figure 1.2, Pearl and Jim Rideout of Long Pond erect a post and rail fence on their property in the early 1940s. In figure 1.3, Pearl and Jim, along with his brothers and sisters-in-law, work in a shared family garden circa 1945.

Figures 1.4, 1.5, and 1.6 Women's work in rural Conception Bay was extensive and varied, including housekeeping and laundry, animal husbandry and gardening, and food production and childcare. Examples from the experience of Phoebe (Dawe) Morgan of Seal Cove, an activist Anglican as well as shopkeeper, include laundry work in the 1930s and cutting seed potato in the 1950s.

branch closed their meetings in early May 1934 with the "sincere hope we will all meet again God willing ... after the busy summer is past."[26] In May 1960, farm-minded Foxtrap branch president Lily Batten wished members "lots of sunshine and the right amount of rain" as they closed for summer recess.[27]

Selina Porter of Long Pond (born 1897) noted that women's household work at mid-century was all-encompassing.[28] She described how "the mother was the cook, doctor, and farmer, all in one," and that women were responsible for "keeping the farms going" when men were away working, on top of "raising the family besides."[29] Arch Morgan described of his childhood women "catching sheep, tearing the ... wool off them and spinning, day and night. That's all you could see was the spinning wheel." He went on to describe his view on women's contributions to the household economy: "They worked … harder than the men. If they didn't work harder they certainly put in more hours. The men punched in plenty hours in fishing time but I think the women punched in more because the women had all the work to do: the hay to make, the fish to make, the children to raise, the washing and the cutting up wood. They done it all … I'd say the women done it all."[30] Of his own family, Arch recalled, "my wife she was good, she was a good partner," referring to long-time CEWA activist Phoebe (Dawe) Morgan.[31]

Elizabeth (Batten) Petten, born 1908 in Foxtrap, described family life during her childhood as "all work, work, work." Elizabeth recalled how she attended the Church of England's Greeleytown School up until the age of ten but had to leave in order to participate in family agriculture. She described how "setting out the gardens" in the spring and "taking up the vegetables" in the fall meant her generation "missed out" on formal educational opportunities. "[You] couldn't make good grades if you were out of school so much," Elizabeth observed, adding that many people she knew would "teach themselves" after leaving school by reading books and writing letters.[32] Berry picking affected children's access to education. "When we were small," Rachel (Batten) Fagan of Foxtrap recollected in 1973, "we'd never get to school in September. We'd spend all that month goin' in on the barrens with the horse and long cart with me father to pick blueberries. We'd spend all day in there and get home at dark." They sold these berries in St John's, to stores on the shore, or, once car traffic increased on the Conception Bay highway, by "stand[ing] on the side of the road." Sarah (Batten) Bussey, also of Foxtrap, similarly remembered that as a child "we usually got to school by the first of October."[33]

Elizabeth (Batten) Petten noted that there was better access to education after confederation, although, like, the rest of Newfoundland and Labrador, the denominational education system operated until 1997.[34] She described a connection between religion and education which was not just sectarian and institutional, in that children of different traditions went to different schools, but in the everyday religious practices that were part of the day. Classes started with morning prayers and hymn singing, grace was sung before and after lunch, and the day ended with evening prayer. This was "really nice," Elizabeth recalled, going on to express her sense of religious declension in schools by adding, "none of that now."[35] Morning prayer was described by teacher Deborah (Emberley) Eddy, who taught at the Church of England school in Upper Gullies in the mid-1900s. For Deborah, this ritual was just as important for her spirituality as it was for the children's religious instruction.[36] In 1954 the first regional high school in Newfoundland, named for Queen Elizabeth, was opened at Foxtrap to serve students living in Conception Bay South, a project made possible by government education funding but also by the "free labour" residents offered in support of the increased educational opportunities the school would create for families.[37] After 1963, post-secondary education became available in the area when a vocational training school opened at Seal Cove.[38]

In terms of religious tradition, the population of the south side of Conception Bay was predominantly Anglican in the mid-1900s. In 1921, 80 per cent (2,556 of 3,206) of the people who lived between Indian Pond and Topsail identified as Anglican. This dropped slightly to 78 per cent (2,666 of 3,450) in 1935 and to 77 per cent (3,124 of 4,055) in 1945.[39] Within parish boundaries, Anglicans made up 83 per cent (2,483 of 2,981) of the total population in 1945. While the population in communities such as Foxtrap, Greeleytown, Hopewell, Indian Pond, Middle Bight, Peachytown, and Upper Gullies were over 90 per cent Anglican, Long Pond and Seal Cove were somewhat diversified in terms of Christian tradition, with significant Roman Catholic populations in Kelligrews and Riverdale.[40] Distribution of population by tradition is summarized in table 1.2.[41] In Long Pond, with a mix of Roman Catholic, Methodist, United, and Salvationist households, Anglicans still made up three-quarters of the population in 1945. They were a minority in Riverdale only, yet still made up 39 per cent of the population. As census data indicate, the Holiness movement was especially successful in Long Pond and Seal Cove, and won enough converts from Anglicanism to warrant the construction of a Salvation Army citadel (Long Pond) and a Pentecostal mission (Seal Cove). As an example of women's Christian leadership, the 1945 census listed "religious workers" Myrtle Hayden (age twenty-three) and Myrtle Sheppard (age twenty-two) among the Seal Cove population.

Some local Anglicans participated in the Loyal Orange Association, which had active Lodges at Foxtrap, Kelligrews, and Upper Gullies. Both men and women could be members of the Orange Order; Joan (Petten) Jefford of Kelligrews remembered that her father Henry belonged to the men's Loyal Orange Association, while her mother Jessie belonged to the women's Loyal Orange Benevolent Association. Orange parades,

Table 1.2 Study area population by religious tradition, 1945

Community	*CofE*	*RC*	*Meth/UC*	*SA*	*Pent*	*Other*	*Total*
Foxtrap	375		2		1		378
Greeleytown	141		1	4			146
Hopewell	84		1		7		92
Indian Pond	82						82
Kelligrews	311	147	3	1			462
Lance Cove	18		7		2		27
Long Pond	644	63	21	119	2	3	852
Middle Bight	275		2	5			282
Peachytown	121			5			126
Riverdale	27	40	2				69
Seal Cove	172	4	2		24	9	211
Upper Gullies	233	15		1		5	254
TOTAL	2,483	269	41	135	36	17	2,981

Key: CofE = Anglican/Church of England, RC = Roman Catholic, Meth/UC = Methodist or United Church, SA = Salvation Army, Pent = Pentecostal.

especially the annual St George's Day Parade at Foxtrap, were a regular part of community life in the mid-1900s. Work on the Orange Order in Newfoundland and Labrador suggests that this group was less sectarian and more "social, fraternal, patronage and recreational" in character, as was seen in other Canadian jurisdictions.[42] While an exploration of the nature of Orangeism and its influence on relations between Anglicans and Roman Catholics is beyond the scope of this volume, evidence suggests there is a need to better understand the dynamics of this organization at the local level, including its ties to assertion of ethnic identity.[43]

Up until 1977, when the separate parishes of All Saints (Foxtrap) and St Peter's (Upper Gullies) were formed, all local Anglicans were members of the parish of Foxtrap and Hopewell. This large parish was served by one rector and two church buildings, one each in Upper Gullies and Foxtrap. There were Church of England schools in other parish communities, such as St Andrew's schoolhouse in Seal Cove, St Alban's in Kelligrews, All Saints in Greeleytown, and St George's in Long Pond. Services were occasionally offered in these buildings, especially during Lent. In all of these schools, one room was preserved for the local CEWA branch and was where the women held their weekly meetings, as well as where they stored their written records, gavel and ballot box, materials, and finished goods, often in a steamer trunk. The room was also fitted out with table and chairs, a cupboard for dishes and kettle, as well as a wood-burning or oil stove for heat and making tea.

The history of Anglicanism in Newfoundland and Labrador has explored the relationship between high and low Anglicanism, sometimes described as the difference between Tractarianism and evangelical Anglicanism. Calvin Hollett identifies how the lived religious practices of ordinary Anglicans in the nineteenth century displayed resistance to official efforts, mostly associated with Bishop Edward Field, to make the Newfoundland church more "high church" in orientation. As was the case in other parishes, the church buildings at Foxtrap and Hopewell (especially) display characteristics of gothic high church architecture.[44] Yet, as I describe in this volume, women's resistance to clerical authority, personal prayer practices, emphasis on the Bible and preaching, and expression of emotional connection with the figure of Jesus suggest a lived religion within the parish closer to evangelicalism than Tractarianism.

Anglican Women in Association

The first Anglican women's association in Long Pond was a sewing class established in March 1905. Sewing classes were likewise operating at Seal Cove, Hopewell, and Kelligrews by the last decade of the nineteenth century.[45] This group was organized top-down by the parish rector, the Reverend Edward K. Caldwell, and the rector's wife, Emily Caldwell, who was also the founding president.[46] Fifteen women turned out for the first meeting, and while thirteen promised to join, initially only nine became members. This number increased steadily over the following months, especially when the group decided to change their Thursday meeting time from 4:00 p.m. to 6:30 p.m., a more practical time for women who had to get family supper on the table.[47] Some women may have needed time to save up the required twenty-cent entrance fee. Within a few years, there were forty members in the Long Pond Sewing Class. During the first winter of communal sewing, women produced aprons, pinafores, overalls, handkerchiefs, and blouses – practical items designed to be sold to members of the class for personal and household use. Decorative "fancy work" was rare, first mentioned when school teacher and single woman Naomi Andrews suggested "we should buy some pound velvet and sateen to make cushions for sale."[48] Several months later, "two doilies" were "brought in finished" by members, but otherwise the women made functional items destined for use in the course of daily labour in each other's households.[49]

The Long Pond Sewing Class became a branch of the CEWA in 1917.[50] The CEWA was a Diocese of Newfoundland–wide women's organization, the founding of which is credited to the Reverend George Gardner, who in 1876 developed its name, structure, and rules during his work in the Mission of Heart's Content, Trinity Bay.[51] In April 1917, Enid Colley, president of the Kelligrews CEWA branch and wife of then-rector the Reverend Canon Edward Colley, visited Long Pond with two members of her executive, Matilda and Susan Butler. Enid "spoke at some length on the work of the association in every part of Newfoundland and impressed upon those present the honours and importance of belonging to an Association of this kind which was doing such good work." After she "read and carefully explained" the CEWA rules, the women of Long Pond "expressed their willingness to [join] … [and] were duly received and initiated by the three officers present."[52] Showing a sense of continuity between the former Long Pond Sewing Class and the CEWA, a May 1917 discussion "as to future work" ended with the women settling on "a little sewing" and making a decision to transfer funds and "scrap material left over from the Sewing Class" to the new organization.[53]

The CEWA was different from the sewing class in the formalized Christian ritual that women used to open and close meetings as well as to initiate new members, or "sisters" as they were known, upon joining.[54] In the fall of 1937, Lillian Greenslade sat at her kitchen table and copied rules and rituals associated with the CEWA onto the first fifteen pages of a new minute book.[55] Lillian was the second vice president of the Long Pond branch when she wrote out the prayers and scriptures to be read at weekly meetings, but religiously her past included conversion from Anglicanism to follow an evangelical "gospel preacher" who had conducted meetings at Long Pond twenty years before. In 1921, while census takers identified her husband Matthew as "Church of England," they listed Lillian as a member of the new religion, as they did her children.[56] Back in the Anglican fold by the time census takers revisited Long Pond in 1935, Lillian's past demonstrated that she was a spiritual seeker who craved fulfillment and meaning within her religious life.

For her, transcribing association ritual, including passages of scripture, would not have been a simple clerical task but an encounter with what she believed to be God's word and an exploration of the relationship she understood to exist between herself, as a woman and CEWA member, and the divine.

The "worthy president," a woman the sisters elected annually, was responsible for leading CEWA ritual, as well as for providing leadership on other association activities. Women opened meetings by praying to "our Blessed Master" who "has spared us to meet once again," singing the hymn "Soldiers of Christ Arise," and jointly reciting the Lord's Prayer. After a prayer of supplication to ask for divine blessing on "thy Church" and the "work of this association to the good of thy church," an officer read a scripture passage aloud, and the worthy president would declare: "Sisters, having sought gods [*sic*] blessing in Prayer and the reading of his Word, our class being met together in Faith, Hope and Charity ... I do declare this meeting ... duly opened." The closing ritual was briefer and started with the words "Dear Sisters, let us postpone our Christian Work for a short time, hoping soon to meet again and by gods help to renew the same." The women then prayed for the parish, including a request "that we may all be knit together in the bond of Christian Care," and for the CEWA: "Almighty god, we humbly beseech thee to bless the work of our Association and to further with thy continual help us who labour in it. In thy fear and to thy glory grant us lowliness of spirit, steadfastness of faith, perseverance in all good works and bring us at last to thy heavenly kingdom through Jesus Christ our Lord. (Amen)."

The worthy president read the same passage of scripture each week to open meetings: Acts 9: 36–42, which tells the story of Tabitha (or Dorcas), a woman "full of good works and alms deeds" which she demonstrated through making "coats and garments." Stories about women of the Bible helped to shape activist church women's understanding of God's relationship with, and expectations of, female Christians.[57] The Biblical role model of Tabitha was crucial to CEWA members' understanding of their place within the Christian universe. Her death and resurrection from the dead by the miraculous intervention of Christ's apostle Peter, which took place after "all the widows" showed Peter clothing that Tabitha had "made while she was with them," informed the CEWA view that benevolent textile-making was pleasing to the almighty and, as such, sewing could be elevated from a matter of household labour (as it was for most rural working women) into a means of Christian salvation.

The CEWA initiation ritual reinforced this understanding. Participation in this ceremony was extended only to women who had been approved for membership by current CEWA members, a process that started when they were nominated by a current member and "balloted in" (or out) using special buttons kept for that purpose. Association women were given two buttons, black and white, which they cast to approve or disapprove of a potential new member. Mary (Petten) Porter of Kelligrews described the process, as well as how new members were immediately turned to apprenticeship in textile work:

> You had to have two buttons, a black one and a white one … to ballot you in. The white one balloted you in and the black one said no … [Once we were] joined … the ladies you know greet us in and they come along with the needles … and the wool where we could knit squares … [T]he ladies used to cut out the aprons and make them on the sewing machine, then we sew on … the trim that would go around the tail of the apron.[58]

According to Mary, a majority of white buttons meant approval, even if some black buttons were cast against a candidate. She called the initiation ceremony that followed "beautiful," and described how "you had to go up and stand in front of the desk and they read out the questions and if you are going to be faithful and honour and do this of free will."

The formal initiation ritual, as Lillian Greenslade recorded it, started when an assistant announced that "there is a friend outside who wishes to become a member" and the president directed two sisters to "go and see if the friend outside is a true one and has an earnest wish to join us to do good." Once she joined them, members read the CEWA rules and shared the secret password, and the candidate "[took] the obligation": "I _______ do promise that I will continue a faithful member of the Church, that I will endeavour to promote to the best of my power the objects of this Association, that I will obey its rules and never tell the password to anyone not a member." The women next sang "O Praise Our God Today" and one of the association officers read aloud Matthew 25: 31–46, a different Bible lesson than that used at regular weekly meetings. This passage contains the story of Christ's instruction to his followers of any gender to feed the hungry, give drink to the thirsty, clothe the naked, and visit the sick or imprisoned, concluding that "inasmuch as ye have done it unto one of the least of these my brethren, ye have done it unto me." The "righteous" who chose to serve others in this way would enjoy "life eternal," the scripture writer promised, while "ye cursed" who did not "shall go away into everlasting punishment."

Beyond the threat of eternal damnation for the disobedient, several aspects of this initiation ritual illustrate the connections between women's household production and Christian belief and practice. First, the secret CEWA password women shared at the ceremony was "Tabitha," a constant reminder of the Biblical role model whose story of sanctifying textile work members heard each week.[59] Mary described how her association sponsor told her about the password: "Rachael said now Mary you know what you got to say when you go to the door ... I said Rachael do I say breakfast and she said no, Tabitta [*sic*]. All saying the one thing: Let no one know." In addition, the "objects" of the association to which the women referred were "to further the cause of Christian unity and fellowship and promote the spiritual and temporal welfare of its members." Anglican Church leaders conceived of the CEWA primarily as a benevolent women's voluntary organization, distinguishable from "ladies' aids" dedicated to fundraising for church purposes and missionary societies.[60] The practice of benevolence in rural settings, where "women living on farms and in villages readily observed the illness and want of their neighbours" and worked to benefit each other, was distinct from that in urban centres, where middle- and upper-class women directed charitable work at "the other," usually "the lower order" or working classes.[61] Such relief associations were commonly named Dorcas societies by the bourgeois women and church leaders who established them.[62] Christ's call to do "unto the least of these" motivated some activist women to engage in social reform work. For middle-class, urban women, the Biblical instruction to feed, clothe, and care for others became a way to use socially prescribed women's work to move from the private to public sphere of influence while retaining their Christian respectability. In Conception Bay, as in other rural settings, women understood this call to serve others (and to emulate Dorcas/Tabitha) in terms of mutual aid. At Long Pond, women chiefly expressed mutuality by providing each other with affordable household textiles and children's clothing. At Seal Cove, they expressed it by providing financial, spiritual, and emotional support to sisters in need.

Reforming Anglicanism

Religiosity, along with their identity as Anglicans, was important to Conception Bay residents. A description of the 1930 confirmation service held at All Saints Church shows the mixing of official church ceremony with popular practices and rituals, including the building of evergreen-bough arches to welcome the diocesan bishop:

> On arrival within the precincts of Foxtrap it became apparent that the people had been fully alive to the importance of the occasion, and had taken a great deal of trouble to give the church and its surroundings a gala appearance. Two very pretty arches had been erected on the church road, an avenue of trees had been planted along the approach to the church itself and the church grounds resplendent with streamers and flags.[63]

Bishop's chaplain the Reverend H.L. Pike reported that an "overflowing congregation" participated in the confirmation of "65 men and boys" at the morning service and the confirmation of "75 females" at the evening service. In the afternoon, Pike added, the bishop travelled to Hopewell, where thirty-four boys and eighteen girls received the sacrament.[64] While many parishioners had little spare cash to donate to the diocese, agricultural Foxtrap and Hopewell was especially noted in the mid-1900s for annual gifts of vegetables and fruit to the Anglican seminary at Queen's College, and to the Church of England Orphanage in St John's.[65]

Despite these local traditions and religious practices, in the early 1960s rector Mark Genge encouraged people of the parish to engage in a program of spiritual and material renewal in church life.[66] Changes included the start of a Sunday school program for children; the construction of a new rectory at Kelligrews; extensive improvements in church furniture and vestments at both St Peter's and All Saints churches; and the installation of central heating systems, artesian wells, and flush toilets at the Anglican schools of Foxtrap, Kelligrews, Upper Gullies, and Seal Cove.[67] Spiritual renewal was sought through a preaching mission in 1963, which featured brothers from the Order of the Holy Cross in Brooklyn, New York, as well as through the Parish Life Conference to "assess the life and ministry of the Parish" in 1965.[68]

While better sanitary conditions at schools and greater access to higher education were changes with which few would argue, other efforts were designed to transform the religious practices of Conception Bay Anglicans into a middle-class, Protestant, and suburban practice of church life. Mark Genge was unimpressed with some people's reaction to his vision of attractive, warm, "home-like" churches and his launch of ministries designed for families and youth. Approximately one hundred "bewildered" persons attended the Parish Life Conference, he reported in the pages of the *Newfoundland Churchman* in 1965, and "surprised" their rector by suggesting his new Sunday schools were "only babysitting" and that "altar boys and servers" should go as well. "They were not necessary in days gone by," the people of Foxtrap and Hopewell argued, "so we can do without them now."[69] Efforts to change the character of local Anglican practice particularly affected CEWA women by placing new fundraising responsibilities and gender expectations upon them. Coupled with this, local Anglican women faced diocesan-level efforts to "reorganize" their church work, a movement grounded in middle-class gender ideology related to appropriate roles for Christian women, especially motherhood and homemaking.

During the first half of the twentieth century, official Newfoundland Anglican discourse included little promotion of prescriptive ideas about motherhood, especially bourgeois ideas about mothers as the primary religious influence within the home and the person most responsible for children's religious education. In the 1940s, the new diocesan Bishop Philip Selwyn Abraham began to promote "deaconess" training for Newfoundland, including establishment of a Deaconess House in Brooklyn, Bonavista Bay, where women called to church work could prepare for work as "assistants" in parishes as one solution to the rural priest shortage. While the plan opened up new opportunities for paid employment among faithful Anglican women, and was generally supported by the CEWA, it did not succeed as Abraham had hoped. The vision of deaconess as helpmeet to male parish clergy, primarily assisting with ministry to women and children, overseeing CEWA branches, and setting up Sunday schools, drew few recruits, perhaps because its vision of gender relations and roles did not resonate with ordinary Anglican women. While a few women were called from city parishes to work in urban settings, very few were called from rural areas, despite financial support coming from CEWA branches.[70]

While the deaconess movement assumed that women were interested in working with families and children, the church's effort to encourage Anglican women to think of themselves primarily as mothers and home-makers, and to offer a model of associational life that supported this new, largely middle-class vision of womanhood, came to prominence in the late 1950s. Much of this discourse centred on the Diocesan Board of Women's Work, a committee of women Anglican leaders, mostly rectors' wives, organized in 1951 to reform and "rationalize" women's voluntary labour following the merger of the Newfoundland Church with the Anglican Church of Canada in 1949.[71] While the CEWA was established as the primary women's group in the diocese in 1926 (although first organized in the Mission of Heart's Content in 1877), other voluntary women's groups were operating in the province during the early 1950s. These included the Women's Auxiliary, the leading association of the Anglican Church in Canada, the Girl's Friendly Society, and assorted church guilds.[72] The Anglican Church of Canada's Women's Auxiliary had a longer history of emphasizing "pious motherhood" than did the Newfoundland CEWA, and Anglican leadership was quick to embrace and promote this rhetoric.[73] The July 1959 edition of the newly renamed *Newfoundland Churchman* carried the front page headline "The Religious, Educational and Social Development of the Child" and presented on its leading pages the text of an address by then-Parish of Grand Falls rector's wife "Mrs R.S. Sheppard," who was a promoter of the Women's Auxiliary in Newfoundland.

Sheppard delivered her speech at the diocese's first conference of Little Helpers secretaries and assistants.[74] The organization and activities Sheppard described were of the "friendly visitor" type that middle-class women's reform associations, although largely in urban settings, had practised since the nineteenth century.[75] Little Helpers secretaries, she explained, visited parish homes to see how well mothers were doing in their efforts to teach religion to children. Referencing the twenty-four delegates in attendance, Sheppard told her audience that "we have encountered few mothers in Newfoundland who do not believe in teaching children religion," and that women welcomed such visits and the opportunity they provided to learn "the right thing" to teach. Sheppard may have been concerned with preserving and promoting orthodoxy, but other advocates focused more on the benefits of outreach to Anglican families. In 1962, *Churchman* editor Charles Abraham stated that "no well-run parish of any size can do without some such group as the Little Helpers or the Font Roll of the Mothers' Union" as a means for "keeping in touch" with families who brought their children to be baptized but were otherwise not involved in church life.[76] An article that explained the duties of Little Helper parish secretaries, which included making home visits, keeping up the font roll (list of children baptized in the parish), organizing an annual gathering of parents and children, and being ready to help parents select "suitable ... books, records, and pictures" for Christian training in the home, appeared in 1965.[77]

Newfoundland Anglican Church leaders' acceptance and promotion of middle-class discourse on pious motherhood in the 1960s can be seen also in *Churchman* articles. One article, entitled "The First Three Years," originated from the Church of St Mary the Virgin in St John's and was likely written by Anglican Training College for Women-educated parish worker Joyce Payne, who travelled to Toronto to study at ATCW in 1959.[78] "The mother feeds baby at the breast of her own religious life," Payne wrote, while describing how women with "pram" and "carry-cot" should bring very young children to church regularly and teach them to pray at home morning and evening. "You are to teach your baby to DO religious things long before he can understand them," she instructed mothers, and "you are to awaken in him loves and loyalties towards God and His holy church."[79] Efforts to promote Altar Guilds in Anglican parishes throughout the diocese also came from church leadership in the 1950s, and Mark Genge organized branches at Foxtrap and Upper Gullies in 1959.[80] Sometimes referred to as "God's housekeepers," women active in Altar Guilds cleaned and "kept in order" church sanctuaries, vestments, and linens.[81] The devotional aspects of this work were promoted, and reported, by women, yet, like the push to form Little Helpers and Mother's Union groups, Altar Guilds spoke to a vision of women's place within the church which presumed their domesticity and was part of the church's efforts to construct a new model of Christian womanhood for the new post-confederation Newfoundland.[82]

Conclusion

The Anglican women of mid-twentieth-century Conception Bay lived in times of change and transition. Political changes included recognition of their right to vote, the loss of responsible government, and confederation with Canada in 1949. With new and diversified employment opportunities during and after the Second World War, local families that had depended on the household economy before 1940 increasingly relied on male breadwinners' wages, although agriculture remained an important economic activity into the 1960s. After 1949, especially, women of the rural, coastal communities of the south side of Conception Bay encountered new social and cultural expectations around domesticity and motherhood. For Anglicans, the Diocese of Newfoundland became an important agent of middle-class gender ideology as leaders and clergy promoted its vision of Christian women as mothers and homemakers. Yet Conception Bay women already had an understanding of what it meant to be women, and Christians, in their households, communities, and churches – an understanding grounded in their own material and social circumstances. We can begin to appreciate this understanding, this conception of Christianity, by looking at the gender dynamics surrounding everyday religious practices within Anglican homes.

CHAPTER TWO

Families That Work Together, Worship Together: The Practice of Everyday Religion in Anglican Households

Like Protestant and Catholic clergy in other parts of North America, Newfoundland Anglican Church leaders were concerned with home religion, and in the twentieth century they increasingly placed responsibility for pious families at women's feet.[1] The emergence of the prescriptive ideal of the "Christian mother" was closely tied to economic changes, especially the transition from a subsistence/household economy sustained by family labour to a consumer economy that supposed a male breadwinner who earned wages in a workplace distinct from the family home and a female homemaker who was responsible for the quality of family life.

Rural economic settings are associated with a different vision. Despite growing industrialization and urban expansion elsewhere, in rural settings, including on the south shore of Conception Bay, the family-based economy of household production continued into the twentieth century, with "the work of women, men, and children … [remaining] strongly connected."[2] From this came the idea of father as "instructor of the family," including in matters of religion. The vision of fathers as heads of households and "family priests" who conducted daily prayer services for their families was a patriarchal ideal envisioned by nineteenth-century Protestant church leaders in response to industrial economic and social change, and sought to preserve "a simpler, more religious past."[3]

By the late nineteenth century, another gendered ideal, of the "naturally religious" woman well-fitted to be "the moral and spiritual mentor and guardian of her children" and spouse, had begun to displace the notion of father as family priest. Linked to the ideology of separate spheres, which assigned women to home and family and men to business and politics, these prescriptions for family religion were largely middle-class and urban in origin.[4] Concern about the "feminization of religion" led some theologians to embrace the "muscular Christianity" movement, which tried to encourage more men, especially young men, to engage with church life by emphasizing "action" and "manly" pursuits such as sports as part of a Christian lifestyle.[5] Organizations such as the Young Men's Christian Association originated within muscular Christian ideology, and in Newfoundland the life and work of medical missionary Sir Wilfred Grenfell can be understood as an example of this impulse within late nineteenth- and early twentieth-century religious practice.[6] By the mid-1900s, theologians redirected efforts to address what they understood to be men's disinterestedness in religion towards "masculine domesticity."[7] This was an effort to encourage fathers to take a more active role in family religious life and, like the muscular Christianity movement, was rooted in a notion that the feminization of religion was a real problem for which solutions had to be found.

Despite the prescriptions of church leaders and the pervasiveness of gender ideology within middle-class discourse, many people did not conceive of family relationships in terms of separate spheres. As Nancy Christie argues, gender relations within families often were shaped instead by factors such as religious experience and discourse, including "the ideological constructs of Christianity," which created a "patriarchal piety" of male authority which flowed "from God the Father to earthly fathers" and thereby informed the social order and social relations.[8] Among Anglicans in nineteenth-century Ontario, for example, fathers were as active as mothers, if not more so, in providing religious and moral instructions to children within farming families. Believers considered this domestic role to be consistent with their lived Christian ideals.[9]

These prescribed gender roles (father as family priest and mother as naturally pious spiritual mentor), and the extent to which they were evident in the lived religious practices of Anglican families in Conception Bay, are at the heart of this chapter and the next, which consider patterns of Sunday observance and church attendance within households based primarily on evidence gathered through interviews and observed in material culture practices. Understanding the impact of gender on religious belief and practice requires attention to both feminine and masculine experience and expectations, especially in the context of family-based practices.[10] In the case of Conception Bay, these practices included family prayer, Bible reading, and hymn singing, along with use and display of Christian images and objects. Religious role models for Anglican women could be either female or male and could come from the broader church community as well as from the home.

Family Altar and Family Devotions

In Conception Bay, the transition from a family-based economy to a wage-based economy influenced the practice of family prayer. Prescriptions for domestic spirituality that appeared in nineteenth-century Canadian church periodicals, both Protestant and Catholic, agreed "that daily family prayer was crucial, not only to keep the family Christian, but to maintain harmony and strengthen domestic ties."[11] While father-led prayer was considered ideal, by the end of the nineteenth century editors increasingly suggested that women were to take the lead in family devotions.[12] By the 1950s, "the requirements of paid work limited the involvement of fathers in postwar domestic life," including family religious practices. In urban, middle-class, Protestant families, men were "drawn away not only by the demands of bread-winning but also by the assumption that mothers were ultimately responsible for spiritual care-giving."[13] Religious tradition could impact the clerical prescriptions regarding family prayer as well, with Pentecostals more likely to promote men-led devotions.[14]

By the early twentieth century, regular family prayer was more common among working-class families than among middle-class ones.[15] Those Conception Bay Anglicans who were children in the 1920s and 1930s especially recalled the practice. Sisters Mary (Petten) Porter and Joan (Petten) Jefford independently described the important place of family prayer in their Kelligrews home, with Mary describing how group prayer was led by their father, Henry Petten. Mary recalled her upbringing as: "Really, really religious … we would get up in the morning and Mom would always say now everybody sit down 'till Daddy come down. We would all have to kneel down and Daddy would say prayers with us." Mary remembered her father, a farmer, saying both the Lord's Prayer and a special prayer for workers in the fishing and forest industries:

"Poor Daddy, in his prayer he asked God to forgive him and care for his family … He would remember all in his prayers. He used to even remember those gone overseas because he was overseas. He would pray for those out on the water … Poor Daddy would have prayers and he would even pray for men in the forests." Mildred (Butler) Porter likewise recalled domestic prayers for working people, although from her mother: "My mother when she was praying you could hear her, what she was saying … I would kneel down by her side and she would be praying for the poor sealers out to the ice and the poor men on the water. I would listen to her, you know. You could hear her when she be saying her prayers." While Mary's daughter Enid (Porter) Haines remembered family devotions from her 1940s childhood, she did not specifically recall her father leading the service: "We would all be kneeling down. Mom, Dad and my grandmother [Porter] would be there … it would always be in the kitchen … Our prayers were basically the same all the time. We would have the Lord's Prayer and we would God bless Mom and Dad and name off everyone in the family and then of course the Grace on the end and it was always Now I lay me down to sleep [at bedtime]." Marge (Saunders) Dawe described how her father said morning prayers and how in the evening "we would kneel by the bed and Dad would listen." Grace before meals was an important prayer ritual, and Marge noted that "[we] always said grace before we ate, and we would wait for everyone to get to the table … Dad always said the prayer. He would ask for a blessing on the food and thank God for it." She also recalled her father reading the Bible.

Morning and bedtime prayers were often said in the kitchen of Conception Bay homes, since before central heating was common the woodstove made it the warmest room in the house. Pat (Morgan) Woolgar recalled of her mother Marion (Tilley) Morgan, who grew up in Kelligrews: "My mother would talk about when they said their prayers they would say it down in the kitchen because it was warm, instead of going up in the bedrooms. They all had to kneel down before they went into their bedrooms to say their prayers and they did that in the kitchen." While Pat did not recall her father describing family prayer in his home growing up, a mixed Kelligrews household of Anglican father and Bible Christian mother, she did remember how "the Bible was read [aloud] every single day in dad's home by his mother, whether they wanted to take part or not."

Like Mary and Marge, Mildred (Butler) Porter recalled the 1930s family devotions led by her father, Henry Butler, and how he conducted these services in the kitchen. One distinction was that Mildred's mother, Caroline, rather than her father, said grace before meals. This was captured in one of Mildred's favourite childhood memories, which also demonstrates rural women's myriad responsibilities:

> Before we go to bed in the night, Dad had his prayer book and he read prayers. If we was all home, we had prayers. We got up in the morning and we had prayers. Never sat down to a meal without saying grace. You had to keep your hands folded. Mom was sitting to the end of the table one day and she said, "God bless this food which now we take and save our souls for Jesus' sake is that my fowl out there?" Well, the table went up. Things like that stick in my mind. She had her hens barred up and one of them got out. She was at the end of the table and could see [through the window].

When she went on to raise her own family, Mildred noted how "they said their prayers, but not prayers like that," referring to family devotions. She added, "But I often thought about it." In daughter Myra (Porter) Rideout's family, "the boys said their prayers [at bedtime] and their grace. That was it," with Mildred explaining, "it was a different day and age then, see." Like many women interviewed, Mildred's words reflect a sense of religious declension in the face of economic and cultural change.

The recollections of Prudence (Morgan) Rideout and daughter Judy (Rideout) Dawe reveal how family prayer changed between generations, as well as how it varied between families. In contrast to the father-led family altar prayer Mary described, Prudence recalled how "when we were young" her family would sometimes pray as a group "if we were together," but "most of the time each would have their own." She described how her father would pray alone in the kitchen of their Seal Cove home: "When I got up in the morning, as I would come out the hall, downstairs and out through the hall … me father had a rocking chair and he always had it in that first corner we would call it. He would be down there … that was his place to say his prayers … He would kneel in the big rocking chair. We had to stay still … we didn't have anything said to us, because we knew what we had to do and we just automatically go and get in the rocking chair." Of her Methodist mother, Effie (Morrie) Morgan, Prudence noted, "She wouldn't be like him. I think she would say her prayers in her bedroom." This may have reflected Effie's preference for private, individual prayer, in keeping with the Methodist emphasis on personal religion.[16] Prudence's daughter Judy noted the change between generations, and described how when she was growing up they did not pray "as a group, but we always said our prayers … before we went to bed. I don't remember in the mornings, but I remember before we went to bed."

The busyness of family life in the 1950s and 1960s displacing family prayer was described by Doris (Nagle) Bishop, raised as a Roman Catholic, who noted that the family rosary was said in her childhood home ("everyone knelt around and said the rosary on their prayer beads. That was really important"). While she converted to Anglicanism at the time of her marriage, domestic demands rather than differences between traditions were the primary reason there was no family prayer in her own home. "It wasn't the same here. I had me hands full. I had six children," she explained, "[all I had time for was] 'you better say your prayers.'" While she taught her children bedtime prayers, Doris admitted that "sometimes they were hurried." This was not unusual in postwar households, where "busy schedules complicated the religious education of children." Historian Tina Block uses the term "toilet-seat prayers" to illustrate the "often unceremonious ways in which religion was lived" by ordinary families in 1960s Victoria and demonstrates how family religion was "quite different from the formal, routinized, and male-led family altar advocated by clergy."[17]

Grace at Mealtime and Bedtime Prayers

For Conception Bay families who practised family altar-type devotions in the 1920s and 1930s, use of such rituals declined over time. Saying grace before meals and praying at bedtime were the practices most likely to persist into the 1960s and beyond.[18] Mary (Petten) Porter and Joan (Petten) Jefford described how they, as the oldest of fifteen children, were responsible for their younger siblings' bedtime prayers on nights when their parents were away. Joan noted how "Mary washed their face and hands and got them ready for bed … and [they] said their prayers to me," including the Lord's Prayer. Mildred and Myra also described the Lord's Prayer at bedtime. For Eileen Morgan of Seal Cove, it was "always the Lord's Prayer" morning and evening: "There was always prayers going to bed and getting up in the morning, and grace said over the food. That was a ritual. Mom was always on that department." For Mary, her father said grace: "We set down to the tables and how hungry you was but you couldn't touch anything till daddy sat down and said the blessing ... He wouldn't let nobody touch anything, not even pick up your spoon to sweeten your tea, until he said the blessing."

The same grace, with minor variations, was reported by most women during interviews: "God bless the food which now we take / And feed our souls for Jesus's sake. Amen." The exceptions were Emma (Petten) Warford, raised by a United Church woman, who reported saying "For what we are about to receive may the Lord make us truly thankful, for Christ's sake, Amen," and the "granny's grace," learned from their grandmothers, reported by Reta (Morgan) Hill and Prudence (Morgan) Rideout.[19] Sandra (Taylor) Tilley likewise reported a grace preferred by her father, although less admired by her brothers:

> There wasn't a morsel go in anyone's mouth until the grace was said ... There was always a bit of a joke because with our older brothers and a farm they were often hungry and when it was time for food they wanted to eat. Someone would always say, "say the grace before Dad gets a chance." Because when Dad got a chance he would always say ... "Be present at our table, Lord / Be here and everywhere adored / Thy creatures bless and grant that we / May feast in paradise with thee." That was always his grace ... If the boys could beat him to it or they could prompt somebody else it was always God bless the food ... Amen. They were like, "say the grace and let's eat." That was a bit of a running joke. But I think it is safe to say we all know "Be ever present at our table, Lord."

While in some jurisdictions no family prayer beyond grace became a norm in the 1950s and 1960s, this was not the case in Anglican Conception Bay, where bedtime prayer remained important for both children and adults.[20]

Violet Warford of Upper Gullies described her family having no formal prayer besides grace before meals in the 1940s, yet noted how her mother "had her own prayer" and that she had witnessed her parents' private prayer ritual ("one night I went in the [bedroom] and I seen the two of them kneeling down, saying their prayers together"), which "made a big impression" on her religious life. Couples praying together has been described as a largely Pentecostal practice, where such mutual prayer can be understood as a "sacred forum" in which women found a "neutral space" to "discuss marital problems." Mutual prayer was believed to contribute to more "compassionate and forgiving" marriages by women who practised it.[21] Evidence in Conception Bay suggests this was also part of popular Anglican practice.

Other women besides Violet reported how seeing parents or a parent at prayer "made an impression" on them. Sandra (Taylor) Tilley recalled:

> My father was sick lots. So even though we were farmers, lots of time … he wouldn't really be able to work in the garden … He would drive us to the garden and he would give the direction even though he might have to lie down in the truck or … go in the shack and lie down … But I always remember, my vision of him is kneeling with his long underwear on at the side of the bed every night saying his prayers. I remember that. Then, of course, that transferred into us kneeling and you always knelt by the bed in the cold nights when you didn't have heat in the bedrooms [but] we always had a mat on the floor.

Sandra remembered her bedtime prayers: "Now I lay me down to sleep and also God bless and listing off all the people. It always ended with 'and make Sandra a good girl.' That was the last, pre-amen, 'make Sandra a good girl.'"[22] Edna (Roberts) Haines, Joyce (Andrews) Morgan, Pat (Morgan) Woolgar, and Marjorie (Bullen) Morgan also said bedtime prayers as children, and continued the practice as adults when they had their own.

Bible Reading

Conception Bay women recalled the central place of the Bible in home religious practice. This included reading scripture, whether aloud for the benefit of the entire family (calling to mind "The Cotter's Saturday Night," which Protestant theologians through the nineteenth century held up as the domestic ideal) or silently as a matter of private study and meditation.[23] Reading scripture was an essential aspect of Christian practice promoted by nineteenth-century evangelical Anglican missionaries to Newfoundland.[24] In addition, Bibles could hold significance within families as sacred objects. Methodist households often displayed the family Bible "in a position of honour," which for middle-class families could be the "centre table that was the focus of the parlour of a respectable Victorian family."[25] Objects important to a family's history and religious life were often preserved between the pages of large family Bibles, and could include religious pictures or poetry cut from other publications, memorial or prayer cards, obituaries, flowers preserved from a wedding or funeral service, and photographs of children's rite of passage ceremonies such as a baptism or confirmation. While a "four-leaf clover" or other "magical" secular object might make its way into a family Bible, most objects preserved in this way were overtly religious by character or by association.[26] Preserving sentimental and religious items in the family Bible was part of Christian practice among some women of Conception Bay, including that of Beulah (Porter) Morgan and Marjorie (Bullen) Morgan.

While the display of the Bible is often considered to be primarily about demonstrating respectability, memories of the place of the Bible in Conception Bay homes indicated families actively engaged with scripture as part of their lived faithfulness. Mary (Petten) Porter described Bible reading as part of her family' devotions: "Dad's mother lived with us for a few years and she and Mom would sit down on the bench, we didn't have a chesterfield or anything then and ... Dad would always set over across and ... when he would finish prayers he would look over and said 'Mom have you got the [trailed off]' ... I don't know what part of the Bible she read, and she would pass it over to him because she was partly blind ... He used to read it for her." Mary stated that in her childhood home the Bible was "in the middle of the [kitchen] table" and that "Dad would always read the Bible ... he put the Bible on the table, he would never close the Bible," a practice possibly linked to his participation in the Orange Order, which actively promoted Bible reading among its members and included the image of an open Bible among its devices.[27] While a number of women remembered their fathers reading scripture daily (Prudence [Morgan] Rideout) or on Sundays in lieu of going to church (Violet Warford), they did not recall the Bible always left open in this way. In Violet's home, the Bible was kept on a centre table in the front room, where it remained after her parents' deaths.[28]

Figure 2.1 Along with an understanding of Bibles as sacred objects, daily scripture reading was a common religious practice in many mid-1900s Anglican homes. Here, Sarah Elizabeth Dawe of Seal Cove pauses in her Bible reading to enjoy a visit with her great-grandchild.

For Emma (Petten) Warford, raised by Methodist Harriett (Newell) Petten, evening ritual included scripture as well as prayer: "I never went to bed, I am sure I didn't, any time without saying prayers and read a scripture from the Bible. I still do it … I brought up my daughter the same way." She summarized the importance of scripture in her childhood home: "We went by the Bible really … [on Sunday] you would read a script from the Bible … Our Bibles were always out in sight. You had to go by the Bible in them days … The Bible was took out and read before you went [to bed]. Most everything was taken from the Bible. That is really true and I guess there was a lot of people like it." Pat (Morgan) Woolgar likewise described her father's mother, Susannah (Dawe) Morgan, a Bible Christian who maintained her religious identity despite her marriage to an Anglican, and her commitment to reading scripture: "I remember her all through the years … she would always have the Bible out all day long. When you went over to visit her she was in her rocking chair reading the Bible." Other women discovered Bible reading as a result of conversion. Doris (Nagle) Bishop described how participation in Bible study was one of her favourite aspects of becoming Anglican: "I don't remember much about the Bible growing up. Maybe it was there on a shelf or something but you know you didn't ... not the same. But the Bible is more important it seems like in the Church of England ... I really enjoyed Bible studies."[29] For Anglican women, both personal encounters with scripture and participation in clergy-led Bible study could be important aspects of their religious lives.

Hymn Singing

Another domestic religious practice that women reported was family members singing hymns, sometimes as part of Sunday observance but more often to accompany daily labour. The introduction of hymns and hymn singing into Christian worship is associated with the seventeenth-century dissenting movement, a critical response to Church of England practice. Hymnody is especially linked to Methodism, which emerged in eighteenth-century Anglicanism under the leadership of John and Charles Wesley. Controversial at first, by the late nineteenth and early twentieth centuries hymn singing was "a central part of religious and social culture" for Anglicans. Hymns were sung at public worship, in families, and by individuals who "could learn them by heart, quote them in their journals, and recite them on their deathbeds."[30]

Marjorie (Bullen) Morgan, who grew up on Bay d'Leau Island in Fortune Bay, noted how her family practised home prayer and informal worship in the absence of a church building and ordained clergy, and stated that "we only saw the minister three or four times a year" and "where there wasn't a minister very often, sometimes you would have little hymn sings or whatever" on Sundays. Like others, Marjorie recalled men, especially, singing hymns as they went about their work: "Uncle John James, mom's brother, lived over in Red Cove. He used to sing 'How Sweet the Name of Jesus Sounds.' I still remember it. Sometimes he'd be building a boat, you'd hear his hammer and he'd be singing away. It would echo up around the cliffs. I always think of him when we sing it in church."[31] Joan (Petten) Jefford recalled of her father, Henry Petten:

> I used to go into the wood's garden with him when he was cutting hay and stuff like that and we would always have a boil up. He always had a smoke after. I would go ... picking berries or

> whatever. He had a field of hay, I would watch him cutting it and he would sing. I can remember him always, "The king of love my shepherd is / Whose goodness faileth never / I nothing lack if I am his / And he is mine forever." He was singing and smoking. Things [like] that you really remember. I used to love to hear him singing that.

Edna (Rideout) Warford recalled that her maternal grandfather, John Scott of Upper Gullies, "was always singing those mission hymns, those real old hymns ... he'd sit in the chair and he is always singing hymns." Reginald Morgan of Seal Cove likewise remembered Indian Pond shopkeeper Heber Morgan singing, "There were ninety and nine that safely lay in the shelter of the fold / But one was out on the hills away / Far off from the gates of gold / Away on the mountains wild and bare / Away from the tender Shepherd's care."[32]

Women and children sang hymns as well. Pat (Morgan) Woolgar recalled of her Bible Christian grandmother: "[She] went to her own church. Religion was real big in her life. She sang hymns all the time. She wore long skirts, wore her hair up in a bun ... We used to play the piano and we had to do different [hymns] for her ... 'Nearer my God to Thee' ... 'Bringing in the Sheaves' ... 'What a Friend We Have in Jesus.'" Emma (Petten) Warford noted how during her childhood, "I often sang hymns, like Sunday night late at night before you go to bed. Maybe my dad would say, how about singing this one 'Jesus Loves Me' or whatever. That was the way it was." Emma's mother also enjoyed hymns, which could be sung on days besides Sundays: "My brother and I used to sit down a lot. Dad was a butcher – this wouldn't be on a Sunday now – he used to go to town with all his vegetables and go around with his meat ... While we were waiting for him to come, because them days it was a long haul to St John's and back again to Foxtrap, we would sing hymns to Mom ... We would sing hymns for her and songs also ... [but] she liked hymns." Emma recognized music as integral to her religious upbringing ("you had to sing your hymns"), as did Edna (Roberts) Haines of Upper Gullies, who recalled "playing hymns on the gramophone" on Sundays "when it was raining or not fit to go to church." Hymn singing was also important in the religious rituals of CEWA members, with Anglican women recognizing the place of sacred song in the spiritual lives of others.[33]

Religious Pictures

The popular religious beliefs and practices of Christians, both Catholic and Protestant, are affected by use of religious images.[34] Warner Sallman's *Head of Christ* and "countless variations of the Sacred Heart of Jesus" demonstrate how such images "portray a Saviour whose appearance, though it is never described in the New Testament, is instantly recognized" by believers of any denomination.[35] "Despite frequent assertions to the contrary, Protestants as well as Catholics make, buy, and otherwise consume material objects" which they believe to offer supernatural protection and comfort, as well as religious instruction.[36] While there has been a deeper emphasis on objects and icons within Catholic practice, and "although historians and critics have often drawn sharp distinctions between Protestant and Catholic sensory cultures, some of which surely pertain, the overstated case for binary difference has tended to lump together all Protestants in visual and material opposition to all Catholics, rather than to notice more finely grained similarities and differences within and across individuals and groups."[37] Practices of Conception Bay Anglicans, which included visualizing religious figures and encountering religious messages through images and objects displayed within the home, support this view.

The nineteenth-century Protestant vision of middle-class home religion included interiors decorated with "tasteful" Christian prints, which were believed to impress young minds as much as access to religious reading material. Like other aspects of home religion, proponents considered providing such pictures to be mothers' responsibility.[38] Religious prints reproduced and distributed as mass commodities for Christian consumption usually featured a combination of Bible imagery, crosses and hearts, flowers, leaves, and trailing vines.[39] This decorative approach suggests an understanding among manufacturers that such images would appeal to middle-class women.[40] While displayed in Catholic as well as Protestant homes, within Protestant interiors such prints often became the focus of home altars just as images of particular saints or the Sacred Heart could anchor home altars within Catholic households.[41] Within Conception Bay Anglican homes, most religious pictures were not of the Bible-with-trailing-vines variety. Instead, images of Jesus predominated, with representations of his mother Mary a distant second.

Figures 2.2 and 2.3 Owning and displaying religious pictures was common among Anglican women of Conception Bay. Such images provided a feeling of comfort and protection, with many women preferring pictures of Jesus, especially when portrayed as the Good Shepherd, to other kinds of religious prints available to them. While often associated with instruction of children, such images were kept and displayed by women without children at home, too. In figure 2.2, images of Christ in Gethsemane are displayed in Violet Warford's home; in figure 2.3, Christ as the Good Shepherd is displayed in Eileen Morgan's home.

Like elsewhere in North America, Conception Bay Anglicans associated the keeping of these religious pictures with women. Marjorie (Bullen) Morgan described an image of *The Holy Family* displayed in her bedroom as a gift of her mother-in-law, longtime Seal Cove CEWA president Phoebe (Dawe) Morgan. Pat (Morgan) Woolgar's illustrated "Prayer of St Francis" was the gift of an aunt; another woman described of her childhood home a "picture of the Lord with children and a sheep in his arm … the little lamb that went astray … on the wall in mom's bedroom." Judy (Rideout) Dawe remembered how her grandmother Effie (Morrey) Morgan "always had religious pictures in her house … hung up in the living room," while Reta (Morgan) Hill recalled admiring "a picture in my grandmother's living room. It was the Lord's Prayer with pictures."[42] Few religious images were associated with men. Edna (Roberts) Haines recalled having a picture of "William of Orange on a horse" in her living room "because George [her husband] was a member of the Lodge."[43]

Conception Bay families acquired religious pictures in various ways. Joan (Petten) Jefford described the purchase of an illustrated print of the Lord's Prayer, which hung in her and her sister's bedroom, as a combination of piety and patriotism: "We had [it] after the First World War. My dad was in the first. And this day this man came around with one arm. He was selling pictures and one of them was … the Lord's Prayer. My sister and I … that is where we learned the Lord's Prayer … it helped so we didn't forget it." Joan's recollection demonstrates the instructional value of such images. Several other women described decorative religious items such as illuminated certificates and pictures as gifts from Sunday school, reflecting a local official Anglican position that such items were useful in children's religious education.[44] In some cases, images encouraged attendance. Reta (Morgan) Hill recalled of Sunday school in 1920s Indian Pond: "We used to get a picture … they got larger and larger, you know. So I was anxious to get the pictures and often times I walked alone [to the classes]." Other women inherited images. Emma (Petten) Warford described moving into her husband's family home at the time of her marriage in the 1940s: "I remember a picture of Jesus hanging on the wall … That was in the bedroom. I remember that and I let it stay there. Whenever I did my cleaning that went back again … Jesus with the lamb."

The religious print can be understood as twentieth-century commodity, yet social and economic factors influenced which images Anglican families preferred. Some religious pictures were manufactured in the United States primarily for missionaries to use to illustrate Christianity to non-Christian peoples. Prints of Warner Sallman's *Head of Christ* (1940), which American military personnel also distributed, are a good example of this.[45] This particular image of Jesus was displayed in several Conception Bay homes. Given its mid-century date of production, and its widespread distribution to American service personnel, the popularity of this print in Conception Bay may be associated with the American presence in Newfoundland during the Second World War, especially given that many men in the study area were employed at the American base at Argentia during the 1940s and 1950s.[46] At the same time, the equally well-known Sallman image *Christ Our Pilot* (1950), which illustrates Christ offering comfort and direction to a young male sailor at the helm of a ship upon a stormy sea, was not noted in Conception Bay homes despite "the motif of the sailor guided by Jesus ... enjoy[ing] far-flung circulation" during the Second World War.[47] For the most part, mass-produced religious images associated with masculine or muscular Christianity, including the sea-faring themed *Christ Our Pilot*, were not common in Conception Bay homes.[48]

Gender issues surround Sallman's *Head of Christ*, as do matters of class. Through the 1950s and 1960s this print was singled out for "special condemnation" by male, educated, liberal, Protestant theologians in the United States who, despite the image's popularity and religious significance to average practitioners, considered it a good example of overly sentimental, "effeminate," and "low brow" religious art. Striving to "reform visual habits" in mass religious culture to a "modernist aesthetic," elite professionals in art and religion cooperated in the years after the Second World War to promote replacement of "domesticated" art with "serious" or "authentic" art, and effeminate images of Christ with "virile" ones.[49] They directed the same impulse towards church buildings: "One desired impact of these efforts was to reconfigure the interior decorative culture of the liberal church, to make it less the apparent domain of women and children, to distance it from the visual program of 'home' – and then to encourage domestic religious taste to follow suit."[50] The taste culture this campaign encouraged was "white, heterosexual, liberal Protestant" (and middle-class) male. It reflected the Cold War politics of the time, since masculine and serious images were thought to "reclaim the modern church for the men of America. In the battle against 'godless communism,' it would pay to have 'real men' in the pews."[51] The continued popularity of religious art such as *Head of Christ* among practising Christians, including those of Conception Bay, reflected not only the disconnect between "promoters of the high-modern taste culture" and the day-to-day religious lives of believers who found spiritual meaning within mass-produced images, but also "the difficulty of linking revelation to a single style or set of expressive styles."[52]

Neither could particular images be limited to use by Christians within specific traditions. By the mid-nineteenth century, Sacred Heart and Marian portraiture, traditionally associated with Catholic practice, were visible in Protestant homes. As the commercial production of religious images increased, such prints became more accessible to Christian families concerned with home religion, and Protestant leaders promoted their display in domestic settings as just as important to children's religious training as "prayer, catechism, and family devotion." This impacted home religion: "The gaze of Jesus or Mary that followed family members about the domestic interior provided a constant sense of presence and made the heavenly person portrayed accessible to petition and prayer. The devotional sensibility allowed Protestants to practice a visual piety that Roman Catholics had long enjoyed: one that visualized a personal relationship with the sacred other."[53] This type of devotion, based on a sense of relationship between the secular and sacred realms, was practised by Conception Bay Anglicans. Besides other images of Jesus, several homes displayed what are often seen as Roman Catholic objects and images, including the crucifix and the *Sacred Heart of Jesus*. Two homes, largely preserved as they would have been in the mid-1900s, also displayed the *Sacred Heart of Mary* and other Marian iconography. That being said, some of the most popular images identified in Conception Bay households are associated especially with Lutheran and Methodist practice. These included *Christ at Heart's Door* and *The Lord Is My Shepherd*, both linked to ministry to children in that "they are icons of the tender Saviour devoted to his flock."[54] *Christ at Heart's Door*, which shows an image of Jesus standing on the threshold of a home and preparing to knock on the door, was also especially popular. Cynthia (Scott) Dawe recalled how she "always thought that our lord was at the door to be invited in" when she looked at the print in her childhood home. *The Lord Is My Shepherd*, with Christ standing in a verdant landscape cradling a lamb in his arms, was the religious image that informants most often described or displayed. This popularity may have been linked to the agricultural setting of Conception Bay South, where pastoral views resonated with meaning for farming families.[55]

Other widespread popular religious prints, such as *Christ Blessing the Children*, images of the nativity, or *Madonna and Child*, with their overt familial and maternal images, were less popular in Conception Bay homes.[56] Devout mid-twentieth-century Anglicans were more likely to own and display Sallman's *Christ in Gethsemane* (1941), usually in a bedroom, or some variation of *The Last Supper*.[57] While not maternal in content, these prints nevertheless communicated an evangelical message associated with women: that "subordination of the self to the good of others" was a primary way to express Christian piety. Similarly, *The Lord Is My Shepherd* or *Christ at Heart's Door* represented a feminine Jesus, "sympathetic, gentle, and tender saviour," in contrast to images of Christ crucified which emphasized sacrifice, suffering, and pain.[58] Notable in their absence from Conception Bay homes are images associated with evangelical construction of social and ontological hierarchies, mostly portrayals of "the other" (the poor, "sinners," or non-Christians) designed to elicit viewers' sympathy rather than empathy.[59] Anglican women's rejection of such images demonstrates an understanding of Christian benevolence and mercy based in mutuality – a series of social relations associated especially with rural communities and households.[60] This notion of helping "each other" rather than "the other" was likewise demonstrated in the local CEWA.[61]

Despite some critics' condemnation of feminized religious art, prints that portrayed an image of God as male other could alienate some women. Sandra (Taylor) Tilley contrasted two religious pictures from her childhood: "One we had for sure was the guardian angel in the bedroom. The picture of the guardian angel with the children down under ... [it] was a comforting picture. It wasn't a frightening picture. And it wasn't dark and it wasn't one that children were in trouble. It wasn't that black cloud stuff ... the angel was light." The second picture was "God being an old man with a beard with a black book sitting in the clouds. Now we didn't have that picture at home but it is a picture in my mind that I got somewhere, either in books or church or school." Sandra described how this was an "image of God that I never really related well to. I always

Figure 2.4 Reta (Morgan) Hill owned and displayed two versions of the popular American print *Rock of Ages*. An image seen as Protestant crucifix, with the body of a female believer substituted for that of Jesus on the cross, it may have appealed to Reta (who was living in the United States at the time she acquired it) for its setting of a rocky coastline, reminiscent of Newfoundland.

felt 'I am in the black book again.' That image brought guilt and a 'you are bad' kind of thing." Pat (Morgan) Woolgar likewise spoke of "fear" in relation to some religious pictures displayed in her childhood home, mostly related to concern about not "doing the right thing." While scholars have written positively about "sacred presence" evoked by religious objects and images, for some women of Conception Bay this presence could have a menacing overtone of judgment and looming punishment depending upon the character of the image portrayed.[62]

Beyond representations of Mary, informants owned few religious images of women. An exception was the *Rock of Ages*, a visual interpretation of the popular hymn reportedly written by clergyman Augustus Toplady "as he sheltered in a cave during a furious storm on England's rocky coast," which Reta (Morgan) Hill displayed.[63] This print gained popularity in the United States during in the late nineteenth and early twentieth centuries and is interpreted as "a kind of Protestant version of the crucifix in substituting the female body of the believer … for the [male] body of the crucified Christian saviour."[64] It features a young woman, clothed in white robe and mantle (as Christ was often portrayed), "clinging" to a large stone cross rendered by the artist as a natural outcropping of rugged coastline around which, and the woman, stormy seas swirl. Reta had two versions of this print in her bedroom. While scholars have recognized the erotic and melodramatic character of this image, the maritime landscape, evocative of Newfoundland's coast, and the loneness of the female figure portrayed may have spoken to the immigrant Reta, who left Newfoundland in the 1930s and lived in the United States for over fifty years.

Religious Role Models

Despite the ideological construction of women as keepers of home religion and naturally suited to the religious instruction of children, few women named mothers as their own most important religious role models. While Beulah (Porter) Morgan said "it would have to be Mom for sure" when asked about religious influences, most women identified a combination of family members, clergy, teachers, and, interestingly, CEWA members (individually or collectively) that they associated with and worked alongside. Clergy encountered as a child or young person could have a life-long influence. Those who moved to the south side of Conception Bay after their marriages found lasting role models among women active in association life.

While mothers could be religious leaders within families, they would not be the sole religious role models for their children. Eileen Morgan described her mother's influence on home religious practices as "95 per cent. Every inch of it. Yes, she was the leader," and noted that as a religious role model, "Me mother was one for sure," yet went on to describe the influence of CEWA members, and especially the spirit of cooperation she felt among the female activists: "My gosh, I suppose they all were [role models] because we were all a group and everybody seemed like they were all in favour of whatever was going on. Everybody agreed." Doris (Nagle) Bishop likewise described her religious role models as "my own mother and father at home," but went on to explain how when she came to Long Pond, the local CEWA community was important. "Coming here, Ray's family wasn't as involved in church," Doris recalled, so "then you go and meet people," adding how helping out with socials facilitated her acceptance in the local community. Coming from a Roman Catholic background, where "there was nuns in the parish and they took a lot of [church work] from the women," Doris saw in the CEWA members a model of how to be a Christian woman within the Protestant tradition.

Marjorie (Bullen) Morgan also described the influence of local CEWA members on her post-marriage religious life, especially her mother-in-law branch president Phoebe (Dawe) Morgan, who "was involved deeply," and her sister-in-law Eileen. Marjorie remembered CEWA member Harriet (Batten) Morgan: "She was pretty, she was a nice person, she was involved and she was friendly." While CEWA women helped Marjorie integrate into the local church community, she considered her father to be the most important religious role model of her life. "He was always involved in anything going on in the church," she noted. "Dad never missed a service. If there was a service ... a minister or anyone around, he was in church." Of her mother, Marjorie expressed a connection between women's work and "goodness" which did not rely on formal participation in church life: "Mom didn't go to church as much [as Dad] but she was a good person in the meantime. She did an awful lot of work for the church in Mose Ambrose ... She didn't get involved in the meetings and the associations ... she was more stay-at-home ... but she worked behind the scenes I suppose you'd call it. She probably done more work than ... some of the people who was in the association." For Marjorie's mother, Laura (Strowbridge) Bullen, this work was largely textile production: sewing, quilting, and crochet.

Clergy were important role models for some women. Edna (Roberts) Haines, while she described her mother as "religious" and noted how both of her parents were active in the church, cited the Reverend Heber Gosse, rector of the parish while she was a teenager, as her most important religious role model. "I always loved Reverend Gosse," she said, "he put his heart and soul into whatever he was saying and doing." Violet Warford also named him as her role model: "He would get up in that pulpit and he would cry his eyes out having the sermon. I never seen a minister cry having a sermon, but he cried." Along with others, Sandra (Taylor) Tilley named parish rector during her teenage years, the Reverend Mark Genge, who "welcomed us young people and he made a place for us. That was an exceptional role model for me." Joyce (Andrews) Morgan named the Reverend Ben Burry, although she stated that her most important role model was her mother. A woman raised in Bonne Bay cited the Reverend Everett Fowlow. Cynthia (Scott) Dawe described the influence of teachers within the denominational school system: "In school then you were taught religion," Cynthia recalled, "We started every morning with the Lord's Prayer." Within the family, she described the influence of grandparents, as well as an uncle "who was my godfather. He was pretty much interested in what I did and how I did." For Pat (Morgan) Woolgar, teacher Ron Clarke, "other than the minister in the church," was a key role model:

> He taught in Upper Gullies and he taught at the university. He taught us in Upper Gullies when I was in Grade 7 and 8 … the age when you would be doing your confirmation classes. And I got to say he really did have a positive [influence] and he was a religious person then even, though he was young … twenty-nine years old. He made us … learn the catechism by heart and be able to stand and do the Gloria and all that … we didn't have to use a book. He took every word of the Lord's Prayer and broke it down to what it meant.

For these women, male teachers and clergy were not role models because of their position of authority, but because of their inclusive and emotional approach to religious instruction.

If anything, a sense of authority undermined religious relationships. Women might mention men, including fathers and grandfathers, as religious role models, but usually not in relation to being "strict" or the family "enforcer." Sandra (Taylor) Tilley named her father, Alan Taylor, as "one of my greatest role models," going on to describe how his religious instruction came "not by his teaching but by his action," including such gestures as helping out a neighbourhood family in need with gifts of food, providing work in his gardens for people in financial need, and organizing a work gang to repair the roof of a house where a single mother and her child lived.[65] Mildred (Butler) Porter described how "Mom came first" in terms of religious role models, while linking religion with discipline and raising children. She discussed the parenting relationship she experienced growing up: "If Mom got mad then perhaps I was doing something I shouldn't do. I go and my father was sitting down … I go and get between his knees and he would put his arms around me like that. He was my guide. If I got into any trouble, [it was] all I had to do. He wouldn't open his mouth; Mom could grumble all she liked." Daughter Myra (Porter) Rideout added, "She might have said it, but he enforced it … I guess he didn't interfere because he knew she was right and you were wrong." For Myra, men were more linked to religious and moral authority within families than women. When asked about role models she stated, "Dad, really," going on to describe how "he didn't say [anything]; like Grandfather … he enforced it. But I knew in the back of my mind what he expected of me," going on to describe how he made her sister wear her long prom dress when she got married, instead of the short wedding dress in style at that time that had been made for the ceremony. Marjorie (Saunders) Dawe also associated religious role models with men's authority and exercise of discipline. In naming her father as role model, Marjorie explained how her mother was "religious" but her father was "more strict."

Conclusion

As official Newfoundland Anglican emphasis on family religion increased in the late 1950s, family devotions declined. By the 1960s, men-led family prayer rituals, common in Conception Bay households during the first half of the twentieth century, were replaced in most families with prayer regimes at bedtime and mealtime only. Yet in many households, fathers remained closely associated with these religious rituals, despite official Anglicanism's increased emphasis on mothers' role in home religion. Neither devotional practices such as personal prayer nor the religious instruction of children were considered women's sphere; women and men alike engaged in home Bible-reading and study and sang hymns as they went about their daily work. Conception Bay women also saw (and heard) their mothers and fathers engaged in private prayer and recognized the extent to which this experience shaped their own religious lives.

Religious prints and pictures displayed in mid-century homes were largely imported, mass-produced images of Jesus, portrayed *At Heart's Door*, *In the Garden of Gethsemane*, instituting *The Lord's Supper*, and, most especially, as *The Good Shepherd*. Condemned as feminine or domestic by serious (and usually male) art critics, these prints were part of women's expression and experience of domestic religion and reveal connections between gender, class, and Christian belief. Conception Bay women rejected muscular Christian images when they selected religious art for their homes. They were not compelled by Christian images that emphasized social hierarchies or made poverty or otherness a matter of pity. They were alienated by images of a strict, judgmental, and masculine god, and preferred pastoral scenes of a caring, merciful, and self-sacrificing saviour who lived and worked, like most of their families, in the rural outdoors. Despite the narrative of bitter sectarianism in Newfoundland and Labrador, Roman Catholic iconography was owned, and displayed, in some Anglican homes.

In Conception Bay, men engaged in domestic prayer and personal devotional activities much as women did, challenging middle-class urban notions of religion as part of women's sphere. The patriarchal piety model of social relations, based on Christian acceptance of men's authority, is equally challenged by women's expression of spiritual alienation from authoritarian conceptions of the almighty. Religious role models could be any gender and were not necessarily family members. Female role models were as likely to be colleagues in church-based voluntary associations as mothers; teachers and clergy were male role models as often as fathers. While any man who held these positions was an authority figure, women connected spiritually only to those who communicated a sense of caring and personal piety. While some women deferred to fathers as authority figures and saw them as role models for the way in which they enforced religious practices and moral behaviour within families, for the most part fathers were named as role models based on their demonstrated personal piety and commitment to church life and community service.

CHAPTER THREE

"Everything Was for Sunday": Living the Holy Days

While in chapter 2 I considered family-based rituals of prayer, Bible reading, hymn singing, and visual piety in mid-1900s Conception Bay, in this chapter I focus on lived religious practices related to Sunday observance and Lent keeping as described by informants, revealed in MUN Folklore and Language Archives recordings, and noted by women in their CEWA minute books. I explore the meaning of "Sabbath" for ordinary families, including patterns of participation in public services of worship and the domestic rituals and practices which made Sunday a distinctive day of the week. For middle-class, Protestant women in urban settings, a typical Sunday in the 1950s and 1960s often meant "dressing their children 'properly' for church, preparing a 'fancy' dinner, and rushing their children to Sunday School."[1] While a typical Sunday for Conception Bay women also included church, Sunday school, and a Sunday dinner, there were significant differences. Rather than recalling the extra household labour they were expected to perform, women of mid-1900s Conception Bay described Sunday primarily as a day of rest. In some families, this weekly break from routine women's tasks such as baking bread, laundry, knitting, and sewing extended into meal preparation, with men taking responsibility for cooking Sunday dinner. Practices such as Saturday vegetable peeling and lighter-than-average Sunday breakfasts and suppers likewise protected women's Sabbath. Both men and women enforced Sunday observance, and men were just as likely as women, if not more so, to take children to church.

There was similarity in the family practices that surrounded the observation of Lent, including Holy Week and Good Friday. Like the keeping of Sunday as Sabbath day, domestic observation of other holy days centred on food practices and rest from household work. Enforced by both mothers and fathers, many families and individuals practised self-denial during Lent, with the emotion of Good Friday confirming a sense of relationship and kinship with the figure of Jesus. Building on evidence presented in chapter 2, especially that related to shared male and female involvement in prayer and other everyday domestic devotional activities, this look at domestic rituals around holy days further indicates a family religious life shaped by social and economic factors, rather than by the prescriptive expectations of an urban, Protestant middle class and perpetuated by local church leaders. I also demonstrate the fundamental relationship between women's household work and Christian belief and practice as lived within ordinary Anglican families.

Remembering the Sabbath

"When I was growing up … everything was for Sunday," Emma (Petten) Warford recalled of her childhood in 1930s Foxtrap. "We went to church in the morning, Sunday school in the afternoon and … after supper you would get to church again." When she raised her own family in 1950s Upper Gullies, Emma followed the model of Sabbath-keeping familiar from her upbringing: "We kept the same thing … it was always church on Sunday and you did nothing else anymore than having your food cooked and stuff like that. No work whatsoever … You wasn't allowed to pick up a bit of wood and bring into the house … this is the way it was. Most people that I knew in Upper Gullies [and Foxtrap] was like that." Emma's views were echoed by Mildred (Butler) Porter: "Oh my dear, Sunday was Sunday I tell you. You got up in the morning, you had to go to church. Came home and got your dinner, went to Sunday school and after Sunday school you got your supper and you had to go to church again. So that was Sunday." Mildred went on describe how, on Sundays, "I wasn't allowed to do this and I wasn't allowed to do that" noting how that was "all you'd hear from my mother." Like Emma, when Mildred raised her own family she followed her parents' example: "I tried to keep as much to my own way of living [as I could]. I tried to give them the same," she said. "Thank God I had no trouble."[2]

Strict Sabbath-keeping was part of many of the women's experience, remarkable to those raised outside the Anglican tradition. Doris (Nagle)

Figures 3.1 and 3.2 Anglicans living in the parish of Foxtrap and Hopewell had two church buildings at which to worship on Sundays. Families in the communities of Long Pond, Foxtrap, and Kelligrews largely attended All Saints Church in Foxtrap (3.1), while those in Upper Gullies, Seal Cove, and Indian Pond gathered at St Peter's in Hopewell (now Upper Gullies) (3.2). Churches are shown as they looked in 1955.

Bishop, who converted to Anglicanism at the time of her marriage in 1949, summarized the difference between Roman Catholic and Protestant approaches to "keeping the Sabbath" and noted that when she was growing up in Bay Bulls, "if you went to Mass it seemed like you had it done and … you could go wherever then." Doris described her move to Long Pond and the different approach to Sunday she encountered: "Although you know we laugh now, and say sometimes when you talked to Church of England people you know they were pretty [strict] – maybe more so than Roman Catholics in – like for instance not peeling vegetables on Sunday and things like that … They wouldn't be able to knit, but to me I don't see any harm in something like that if you are relaxing." While Doris considered knitting to be leisure today, in the mid-1900s it was a demanding aspect of women's household work.[3] Florence Mae (Morgan) Rideout of Long Pond (born 1905) described it as a "chore" and explained how women were expected to produce enough "hats, mitts, scarves, socks and underwear" to supply the entire household.[4] Laundry and sewing were other types of female household labour prohibited on Sunday, to the frustration of some. Marge (Saunders) Dawe recalled how "you would do nothing, just sit down" and that washing clothes was forbidden "no matter how bad it got with a baby in diapers." Edna (Rideout) Warford, whose mother died when she was a young girl, remembered her maternal grandfather enforcing Sunday observance: "He was down one Sunday and I come in and I had the button off me coat. I come in and was going to sew the button on … No, I didn't do it. He wouldn't let me do that."

Prudence (Morgan) Rideout, born 1914 in Seal Cove, described Sundays as a time of prayer and church attendance and noted how she would "walk down and walk up" from St Peter's church in Upper Gullies with her father. In the afternoon, she attended Sunday school at Seal Cove schoolhouse. Reta (Morgan) Hill, born 1914 in Indian Pond, likewise recalled attending Sunday school at Seal Cove, and noted, "I wasn't pushed to go … I went on my own because I wanted to." While adding that her parents "kept Sunday like all the rest in the neighborhood" and "Mother would clean her vegetables on Saturday for Sunday you know," Reta also recalled that her mother had little interest in religion and that her father was more likely to attend church. "I never heard one word of religion or advice or instructions or anything from my mother and father," Reta observed. "All I got was going to Sunday school when it came to religion. Really the whole neighbourhood [at Indian Pond] was like that. The children went to school on Sundays and the mothers and fathers stayed home." While Reta did not receive religious instruction from her parents, she did recall a close relationship with her grandmother, Virtue (Bishop) Morgan, which included memories of a special grace and religious pictures displayed in her grandmother's home.[5]

Prudence similarly remembered the religious influence of her grandmother, Jane Morgan, a woman who wanted to attend church but could not. Prudence's recollections showed the importance Jane placed on Sunday worship, as well as her literacy, sense of spiritual autonomy, and religious leadership within the family:

> My grandmother now she wasn't young … when I used to go in there and she used to go right through her service. She wasn't able to walk to church … I would go in there Sunday mornings and that was like a service for me. She'd get in her rocking chair. I can see her now. She would go through every bit of the service and I got to learn it. You know, the answers. She would tell me a lot … you wouldn't be allowed to go out around the door, jumpin' and carryin' on if she was in there. Every Sunday when she was well enough, she used to go through the whole morning service … She could sing, too. Now Grandfather, I never heard him sing … but he would sit down to the table when she would be there with her books singing and … go[ing] through every bit of the service.

Jane's lasting impact on her granddaughter's spiritual life (and on the life of later descendants) appears in Prudence's recollection of "granny's grace," which she continued to use at special family occasions such as Christmas dinner or weddings.[6]

In the decades following the Second World War, Sundays were still defined for Anglican families by church attendance and restrictions on both work and leisure, although some new traditions and rituals emerged with the increase in material prosperity and consumer culture. Pat (Morgan) Woolgar recalled of Sundays in the 1950s:

> Up early and breakfast and out to church. If you went to early church there was no breakfast, right. So, went up to church and dressed up in all your best Sunday clothes and Sunday shoes and

Figure 3.3 Remembered as a spiritual leader within the family, Jane Morgan, pictured here with husband Abraham and granddaughters, conducted informal Sunday morning worship for herself and Abraham at their kitchen table in Seal Cove because she was physically unable to walk to formal services in Upper Gullies.

> all that … Mom usually stayed home. There was a crowd of us … We usually had dinner cooked in the middle of the day. Turkey, roast, or whatever. Then after dinner we would be rushing to do the dishes and then off to Sunday school. And then, after that … we didn't do too much. We would always go for a drive because we did have a car … so Dad would take us for a drive for ice cream or something like that. As we got older we used to like to walk back to church [with our father] in the nighttime sometimes as well.

Like Pat, Myra (Porter) Rideout and Judy (Rideout) Dawe described wearing "special clothes" or "good clothes" in the 1950s and 1960s, and that "there wasn't much left to Sunday" by the time church, dinner, and Sunday school were done.

Whether to keep children from playing on Sundays appeared to have varied between households and changed over time even for devout families. Marge (Saunders) Dawe noted that on Sundays in the 1930s children were "not allowed to do anything. No skating, no swimming, no sliding." Mildred (Butler) Porter likewise recalled of the 1920s that there was "no swimming" on a Sabbath day. Marge described how such activities were considered "a sin," and how her first husband Chesley Andrews "lived [in Upper Gullies] with his grandmother Aunt Selina Andrews and she did not even wash a dish on Sundays. They got a bite to eat and that's about it." Chesley's brothers, who lived with another family after the death of their father, could go sliding on Sundays, Marge recalled, but "Aunt Selina would not let him out." A more relaxed attitude towards children and Sunday play came in the next generation. Pat described how in the 1950s "we kind of weren't allowed to do a big lot on Sunday when I was growing up ... But now with my children I would let them play and do things ... [such as] skating." Edna (Rideout) Warford noted how on Sunday during the 1960s and 1970s her children would "play ... out around the door [and] ride the bike. I didn't keep the bike from them or anything like that." For some Anglican families in the 1950s and 1960s, recreational activities were acceptable after church on Sundays, more like the Roman Catholic model Doris (Nagle) Bishop described than the strict Protestant approach recalled for earlier decades. Joyce (Andrews) Morgan stated that while "people didn't do any work" on Sunday, "you could probably go off fishing or something like that but you didn't play cards." Eileen Morgan likewise noted that to "go off on a picnic and maybe have a cup of tea in the woods" was typical Sunday afternoon recreation.

Joyce's differentiation of Sunday leisure activities such as fishing (accepted) and playing cards (forbidden) highlights how Anglicans understood Sunday observance as part of a larger pattern of popular religious practice, including the prohibition on playing cards during Lent. Other practices were consistent with patterns of middle-class family religion identified among American Protestants in the late nineteenth century, including "the long Sunday afternoon carriage ride."[7] Edna described of the 1940s: "Sometimes we would visit our aunt in Kelligrews in the horse and carriage. We enjoyed that a lot. Sometimes after supper dad would take us out in the boat, out around [Kelly's Island] in a little old row boat." By the 1960s, the Sunday car drive was a new version of an old ritual for Conception Bay families who could afford private automobiles. A woman who raised her family in 1960s Upper Gullies noted that after dinner "we had to go for a Sunday drive," and while

Figure 3.4 In the 1950s and 1960s, while church attendance and restrictions on work remained an important part of "keeping the Sabbath," family-oriented leisure activities such as going on a Sunday drive or Sunday picnic became a regular part of observing the holy day. Pictured above is Reg Morgan of Seal Cove, enjoying such a picnic with his sons in 1961.

most women described ice cream as part of this ritual, in some families it was considered a Sabbath violation. Myra recalled: "We took [the boys] for a drive and my husband was very strict about [not] giving them an ice cream. I used to say 'that is a sin' and he would say 'No, the day is Sunday. I am helping to keep those fellows open by buying the ice cream.' After a while he gave in as they got bigger." Myra's account is especially interesting in her use of the word "sin" in a traditional Newfoundland way, meaning "a shame" or as a term of "reproach for a cruel or thoughtless deed."[8] While her husband considered the opening of stores on Sunday to violate the Sabbath, for Myra the "sin" lay in denying a special treat to their children rather than in violating the Sabbath, suggesting a less formal and institutional view of Christianity.

Sandra (Taylor) Tilley also described the Sunday drive, and recalled Sunday evening after church as a social time in her childhood home:

> We would go for our Sunday afternoon drive, often up to Holyrood to get ice cream or something. I don't remember going to church at night myself, but there was somebody going to church, because what I remember is the after church. We had a woodstove and a wood box and couch and table and chairs in the kitchen and I remember Sunday evenings there would be people in our house. Godfather and Aunt Lizzie and other people would come after church and Mom and Dad and … we just sort of sat … I was the youngest of the family … I remember many nights on the wood box and just listening as they were going on with their talks. Of course that would cover everything from family to politics to religion.

Women participated in these conversations, sharing opinions and experiences, and while Newfoundland yarns are often associated with men's voices, Sandra recalled that "Mother was a phenomenal story teller." Other Anglicans, especially those who lived in the west end of the parish, attended worship at the Salvation Army citadel in Long Pond as part of their Sunday evening "after church" ritual.[9]

Children and Church Attendance

While middle-class prescriptive literature envisioned entire families attending services of public worship together, within Conception Bay households this was rarely the case.[10] Decisions about which adult(s) would take children to church varied from household to household. Enid (Porter) Haines attended church with her paternal grandmother, who lived with her family. "She would be going off to church in the morning," Enid remembered, "and she would just hold out her hand to a couple of us and whoever be there we just go on." Enid went on to describe how "we came home from church to cooked dinner," usually prepared by her mother. In other families, men took responsibility for preparing the midday meal on Sundays while other family members attended formal worship.

The practice of Conception Bay men taking their children to church while women stayed home was noted by newcomers to the area. One woman, who grew up Anglican on the west coast of Newfoundland, compared church life in her hometown with that of Upper Gullies: "Men with their children. I found that [different]. Men went [to church] with their children." Upper Gullies native Cynthia (Scott) Dawe recalled of the 1940s: "A typical Sunday when I was a young girl I went to church with my father and we sat in the back seat of the church. That was the only place he would sit. My mother then would be cooking dinner and then in the night my mother and father went to the 7:00 p.m. service." Mildred (Butler) Porter described how "I would get up lots of Sunday mornings longing to stay in the bed but I had to get up and go to church with me father." After service, during Sunday dinner, Mildred and her older sisters would tease their father and his efforts to encourage her to take a more pious approach to church attendance:

> I was the only one that went with Dad. We come home and sit down to the table. [Someone would ask,] "What did you see in church this morning?" [I'd answer,] "So and so had a beautiful hat on, or a new pair of shoes or a new coat." Dad would pipe up, "Is that all you goes to church for? Sitting and seeing what you can see? This one got something new on and someone else got something else on." Well, he would pick it up every time. My other two sisters would do it for badness, and I would try to rhyme out what I seen.

Emma (Petten) Warford remembered how her husband and daughter "would go to church in the morning and I would stay and cook dinner, then I would go at night." Emma felt "it was wonderful" to be left at home, in that it showed her husband was interested in their child's religious upbringing.

Emma's contentment reflects her experience growing up, when "my grandfather was there in the church all the time" but her grandmother "didn't go as much as she was the one who looked after the children." Similarly, Marge (Saunders) Dawe described how her first husband "went to church continually" while she "stayed home with the youngsters and cooked dinner." Like Emma, Marge grew up with her father attending church while her mother cooked, and wryly noted his habit of bringing home guests for dinner that "Mom would have to feed and if there was anything left over, she'd get it." Marge bluntly recalled of the 1950s that parents did not take children to church until they were old enough to "sit down and shut their mouths," a view Edna (Roberts) Haines echoed: "you couldn't take children to church; you had to get someone to mind them." While Beulah (Porter) Morgan's husband "took [the children] to church every Sunday," she noted how there was afternoon Sunday school "for the children that were right small." The practice of men taking children to church while women stayed home was not part of Beulah's childhood experience, and neither was her husband Gordon raised with regular church attendance. Beulah described attending weekly Pentecostal services with her mother as a child, with Gordon noting how religion "wasn't forced on us or nothing like that. We would please ourselves if we went to church or not or Sunday school."

This change from "pleasing ourselves" to "church every Sunday" reflects the emphasis on family religious life that the Reverend Mark Genge and other clergy brought to the parish of Foxtrap and Hopewell in the wake of the Diocese of Newfoundland's union with the Anglican Church of Canada in 1949, an emphasis consistent with trends in other Christian traditions across North America.[11] Moving to Seal Cove in the late 1950s, Marjorie (Bullen) Morgan remembered how "it was important to go to church and I think an awful lot of people was under that same frame of mind." She recalled of raising children in the 1960s that it was important that parents "took them to church," even though in her own experience of growing up Anglican in Fortune Bay, "We didn't go to church because there wasn't a church [in our community]. We didn't have a lot of services but still you were taught the value of what it was to be a Christian, I guess. You certainly were taught the Commandments and taught to obey them. When we were growing up that was important." When asked to explain what she meant by "to be a Christian," she elaborated: "You didn't steal, you didn't lie, you weren't jealous of other people's stuff. You honoured your father and your mother. You looked up to your elders. You know, you didn't swear, if you did, you knew about it. [Mom and Dad] sort of lived by the Commandments and the Bible I think more … they never done any work [on Sunday] unless it was absolutely necessary … Sunday was really the day when you behaved better than you normally did if you could." For Marjorie, the absence of institutional church structures and services meant that religion and religious instruction was centred on family life, with both parents responsible for teaching children how "to be a Christian."

Sunday Observance and Popular Religious Rituals

Popular Sabbath-keeping for Conception Bay Anglicans included a prohibition on using scissors or any other kind of blade on Sundays. This included razors, paring knives, and vegetable peelers. Judy (Rideout) Dawe recalled of the 1950s: "I tell you one thing I remember distinctly. We used to have dolls and cut outs and stuff like that. You weren't allowed to use scissors. Weren't allowed to use scissors on Sunday." Sandra (Taylor) Tilley echoed her memory: "You weren't allowed to use scissors on Sunday and you certainly weren't allowed to cut hair on Sunday."[12] This prohibition on hair-cutting extended to shaving and could reveal interesting aspects of popular morality. As Myra (Porter) Rideout recalled, some men considered shaving on Sunday worse than heavy drinking: "My [first] husband, he would not shave on a Sunday. He drank, but if he came home [Saturday night] and it was five to twelve say and he knew he couldn't shave in that length of time he said he would bear the shame the next day." Myra went on to describe more fully the prohibition on using scissors and one clergyman's dismissive response to her inquiries about the tradition:

> [One time I asked the minister] is it right? I was brought up that you shouldn't cut horn nor hair on the Sabbath day. He just dismissed it all ... I still don't know, if it is in the Bible or it is out. He kind of laughed at me, you know ... I said I was brought up you didn't take the scissors in your hand. You be a little girl playing cut outs, you make paper dolls you know and you cut out outfits for them. That was a Sunday, you didn't do it. And then to cut your fingernails. That was done Saturday night, you got in the washing tub and you got your bath and your fingernails were cut and your toe nails as you were getting prepared for Sunday. All that had to be done Saturday night.

Myra's curiosity about the official status of a popular tradition demonstrates how some women struggled to reconcile their personal beliefs and practices with what they believed the church expected of them, as well as a desire to do the right thing in terms of religious observances.

Sunday Dinner

The cooking and eating of Sunday dinner was (and remains) an important domestic ritual in Newfoundland, especially associated with preserving the family unit by bringing together members to share a weekly meal.[13] In many parts of North America, preparing, cooking, and serving Sunday dinner could conflict with official expectations to "remember the Sabbath and keep it holy," especially for women: "A Sunday under the conditions of 19th-century, white, middle-class domesticity … with food on the table for a large family and guests, would not have been the same 'day of rest' for the wife that it was for the husband."[14] The example of Conception Bay reflects more complicated gender relations and sexual division of household labour, as well as the development of practices designed to help preserve Sunday as a day of rest and religious observance for all family members.

Many women described peeling vegetables for Sunday dinner on Saturday night, a ritual associated both with the prohibition on using blades on the Sabbath and with keeping Sunday a "day of rest." Salvationist, Anglican, Bible Christian, and Pentecostal households all reported peeling vegetables for Sunday dinner on Saturday evening.[15] While not common among Roman Catholic households, doing so was usual for Anglicans in other parts of Newfoundland. Doris (Nagle) Bishop, who grew up Roman Catholic on the Southern Avalon, described how the "Church of England people" she met after her move to Long Pond in 1949 had a different view of keeping the Sabbath than she was used to in Bay Bulls. She noted especially the practice of "not peeling vegetables on Sunday" and added, "I never remember that at home." In contrast, Marjorie (Bullen) Morgan, raised Anglican in Fortune Bay, recalled how her family "lived by the Commandments and the Bible," and added, "they never done any work [on Sunday] unless it was absolutely necessary … Saturday evening, everything was got ready for Sunday dinner." Pat (Morgan) Woolgar reported of her Bible Christian grandmother: "I often heard my dad say that his mother made bread twice on Saturday and of course they always peeled their vegetables on Saturday for Sunday and my mom did the same thing for many years. Saturday night she prepared for Sunday dinner." Beulah (Porter) Morgan, whose mother was Pentecostal and father Anglican, likewise recalled how the Sunday meal "would be ready in the night, the vegetables peeled and stuff."

Along with the rituals surrounding its preparation, the Sunday dinner had special status as a family meal based on the religious character of the day on which it was eaten. Selina Porter of Long Pond remembered that Sunday was "the day of worship" upon which work and play were forbidden, and that Sunday dinner was a "thanksgiving" and "special meal of the week." Her description of a 1920s Sunday dinner is a meal still familiar to many Newfoundlanders: "Carrot, turnip, parsnip, cabbage, and onion boiled with salt meat or salt pork. Peas pudding … cabbage … some type of fresh meat roast[ed] in the oven … gravy. The meat ranged from beef, salt water birds, rabbit, to hens owned by the family or wild fowl. The specialty of the meal was a duff (pudding) of some sort, either plain, blueberry, or raisin. To top off the meal, bottled beets were sometimes available."[16] Selina described the prayer ritual surrounding this meal: "The blessing of the food and of all around the table occurred before any eating and when everyone was finished thanks had to be given for the meal before anyone moved from the table."

In the 1920s Sunday supper was not a "cold plate" of sliced meat, potato salad, pickles, lettuce, and tomato, as grew popular in Conception Bay in the 1940s and 1950s as commercial food products such as processed meats and mayonnaise became available, but "a light but sweet and satisfying meal" of jam, stewed apples, or prunes served with fresh cream, buns or cake, and tea.[17] This lightness and sweetness made Sunday supper distinctive for rural families, especially in the consumption of "slightly elevated baked goods" such as cake, which required refined sugar, instead of "basic, unpretentious" everyday baked goods such as plain bread and biscuits.[18] While Selina believed the simplicity of this meal was rooted in a popular understanding that eating a second large meal in one day was wasteful, the preparing, serving, and cleaning up from a large Sunday supper would also add significant labour to the "day of rest" for women. Its simple nature therefore helped to protect women's Sabbath, as did the Sunday breakfast, which according to Selina was usually brewis (hard bread) put to soak the night before and eaten "with a bit of butter on it," rather than the cooked porridge prepared on other days of the week.

When asked to describe a typical Sunday, women routinely discussed the Sunday dinner. For Conception Bay households, eating this meal was as important to observing Sunday as participating in services of worship or Sunday school. A particular combination of foods (root vegetables, salt meat, gravy, "duff"), eaten at a set time of day (noon "dinner," never an evening "supper") was a well-established and widespread family ritual of Sabbath observance. Significantly, the women of the household were often not responsible for cooking this meal. Instead, families came up with a variety of strategies to ensure that the "cooked dinner" was ready at noon, yet no single family member was unable to attend church. Sandra (Taylor) Tilley and Marjorie (Bullen) Morgan described how family members took turns staying home to cook while the rest went to church, with the person who stayed home attending services in the evening. In the words of Myra (Porter) Rideout, who was responsible for meal preparation and childcare during her first marriage: "Sunday dinner had to be cooked," and so she took her children to church "in the night."

In other families, men cooked Sunday dinner. Violet Warford recalled of the 1940s how "Mom always went to church and Nan went to church and of course I always went too." While her mother "had her vegetables cleaned and everything Saturday night," it was her father who "stayed home and cooked dinner." Judy (Rideout) Dawe also described how her mother "always went to church on Sunday when we were growing up. Dad used to cook dinner and we had to go to church." Judy's mother, Prudence (Morgan) Rideout, recalled how the practice in her childhood home was for her mother Effie (Morrey) Morgan to stay home to cook while her father took the children to church. This may have reflected Effie's sense of dissatisfaction with Anglicanism and feelings of isolation in Seal Cove.[19] Likewise, Beulah (Porter) Morgan, who faced Anglican bigotry over her Pentecostal upbringing, stayed home while her husband and children attended worship – the reverse of her experience as a child, when her Pentecostal mother had attended services while her Anglican father stayed home. Responsibility for cooking Sunday dinner could change as families changed, especially as children grew older. Mary (Petten) Porter described how "Saturday night I would get my Sunday dinner ready and my husband or one of the girls would stay," while daughter Enid (Porter) Haines, possibly recalling when she and her siblings were younger, noted that "Mom didn't go because mom had fourteen children. She always cooked Sunday dinner. So she would go eight o'clock in the morning to the early service. Then dad and my grandmother would take us all off to the eleven o'clock service." Mary, who came from an equally large family, similarly recalled how she and her siblings would "go to church with Dad," suggesting her mother prepared dinner, although "some Sundays Mom would go" as well.

Staying home from church did not mean women did not worship informally. After radio arrived in Conception Bay, some women listened to religious broadcasts as they cooked the Sunday meal.[20] Pat (Morgan) Woolgar recalled that her mother would listen to a religious program such as VOCM's "Chapel for Shut-Ins" as she worked. Myra (Porter) Rideout noted how on Sunday morning once "you have the pots cooking" it was nice to "take a blow" by sitting and listening to a religious program on the radio. Men who stayed home from church to cook Sunday dinner may have listened to these religious broadcasts as well.[21]

Keeping an Anglican Lent: Official Perspectives

In the February 1925 issue of *Diocesan Magazine*, Bishop William White published a lament about the many "careless and indifferent" Anglicans in Newfoundland who did not "keep Lent" and were unwilling "to alter in the slightest degree their habits and customs if thereby self-denial and self-sacrifice become necessary."[22] White emphasized Lent as an opportunity for spiritual renewal among Christians, especially needed in what he described as increasingly demanding and complex times. He encouraged the faithful to lead nonparticipants by example, and to show "earnest zeal and devotion to Christ" by keeping Lent through "something quite elementary – the conquest of some doubtful habit, the breaking of a questionable friendship, the adoption of some desirable practice, or the making of some quite general good resolutions." Regarding fasting during Lent, White explained to readers in 1936 that the Church of England "has not imposed upon her people the obligation of rigid adherence to a set of rules," and encouraged Anglicans to "place Christ first" and mark the season with personal prayer, participation in worship, and the giving of self-denial offerings.[23] In 1944, the Reverend John Meaden similarly advised *Diocesan* readers that "the freedom which we enjoy in the Church of England from minute regulations increases rather than diminishes our responsibility for a proper observance of Lent."[24]

Anglican Church leadership could be mindful of the impact of economic hardship on observance of Lent, especially in some members' ability to give extra financial offerings. In 1927, while outlining to

Anglicans that all Lenten self-denial offerings that year would go towards the cathedral restoration and Queen's College building projects, White wrote that "self-denial to not a few is a daily experience by reason of their straightened circumstances. These cannot be expected to give much, if anything, but in almost every locality there are some who would be better in soul, and in body, too, very likely, if they did without something and gave what they save for the Cause of Christ and his Church."[25] For class-conscious White, the potential health benefits of fasting outweighed the risks, especially for the prosperous.

Throughout the mid-1900s, leaders of the Anglican Church in Newfoundland repeatedly encouraged members to approach Lent as a time of spiritual renewal, rather than simply engaging in the "superficial religious effort" of fasting or self-denial. "There is danger that Lent may degenerate into an outward conformity to custom, and nothing more," *Diocesan* editor the Reverend Leslie Pike wrote in 1929, "without the corresponding inward reaction. Formality, whether in the keeping of Lent or in the performance of any other religious exercise is of little worth."[26] To help ordinary Anglicans realize the spiritual benefits of Lent, in 1937 the diocese began to distribute "simple reading material" to church members, including the "little booklet, 'Forward, Day by Day,'" which provided Bible readings, prayers, and meditations.[27] Yet attention to the body and conquering physical and material "inclinations" remained an important aspect of the season. In the mid-1930s, at a time of economic, social, and political uncertainty in Newfoundland, the church was especially keen to focus attention on Christ's physical sufferings; to encourage Anglicans to meditate on "the process of crucifixion [as] real pains in the tender human body of Our Saviour," and to compare this with their own physical beings.[28]

By the late 1930s, the church had summarized a balance of the physical, spiritual, and financial aspects of Lent in what was to become the official expectation of the pious Anglican up until the 1960s: "The evangelical virtues taught us by Our Lord ... Almsgiving, Prayer, and Fasting."[29] That being said, at times the church's emphasis for Lent changed. In the early 1940s, language of "penitence for past sins" briefly entered official Anglican discourse on keeping Lent.[30] This may have been a response to what the church labelled the "special circumstances" of the Second World War and the increased "over-drinking and un-chastity" it identified among the Newfoundland population.[31] By the 1950s, Anglican leadership was responding to increased prosperity and consumerism by placing new emphasis on self-denial. In 1939, "giving up some pleasure, however innocent" formed only one part of an eight-part guide to Lenten observance published in the *Diocesan*; in 1944, *Diocesan* editorials stressed how Lent was not primarily about giving up "a few trifles" such as cigarettes, sugar, or movies.[32] By the 1950s, however, Abraham was calling Lent a time to practise "restrictions on our liberty" and "mortifications of the flesh."[33] A third of the practices for keeping Lent recommended in 1955 related to self-denial in matters such as "food and drink," "ordinary social amusements," "gaieties," "light reading," and "betting." A piece recommending fasting appeared in 1960 and called for "abstinence from food and drink" so that "the flesh may be subdued to the spirit." In 1961, a list of "What to 'Give up' in Lent" included "television one evening a week" and "buying anything but essentials."[34] "We need to discipline the body," Bishop John Meaden wrote, "not because the body is evil, but because our body is, or is intended to be, holy. Our whole being, including our bodies, is meant to be spiritual ... and it is here that fasting comes in and, unpopular as it may be, confronts our self-indulgent age."[35]

Popular Lenten Practices

Despite church leaders' concern that many ordinary Anglicans did not observe it as they should, for many Christians of mid-twentieth century Conception Bay, Lent was a particularly holy time of year when daily and weekly routines changed as part of religious observances. Starting with Shrove Tuesday (locally known as Pancake Day), and proceeding through Ash Wednesday to Good Friday, families increased their church attendance and, especially, engaged in the embodied practices of fasting and/or "giving up something for Lent." Women remembered that both fathers and mothers practised, and enforced, Lenten self-denial. Mildred (Butler) Porter, who grew up in the 1930s, summarized: "Lent was Lent and it was kept. You didn't do this and you didn't do that. ... You knew ... what you was allowed to do and what you wasn't allowed to do."

In most households, observing holy days such as Ash Wednesday or Good Friday centred on preparing and serving particular foods or avoiding others. Salvationist Selina Porter described the typical Ash Wednesday meal as salt fish and bread without butter, drawing the comparison with abstinence from butter on Good Friday and noting that on Ash Wednesday "you'd start in then, not eating, you're fasting then."[36] Anglicans Rachel (Batten) Fagan, Sarah (Batten) Bussey, and Charles Bussey recalled Ash Wednesday as a fast day on which no butter or "grease" was eaten. While Charles remembered eating herring on Ash Wednesday, his wife Sarah described "dough b'ys and lassy" instead.[37] Meal choice on Ash Wednesday reflected how primary occupation could shape religious observance: while Sarah was raised in the farming household of James and Rebecca Batten, Charles's family fished from Kelly's Island, in Conception Bay, and only lived in Foxtrap during the fall and winter months.[38]

Women also remembered special Ash Wednesday church services. Marge (Saunders) Dawe described parading from Long Pond schoolhouse to All Saints Church, where there was a service for the students. She told how local Roman Catholic children only went to school after dinner on Ash Wednesday and how St Patrick's Day fell during Lent and "RCs could do what they like" including have a dance in the Star Hall. For Anglicans, no social activities such as dances, concerts, or card games were held during Lent, even as church fundraisers. Marge noted that she and her siblings were not allowed to go to the St Patrick's Day dance, but as they got older they would go anyway, even though "Dad didn't like it." She described the extra church services of Lent: alternating Wednesdays at St Peter's and All Saints (due to shared clergy), and every Friday evening at Long Pond school.[39]

While Conception Bay women recalled that participating in mid-week Lenten church services was central to observing the season, of equal importance was "giving up something for Lent," an act of devotion which everyone practised. As Edna (Roberts) Haines stated, deciding what to give up was the "first thing" done during Lent. Self-denial could be food-related, but could also extend to anything considered recreational, such as playing games, drinking alcohol, or smoking. Cynthia (Scott) Dawe of Upper Gullies recalled: "We … went to church and observed Lent and you tried, I guess, to give up something for Lent … You would give up candy and any kind of sweets. I think some of the men would give up drinking. That was one thing the men tried to give up. I can't think right now about what my mother did. But we as children always gave up something and it was usually sweets." Other women also described giving up sugar or candy. Mary (Petten) Porter recalled that normally, "if Dad went to the store, he'd bring back maybe a bag of apples or, maybe a candy each for us," but "once Lent come you didn't get no candy or nothing."[40] Giving up smoking for Lent was described by several others, including Joan (Petten) Jefford, who recalled how her father loved to smoke but would give it up each year.[41] Giving up butter for Lent was mentioned by Marjorie (Bullen) Morgan, Emma (Petten) Warford, and Beulah (Porter) Morgan. In contrast, Marge (Saunders) Dawe simply stated of her childhood: "It was in the Depression, we had nothing to give up."

In separate conversations, sisters Joan (Petten) Jefford and Mary (Petten) Porter remembered how no games would be played in their family home during Lent. Joan told me, "we used to love to play cards" but never played "any game of cards" during Lent, likely to distinguish between competitive bidding games such as hundred and twenties (known as "growl" in some parts of Newfoundland) and more benign games such as go fish. Joan recalled that the checkers were put away and that "we had to do our lessons and studying and all that," while Mary recalled that "Lent was really religious for us in our house. Yeah. We used to play different games through the winter and playing cards and as soon as Ash Wednesday came everything, you know we had lots of games to play ... Dad would take [them] and put [them] down in the bag from us." Within the prohibition on games, the most widespread practice among Anglicans appears to have been not playing cards.[42]

The Lenten prohibition on playing cards affected the social life of the community,[43] and apart from food restrictions was the aspect of Lent most discussed by informants. Sarah (Batten) Bussey, Charles Bussey, and Rachel (Batten) Fagan remembered of the 1920s and 1930s that during Lent no one in the community would organize entertainments, dances, or card games.[44] Beulah (Porter) Morgan recalled "nobody gettin' married" during Lent since there could be no dances. Yet other traditions developed to fill this social gap, especially among women. When asked about Lent, Myra (Porter) Rideout answered, "Mom always brought in the matting frame," to which her mother Mildred added, "Oh yes, that was in place of cards." Myra went on to describe this woman-centred Lenten ritual: "Something had to take the place of [cards]. Maybe your sister-in-law would come from Foxtrap and someone else for a day hooking a mat. Or maybe, I heard some of them had a quilt. They probably didn't have a matting frame or anything like that. It was a wonderful feeling because you had this coming together." "We knew when the time of the year came, what was expected," Mildred explained, with Myra adding that when the season came, "that was it, Aunt So-and-So coming today for a day of matting" and "although it [Lent] was more restricted, you really looked forward to it."

The Conception Bay practice of women cooperatively matting or quilting during Lent was reflected in local CEWA branches. At a meeting in Long Pond on 4 March 1931, "some of the Sisters ... started hooking the mat," and by 25 March they had "finished it, and put it away." Members worked cooperatively at mats and a quilt during Lent in 1938 and 1939 as well.[45] In 1939, Seal Cove branch secretary Lizzie Dawe described how during Lent "some of the Sisters went busy matting while some more of them went sewing the quilt."[46] In Seal Cove, however, members saw working on common projects such as quilts primarily as a way to cooperatively raise funds, which could be worked on at various times during the association year.[47] The ritual of women working together on a mat or quilt during Lent appears to have been particularly important to the women of Foxtrap and Long Pond, which perhaps reflects the enhanced connection between textile work and religiosity displayed in that branch's activities.[48]

The ways in which CEWA women "kept Lent" as an association changed over time, especially in matters of self-denial. In the early 1920s at Long Pond, the women interpreted self-denial in terms of fasting and abstinence from social pleasures such as playing games, as was practised in families. In 1921, members of that branch celebrated the end of Lent by having tea and playing games at their weekly meeting of 6 April, with secretary Lilly Greenslade noting that twenty-nine women attended (the largest turn-out in months) and "everybody enjoyed themselves thoroughly."[49] In 1923, tea was served at a Long Pond meeting during Lent (described as an "indulgence" by branch secretary Winnifred Dawe) but only because the Reverend Hugh Facey was in attendance.[50] Although serving tea was not part of the weekly meeting at Long Pond at this time, on 18 March 1925 the women agreed that during Lent they would "have a ten cent tea among the members to raise our Self Denial offering," a financial contribution to the diocese expected each year. Through most of the mid-1900s, this tea was the primary Lenten observance at Long Pond CEWA meetings.[51] While their personal and domestic practice of self-denial during Lent focused on food restrictions and other embodied practices, women of Long Pond, when in association, interpreted self-denial as a financial obligation to be met through additional food consumption.

In contrast to members of the Long Pond branch, during the 1920s women of the Seal Cove CEWA paid little attention to Lenten self-denial. During Lent in 1929, the branch secretary noted a "nice cup of tea" was served at most meetings, although the worthy president Susie Lear suggested on 19 March that "there should be no tea next Tuesday night as it was Holy Week." During the 1930s, not only did women continue to have tea during meetings in Lent, but they appear to have put extra effort into association lunches. Branch secretary Annie Dawe reported on 9 February 1937 that in recognition of Shrove Tuesday, "Sisters Sarah Dowden and Harriet Morgan fried pancakes and prepared a nice cup of tea which was greatly enjoyed by all." Likewise, "during the evening" of 3 March 1937, "soup was cooked by Sister Priscilla Morgan which she served to the sisters after work was concluded." On Shrove Tuesday 1939, "sisters Lizzy Dawe and Ethel Lear fried pancakes and prepared a nice cup of tea" while soup was served when meetings were held during Lent in homes of members whose limited mobility kept them from attending meetings during the winter months.[52] Several factors appear to have been at play in the Seal Cove CEWA's approach to observing Lent. One was practical and related to the serving of "extra" food at meetings. In Newfoundland, the season of Lent fell during the coldest winter months, February and March, and women who usually walked to and from meetings needed the extra nutrition despite the connection between self-denial and food that was part of popular religious practice. Other factors were more spiritual in origin. Seal Cove women tended towards "cooperative benevolence" or "benevolent mutuality" in their CEWA work, in that they supported each other spiritually and financially as a way to express Christian charity rather than directing their efforts towards those of a different social status.[53] Cooking and serving soup at meetings during Lent, therefore, was seen as a Christian act, suitable for a time of year when Church leadership called on Anglicans to think about and serve others as part of their spiritual development, rather than "going through the motions" of physical self-denial. An orientation towards others' needs would have also informed their practice of visiting the homes of members with limited mobility during the Lenten season.

This approach is consistent with some women's discussion of the importance of "taking up" rather than "giving up" during Lent, a practice which many associated with spiritual maturity. Pat (Morgan) Woolgar described how during Lent her mother "would always remind us that you had to take something up, too ... Give up and take up. Reading the Bible and going to church." Violet Warford described "taking up" extra choir practice in preparation for Easter Sunday. Eileen Morgan described how "in the younger years you dropped off something that you really liked, but when I got older I always took up something, like visiting the elderly." Doris (Nagle) Bishop echoed this: "We always thought about ... giving up something for Lent ... But now I feel you should take something up instead of giving it up. Do something good."

Holy Week and Good Friday

Conception Bay Anglicans observed Holy Week through a combination of domestic food rituals and church attendance. As Violet Warford summarized, "Holy Week was ... very special, especially Good Friday ... We would have dumplings and molasses for dinner around 11:30 and we would go to church ... [for] three hours." Myra (Porter) Rideout recalled that there would be church service every night during Holy Week, and termed this "a warm up for Good Friday." Church every night was also remembered by Doris (Nagle) Bishop, who acknowledged "maybe you couldn't go every night" even though the services were offered. For farming families, the season of spring, even a Conception Bay spring where cold weather could linger until June, was a busy time. Marge (Saunders) Dawe remembered Holy Week not for church, but for "going to school and working like a dog in the garden." Sandra (Taylor) Tilley likewise recalled agricultural practices around Holy Week, such as setting out cabbage seed on Good Friday. For Judy (Rideout) Dawe, doing agricultural work on Good Friday violated what she considered a holy day, and a practice that distinguished Anglicans from Pentecostals. She described of her early married life: "[My husband's] parents were all Pentecostal. They didn't observe Good Friday and I found that very strange. I found it weird. It just wasn't right. To give you an example, they used to do all their gardening. On Good Friday they would get all their gardens ready to plant their vegetables."

For Anglicans, Holy Week observance started on Palm Sunday, which Rachel (Batten) Fagan recalled as an especially religious day. She described how "on Palm Sunday everybody went to church with their palm in their coat. They were little green boughs picked in the woods from the real palm tree." Rachel condemned the imported "white" palms that had come into common use in Anglican churches for Palm Sunday celebrations in the 1960s, preferring local greenery. When asked to identify what local people considered the "real palm tree," she consulted with her husband, Gordon, who described it as a small tree "not very high off the ground and something like a pine tree and green in colour."[54] Rachel's gesture in asking her husband to identify the real palm tree suggests that men gathered these branches for use in religious ritual, consistent with woodswork as a traditional area of male labour in rural Newfoundland.[55] This belief in the "real palm tree" growing in Conception Bay demonstrates the popular Newfoundland Christian practice of making sacred local landscapes and environments by associating particular geographic features or flora with stories from the Bible. While some widespread popular religious beliefs around local trees were commonly heard in Conception Bay South (such as the cross on which Jesus was crucified being made from juniper or larch), traditions surrounding the real palm tree do not appear to have been common elsewhere in Newfoundland.[56]

Many Anglican families observed Good Friday by abstaining from particular foods, especially meat and butter. Violet Warford described her parents going to church on Good Friday and "not having any butter on your bread." Most women, including Mary (Petten) Porter, recalled observing Good Friday by not eating butter: "We maybe have raisin bread there but you couldn't put butter on [it]."[57] Both parents enforced this tradition.[58] While abstaining from butter was an important Anglican ritual, it was not practised by all Conception Bay Christians. Salvationist Selina Porter recalled a time when her son was working for Anglicans Edward J. and Emma Jane Kennedy, who owned and operated a general store on Anchorage Road in Long Pond: "Edgar used to be out to Kennedy's working and he was out there working one Good Friday and he had butter and poor Aunt Emma Jane, she was a real church woman, she said, 'My blessed, you're not eating butter this day!' 'Cause we wasn't like that see, you know, we didn't mind eating butter."[59] Selina's characterization of Emma as "a real church woman" reflected Emma's leadership in the Long Pond CEWA.[60]

While families did not eat meat on Good Friday, a long-standing Christian fast seen in many jurisdictions and traditions, in Conception Bay particular meatless meals were associated with observing the day. Several women described "dumplings and molasses," with Enid (Porter)

Haines noting that "when we came home from the three-hour service Mom would have dumplings and molasses and she would boil the molasses on the stove."[61] Like Sunday dinner, some men prepared this meal in order to accommodate women's attendance at services of worship. Gordon Morgan described how "my father would make dough boys for dinner" while his mother was at the three-hour service. This was not a uniquely Anglican tradition. Selina recalled that "dough-boys and molasses" was typical Good Friday fare in Long Pond.[62] Eating this meal did not represent sacrifice or self-denial in some households. Myra (Porter) Rideout described her three sons excitedly asking, "Is this dough-boy day?" on Good Friday morning, with her mother adding wryly, "I never see such a crowd for flour and water in all me life." Myra went on to explain that even though Good Friday church services changed, and self-denial through Lent "started to fade out," food practices remained important and helped her family to recognize Good Friday as a holy day even when they no longer wanted to attend church: "You kept the things, your meals and what not as much as you could. But that is about all. Now as [my children] got older well … they weren't going [to church]. Three boys, you know. But they knew it was Good Friday once Good Friday came. They knew it was a holy day … If they didn't go to church, they kept it." Boiled salt herring or salt cod served with raisin bread was another specific meatless meal eaten on Good Friday.[63] Eileen Morgan described how "we all used to go to church on Good Friday and had our salt herring when we came home." Pat (Morgan) Woolgar and Joyce (Andrews) Morgan, recalling the 1950s, remembered having fish on Good Friday but not necessarily the "feed of boiled herring" described for the 1920s and 1930s.[64] Enid (Porter) Haines recalled of the 1950s and 1960s that there was "fish for supper with no potatoes or anything and no fat just the fish and bread … molasses bread with raisins."[65] While many Conception Bay families ate a combination of fish and dumpling meals on Good Friday, others kept a strict Good Friday fast.[66] Emma (Petten) Warford, raised in a mixed Anglican-United Church home, described how "we weren't allowed to eat anything until Lent was over" and added that "when six o'clock came it was over, right" and they would be permitted to have a meal.

Many women remembered attending the three-hour Good Friday service at All Saints or St Peter's churches, with most emphasizing how their families stayed for the duration although some stated that "you didn't have to go for three hours but usually some part thereof."[67] Marge (Saunders) Dawe remembered attending the Good Friday service with her father "from the time that she could walk," and added that other than attending service, her family would stay indoors all that day. Emma (Petten) Warford described the emotion of Good Friday: "I remember it very well. We went to three-hour service … They told all about Jesus then, sacrificed you know and died on the cross. There was a lot of crying going on … it was all into what Jesus went through. There was a lot of tears shed. Our service was really sad on that day." Edna (Roberts) Haines described how the Reverend Heber Gosse would cry during "especially sad parts" of the three-hour service, which he conducted as a series of readings, reflections, and prayers based on the "seven words from the cross."[68] Myra (Porter) Rideout likewise noted how "you had seven words from the cross and there was times you cried" during the service. Sadness could be felt in households as well as in the church. Cynthia (Scott) Dawe described how Good Friday had a feeling "just like it was a death [in the family]," and added that at home, "we were very somber." Enid (Porter) Haines noted: "I always found Good Friday very emotional. Really, really did always. And I still do … For us, we were always taught that it was a very, very holy day. Our grandmother was alive then and it was a very very strict day. Not strict in a bad way, but very spiritual." Pat (Morgan) Woolgar likewise recalled Good Friday as "a pretty solemn time" but one that did not create a positive impression. "Right to this day I don't like it," she said, "not just Holy Week, but all of Lent. The feeling of Lent, I don't like it."

In contrast, Joyce (Andrews) Morgan recalled the day as "a bit somber, you know, reflecting on the death," but it was mainly "like a Sunday, you didn't do much that day. It was kind of a family day … a holiday." Joan (Petten) Jefford also remembered Good Friday as "a holy day, but not a strict day," and recalled the three-hour service from a child's perspective: "We had to go to church. You go to church at twelve o'clock and you come home at three. It was long services you know. I was never very interested into it because it was awful boring. It wasn't saying anything that you could understand. But now it is a lot different." Along with church attendance, Joan's parents Jessie and Henry Petten recognized the day with family ritual, which another of their children, Mary (Petten) Porter, described: "Good Friday we would get up and Dad would have prayers with us all, but it is like, we loved it. We really did like it. Mom would say, now be good ... Dad would have prayers with us, then Dad would walk around the room and give us all a kiss and then we, of course, all repeat and go kiss Mommy." In contrast, Anglican-raised Reta (Morgan) Hill of Indian Pond did not remember any special practices around Lent-keeping in her family, and noted, "I don't think Mother and Father were too religious, you know." While she recalled that her parents "kept Good Friday" and there was "church service down to the Gullies," as children at home they did not feel the day was different from any other and "played as usual."

Several women compared Good Friday and Sunday, especially in terms of abstaining from household work.[69] Edna (Rideout) Warford described how Good Friday "was a lot like Sunday really. That was the way it was kept, like it was Sunday," with Judy (Rideout) Dawe noting that "Good Friday was ... worse than Sunday. You could not do one thing on Good Friday." Cynthia (Scott) Dawe recalled: "You didn't do anything on Good Friday. No work. Only whatever had to be done. My father was a farmer so we had to do things related to the farm. But you never did anything else."[70] Edna (Roberts) Haines, whose father was a butcher, recalled how Good Friday was "really kept holy," and while her family would pray and read the Bible, no work "was done at home, not even splits made."[71] Sandra (Taylor) Tilley told me: "I remember [after church] the only thing you would do on Good Friday is probably go for a walk ... No work at all was done on Good Friday ... I grew up on a farm ... there would be no gardening or anything ... Good Friday was very solemn ... [I remember] you weren't allowed to throw water out because you were throwing it in the face of the Lord. That is one story I remember." Marjorie (Bullen) Morgan, who grew up in a fishing and seafaring family in Fortune Bay, echoed this tradition: "You did absolutely nothing. You didn't even throw water out the doors because that was the belief." Similarly, mindful of the nature of Christ's crucifixion, Marjorie noted that "no one would ever drive a nail" on Good Friday.

Conclusion

When it came to discussion of Sunday observance and keeping Lent, many women expressed a sense of declension, especially in relation to church attendance, Lenten self-denial, three-hour Good Friday services, and the availability of religious programming in the broadcast media. There was a more relaxed attitude towards domestic observance of holy days when it came to restrictions on children's activities, which coincided with the late 1950s and 1960s campaign by Anglican leadership to increase family attendance at Sunday worship. Taking children to church was a usual practice in mid-1900s Conception Bay, a responsibility shared by any adult who lived in the household. Just as bringing children to church was not considered specifically women's responsibility, neither was the preparation of the special Sunday dinner enjoyed in most families. Sundays were understood to be a day of rest for all family members, with popular practices demonstrating an effort to protect the Sabbath for women as well as for men. This understanding reflects the continuing household economy of the area, in which the labour of all family members was visible and valued, rather than a wage economy in which the male breadwinner rested on Sunday and women continued to labour at food preparation, serving, and childcare.

Increased prosperity in the 1950s and 1960s affected some aspects of domestic religious observance. The Sunday drive became common in families who owned cars, an outing that invariably involved ice cream, the eating of which became as much a part of Sunday as consuming salt meat, root vegetables, and gravy. Food was central to domestic religious observance not only of Sunday, but of the season of Lent. Certain foods, such as sugar, were commonly given up for the season, while holy days were marked with boiled salt fish, the absence of butter, dumplings, and molasses. Although church leaders suggested that most Anglicans did not observe Lent in their daily lives, recollections of Conception Bay women as well as the records of local church associations demonstrate this was not so. For CEWA women, the approach to observing Lent was to take up extra spiritual activities (promoted by the church during hard economic times) rather than to give up material pleasures (the renewed focus of church teaching in the prosperous decades after the Second World War). While "giving up" was common in personal and domestic observance, at mid-century women did not practise this approach in weekly meetings and preferred instead to focus on the perceived spiritual benefits that came from caring for each other.

Good Friday observance demonstrates the emotional aspect of religious life and the degree to which Anglican everyday practice built a sense of personal relationship and kinship with the figure of Jesus. As noted in chapter 2, devotional practices involving the display of images of Jesus in homes encouraged a sense of sacred presence and personal connectedness with Christ. On Good Friday, "tears were shed" at three-hour services, by people and clergy alike, as they remembered Christ's crucifixion on that "very emotional" day. As Cynthia (Scott) Dawe stated of her childhood home: Good Friday felt the same as when there was a death in the family, a telling comment about the relationship between spiritual and material worlds that informed religious practice in the households of Conception Bay.

CHAPTER FOUR

"We Had Lots of Trouble": Mixed Marriages, Women's Conversion, and Religious Experimentation

While in the previous chapters I examined domestic rituals related to the preservation of religious identity within households, including family prayer, Sabbath keeping, and participation in Sunday services of worship, in this chapter I consider the impact of religious change within families and communities. In the twentieth century, women and men in Anglican households appear to have been equally engaged in family religion and children's spiritual instruction, suggesting little influence of the nineteenth-century prescribed "Christian mother" stereotype. The ideal of fathers as family priests, associated with the preindustrial family economy, was part of lived practice and suggested the place of patriarchal piety within local Anglican culture. Yet this Christian-inspired vision of gender relations did not go unchallenged. Women's influence on family religious practices, as well as family's influence on women's religiosity, became especially apparent at moments of household religious disruption brought about by mixed marriages (in which the partners maintained separate religious identities) or by women's decision to convert to new traditions. The Anglicans of the south shore of Conception Bay lived in community with other Christian traditions, and relations with Roman Catholics, Methodists, Salvationists, and Pentecostals reveal much about the lived religious practices of ordinary believers.

Religious conversion is a complex issue, and scholars are often divided between "deterministic" views, focused on the personality traits of those people most likely to convert and the particular methods that religious groups use to encourage new members to join, and "agent-centred" views that consider conversion as a conscious voluntary act by a person seeking to change their identity and/or establish new commitments, whether social or spiritual. Conversion is often evolutionary in character, with "the fundamental personal transformation" it represents deserving scholarly attention.[1] Yet in this chapter I do not explore in depth the psychopathology of converts to and from Anglicanism, but instead consider how women's decisions to change religious identity could affect, and were affected by, gender relations, family dynamics, and personal spiritual needs. Women's conversion can be understood as an act of resistance against patriarchal Anglican authority within families, with such acts constructed by disapproving church leadership as examples of "women's excessive religious fervor" or "female madness."[2] This was especially so when Anglican women converted to Salvationism, which some Anglican clergy saw as evidence of "mental crisis" brought on "by the excitement of the Salvation Army meetings" rather than a deliberate spiritual choice.[3]

Sectarianism and denominational rivalry are dominant narratives within the Newfoundland historiography, with most work on religion written from an institutional perspective.[4] There has been little attention to relations between traditions as expressed in lived practice, especially women's lived religiosity. Mixed marriages were part of the religious landscape of Conception Bay, as were households in which individual family members identified with different Christian traditions. In this chapter, I consider how contact with other traditions led to religious change within households, and identify patterns of conversion and religious experimentation as nominal census data of 1921, 1935, and 1945 reveal. Other evidence of relations with people of different traditions was found in CEWA minute books and described in interviews. Anglican families of Conception Bay South were especially affected by the arrival of traditions associated with the nineteenth-century Holiness movement, including Salvationism and Pentecostalism. Women's narratives of conversion and mixed marriage demonstrate how religious change was often about preserving familial relations rather than about seeking personal spiritual fulfillment, and show how religious intolerance could be manifested in relationships between women and expressed in gendered terms.[5] At the same time, an individual woman's decision to convert can be seen as an act of resistance against patriarchal Anglican structures, especially the male-only clerical hierarchy of the official Church.

"Springing Up like Mushrooms"

In the 1920s and 1930s, as religious movements such as Pentecostalism and Seventh-Day Adventism spread across Newfoundland, Diocesan Bishop the Right Reverend William White instructed his flock. "A religion is not necessarily true because it is new," he wrote in his monthly pastoral letter of April 1926, complaining about the "sects" that were "springing up like mushrooms in every city of this western world." Echoing standard language of nineteenth- and early twentieth-century middle-class moral reformers in Great Britain and North America, White described how young rural people arriving in urban centres for work were "prey" for these new religious sects, and charged mothers with the duty to protect their daughters, in particular, from falling into the wrong religious ways when they took domestic service jobs in St John's. White described membership in the Girls' Friendly Society, a prescriptive middle-class organization aimed at working-class girls, as the best way for girls "to keep in touch … with their church" when away from home. He advised Anglican mothers that there were branches of the Girls' Friendly Society all over Canada and the United States for those girls who left Newfoundland to find work.[6] Yet, as the people of Conception Bay were aware in the early years of the twentieth century, religious conversion happened in rural communities as well as in urban settings. They understood also that mothers, singled out by White as the guardians of their children's religious lives, could encourage acts of conversion as well as foster loyalty to Anglicanism among members of their families.

By the 1930s, the Anglican diocese of Newfoundland knew it was losing members to other traditions, especially Pentecostalism. Confronted with this problem, White placed blame at the feet of "self-centred" Anglicans for whom religion "is merely a matter having to do with their individual comfort or their own personal tastes" rather than loyalty to the Church.[7] He criticized Anglicans who, offended "at the slightest provocation," are "sometimes unmeasured in their condemnation of [the church] and all her ways." He pointed to a shortage of Anglican priests, especially for work in rural and remote parts of the Island and Labrador, and the consequences of having parishes and missions where there was little contact between "the pastor and the individual members of his flock." Somewhat condescending in his notion of "defenseless" rural Newfoundlanders (although he was himself born in rural Newfoundland), he lamented: "Is it any wonder then that people are tempted to listen to any 'good man' [or woman] who may happen along purporting to 'preach the Gospel' … Prowling sectaries are often only too ready to take advantage of the defenseless state of some little flock to descend upon them and hustle them into a new fold." To White's credit, he recognized the work of female as well as male preachers and missionaries, yet he was unwilling to acknowledge that other traditions could appeal to ordinary Anglicans because they found in them a form of worship and/or doctrines that met personal spiritual needs in a way that Anglicanism, often a religion of birth rather than choice, no longer could.

An example of such a conversion, and of the family consequences that could follow, was provided by informant Reta (Morgan) Hill, who became a Seventh-Day Adventist in 1928 while working as a domestic in St John's. She went to the city at age fourteen and recalled "the hard work that we had to do" and how "we wasn't considered very much" by employers. Reta became close to her mother's sister, Maria (Morgan) Duffett, who lived in St John's and converted from Anglicanism to Adventism after attending camp meetings at Buckmaster's Field. When Reta decided to follow "Auntie Ry" into the Seventh-Day Adventist church, she faced "abuses and objections" from other women of her family, especially her mother Caroline (Morgan) Morgan, who "was bitterly against it … very prejudice[d]." Reta recalled how her grandmother Virtue (Bishop) Morgan "wasn't in favour of it" either and how Adventism "was a strange religion to the all the Protestant people out in Indian Pond." She noted how her grandfather, Virtue's husband Joseph, was sympathetic, as were her father Beniah and brother Joseph. "But the rest of them, they didn't have no patience with me. Hard words and not welcome in the house and things like that." When questioned about the main objection to her conversion, especially among female relations, Reta answered simply: "Because of leaving the Church of England … I was a lost person, you know."

By the second half of the 1930s, White was more willing to concede that people were leaving Anglicanism of their own free will, but he felt that free will was compromised by naïve ignorance of the church's doctrine and discipline. In his 1936 charge to Synod, White confessed to the assembled delegates, lay and clergy, that "sometimes we wish that

Figure 4.1 Reta (Morgan) Hill with her mother, Caroline. When young women converted for personal spiritual reasons from the tradition in which they were raised, doing so could create conflict with other family members. While Reta's conversion from Anglicanism to Seventh-Day Adventism led to "hard words" with her mother, the relationship was somewhat healed by the time this portrait was taken in 1942.

[Anglican] churchmanship were based on a more intelligent grasp of church principles; that they were not so easily influence[d] by wandering uplifters to whom the kind and hospitable Newfoundlander is an easy prey."[8] His patronizing tone, directed at ordinary believers, resurfaced during the 1938 Synod meetings: "How easily are [young Anglicans] drawn away from the Church, accept the teaching of some other religious body and embrace it with enthusiasm as though they were hearing the Gospel for the first time!"[9] The response of some church leaders to Anglicans who chose alternative spiritual paths was revealed when White went on to state that he could not agree that the diocese was "better off without" those who joined other traditions. He likewise rejected "the rather popular assumption that after all, so long as they become good Christians where they have gone it does not matter very much. We do not really believe that; and if we do it hardly seems necessary that we should go on teaching a great deal of what our Prayer Book contains." While White tended towards a sectarian response to different Christian traditions, in the years following the Second World War, the diocese began to take a new approach focused on calls for tolerance and Christian unity. This effort was led by English-born the Reverend Philip Abraham, who became the bishop of Newfoundland in 1942 after serving as co-adjunct bishop alongside the ailing White since 1937.[10] By the 1960s, Anglican Church leaders were promoting the Ecumenical Movement, with its emphasis on tolerance and cooperation between Christian traditions, at both the diocesan and parish levels.[11]

"We Didn't Know the Difference, Only Sundays"

While women spoke generally of the tension that could exist between people of different Christian traditions, they often described ways their own families tolerated religious difference. Many noted similarities between Anglicans and Roman Catholics especially, though tensions seemed to surface on issues related to work and family. Joan (Petten) Jefford of Kelligrews, which had one of the largest Roman Catholic populations in Conception Bay South, described how "when the railway went through, everyone [who] worked on the railway were all Roman Catholics," clearly repeating stories she heard as a child. "No Anglicans allowed or whatever [other] religion was around." This construction project took place in the 1880s, decades before Joan was born, but stories of unequal treatment in access to paid work may have been part of family lore in a household where both parents were active members of the Orange Order, with its ties to anti-Catholicism.[12] Joan described how there were few mixed marriages in the area, and noted the consequences faced by couples who chose to marry despite religious differences. "My grandmother's sister, she married somebody Roman Catholic on Topsail Road somewhere," she related. "She never came back after [although] her family did see her." Her latter comment suggests that being shunned by other family members was a common outcome of such matches.

At the same time, Joan recalled of her childhood that "we didn't know the difference, only Sundays" when it came to relations between traditions. She went on to describe how a Roman Catholic family named

"Farrell was next door to my father. We didn't know the difference growing up whether we were Roman Catholics or Anglicans. There was no such thing as talking about stuff like that … The only difference we knew is we wasn't allowed to go to Kelligrews RC church and they wasn't allowed to go to Foxtrap Anglican church." Once church and Sunday school ended, "we would meet each other" and socialize for the rest of the day, Joan recalled. Joan's younger sister, Mary (Petten) Porter, likewise described her close friendship with one of the Farrell girls, but, in contrast to Joan, remembered participating in worship at the Roman Catholic Church:

> They had a daughter … we were just like two sisters. When she go to mass in the morning, if was a Sunday we didn't go [to church], she would always come [over and] I used to go to mass with her. I was terrified. You'd go in and sit down in the Catholic Church and you wouldn't move your head and you wouldn't say anything. It was much like our own service. We really enjoyed [it] but then when we got old enough when we could go to our own church we did.

Mary recalled how she would join with the Farrells while they said the rosary, if she happened by their house during family prayers, and that the Farrell girl would likewise join in with their family prayer service.

In contrast, Edna (Roberts) Haines, who grew up in Upper Gullies during the 1930s, described relationships between members of different denominations as "some bitter." You would never bring up religion, she reported, and people were convinced their way was the best way; many would never step inside a church other than "their own." Emma (Petten) Warford, who grew up in a mixed Anglican-United Church household in 1930s Foxtrap, echoed Edna. She recalled wanting to go into the Roman Catholic Church in Kelligrews when she was a little girl to see a figure of the Baby Jesus, but "I wasn't allowed to go … I don't know why but you had to go to your own church and that was it." At the same time, Emma remembered, "there wasn't much difference" between the Anglican and Roman Catholic traditions. Violet Warford of Upper Gullies recalled her mother describing the Anglican and Roman Catholic people meeting on Sunday morning as they travelled to and from their respective churches, and stopping for a chat before they went on their way. Other recollections demonstrated tensions. Myra (Porter) Rideout and Mildred (Butler) Porter described relations between traditions as "not nice," with Mildred remembering being told by a Roman Catholic playmate in the 1920s that all Anglicans were "going to hell."

Judy (Rideout) Dawe, who grew up in 1950s Upper Gullies, recalled tension between Roman Catholics and Anglicans within local culture, but stressed how her mother Prudence (Morgan) Rideout encouraged tolerance:

> Back then when I grew up there was a big difference between Protestants and Catholics. That was a big thing. One time you didn't bring a Catholic person into your house. Now, I remember my home wasn't like that ... But I remember one time when my younger brother, he married a Catholic girl, before he was married ... he used to call the Catholics "micks" ... he said something about a "mick." Mom said, don't you ever use that word in this house again ... Our house was very open to different religions and stuff like that ... Salvation Army person, Pentecostal, Roman Catholic, same thing, you were just as welcome and they were just as good as you were. Even though we were brought up in the Anglican religion and religion was a big part of [our upbringing], it was never brought to the fact that [Anglican] was the only religion.

Marge (Saunders) Dawe described similar experiences from 1930s Long Pond. She recalled how people of different traditions did not mix, with some Anglican people so bigoted that they would not even speak to a Roman Catholic child. Roman Catholics were not allowed in an Anglican church, Marge remembered, and "hundreds" of Anglicans would not participate in Roman Catholic worship. Yet within her own family, her father taught them that despite "different rules and different doctrines," there was "one Bible," "one God," and "we were all God's children." Marge recalled that her father did not care which church his children went to as long as they attended worship services. He would never miss the New Year's mass at Topsail Roman Catholic church, she said, and, like Prudence in Upper Gullies, he would not tolerate negative comments about other religions.

Mixed Marriages: "A Black Protestant He Was"

Doris (Nagle) Bishop was Roman Catholic until the time of her marriage and move to Long Pond in 1949. Her experience reveals how difficult a mixed marriage could be in mid-twentieth-century Newfoundland. Doris grew up in Bay Bulls, and met her future husband Ray, an Anglican, when he was driving for a local bus company. She remembered their earliest meeting:

> He came into our home with my sister, she was older and he was a new man on the block. Then, of course, everyone in Bay Bulls [was RC] and … a black Protestant he was, you know. So he came into our home with my sister and they were singing and whatever. He was twenty years old, but I was only ten. So he said to Mom, "I don't think I am going to have Irene" he said, "I think I am going to wait for Doris." Mom laughed and said, "A lot of water will run under the bridge before she will be ready to be married."

Doris described how she finished school and started to work as a nursing assistant at the Waterford Hospital, located in the west end of St John's. One day when she caught the bus back to Bay Bulls, "I met him again. So it had to be." When they decided to get married, they had problems "in the Catholic part" of the family but not in her family, which knew and liked her prospective husband. "But friends and things," Doris said, "I had more problems there." She also described facing institutional barriers: "The big thing at that time then was that he should sign a paper if he was going to be married in the Catholic Church; he should sign a paper that the children should be Catholic. That was the thing." She said Ray went and spoke to the local Anglican rector at that time, the Reverend Gordon Elliott, who confirmed that "he had to sign a paper that the children would be Catholic if he went to the Catholic Church." Doris recalled how Ray "didn't seem to be prepared to do that. To be married in the Catholic Church was no problem, but he had seen people, I can nearly name them, that done that and then didn't carry out … and he wasn't prepared to sign." Hoping things might be different on the west coast of the Island, Doris and Ray got on the train and headed for Deer Lake: "But he still didn't have whatever was needed, permission or whatever. So he went to someone in Corner Brook, he went to a Catholic place in Corner Brook, but the rules were still there that the children had to be Catholic." The next stop was St George's, where Ray's uncle, the Reverend Isaac Butler, was the Anglican rector: "He gave us a letter to bring back to Reverend Barnes in Deer Lake. When we got off the train in Deer Lake we brought this letter to Reverend Barnes and that is who married us, an Anglican in Deer Lake. We had lots of trouble … Really had to do with religion. We wouldn't have went there if it was otherwise." Once married, Doris found she faced little trouble in the community or church because of her Roman Catholic background. She said the issue of religion "was settled as far as the Church of England was concerned" and that "I was accepted here because Ray was well known." She described being invited to join the CEWA by new friends, who were mostly women who had grown up in the local Anglican community.

As Doris and Ray's experience demonstrates, the Anglican and the Roman Catholic institutional churches discouraged mixed marriages.[13] In November 1949, the same year Doris and Ray were married, the advice column "Your Own Problems," which had become an occasional feature of *Diocesan Magazine*, answered an inquiry supposedly received from an Anglican man engaged to a Roman Catholic woman: "Can I keep my own religion if I marry in the Roman Catholic Church?" The answer summarized the official Anglican position: "If such marriages cannot be avoided, the one to whom religion means less must give way." At the same time, the writer was careful to point out the pitfalls of marrying in the Roman Catholic Church, many of which Doris described: the non–Roman Catholic would have to convert, or else the couple would need to get a special dispensation to wed and the non–Roman Catholic would have to sign a paper swearing that any children would be brought up as Roman Catholics. In contrast, marriage in the Anglican church could occur without the Roman Catholic party "coming over" and would preserve the religious freedom of all parties, including future children. "If she doesn't see reason," concluded the writer, break off the engagement, "[there are] lots of fish in the sea."[14] Similar sentiments were expressed a decade later in a *Diocesan* editorial discussing the consequences of marrying outside one's own tradition. In that case, readers were advised that "it takes more than romance to make a Christian marriage" and that matters of religious difference between spouses should be taken seriously.[15]

Newfoundland census data demonstrate how families with parents from different Christian traditions (and who preserved their separate religious identities after marriage) dealt with the question of in which tradition to raise their children, as well as the numbers of households within the geographic boundaries of the parish with members of mixed religious identity. In 1921, there were only twenty-one mixed families, a clear minority within the overall population of 544 households. Of these, just over half were cases of mixed marriage where neither partner converted to the tradition of the other or where conversion occurred after the marriage. Mixed marriages where a conversion took place are largely hidden in census data, although conversion is suggested when in-laws living within the household are of another tradition. A couple of largely Anglican households, for example, included widowed parents, women and men, who identified as Methodist.[16] Some women who chose to keep their own religious identity upon marriage nevertheless agreed to raise their children within their husband's tradition. This was true of the four 1921 families where Methodist women were married to Anglican men. By 1935, census takers recorded most of these formerly Methodist women as Anglican. This may have been a rejection of membership in the newly formed United Church of Canada, which appeared to be the trend among Methodists living on the southwest shore of Conception Bay.[17]

For marriages between Anglicans and Roman Catholics, the choice of in which tradition to raise children was not so clear cut. In the four 1921 households where Roman Catholic women were married to Anglican men, children were raised Roman Catholic in two instances and Anglican in one. (The fourth household listed no children.) Interestingly, there was only one Anglican-Roman Catholic partnership raising children as Roman Catholics in 1935. By 1945, there were five Roman Catholic-Anglican marriages reported and one Roman Catholic-United Church family.[18] With the exception of one family where the children were being raised Anglican (the father was Roman Catholic born in Canada, and the mother was Anglican born in Newfoundland), the children were being raised Roman Catholic, largely after the mother's tradition. While census data from 1921 and 1935 contained no examples of Roman Catholic men married to women of other traditions, half of the mixed Protestant-Roman Catholic families reported in 1945 involved Roman Catholic men. This suggests that earlier in the century there was either less interest in intermarriage with other traditions among Roman Catholic men, or else greater likelihood that women would have converted to Roman Catholicism at the time of the marriage. In 1963, Parish of Manuels parish priest Father Francis Jackman reported twenty-four converts to Roman Catholicism in the five years since 1957, mostly the result of mixed marriages, but did not indicate the converts' genders.[19]

During the 1920s and 1930s, in families where Anglicans were married to Pentecostals or Salvationists, the mother's religious identity appeared to determine the tradition in which her children were raised. There were only two examples in 1921, both from Long Pond. In one, a Salvation Army man was married to an Anglican woman; in the other, an Anglican man was married to a woman who identified her tradition as "gospel preacher," a possible forerunner to Pentecostalism. In both cases the children were identified with their mother's tradition. Likewise, in 1935, in families where Salvationist or Pentecostal women were married to Anglican men, the children were identified with their mother's tradition.[20] Data from 1945, which included fifteen families of mixed religious identity, reveal a changing pattern of gender relations and how religion could shape these relations. In households where the father was reported Salvation Army or Pentecostal, the children were reported in the mother's tradition, be it Anglican or United Church. This included a case of a second marriage, where a United Church woman married a Salvation Army man. While her four step-children remained Salvationist, her newborn infant was described as United Church. However, in families where the father was reported Anglican and the mother was identified as United Church, Salvation Army or Pentecostal, children were raised Anglican. This shows the patriarchal piety of some Anglican households, likewise reflected in men's leadership of family religious practices. For men who identified with Holiness religions, bringing the family into line with his beliefs and practices was less important, which perhaps reflected the evangelical notion that individual consecration took priority over earthly concerns, including "first allegiance to God, not family."[21] In addition, Roman Catholic mothers raised Roman Catholic children even when married to Anglican men, which suggests a level of matriarchy within households consistent with patterns in the largely Roman Catholic communities of the southern Avalon.[22]

"They Put Her Out of It": Methodism

In 1925, the United Church of Canada formed from a union of formerly Methodist, Presbyterian, and Congregational Churches. This included the Methodists of Newfoundland, despite a majority of clergy and members voting against union in 1923.[23] According to the 1921 *Census of Newfoundland*, there were 201 Methodists living in Conception Bay South. While it would be easy to assume that these individuals became the 192 United Church members listed in the 1935 *Census*, cross-checking their names in the 1935 *Census* reveals a different trend. While many former Methodists who lived on the southeast side of Conception Bay, especially around the communities of Chamberlains and Topsail, identified as United Church in 1935, those who lived in communities within the parish of Foxtrap and Hopewell tended to become Anglican instead.[24] This could reflect memory of Methodism's origins within the Church of England, or simply practicality. The only United Church in Conception Bay South was located in Topsail, close enough for the people of Manuels and Chamberlains to attend, but less convenient for those of Seal Cove or Kelligrews.

Some former Methodists chose an alternate spiritual path. The Methodism practised on the northside of Conception Bay during the nineteenth century was perceived by some missionaries as particularly "sedate," with one observing in 1829 that "he rarely saw his congregation in tears" and "the Methodists themselves will tell you they do not like Ranters."[25] In the years between 1829 and 1832, the practice of Methodism in that area underwent a spiritual revival, largely led by lay members, and became more emotional, demonstrative, and, in the language of missionaries, "vital."[26] Given that many south shore Conception Bay settlers originated from older communities on the north shore of the bay, this may explain why, in terms of worship, the Long Pond Methodists fell within this vital category. This vitality may have influenced their decision to reject both the United Church and the Church of England, and to instead form the heart of a new Pentecostal community.

Vital Methodist worship was sometimes ridiculed by people from other traditions, a tendency that continued in Anglican views of Pentecostalism. One Long Pond resident recalled:

> I remember a kind of funny story about my grandfather. He always said when his father was dying there was a church just out the road, and it was an old-fashioned Methodist church, and the Methodists back in those days liked to sing loud and kick up a noise in the church, and this evening they were making such a noise that somebody had to go out from the house and knock on the church door and tell them to keep the noise down because a man up the road wanted to die.[27]

Some Anglicans' treatment of Methodists was less amusing. Prudence (Morgan) Rideout described how her mother Effie (Morrey) Morgan, originally from La Scie on Newfoundland's northeast coast, came to Seal Cove after her marriage to Isaac Morgan. Effie was Methodist and identified herself as such in the 1921 *Census*. Isaac was Anglican, as were their children. When Effie came to Seal Cove she decided to join the local Anglican women's association, but was subjected to bigotry from CEWA members. As Prudence recalled, "they said as much that they put her out of it. She was United, see. She was reared up United." Prudence described how her mother "left [the CEWA] for a while after that," but wanted so much to fit into the local women's community that she converted from Methodism to Anglicanism and "went back" to the meetings. While the association had no official reason to exclude her, in that she could now meet the "true and faithful member of the Church" test required of all members, Effie became the victim of back-biting and gossip.

Prudence described how her mother "caught a couple of the women talking about her one day and what was going on" and was so angry and hurt that "she didn't feel like going to church" anymore. Prudence's daughter Judy (Rideout) Dawe described how eventually her grandmother "went back to church, but she never went back to the women's group after that." Effie's treatment by the Seal Cove CEWA members had a lasting impact on Prudence. She never officially joined any women's groups herself, although she was always willing to help out for special events such as church sales or the annual garden party. She practised religious tolerance and taught her children to do the same.[28] Effie's experience shows the informal power that some women gained through gossip networks, and how this behaviour was practised as much by the Anglican women of Conception Bay as by the Roman Catholic women of the southern Avalon.[29] Yet Effie's story also demonstrates how some women's empowerment came at the expense of other women. In this case, a religious majority shunned and isolated a newcomer of minority faith, despite her best efforts to fit in, and so reveals the limits of women's solidarity as well as of Christian unity.

Effie's story provides insight into what motivated some women to convert to another faith, the destiny of Methodists in Conception Bay, and how spiritual needs were not always met by a changed religious identity. Methodists who lived within parish boundaries, especially those who lived in largely Anglican households, tended to become Anglican rather than join the United Church. Effie's experience suggests that this was done not necessarily for the sake of domestic unity but in order to fit into the religious majority of the local community. In addition, women could place children's religious education above personal spiritual needs. Prudence recalled that while her father often "towed me to church," her mother only "went to church whenever children could go." With improvements in transportation, especially increased access to private vehicles in the 1950s, Effie finally began to worship in a personally fulfilling way. Granddaughter Judy recalled: "In later years, when we had, I didn't have a vehicle but her sons and that did, she would love to go to Topsail United Church and she would love to go to the Salvation Army [in Long Pond]. That was two religions she really loved." We know little about the spread of Methodism from the north side of Conception Bay to the south side during migrations of the mid-nineteenth century, or the form of Methodism brought to these emerging communities. Members of communities settled by more sedate Methodists may have merged into Anglican practice, while vital religionists sought the more demonstrative worship offered within the Pentecostal movement. Yet Effie's story shows that many Methodists may have walked the line between sedate and vital religion. Effie converted to Anglicanism and worshipped with her children despite distaste for the local CEWA and its members, yet her spiritual heart remained elsewhere.

"They Could Not Be a Member of Both": The Salvation Army

A Salvation Army corps was first established in St John's in 1886, and by 1891 there were almost 2,100 Salvationists among the Newfoundland population. While most lived on the Burin Peninsula and in Notre

Dame Bay, the Army also attracted members in Conception Bay.[30] In the 1921 *Census* sixteen households within communities that made up the parish of Foxtrap and Hopewell contained one or more persons who identified as Salvation Army, with most living in Long Pond or Manuels. In Long Pond, entire families tended to be Salvation Army, although there were some exceptions.[31] While James and Lavina Baird, along with their three children (aged fourteen to twenty years) identified as Salvationist, the household also included Lavina's mother, Jane Stanley, and a fifteen-year-old dependent, Maud Stanley, who identified as Church of England. Other Salvationists of varying ages and genders were lone adherents within Anglican or Methodist households.[32] Outside the Long Pond area there was only one young Salvationist family in 1921: Charles and Emma Butler of Seal Cove and their three children. Most people who identified as Salvation Army were individuals in larger households or else mature couples. These included seventy-five-year-old widower Samuel Tilley of Kelligrews, George and Naomi Morgan of Seal Cove, and Abram and Annie Dawe of Riverdale. Annie was originally from Seal Cove, where Clarence Morgan recalled there had once been a Salvation Army barracks, but not "in his time." Clarence described "Uncle Abe" in his uniform of red sweater emblazoned with "Blood and Fire," and noted how he and "Aunt Annie" would walk to Seal Cove to attend Sunday evening services of worship.[33]

In Newfoundland, Salvationism may have been most attractive to former Methodists who sought vital worship as their own congregations became more "church-like" and "respectable." Despite the belief that Anglicans rejected Salvationism as a "lower-class phenomenon," evidence from the parish demonstrates the allure that the Salvation Army held for some members of the Anglican community, including women and their families active in church life.[34]

On the evening of 9 March 1921, eighteen women of the Long Pond CEWA gathered to sew and to purchase household linen from the association's stock of member-made goods. Two women bought aprons, one treating herself to a bib-less "tea apron," a garment usually adorned with some kind of trim or embroidery worked by an association sister. A bag was purchased, along with a decorative cushion. Sister Lizzie J. Greenslade, thirty-seven years old and with three small sons, bought a piece of gingham from the association to use in home sewing. After this, "almost every Sister got to work and an enjoyable hour was spent in talking and sewing." However, a point of procedure regarding membership in the association was on some of the women's minds, and there was "a little discussion about joining members not being true and faithful members of the Church." This reference to being "true and faithful" came from the initiation pledge all sisters took and was a membership requirement outlined in the CEWA constitution.[35] The trouble at Long Pond was rooted in association members attending Salvation Army services, which some sisters perceived to be a violation of the CEWA oath. Others "did not think there was any harm in singing and praising God elsewhere," suggesting acceptance of more embodied forms of public worship than was typical in Anglican services.[36] The disagreement ended pleasantly, as "one and all promised to be present at the next meeting unless any unforeseen circumstances prevented them."[37]

Two weeks later, the matter came up for discussion again, with worthy president Susie Rendell providing a clarification on membership rules that seemed to satisfy the women. Secretary Lilly Greenslade, whose own family attended "gospel preacher" meetings while she continued to hold CEWA executive office, summarized: "The Worthy President then explained about new members joining. Anyone could join, only [not] those that had been enrolled to the Army. They could not be a member of both. Each Sister got busy then and a social hour was spent."[38] This explanation was followed by a flurry of "new members joining," most of whom were daughters of current members. Perhaps this was intended to keep the girls from enrolling in the Salvation Army, as nineteen-year-old Eliza Stanley, the daughter of founding member Mary Jane Stanley, had done. The new members included Doris Rendell (age sixteen), daughter of Susie Rendell; Mabel Dawe (age fifteen), daughter of Rachael Dawe; and Emmeline Baird (age seventeen), daughter of Jane Baird. Later that spring, Lucy Stanley (age eighteen), daughter-in-law of Mary Ann Stanley, joined, as did Susan Perrin (age thirteen), daughter of well-known Long Pond midwife and healer Eunice "Aunt Nicey" Perrin.[39]

One of the new members was Margaret Dawe (age sixteen), daughter of Jessie Dawe. Like Mary Ann Stanley, Jessie was one of the founding members of Long Pond CEWA, yet her family demonstrated the flexibility that could exist around formal religious identity. Margaret's sister Selina recalled in 1985 how her formerly Anglican family had become "soldiers of the Salvation Army" in 1914, when the movement first came to Long Pond. This suggests that Jessie was Salvationist prior to the formation of the CEWA, but became an active member nonetheless. At the same time, Jessie and Samuel Dawe's family continued to report "Anglican" for census takers, despite the conversion their daughter described.[40]

Many Conception Bay Anglicans felt, like some members of the Long Pond CEWA, that there was no harm "in singing and praising God elsewhere" as long as one remained officially a member of the Church of England. Several women noted how Foxtrap and Long Pond residents would go to Salvation Army services after attending Anglican worship.[41] "You couldn't go to the Salvation Army if the church door was open," Mildred (Butler) Porter recalled, "we couldn't pass our church door, but after church we could go where we liked." Mildred described Army services as "great fun," and her daughter Myra (Porter) Rideout noted that it would be "standing room only" on Sunday nights, with most of the crowd "Anglicans there for the show." Hugh Eason of Long Pond (born 1913) described local courting practices by stating "you'd take her to the Army" and "back home again" as a typical date.[42] For single young people, services of worship were good places to meet potential spouses.[43] Elizabeth Petten of Kelligrews, for example, described in 1981 how she met her then-future husband, Nathaniel, in the All Saints church porch one Sunday night after Evensong.[44]

"The Other Religion": Pentecostalism

The official Anglican position on Salvationism walked the line between disapproval and admiration. A September 1944 *Diocesan Magazine* editorial explained that Anglicans "cannot approve of the teaching of the Salvation Army," yet could "learn from [the Army's] evangelistic zeal."[45] Clarence Morgan of Kelligrews expressed the general admiration of the Army among people of other traditions: "Catholics, United Church, Anglicans, they all respected the Salvation Army more than their own religion. Maybe it was because of the uniform, like police, so people would respect them. They also do good for people who are poor off." The church's position on Pentecostalism was not so generous; neither were the opinions of ordinary Anglicans. Bethesda Pentecostal Assembly, the first in Newfoundland, opened on New Gower Street, St John's, in 1911 under the leadership of American Alice B. Garrigus.[46] Alice described the Pentecostals of St John's as "somewhat despised" by the general population, but noted that despite this "a large part of the city turned out" to watch public baptisms at Mundy Pond.[47] By

1929, Pentecostal converts were active in Long Pond, with first meetings at Seal Cove conducted in 1933.[48] Census data reveal Pentecostalism's impact on the local Anglican community, including women's role in influencing families' religious affiliation. In 1935, seventeen separate households within the study area included some, if not all, members who identified themselves as Pentecostal. In Long Pond-Manuels, these included the families of Charles and Elfrida Eason (four children), Harold and Mary Tilley (three children), and William R. and Annie F. Porter (eight children). While the Easons identified as Anglican in 1921, by 1945, following Elfrida's death, widower Charles and the children identified as Anglican once more.

The family of Harold and Mary Tilley was likewise Anglican in 1921, and mostly so in 1945. Like Elfrida Eason, Mary died sometime after 1935, with Harold remarried in 1940 to Anglican Irene (Anthony) Warford, a widow with three children.[49] By 1945, Harold and two older sons living in a separate household once again identified as Anglicans. The youngest of Harold and Mary's sons, still living at home, held on to the Pentecostal identity of his late mother but converted to Anglicanism later in life. This family is particularly interesting in that "the Harold Tilleys" were central figures in the spread of Pentecostalism from Long Pond to Seal Cove, and led "many old-fashioned Pentecostal services" in James Morgan's home. Despite Mary's invisibility in most accounts, she, not Harold, was likely the driving force behind the family's religious enthusiasm and possibly the lead preacher to the Seal Cove mission.[50] When it came to religion, Harold appeared to follow where his spouse led. In December 1958, he dutifully obtained and installed a new stove in the Long Pond CEWA room, where Irene was serving one of her many terms as vice president of that branch.[51]

Two older Long Pond couples who identified as Pentecostal in 1935 had roots in experiential religion. Joseph and Esther Dawe followed the "gospel preacher" by 1921, as sixty-eight-year-old Joseph would later report doing with his new wife Catherine (aged fifty-five) in 1935. The religious background of Zachariah and Mary Ann Dawe (aged eighty-five and seventy-nine, respectively) was Methodist, as it was for Long Pond resident Jabez H. Butler, who by 1935 had moved to Seal Cove and was helping establish the local Pentecostal community there.[52] Jabez and Florence Butler, along with their three children, were listed as Pentecostal in 1935 and remained so. In 1935 their household included twenty-seven-year-old

Canadian Pentecostal preacher Maud Evans, whose ministry was winning converts from among the most committed of Anglican women.[53] The first indication of this came in April 1933, as Seal Cove CEWA women discussed plans for their upcoming Easter tea and sale. Some sisters, secretary Lizzie Dawe noted, "said we should not have dancing with our sale," reflecting the Holiness belief that "dancing acted as proof of sanctification," much as it did for vital Newfoundland Methodists. Recreational dancing to secular music, rather than in response to the Holy Spirit, was "forbidden to those who sought to live the sanctified life."[54]

As soon as the matter of dancing was raised, the meeting turned contentious, perhaps because Lear was absent and unavailable to keep order. Perhaps the religious divisions, starting within a once largely homogenous Anglican community and indicated by the protest against dancing at the CEWA "time," may have shortened the women's tempers. The impact of 1930s economic hardship on local families did nothing to lighten the mood: some women opined that they should not "have [the sale] at all, because there was some of the sisters could not provide much for the tea." Lizzie recorded that the sisters decided "to leave it and speak to the Worthy President about her intentions," but the arguments were not over. A sample roll of wallpaper for the association room, selected by the president, was produced "to see if all the sisters were satisfied with it but they were not." A frustrated Lizzie pointed out the procedural irregularities and lack of deference in her account of this meeting, noting that "when the 1st Vice President [Harriet Morgan] asked if there was any remarks to make" at the beginning of the meeting, "there wasn't any but after the meeting opened ready for work there was none done" because of bickering. "We all have to be governed by [the Worthy President] while in our Association room," was Lizzie's final comment on the contentious meeting, "if the paper is suitable it will be put up soon."[55]

Two weeks later, the Easter sale was cancelled and the Seal Cove branch closed for the summer season. When it reopened in November, Lizzie reflected on the amount of goods "that was made up" and "wished we could proceed with our work."[56] The shake-up continued, however, as only one officer (treasurer Ethel Lear) was willing to stand for re-election. Lizzie was elected the new worthy president, with one of her first tasks to write to the Diocesan Council of the CEWA "concerning the members who have joined the other religion … if their names should be taken from the Roll."[57] Comparing names in the 1928–1931 Seal Cove CEWA roll book with the 1935 *Census* reveals at least a few of the dissenting voices who embraced "the other religion" in 1933: Emily Morgan of Lance Cove (spouse of Abe), Emily Morgan of Seal Cove (widow of James), and Elizabeth Anthony.

Based on census data, most Seal Cove and Indian Pond Pentecostals in 1935 were formerly Anglican, as were most in Long Pond. Alice B. Garrigus herself was raised within the American Episcopal Church of New England.[58] Anglicans, however, remained numerically dominant within the local population. As in Long Pond, there was religious experimentation among the Anglicans of Seal Cove and a distinct pattern of women influencing families' religious affiliation. Among the Seal Cove converts to Pentecostalism were elderly widower William Morgan (late wife Esther was Anglican) and Emily A. Morgan, widow of James Morgan. Emily's son Gilbert, his wife Sadie, and their three children, as well as Reuben and Elizabeth Morgan and their three children.[59] As in Long Pond, several Pentecostal families returned to the Anglican fold by 1945. While Emily Morgan and her twenty-four-year-old son Eddie John were Pentecostal in 1935, Emily's husband Abe remained Anglican. By 1945, Eddie John had married Harriet Batten, the daughter of George and Susan Batten, a committed Anglican who threw herself wholeheartedly into the work of Seal Cove CEWA after she transferred from the Foxtrap branch in March 1943.[60] Harriet moved in with her in-laws, and by 1945 the whole household was Anglican once more.

Likewise, Robert and Elizabeth Anthony (with four children) and Joseph and Ada Morgan (with three) were Pentecostal in 1935. Ada, sometimes described as "William Joe Morgan's wife," was reportedly the first Pentecostal convert in Seal Cove, although seventeen-year-old Dorcas Morgan, who converted at Bethesda while she worked, likely as a domestic servant, in St John's, was the first Pentecostal convert from Seal Cove.[61] By 1945 both Elizabeth and Ada had died, and with their husbands' remarriages to Anglicans the families returned to the Church of England fold.[62] Two other temporary Pentecostals from Seal Cove were brothers Herbert and Robert Dawe, the children of Eli and Jessie Dawe and the only converts in an otherwise Anglican family. Both identified as Anglican in 1945. While Herbert lived with his widowed father, Robert had married Roman Catholic Charlotte Constantine of St John's and formed a new household. Consistent with practice noted elsewhere in

Conception Bay, "Lottie" Dawe raised their children as Roman Catholics even though Bobby continued to identify as Anglican.[63]

Holiness, Gender, and Embodied Religious Practice

For some Anglicans in Conception Bay, seeing women in positions of official spiritual leadership within Salvationism and Pentecostalism may have made those traditions attractive. The Holiness movement provided opportunity for women's preaching and official religious leadership in ways unavailable in Catholic and mainstream Protestant traditions. The Salvation Army, early Methodists, Holiness, and evangelical traditions each supported the right of women to preach who felt called to do so.[64] Over time, however, women preachers and spiritual leaders became as marginalized within institutionalized Pentecostalism as they were in other religious traditions, a trend linked to backlash against the women's movement and increased requirements for formal leadership training. This training was often less available to women because of family responsibilities and increasingly restrictive seminary admission policies. Some Pentecostal women continued to make a place for themselves within the increasingly patriarchal structures of their church, as revealed in "call-to-preach" narratives which highlight "the importance of uncoupling official discourse from actual practice" when studying religion.[65]

In contrast, female leadership continued to characterize Salvationism, which suggests a tradition more committed to the Holiness movement's "defense of women's right to minister."[66] Salvationism appealed to Canadian working-class women because of its sense of gender equality.[67] Women in public ministry characterized Holiness revivals and may have spiritually invigorated Anglican women who were otherwise used to an exclusively male clergy. The Pentecostal concept of a "priesthood of believers" in which "both men and women are equal in the sight of God" may have appealed to women critical of patriarchal Anglican Church structure and practice.[68] The ministry of Maud Evans in Seal Cove drew otherwise committed Anglican women to the fledgling congregation, even if temporarily. Beulah (Porter) Morgan, who had been raised Pentecostal, recalled that women's position in that congregation was "equal to the men," whereas Anglicans recalled their church as a place where women had no official influence. Cynthia (Scott)

Dawe described Anglican women's traditional role as "supporters of the church" comparing this to their "more meaningful role" as participants in twenty-first-century church "structure." Marjorie (Bullen) Morgan was blunter: "Men were more predominant years ago ... women were more or less kept in their place."

Despite the Holiness movement's official support for women in leadership roles, some Anglican women remained suspicious of, and prejudiced against, these traditions. This was especially true when it came to issues of intermarriage or conversion within their own families. Beulah, whose mother Elsie Kennedy was a "lifelong" Pentecostal from Port-de-Grave married to Anglican Fred Porter (he converted in 1964), recalled of her own planned 1961 marriage to Anglican Gordon: "When we were going to get married, Gordon was away, he was in Lab City. And Mom suggested maybe when he comes home, which was just five days before the wedding, we could get married in her church. I went up [to Seal Cove] and I told his parents and they said well if that happens they won't be going. So I said very good we will get married in the Anglican Church in Foxtrap. I couldn't start off on the wrong foot with those people." When asked why Gordon's parents would refuse to attend their wedding if held in the Pentecostal church, Beulah cited difference in beliefs while Gordon noted "different form of service" and disagreement "with the way the Pentecostals was getting on," referring to the emotional, experiential nature of Holiness worship. Beulah's desire to please her in-laws led her to marry in the Anglican Church, but when asked about her own religious identity her ambiguous answer of "Anglican, I guess" reveals the extent to which her experience, like Effie (Morrey) Morgan's, was one of religious change motivated by a desire to "fit in" to a family or community rather than by spiritual conversion.

For Anglican Judy (Rideout) Dawe, marriage into a Long Pond Pentecostal family in the 1960s was no easier. She recalled how her in-laws believed that "Pentecostal was the only religion," yet she was determined to hold on to her Anglican identity: "I suppose it was a problem, but I didn't let it become a problem. I was told quite often that there was only one religion and [Pentecostalism] was it. I didn't let that bother me. I went out and did what I wanted to do. As far as I was concerned, I was no different than they were. I was going to church, and I was bringing my children to church." Describing how her husband remained Pentecostal, how her grown children have since married Anglican and United Church partners, and how her best friend is Roman Catholic, Judy reflected that "to me it is all one big family right now, to me, there is no bars," a perspective she linked to her upbringing in a home where people of different Christian backgrounds were treated with equal respect. At the same time, she noted how Pentecostal services "aren't what they used to be" and are now "like going to our church." Judy went on to describe her religious identity as "between the two of them," referring to both the Anglican and the Pentecostal worship communities.

Judy's and Beulah's experiences demonstrate the tense relationship that could exist between Pentecostals and Anglicans. Beulah recalled of 1950s Foxtrap: "The Pentecostal and the Anglican people didn't like each other. I got made fun at. I did, I did, yes I did. And I resented it … Because I went to the Pentecostal church I was made fun at. That is why I don't go to church very much because I still resent it." This bullying was made worse for Beulah by the fact that she was a child at the time, "And I was forced to go, you know." Her husband Gordon described how Pentecostal children went to the Church of England school in Seal Cove but were not allowed to attend the annual school-closing picnic: "Someone else used to take them to somewhere so, you know, they wouldn't associate with us at the picnic. Just didn't want to play the games we were playing, I guess." While parents may have kept their children from participating in secular games as part of their commitment to preserving the Holiness of their bodies, such actions also showed how adults used children (and children's bodies) to express their own religious commitment and beliefs.[69]

The Pentecostal movement encouraged believers to think less about "right" theology and liturgy, and to instead embrace the Holy Spirit's workings within their own lives. Manifested often in "exuberant worship," Pentecostal meetings could include tongue-speaking (glossolalia), testimonies, dancing and clapping, singing, acts of healing, shouting, and crying.[70] Among Conception Bay Anglicans, embodied and emotional Pentecostal worship seemed to be the most misunderstood aspect of the tradition and was singled out for far more criticism than women in leadership roles. Myra (Porter) Rideout recalled attending a Pentecostal service as a child and how the sight of a woman preacher had "made an impression" on her. At the same time, Anglican gossip about Pentecostals often contained sexual innuendo, perhaps as a response to the greater gender equality in Holiness worship than in their own church. In the early years of the movement in America, Holiness meetings led by women were labelled "promiscuous" because both women and men attended, rather than women only.[71] In the parish of Foxtrap and Hopewell, Anglican families told stories of Pentecostals "crawling around in the dark sniffing each other's arses" during worship services at Seal Cove. Teenagers were cautioned about "goings on" at the Pentecostal youth campgrounds in Long Pond, which Anglicans hostile to the local Pentecostal population described as "a good place to get knocked up."[72] The official Anglican position was more muted, but equally condemned "the Pentecostalists" for their "anti-liturgical spirit" and "unrestrained freedom in worship."[73]

As was the case in St John's, the Pentecostal practice of full-immersion baptism, especially of adults, was a source of curiosity in Conception Bay. Mildred (Butler) Porter and Myra (Porter) Rideout described Pentecostal baptism ceremonies on the shores of Long Pond, an inlet of Conception Bay close to the Pentecostal meeting hall on Anchorage Road, and how Anglicans would travel down from Foxtrap by water for the event. "Everyone would get out in the boats, as many as a boat could hold," Myra recalled, "and go down to watch the dipping." Yet adult baptism aroused as much suspicion as curiosity. Census data reveal that women were more likely to convert than men, and stories that circulated in Conception Bay about the health risks of immersion were not only gender-specific but also sought to control women's bodies by suggesting that conversion could compromise their reproductive capacity. Mildred and Myra recalled stories of how a woman baptized while menstruating "caught a chill" and died. Another, baptized while pregnant, was reported to have given birth to a disabled "blue baby" as a result of her experience in the Long Pond waters. In comparison, informants did not repeat any negative stories about women preachers, which suggests that Anglicans found female religious leaders more socially and culturally acceptable than emotional and experiential worship.

Conclusion

In situations of conversion to and from Anglicanism, women exercised considerable spiritual authority and leadership within Conception Bay households. Census data on children's religious identity in cases of mixed marriages suggest that children would be raised within the mother's tradition, rather than the father's, although by 1945 Anglican fathers increasingly meant Anglican children, regardless of the mother's religious affiliation. Women described efforts by parents in some Anglican families to teach their children to accept religious difference in the face of a society marked by official denominational divisions and a history of sectarianism. Women likewise recalled grassroots-level relationships with people of other traditions despite institutional divides, including the denominational school system.[74]

While a dominant narrative within the writing of the history of Newfoundland and Labrador has been sectarian rivalry, especially between Roman Catholics and Protestants, evidence from mid-twentieth-century Conception Bay suggests that relations between Methodists and Anglicans, and between Anglicans and Pentecostals, could be more strained than those between Anglicans and Roman Catholics. Anglicans could recognize similarities in worship with Roman Catholics, but ridiculed and reviled the experiential, demonstrative worship of Holiness groups such as Pentecostals and vital Methodists. Gossip about members of these traditions was often gendered, reflecting a perception among Church of England households, as well as in CEWA meeting rooms, that women were most likely to convert. Cautionary tales about the impact of conversion on women's reproductive capacity – and mortality – demonstrated a local population who felt that women's primary responsibility should be to their families (and the reproduction thereof), rather than to their personal spiritual fulfillment.

Despite their distaste for enthusiastic worship (with the Salvation Army the exception), Anglicans accepted women in official leadership roles as practised within Holiness traditions. This may have reflected women's and men's shared religious leadership within families and the blurring of lines between indoor (women's) and outdoor (men's) work, and therefore of gender expectations, within Conception Bay households. Religious authority that originated within the household could be exercised in the community. Anglican mothers in Long Pond used church associational life to try to prevent their daughters, like other young women in the area, from joining the Salvation Army. While sometimes conversion was a personal choice for individual Anglicans, at other times entire families embraced a new spiritual life or were shaped by religious experimentation. Census data show that women often led family religious change (both permanent and temporary), yet CEWA records demonstrate how at the community level they could resist (and resent) religious change in others.

Reta (Morgan) Hill's conversion from Anglicanism to Seventh-Day Adventism fit the stereotype of "domestic servant gone astray" as White described in the 1930s, yet her experience demonstrates how an older female family member could inspire religious change as well as anchor the young within a familiar tradition. The Diocese of Newfoundland's call for loyalty to Anglicanism did not discourage CEWA members or long-standing Anglican families from embracing new Christian identities, and narratives presented by Conception Bay women demonstrate how women's conversion could both disrupt and restore families.[75] Women in mixed marriages often converted to "fit in" and put family stability and social needs before their own religious identities. Some, like Effie Morgan, continued to carry personal spiritual desires quietly within their own hearts, while others, like Mary Tilley, were determined to seek their own religious paths and brought their children and husbands along for the journey.

CHAPTER FIVE

"Aunt Dorcas and the Babies Was a Revered Thing": Midwifery, Childbirth, and Embodied Religious Practices

During the past decade, scholars of religion have become interested in questions of embodied religious practice and the ways in which spiritual belief can inform perceptions of, and relationships with, the physical self.[1] Exploring how "sacred presence becomes real in particular times and places" includes looking at how human bodies help to create religious cultures, as Robert Orsi writes: "The materialization of religious worlds includes a process that might be called the corporalization of the sacred. I mean by this the practice of rendering the invisible visible by constituting it as an experience in a body – in one's own body or in someone else's body – so that the experiencing body itself becomes the bearer of presence for oneself and for others."[2] In this way, as one Roman Catholic sister wrote in the 1930s, the "spiritual" is "made concrete."[3] In Conception Bay, consideration of how women expressed Christian belief through their work in childbirth, traditional healing, and death rituals helps us to understand "how believers think about body and spirit and how religion influences practices involved in caring for the body, coping with illness, and understanding death."[4]

This includes how gender informs, and is informed by, embodied religious practices. Work on women and faith healing in the late nineteenth and early twentieth centuries has found that "women were not simply a part of the divine healing movement, their bodies were the movement. It was primarily women's bodies that were healed, and it was primarily women who testified to their experience."[5] By "encountering the divine within the body" through faith healing, women found a sense of personal holiness and physical "perfection" which contrasted to male medical discourses that characterized the female body as "other" and "prone to sickness."[6]

Concepts of women's bodies as "despised other" also informed male theological discourses, which in turn shaped official beliefs and practices. Negative constructions of women's bodies led to theological thinking in which "women could share in the redemptive experience but only through negation of their identities as sexual beings and mothers, only through them becoming the male spirit … In Christian theology this led often to presenting the soul as separate from and superior to the trappings of the body."[7] Women's traditional role in "the processes of life and death," and particularly in childbirth, was perceived by many male theologians as a threat to patriarchal social and cultural power. For this reason, mainstream (male) theologies tended to present female sexuality and maternity as an "inferior aspect" of human experience.[8] Yet for the Anglican women of Conception Bay, experiences of the female body, like the definition of sacrament contained in the *Book of Common Prayer*, could be an "outward and visible sign of an inward and spiritual grace."

Based on interviews housed in MUN's Folklore and Language Archives and those I conducted with informants, along with official church registers and CEWA minutes, in this chapter I explore the Christian practices and beliefs that surrounded childbirth in mid-twentieth-century Conception Bay, including midwives' place in local religious culture. Along with popular religious discourse and rituals surrounding labour and delivery, I consider ordinary women's perspectives on two official Anglican ceremonies associated with childbirth: the baptism of infants and the churching of women. Male clergy considered the baptism ceremony to be necessary for establishing membership in the Christian community; it was of such central theological importance for salvation that both Catholic and Protestant churches recognized (and encouraged) emergency baptisms by midwives at a time when women were otherwise barred from ordination and priestly functions.[9] Churching, a Christian ritual centred on newly delivered mothers, has a history of dual meanings related to purification and thanksgiving, and is of special interest to feminist theologians and liturgists.[10] In Conception Bay, popular beliefs and practices surrounding churching reveal a lived religiosity that was informed by gendered notions of cleanliness and female sexuality in ways that official Anglican discourse and doctrine was not. I conclude this chapter with consideration of some of the reasons why women themselves would enforce such beliefs at the family and community levels.

Midwifery and Spirituality

Sandra (Taylor) Tilley recognized the religious aspects of midwifery as she recalled her aunt, Dorcas Taylor, and the way in which Dorcas's work with labouring mothers and delivering children gave her a "revered" local status. Sandra associated this special spiritual status with midwives' work with mothers and children at a time of high infant mortality, and remembered of her aunt:

> She born all of Mom's children, she would have been there to born the children and she was up and down the shore … That was always kind of revered. I guess it was revered because back then it was common that … one child in every family seemed to die … I know my sister died only months old and my husband Frank had a sister died only months old … things that today they would never die. I don't know if it was because [midwives] were so tuned into this, you still go through our cemeteries on Foxtrap Church Road, you see all these one month, two months, three months … So I always seemed to recall that Aunt Dorcas and the babies was a revered thing.

Sandra recognized how a midwife was intimately tied to another woman at a moment of potential joy or sorrow, and how the outcome of any delivery had profound religious and emotional effects on families and communities. Historically, the "fear of death in childbirth," whether of women or infants, created a special religious status around midwives, especially in rural settings, and midwives often carried a "spiritual demeanor" that could include private prayer rituals after a child's safe delivery.[11] The death of a child, or children, shaped women's theology, and even the most committed Christians experienced feelings of doubt and questioned the meaning of "God's will" when faced with such a loss.[12] Midwives felt mothers' sorrow firsthand when a birth went wrong or a child died in infancy, as well as their own sense of loss. Midwife Eliza Jane (Anthony) Dawe of Upper Gullies described in 1977 her lingering sadness at being present for births of dead or deformed and dying children, and remembered especially one woman who faced the sorrow of three stillborn deliveries.[13]

Like other Conception Bay Anglican women, midwives such as Eve Morgan of Seal Cove and Rachel Dawe of Long Pond participated in the religious life of the community and expressed their need for female-centred Christian practice and service through active participation in the CEWA. The women of Seal Cove demonstrated their respect and affection for Eve in the financial and spiritual support they provided to her in the late 1920s and early 1930s, as she experienced a period of sickness in an otherwise long and healthy life. Eve was born in Green's Bay, Trinity Bay in 1860, and moved to Indian Pond after her marriage to Abraham "Valley Abe" Morgan.[14] She was the midwife for Seal Cove and Indian Pond, and was remembered for delivering babies in two separate households during a February blizzard in 1914. In a recollection that echoes Laurel Thatcher Ulrich's description of midwife Martha Ballard's travels and tribulations, informant Reta (Morgan) Hill, who was one of those babies, described hearing how "Aunt Eve," who was fifty-five years old at the time, struggled through snowdrifts in her husband's long rubber boots and faced blinding winds in order to simultaneously help the two labouring mothers.[15]

In February 1929, Seal Cove CEWA president Susie Lear reported to the women gathered for their weekly meeting that Eve was sick in hospital, and suggested "if any of the sisters went to St John's they should visit her."[16] At a meeting three weeks later, there was a "remark made about giving Sister Eve Morgan a sick benefit," to which the assembled women responded with extraordinary generosity. Not only did they take $1.50 from their funds (the standard sick benefit was $1.00), but "a collection was made among the members which amounted to 50 cents" more.[17] Along with a double cash benefit, during the following week's meeting the women agreed to go to Eve's house "on Good Friday night and hav[e] prayer with her."[18] The women's decision to gather and conduct a private prayer service with "Aunt Eve" on one of the holiest days of the church year reveals not only how much they esteemed her, but also the extent of their respect for her as a Christian and their desire to offer her spiritual support, as well as temporal assistance, in her time of need – reciprocity, perhaps, for the times she gave them support, advice, and assistance, and indicative of rural mutuality.

Eve recovered from her illness and actively participated in the CEWA for many more years. Five years after the Good Friday prayer service of 1929, she handed around cups of tea at a weekly association meeting; ten years later, branch secretary Harriet Morgan noted her attendance and that the women were "all glad to see one of our old Sisters with us for the evening."[19] In April 1946, Harriet wrote, "[we were] pleased to see our oldest member with us in the person of Sister Eve Morgan who told us that she is 85 years old which we all agree a Ripe Old Age and glad to see her so smart."[20] Eve's energy and stamina at the Easter sale of 1946 so impressed rector's wife Elizabeth Gosse that she made special mention of it at the CEWA district branch meeting held on 3 May 1946. In response, visiting sisters from St John's proposed that "it would be right and proper to send this old lady a word of congratulations," to which all present agreed. Eve, "our oldest member," was reported sick during the winter of 1947, but sent word along by neighbour Ethel Morgan that she "would like for all sisters to visit her."[21] At the end of 1947, Eve, "who despite her age seems very active yet," still attended CEWA meetings whenever she could.[22] A survey of the Anglican cemetery in Upper Gullies reveals that Elizabeth Eva Morgan, wife of Abraham Morgan, died in 1950 at the age of eighty-nine. The epitaph on her headstone is rich with religious imagery and the language of childbirth and evokes the February 1914 deliveries which made her reputation as a midwife: "Sleep on mother, thy pain is over / Thy mortal pain is past. / Jesus has called and borne thee home / Beyond this stormy blast."

At Long Pond, CEWA women demonstrated their respect and appreciation for midwife Rachel Dawe (born 1878) at the time of her death in 1953. Their tribute to her, offered at a meeting held on 14 October 1953 was captured by association secretary Elsie Baird: "The Worthy President [Annie Jefford] now spoke of our late sister Rachel Dawe who passed away during the summer. She was a lifelong member of the CEWA and did much for this community being a Maternity nurse. The sisters were asked to stand for two minutes of silence in her honour. This was done. May she rest in peace and light perpetual shine upon her." After this final sentence, a benediction taken from the *Book of Common Prayer* and usually spoken by clergy during burial services, Baird concluded with sadness: "Another of our older sisters passed on."[23]

While Eve and Rachel were identified as midwives through CEWA records and interviews, additional midwives active on the south side of Conception Bay appear in church baptismal records, as clergy often noted the name of the person who administered an emergency baptism if the child lived to be received into the church at a later date.[24] Midwives identified in this way include Eunice "Aunt Nicie" Perrin of Long Pond (born 1877), Elizabeth "Aunt Liz" Taylor of Middle Bight (born 1877), and Matilda Butler of Seal Cove (born 1896).[25] Other Conception Bay midwives include Eliza Jane "Auntie Jen" Dawe of Upper Gullies (born 1900), Elizabeth "Aunt Lizzie" Dawe of Long Pond, and Dorcas "Aunt Dark" Taylor of Foxtrap (born 1899).[26] Midwives travelled to various communities within the parish to help with deliveries, with Gordon Morgan describing how either Aunt Liz (Kelligrews) or Aunt Rachel (Long Pond) assisted his Seal Cove mother in the 1930s. Some midwives' medical knowledge went beyond assisting with childbirth and post-partum care, and earned them reputations as healers within the community.[27] Gladys Butler of Long Pond (born 1901) referred to Eunice Perrin as a "doctor woman" who would "bind up" broken bones; make ointment for boils; treat infections; and cure pneumonia, flu, and bad colds.[28] Likewise, Dorcas Taylor was remembered by fellow midwife Eliza Jane Dawe as the "next thing to a doctor" on the shore.[29]

Lying In and Post-partum Care

Closely tied to the rites of baptism and churching was the "lying in" following childbirth. While it originated "in Levitical blood taboos, which required the separation of the newly delivered woman from the community" during the time of her lochial flow, historians recognize how the lying-in period "offered mothers valuable care, recognition and a chance for celebration during and after what was a physically demanding time."[30] Lying in (and churching) could reorder "traditional gender hierarchies." Through childbirth, women could negotiate their place within patriarchal social structures and, even if temporarily, come out on top within households and the broader community.[31] For aristocratic women of medieval and early modern Western and Northern Europe, lying in could last from four to six weeks. While "all Christian women adhered" to this practice, the duration depended on the household's status, and especially on the amount of help available from "female assistants, relatives, friends or hired midwives."[32]

Women of mid-twentieth-century Conception Bay were aware of the risks associated with childbirth, in terms of both the mother's health and the child's chances of survival. In the 1920s, 1930s, and 1940s an average of one-third of burials in the Anglican cemetery at Foxtrap were infants under the age of two, a rate that dropped to one-fifth of burials in the 1950s and 1960s.[33] As Mildred (Butler) Porter of the 1940s expressed: "it was serious having a baby and you had to be so careful." News that members had delivered babies was included in the CEWA's weekly "sick report," a message sometimes communicated by midwives active in the association.[34] At Long Pond, the sick report of 16 December 1959 noted that "Sister Doris Bishop and Sister Violet Taylor has a baby girl each," while on 23 September 1964 the secretary noted that "Sister Joan Jefford reported sick with a new baby girl." On 25 November 1964, "Sister Edwina Porter reported having her baby and better." The language of sickness reflects the women's understanding of the risks of childbirth and the need for a period of rest and recovery after delivery, rather than a notion of childbirth as disease or disability.

As in other jurisdictions, midwives' services went beyond the delivery moment.[35] Gladys Butler of Long Pond described how local midwives would stay all day with a woman while she laboured ("kept you occupied and talking") and, after the birth, would visit every day for nine days to tend to the mother and child, as well as to wash baby clothes.[36] This timeframe for care was mentioned mostly by women from Foxtrap and Long Pond.[37] Other Conception Bay women, including midwife Eliza Jane Dawe, recalled seven days of care.[38] Myra (Porter) Rideout recalled a local midwife's care of her mother, as well as care that she herself provided: "I was thirteen when my sister was born. She was born home, that was by a midwife. She came for six or seven days after. Mom didn't get out of bed. Before I [went] to school I would bring up [the] face and hand [pan] for her to wash. Then you would bring her breakfast. Then the nurse would come and see to the baby … It was complete bed rest." For English women, ten days of lying in before churching appeared to be the twentieth-century standard.[39]

The length of time midwives cared for new mothers in Conception Bay was tied to practices around the sacrament of baptism and the churching service that accompanied it. Whether "six or seven days" or "nine days," the duration of these periods of care and rest recalled by

Conception Bay women has religious significance. Seven days of lying in reflected the timeframe of "uncleanness" following the birth of a male child as described in Leviticus 12, the scriptural chapter most associated with churching. The distinction between giving birth to a male child (seven days "unclean") and a female child (twelve days "unclean") as described in Leviticus did not survive in local popular practice.[40] Nine days was the number informants mentioned most often, and can be connected to the nine days described in a variety of religiously invoked traditional healing practices for the study area.[41]

The number seven was significant in vernacular medicine. Residents asked about religious cures described the healing powers of a "seventh daughter" or a "seventh son," a well-documented European folk belief also common in Newfoundland and Labrador (although usually associated with sons only).[42] Henry Morgan of Seal Cove noted how "a seventh son could charm your tooth," while informant Pat (Morgan) Woolgar related her personal experience of being healed:

> I had a string of warts down my leg, bunch of little warts. This old aunt of my mom's, old Rachael Hennessey, used to come up now and then. She was a real old woman and [Mom] would say Aunt Rachael was a seventh daughter. You heard tell of seventh sons … but she was the seventh daughter. Mom said to me "one day when Aunt Rachael comes up now she will take those away for you." So she rubbed her hand over my warts and I don't know what she said or did. I didn't even think of it but it was four or five days later and when I looked they were gone away, whether she took it away or not. That actually did happen to me and it never came back.[43]

Pat was careful to emphasize that the special powers associated with the seventh born could be found among women as well as men, even if she was skeptical about the source of her cure. She likewise described how another member of her mother's family, "Uncle Ray Tilley," was a seventh son, and how "I do know that people used to come to him … to take the tooth ache away, or take some pain away. So people did believe it."[44]

Sandra (Taylor) Tilley recognized the Christian significance of the number seven, although she was ambivalent about whether or not ordinary people would consider cures by seventh-born children as "religious" per se: "I don't know if they perceived it that way or not, but the seven is a Biblical number. It is completeness. The seven days of the week and seven tribes and you know and all that … So you would hear talks, people would go to somebody about their tooth. So did they see it as religious? I don't know what their interpretation was. They didn't talk about why they did it. They just believed in it. They availed of it." The number seven also appeared in descriptions of traditional healing practices provided by Rachel Fagan and Minnie Bussey. They noted how local women who cared for sick family members believed that the seventh day of a serious illness was the point at which the person would start to either improve or die.[45]

Whether nine days or seven, women connected the timeframe of a midwife's care with preparation for the religious ceremonies of baptism and churching. Mildred (Butler) Porter explained how for nine days after delivering a baby "you had to make sure you didn't go out of doors or wet your hands or anything 'till [the christening]." Other informants echoed her link between traditional post-partum practices and religious rituals. Enid (Porter) Haines, when asked about religious practices around childbirth, said, "you don't take the child out until the child goes and gets baptized. There was no such thing as taking a child outside then before it was baptized," with her mother Mary (Petten) Porter agreeing and adding, "they was only baptized on Sunday."[46] Edna (Roberts) Haines stressed the importance of baptizing a baby "right away," with Gordon Morgan of Seal Cove explaining that "if they thought the baby wasn't going to live they would get someone to baptize him. Like a schoolteacher or somebody." Midwives often performed home baptism in emergency cases, as local church records reflect. However, as the pages of *Diocesan Magazine* indicate, some Anglican clergy questioned such administration by these nonordained rural women.

"Baptism Is So Very Important"

Parish clergy who worked in rural areas of Newfoundland were concerned about the "proper" administration of the sacrament of baptism, whether performed by ordained clergy, male lay readers, or midwives. "An Outport Priest," writing in 1931, explained:

> May I point out to you that pouring water and sprinkling water are two different things? To dip a finger in water and sprinkle it on a child is *not* pouring it. The church distinctly says *pour*. Baptism is so very important that we ought to take no chances. If ever you see a Clergyman sprinkle water, you ought to object at once. Baptism should be administered properly: and there are only two proper ways: dipping and pouring, but not sprinkling.[47]

This letter is remarkable in its suggestion that the laity, including women, had the right – even the duty – to correct a priest's errors. At the same time, this somewhat liberal notion of spiritual equality among believers is coupled with a conception of the almighty as "God of Judgment," a stickler for details who might consider unbaptized those persons upon whom water has been merely sprinkled rather than poured. The need to pour water in baptism was again taken up in 1947 by the Reverend A.L. Parish, then-rector of the rural Mission of Rose Blanche, located on the southwest coast of the island. In a letter to *Diocesan Magazine* he described lay acts of baptism, as well as popular notions of clerical prerogative when it came to use of water:

> It has come to my notice on several occasions that a baptism purporting to have been administered by a lay man or woman was not validly performed. In two distinct cases no water was used, the responsible parties stating that they did not know they were entitled to use water. In other cases I have found that the baptism was administered by affusion, the method having been to dip the fingers in water and touch the head of the infant, or to mark a cross.

"I am not theologian enough to know whether baptism by affusion when the intention was right is completely invalid," he confessed, "but there is no doubt it is contrary to the formalities of the Church of England."[48]

In contrast to "An Outport Priest," Parish did not suspect clergy of improper administration of baptism but considered them guardians of proper Anglican practice. He suggested that education of lay persons by clergy, rather than lay chastisement of priests, was the solution to "the many cases of irregular baptism" he expected would be found throughout the diocese "if careful enquiry was made." Working in a district made up of many small coastal settlements which could be reached only by boat made Parish a pragmatic theologian and tolerant of lay baptisms whether performed by men or women:

> In a diocese like ours baptism must frequently be performed by persons not in Holy Orders, and therefore it seems to behove the clergy to catechize those who are likely to have this important function to fulfill. My own practice is to question such persons as lay readers and midwives on their method of administering baptism (and I have never found my question resented) pointing out that even in the event of an infant's being too sick to be lifted, the water, slightly warmed, can be poured with a spoon and caught with a towel, thus ensuring that the water be made to run – an essential feature, even though the quantity used be small.[49]

The clergy's concern with properly baptizing sickly infants was understandable given Anglican church discipline. Clergy were directed by church law to deny full burial services and interment in consecrated ground to unbaptized persons, a rule most often applied to infants. This distressing practice could alienate parents from the official church and, if one can judge from other jurisdictions, was generally condemned by lay members who deemed it harsh on the innocent.[50] For a Christian woman and her family, the tragedy of giving birth to a stillborn child was made worse when the church denied the child burial in consecrated ground.

In Conception Bay, as elsewhere, the Anglican Church tried to limit these situations by recognizing the validity of emergency infant lay baptisms, including those performed by midwives. While officially emergency baptism was unavailable to the stillborn, entries in the burial registers for All Saints and St Peter's churches suggest that midwives were anxious to ensure all infants received this rite and that clergymen supported them in this endeavour. The age of deceased infants sometimes appears as a few minutes, or one hour, and one telling entry in a burial register that originally described a child as "stillborn" has, penciled in afterwards, an age of "one minute," likely to demonstrate that there was time for baptism to occur. Clergy may not have encouraged midwives to baptize stillborn children, but they were more than willing to look the other way. At the same time, the local community developed its own practices around burial of unbaptized infants. This was seen elsewhere, such as in the Irish use of cillini (burial sites for those denied consecrated ground, especially infants). Bereaved parents treated such sites with the same reverence as cemeteries and engaged in community-led funerary rituals when burying children there.[51] In Conception Bay, families may have taken it upon themselves to secretly bury stillborn children in consecrated ground, even if it meant an unmarked grave. Long Pond resident Tom Dawe recalled of his childhood watching graves being dug in the Foxtrap cemetery and how "sometimes they'd dig down in a place and go right down on top of one they didn't know was there. Especially, I tell you, babies' graves." According to Dawe, "no-name babies, babies born dead" were "scattered around" all kinds of unmarked places inside the cemetery fence, which suggests a popular determination to put a child in consecrated ground whether it was baptized or not.[52]

Reforming Baptism: "More Ecclesiastical … and Less Domestic"

Mid-twentieth-century Anglican clergy had more concerns about baptism than its proper administration. By the 1940s, priests began to worry about parents' understanding of baptism as sacrament, as the transformative ritual which made one a Christian, rather than as "a mere church custom, or a naming ceremony." Writing in *Diocesan Magazine* of 1944, one priest stated that baptisms generally needed to be "more respected and treated with dignity" than what he saw in current practice.[53] This included the choice of name given to infants. While a 1940s catechism lesson published in *Diocesan* described "Your Christian Name" as an assurance to the baptized that she or he was "a particular person – God knows me. God calls me to be his child," regardless of what that name was, by the 1960s the specific name parents selected was considered a test of religious sincerity and commitment. *Newfoundland Churchman* editor the Reverend Charles J. Abraham was outspoken on this matter, but laid as much blame on Anglican liturgical practice of conducting baptisms as stand-alone services, fitted in somewhere between morning prayer and evensong, as on "careless" parents influenced by popular culture:

> The parent who discards a good, strong Christian name in favour of the first name of some crooner or prizefighter is probably under the impression that it is an entirely private matter. Yet

> if that name is received in Baptism, living up – or down – to the name is the concern of the church into which the child is received. However, when Baptism is administered at the dead end of a Sunday afternoon with no congregation present, the family of the child may be pardoned for thinking that they have been through a "ceremony" to which the church attaches no great importance.[54]

Abraham went on to argue for a reformed approach to make baptism "more of an ecclesiastical occasion and less of a domestic one," including having "the whole congregation present as witnesses." Along with promoting this liturgical transformation from private to public, Abraham began to include in the pages of the *Churchman* a new feature, "Some Christian Names and Their Meanings," in an effort to direct new parents away from "frivolous" nomenclature.[55]

These views of Anglican church leaders suggest a binary opposition between baptism as public religious ceremony and baptism as private family celebration, and also discredit the extent to which spiritual concerns informed local domestic practices around a child's christening. Along with women's recollection that babies "had" to be baptized as soon as possible after birth, Elizabeth (Batten) Petten of Foxtrap (born 1908) described how taking a child out to be baptized at church was a joyful occasion, shared by an entire community, just as Abraham suggested it should be.[56] Textile making was part of Anglican women's devotional practice, and included the preparation of garments and wrappings for newborn family members to wear during baptism.[57] The "long white baptismal gown" that could be "passed from generation to generation" showed the importance of this rite of passage within families – a rite which "marked the entry of the child into the community of faithful" and allowed for extension of social networks through the selection of "fictive kin" (godparents).[58] In Conception Bay, new mothers or grandmothers often made white christening gowns which could be shared by all babies within immediate, if not extended, families. A newborn's female kin prepared knitted or crocheted caps, sweaters, leggings, and booties from white wool for the child to wear during the ceremony, especially during cooler weather. Women knitted or crocheted white christening shawls or blankets to help keep the baby warm on its trip to and from the church.[59] Male family members also contributed to the joyous community feeling around baptism. Elizabeth Petten noted that in the 1920s and 1930s local people usually walked to church regardless of weather, but if a family had to get a baby baptized in winter "the men" would take out the horse and sleigh and rig it up with harness bells for the drive to and from the church.[60]

Local families acknowledged midwives' special spiritual status by asking them to stand as godmothers to children they helped deliver, something midwife Eliza Jane Dawe reported in 1977 that she was often asked to do.[61] Along with revering them for their work at the intersection of life and death, local people may have considered midwives especially appropriate godmothers because of their ability to perform emergency baptisms, a sacramental function normally reserved for male priests and lay readers, who were licensed by the church to conduct services in places where ordained clergy were in short supply. Having midwives present as godmothers at baptisms suggests a cultural remnant from English churching rituals. In the sixteenth and seventeenth centuries, midwives (along with other community women) often accompanied new mothers when they went to be churched.[62] The popular treatment of churching as a woman-centred community celebration may have disappeared by the twentieth century, but the Anglican women of Conception Bay nevertheless found a way to include midwives in the official religious rituals triggered by the birth of a child.[63]

The Churching of Women: Official Views

While Anglicans generally agreed about the joyfulness of baptism, the ceremony that accompanied baptism (officially titled "Thanksgiving after Childbirth" but popularly referred to as "the churching of women") was less universally regarded. Some female theologians condemn the rite as "devaluing" women, while others see feminist liturgical potential within a Christian ceremony focused exclusively on lay women.[64] Drawing on the pre-Christian origins of the rite as well as on the Church of England's official emphasis on churching as a service of thanksgiving rather than of purification, one Anglican theologian suggests that modern Christian women need to revive and reclaim this ancient liturgy as a female-centred celebration of women's bodies and reproductive capacity, rather than "dismiss[ing it] as yet another expression of the church's misogyny."[65]

Historians have largely investigated churching in terms of the medieval or early modern European experience, and have relied almost exclusively on upper- and middle-class sources.[66] They have considered churching as an aspect of a female-centred childbearing culture and have argued for its part in gender role construction and expression.[67] Work on late-medieval France has linked churching to social and cultural ideas of female sexuality, purification, social standing (legitimacy), and healing.[68] Churching in Tudor and Stuart England has been interpreted as "an occasion of female social activity, in which the notion of 'purification' was un-contentious, minimal or missing."[69] Churching may have been an empowering, female-centred community celebration at that time, historically valued by Anglican women as a "rare opportunity to be the focus of attention within the liturgy of the church and to have their bodily labours recognized, taken seriously, and celebrated," yet there is a need to be sensitive to the influence of time and place on women's experience.[70] "Churching was about many things," one historian observes, "but not necessarily always the same things. Like many other rituals, its outward form could mask a variety of meanings."[71]

Scholars have sought to understand how women themselves felt about participation in this rite and the nature of its meaning.[72] Despite the belief, as some historians argue, that churching became obsolete after the eighteenth century, increased attention to the working-class experience demonstrates otherwise.[73] In northern English parishes and working-class districts of London, churching was practised into the twentieth century. It remained especially popular among English artisan and labouring families, although interest has declined since the 1960s.[74] The meaning of churching for mid-twentieth-century women can be explored by seeking out the living voices of those who experienced the rite, including the women of Conception Bay.[75]

Purification or Thanksgiving?

Scholarship on churching within the Anglican tradition has considered the tension between custom, including popular understanding of churching as a purification ritual, and liturgy, the church's argument that the service was primarily about thanksgiving.[76] This tension is rooted in the historical development of the rite, which was part of English custom as early as the seventh century and was described by the Venerable Bede in his *Ecclesiastical History of the English People*. Churching became an official church rite in the medieval era. Titled "Blessing of a Woman after Childbirth before the Church Porch" in the twelfth-century *Missal of Sarum*, in 1549 the service of churching was preserved in the Church of England's first *Book of Common Prayer* under a new title: "The Order of the Purification of Women." Under pressure from English Protestant leaders, who associated churching with Jewish and Roman Catholic "superstition," by 1552 the Church of England had removed the reference to "purification" and renamed the service "The Thanksgiving of Women after Child Birth, commonly called the Churching of Women," a name retained into the twenty-first century.[77] Church of England leadership tried to counteract the persistent popular understanding of churching as a purification rite by making liturgical changes to the service for the 1662 version of the *Book of Common Prayer.* These included emphasizing the language of thanksgiving and replacing Psalm 121, with its call for help and protection from evil, with Psalm 116, a song of thanksgiving after delivery from distress.[78] Despite Anglican clergy's tendency to suggest that "churching as purification" was simply a popular misunderstanding, English theologians debated churching as purification or thanksgiving well into the seventeenth century.[79]

Following the Restoration, ecclesiastical and political debates about the rite subsided, yet churching remained a controversial ceremony within the Church of England. Popular notions of women's impurity after childbirth and the need to be "churched" or else "remain unclean" continued up until after the Second World War, especially among older women. In the 1950s and 1960s there were special clerical efforts to "stamp out" churching, including publication of articles in church magazines that "condemn[ed] superstition about the ritual." This included belief that unchurched women would be "unlucky," that their shadows could cause houses to collapse, that they were "impure," and that they could not be seen in public.[80] The Anglican Church of Canada made similar efforts.[81] In Newfoundland, Anglican church leaders were aware of the vernacular interpretation of this service in other jurisdictions, yet believed the island and Labrador were pockets of orthodoxy within a vast landscape of misinterpretation. In March 1926, Bishop of Newfoundland William White described churching as an important gesture of public thanks to God for the blessing of a new family member, and stated that "contrary to some other dioceses,"

Newfoundland women understood the "true" meaning of this service.[82] In saying this, White may have been willfully blind, overly hopeful, or simply out of touch with popular practices. For the women of mid-1900s Conception Bay, beliefs around churching were laden with notions of female cleanliness, sin, and morality.

Churching Practices in Conception Bay

Many women remembered the Anglican practice of churching, including a popular belief that it was about restoration of female cleanliness after childbirth rather than an act of thanksgiving intended by the church.[83] Marge (Saunders) Dawe described the prohibitions new mothers faced at home and in church: "you couldn't take communion 'til you were churched. You couldn't make bread 'til you were churched." Emma (Petten) Warford of Upper Gullies likewise recalled that "you weren't allowed to make bread or do a thing after your baby until your baby was christened … You weren't allowed to touch anything along the food line." She also recalled not being allowed to take communion, and added, "you had to listen to what they said." Based on the interpretation of churching described in *Diocesan Magazine*, the "they" to which Emma referred were not members of the clergy or other official Anglican leaders but members of the local community.

Despite remembering the strict restrictions on new mothers, Emma was positive about her churching experience. "I was so delighted with my baby," she recalled, and, reflecting the women-centred nature of the ceremony, went on to remember the names of other women who were churched at the same time she was. Prudence (Morgan) Rideout was positive also: "that was part of the service [of baptism] … if a woman had a baby it seemed like that was the blessing on her." Other Conception Bay women were more critical of the rules and rituals surrounding churching. Marge (Saunders) Dawe considered the prohibitions on touching food or taking communion as evidence that the community (and the church) believed that a new mother "wasn't clean or something," and went on to point out, "the Lord ordained how babies are born, so how could you be unclean?"

Sandra (Taylor) Tilley described how her mother, who grew up close to St John's and attended Roman Catholic schools, resisted her Anglican mother-in-law's attempt to impose local customs:

Figure 5.1 The churching of women, a formal Anglican service conducted after childbirth, was understood to be both thanksgiving ceremony and purification ritual among those who participated in it. Older women, such as Sarah Ann Taylor (pictured here with granddaughter), enforced a variety of restrictions on newly delivered mothers. These could include not preparing food, not going outside, or, in the case of Sarah Taylor's orders to daughter-in-law Olive, not eating at the family table "until she was churched."

> One [religious practice] my mother doesn't speak very highly of ... When a child was born the mother was not allowed to sit at the table for the meal until after they had gone to church and been churched ... Mom was living on Topsail Road and she married Dad and moved to Kelligrews ... Dad's mother was still alive and living [with them], because Dad looked after her ... [W]hen [my brother] was born [in 1937] she would have come to go to the table, [but] she was told by Nana Taylor that she was not to come to the table 'til she was churched. My mother was a strong woman, I guess too, and she defied that practice. She said having a child was not a dirty thing and she was going to be eating at the table with the family.

An ordained priest, Tilley went on to describe how popular customs around churching had little to do with what she considered to be the official intention behind "thanksgiving after childbirth": "I think we see it today that it was, over the years, a misconstruing of what [it] was meant to be. The churching of women was really wanting [to give] God thanks for safe delivery, safe baby, healthy baby, safe mother. God's hand at work. Somehow it got turned into you put some money on the Bible and you were forgiven your sins for the dirt you were involved in." Mildred (Butler) Porter and Myra (Porter) Rideout likewise recalled how the priest expected a gift of money during churching, and how they felt the amount given reflected their worth as women. Mildred described of the 1940s: "You went to the service, eleven o'clock service in the morning. Now there was churching of women. Perhaps there would be one, two or three. You would go up to the rail and he had a service to read to you. Then, of course, he passed this book to you to put your bit of money on."

Myra, whose children were born in the 1960s, related:

> I remember when mine were [baptized] it was a bit different. They had their service, morning service. So you went with your baby and you sat with your sponsors [godparents] and you sat in the back of the church ... They baptized your babies and then they had the churching of the women. By this time the church was empty unless it was some of your family, you know. It was a little service after ... You would stay in the back of the church and

> he would say we are going to have the churching of women … and all the mothers went up. He'd say a few prayers and then he passed along his book and you put your dollar.

When Mildred added "perhaps it would be twenty-five cents or fifty cents, it wouldn't be no more than a dollar," Myra concluded, "That was all we were worth then."

Many of the beliefs and practices that twentieth century Conception Bay women describe, such as staying indoors or not preparing food, were part of popular Christian practice from the medieval era. Before the eleventh century, European Christian women were expected to wait for a specified period after childbirth to attend public services of worship and receive communion, but the church did not formalize a ritual around this period of waiting and a mother's "return" to the church community. Many popular beliefs about purification, such as that an unchurched woman should stay indoors for fear she would be "attacked by evil spirits" or "defile those around her," were never accepted or promoted by Anglican theologians.[84] Some of the popular beliefs about unchurched women were based on religious language used in the ceremony: they would be burned if exposed to the sun or moon (Psalm 121, verse 6), meat they touched would spoil, and grass would not grow where they walked. Some of these beliefs showed interpretation, by both clergy and laity, of sexual activity as "polluting" and of the physical process of childbirth, with its pain and bloodshed (and its association with the Fall from the Garden of Eden), as evidence that "some stain or other doth creep into this action which had need to be repented."[85] Among early modern clerics, there were theological debates about whether unchurched women were damned and whether or not they could be buried in consecrated ground, a debate tied to the popular belief that women of childbearing age should avoid the grave of an unchurched woman, for fear their own reproductive capacity could be compromised.[86]

Churching, Gender, and Class

Attitudes towards churching were tied to social standing. By the eighteenth century, members of the English middle and upper classes tended to reject popular ideas about churching, female purity, and restrictions on women's movements and activities following childbirth. Yet these ideas remained important to the English working class well into the twentieth century. The practices and beliefs described by women in 1920s working-class London echo those recalled by Anglican women of rural Conception Bay, including restrictions on a new mother's mobility and how such limitations could only be lifted with participation in church ritual: "When I had my Billy I got out of bed to change his napkins [and] they came and caught me and said I was flying in the face of the Lord. You couldn't come out of the door into the open air unless you went straight to the church after you had children and the child wasn't allowed out until it was christened. If you did not you was treated like dirt."[87] While there is a social control aspect to churching, with obedience to prescribed behaviours as a test of a woman's piety and respectability, other factors may have been at play for working women.

In twentieth-century Conception Bay, the limitations on unchurched women were popularly preserved (and enforced) by women who worked long and hard in support of their households. While such limitations suggested female impurity that could only be cleansed by churching, a fact which some women recognized and resented, one can also see the seven- to nine-day lying-in period and the prohibitions on making bread, getting her hands wet, and leaving the house as a mandatory break from heavy household labour. In early modern Europe, lying in provided valuable rest to women after childbirth. During this time, whether several days or several weeks, female needs and concerns became central in otherwise male-headed households. Women of rural Newfoundland may have cherished this break from their working routine after the physical demands of pregnancy and delivery, and may have recognized that engaging in heavy work too soon after childbirth could have long-term health consequences. Churching may have been, as the Canadian cleric the Reverend Dr William Armitage stated, "highly valued" by Newfoundland Anglicans, but part of this value came from rural working women conscripting popular religious beliefs and official ritual into something that benefitted each other physically, if not always spiritually or socially.[88] When Armitage noted in 1922 that churching continued to be important for immigrant Anglicans from Newfoundland and the "mother land," he was focused almost exclusively on ethnicity, to the neglect of other factors such as social class. The working-class or rural background of people likely to immigrate to Canada from the United Kingdom or Newfoundland in the late nineteenth and early twentieth centuries informed continued attachment to this religious ritual.[89] For English families of upper- and middle-class status, churching was largely abandoned by the 1800s.

Important messages about gender and sexuality appear in lived Christian practices around churching. Cultural historians sometimes neglect women's agency and the impact of religion on constructions of modern sexuality, perhaps stemming from unquestioning acceptance (for the most part) of the secularization narrative.[90] The thought and work of largely middle-class, female British writers and reformers of the nineteenth and twentieth centuries show how women used religious discourse to promote sexual purity and pleasure within heterosexual marriage, to campaign for and against birth control, to inform the "social purity" movement against sexual vice and venereal disease, and to provide language for the expression of alternative sexualities, including same-sex relationships and celibacy. In this way it can be understood that "[it] was not the clerical elite but the prominent participation of laywomen as orators, writers and activists throughout the period [between 1800 and 1940] that ensured religion remained an influential arbiter of sexual behavior well into the twentieth century."[91] While some women "by virtue of their gendered occupation of a distinctive space between ordained institutional and lay popular religious cultures" were freer to communicate on sexual matters than ecclesiastical authorities, it is important to remember the impact of class on women's ability to communicate influentially at a national level.[92]

The Anglican women of Conception Bay likewise occupied a gendered space outside the official church where religious discourse could be applied to matters of sexuality, especially sexual purity within marriage. Within this space and religious culture, a woman's sexual purity was understood to be compromised by pregnancy and childbirth, leading to series of prohibitions on her domestic activities, largely enforced by female kin. The tendency for female relations of a new mother, rather than clergy, to enforce twentieth-century working-class churching practices also occurred in English parishes.[93] In Conception Bay, a new mother's "uncleanness" was thought to compromise especially her ability to prepare and serve food, and even to sit at the family table during mealtimes. Only after churching would an Anglican woman be considered cleansed and ready to assume her full household duties. Her domestic status was restored hand-in-hand with her religious status, as it was popularly understood that a woman was forbidden to take communion until she was churched. While some women remembered popular practices around churching with resentment, others understood the service as White believed all Newfoundland Anglican women did, as an act of thanksgiving and a blessing, which suggests variety in religious belief and practice between households as well as various levels of gender consciousness among women. As with enforcement by female kin, this pattern of mixed responses to churching was noted also among English working-class women.[94]

Conclusion

Christian rituals around childbirth are examples of female embodied religion in Conception Bay. Spiritual beliefs and practices were tied to women's physical experience of labour and delivery, a vitally important aspect of their work in support of households. Midwives, often active participants in church life and members of local CEWA branches, had, by virtue of their work with mothers at a time of high infant mortality, a special religious status within the community. This status demonstrates a "premodern sense of the symbolic connectedness of birth and death," although midwives were not expected to perform undertaking duties within the study area as they were in other jurisdictions.[95] Families relied on midwives to baptize children dying or stillborn children and, when things went well, often asked midwives to stand as godmothers to children they delivered. This created ties of community, religion, and family. Rural mutuality and Christian charity are evident in the way midwives, in their own time of need, could receive spiritual and material support from the female communities they served.

While male Anglican clergy accepted and accommodated midwives' emergency baptisms, some expressed concern about the method of administration. Other clergy criticized Anglican families for treating baptism as a private or domestic affair and a mere naming ceremony rather than a public sacrament of the church. Yet evidence from Conception Bay suggests that the religious and the domestic intertwined in this key rite of Christian passage. Ordinary Anglican families were mindful of the spiritual aspect of baptism, with women producing special christening garments and shawls to be shared by multiple siblings and seeking to have a child baptized as early as possible after its birth. Along with religious concerns, baptisms also celebrated successful reproduction of the family unit, key in a time of household economy. For families who faced the tragedy of stillborn children, one compounded by the church's refusal to bury unbaptized infants in consecrated ground, secret cemetery interments defied official Anglican practice. This demonstrates a popular belief that a child should not be denied Christian burial, even when not "officially" a Christian: an act of mercy for both that child and those who grieved its loss.

Churching has a complex history within Anglican practice and theology. In Conception Bay, different views of it reflected a gap between official and lived religion stretching back to the medieval English church. The dual meanings of churching – purification and thanksgiving – affected how the rite was understood by women who participated in it. Evidence from Conception Bay suggested ordinary women were divided on its meaning. They also reveal the influence of class and gender on Christian ritual. The female-centred events of childbirth, lying in, and churching included embodied practices and beliefs informed by Christian scripture and doctrine, recognition of women's labour within rural households and communities, and prescribed notions of female sexuality and reproductive capacity. In this way, women's work, including the work of childbearing, shaped religious belief and practice into a lived Christianity that reflected the material circumstances of women's lives. It was also a lived Christianity experienced through, and located in, female bodies as they laboured (in various ways) within the coastal communities of Conception Bay.

CHAPTER SIX

"Our Sisters ... Placed Bows of Ribbon in Her Grave": Exploring Women-Led Funeral Rituals

The Burial of the Dead is the [service] most highly charged with emotion, and therefore the least easy to get people to think about clearly ... The Church has the right and the duty to direct the details of burial in so far as they may affect a truly Christian understanding of death and the life to come.

Charles Abraham[1]

The church recognized how the death of a family member, friend, or neighbour (especially in close-knit rural settlements connected by kinship ties) could be a time of intense emotion for surviving community members. While Abraham expressed the "right and duty" of the institutionalized church to "direct" funeral services, popular practice in Conception Bay, as MUN Folklore and Language Archives collections detail and CEWA minute books describe, reveals the extent to which people developed their own ceremonies and customs surrounding deceased community members and the degree to which ordained clergy accepted informal Christian ritual alongside official liturgy. Women participated in, and sometimes led, death and burial rituals in Anglican Conception Bay, including those surrounding wakes, funeral processions, and public burial services. As noted for nineteenth-century New England, "practices surrounding illness, death, and loss are socially constructed and culturally embodied. Death may be a natural, biological process, but the way it is manifested in a community is laden with social, cultural, and psychological dimension."[2] Funeral practices in nineteenth-century Montreal also show how "particular rituals following deaths varied with class, religion, and ethnicity."[3] Among the social and cultural matters discussed in this chapter are gendered practices around laying out and dressing deceased persons, as well preparing houses for wakes. In Conception Bay, these practices were influenced partially by the sexual division of household labour, including blurred lines between indoor (women's) and outdoor (men's) work in rural Newfoundland, and were consistent with rural women's experience elsewhere in North America.[4] Gendered expectations of women's physical appearance, even in death, are considered, as is their participation in what were male-only wake rituals in other jurisdictions.

Many historians have approached the study of funerals from a secular perspective and have not considered the spiritual beliefs surrounding burial service and interment. This has been especially evident in histories of working people.[5] Despite some nineteenth-century English reformers' assertion that the "lower orders" had little respect for the dead or interest in burial services, evidence from the working-class and immigrant communities of Massachusetts, as well as of Great Britain, contradict this suggestion.[6] The immediacy of encounters with illness and death characterized the lives of people in mid-twentieth-century Conception Bay. Friends and loved ones most often died at home in the case of old age or illness, or within the familiar community landscape (and workspace) of sea, gardens, highway, and woods in the case of accidental ends. Tending to the dead was not a matter for hired mortuary specialists, although one could see the beginning of a shift towards professional, commercial, and, ultimately, masculine care in the 1930s and 1940s as embalming and undertaking services were established in the area. James and Josephine (Brophy) Hickey of Holyrood, for example, began to offer funeral and undertaker services in the 1940s, and later expanded their mortuary business to include a Kelligrews branch.[7] Yet into the 1960s many families continued to wake their deceased loved ones at home, making the domestic sphere into a place of transition from life to death and, for the religiously minded, from mortality to immortality.

In this chapter, I consider female-centred and -led commemoration ceremonies, publicly practised by CEWA members for the benefit of the deceased, her family, and themselves. On 31 March 1966, for example, Annie Greenslade, secretary for the Long Pond branch of the CEWA, noted in her minute book that "since our last meeting the Worthy President and Sisters were very sorry to hear of the passing of two of our sisters."[8] One of these was Elizabeth Tilley, a longtime active member and former president of the Long Pond branch. Annie noted that current "Worthy President [Marjorie Jefford] and some of our sisters attend[ed] her funeral and out of respect for her placed bows of ribbon in her grave." The women's use of a sewing notion to pay tribute to their former leader is significant, given the central place of textile production in the spiritual lives of Long Pond CEWA members.[9] The second deceased sister was Ruth Dawe. The women's response to her death demonstrates the importance of procession, prayer, and hymn singing for expressing popular female religiosity, as well the way in which Anglican women could act publicly as spiritual leaders while officially barred from ordination.

Laying Out and Dressing the Dead

Before the advent of professional mortuary services, death and corpses were part of the domestic space of Conception Bay, as they were for other Anglo-American and European peoples. In nineteenth-century Montreal, whether the family was Roman Catholic, Protestant, or Jewish, "[the] bodies of husbands, wives, and children normally remained at home until their funeral and burial."[10] By virtue of being "indoor" or domestic labour, laying out rituals and practices in England, Ireland, Australia, France, and Sweden were considered women's work, and such tasks brought women special spiritual status within their communities. The early modern Irish practice of a particular woman from a community being identified as a specialist in laying out the dead (the an bhean bhán, or white woman) was largely a result of women's association with indoor work, and men with outdoor, following the separate spheres notion of household labour. This white woman, by virtue of her work with the bodies of people thought to be somewhere between an earthly and spiritual existence, was simultaneously venerated and feared by other members of her community.[11]

In working-class England, laying out corpses was likewise "the preserve of women," although it could be performed either by a group of "friends who wished to intimate their sympathy to the bereaved" or by an individual woman "renowned within the neighbourhood for her cleanliness, efficiency and experience." This woman was sometimes the local midwife, "remembered as solemn and respectable ... perform[ing her] task with tact and skill" despite the criticism she often received from urban reformers who preferred the male professional mortician over the female "amateur."[12] In rural England, it was more likely that a group of women, rather than an individual, would work together to lay out a body, which scholars interpret as evidence of "a wider female culture of mutual aid [and] pragmatic support" outside urban centres.[13] In nineteenth- and early twentieth-century Australia, laying out the dead was a spiritually charged female responsibility. Women, who were expected to complete this work as part of the gendered division of labour, considered laying out a dead body to be "sacred ritual," performed largely in silence and accompanied with prayer. As in England, working-class Australian women looked after the bodies of deceased persons from their own community, sometimes with the local midwife's help, while middle- and upper-class families left this work to a female domestic servant or to the nurse who tended the deceased during their final days.[14]

In Conception Bay, laying out and dressing the dead was not considered an exclusively female activity, but depended upon the sex of the deceased. While men in rural Sweden could, very rarely, wash and dress a dead body, Rachel Fagan of Foxtrap remembered that in Conception Bay "men always prepared the men, and women always did up women."[15] Likewise, Tom Dawe of Long Pond related that "in every place there'd be men and women who'd prepare the body for burial. There was a group of women who'd undress the woman corpse and get her all ready, and there'd be a group of men who'd do the [adult] men."[16] Informant Marjorie (Bullen) Morgan reported the same practice in Fortune Bay, on the south coast of the island.[17] "The act of washing and laying out a corpse," notes one historian of nineteenth-century working-class England, "represented a final gesture of intimacy and affection."[18] In Conception Bay, men as well as women could engage in this last emotional and spiritually charged encounter with the deceased.

When it came to dressing the dead, the kinds of garments varied in different jurisdictions, and the choices reflect particular religious perspectives and gender expectations. Among the English working classes a nightgown or "simple shroud" was used for burial, while in rural Ireland the corpse would be dressed in his or her best clothes, usually ones worn to public worship services, or else clad in a brown or black burial shroud.[19] Shrouds can be considered gendered and largely influenced by separate spheres ideology. By the late nineteenth and early twentieth centuries in New England, men were increasingly buried in suits, reflecting how for them the "world of commerce" had displaced "the sacred domains of family and church." Women were still buried in shrouds due to the popular perception that they were more pious and the "guardians of home and faith."[20]

The use of burial garments among Conception Bay Anglicans was a hybrid of the traditions described for England, Ireland, and New England, and while the influence of gender roles and expectations was clear, it was not entirely about perceived distinctions between "worldly men" and "pious women." Anglicans in Conception Bay leaned more towards the Irish tradition of dressing corpses in their best clothes. Rachel Fagan and Minnie Bussey of Foxtrap described how men were dressed in "Sunday suit with a white shirt and black tie," while women were clothed in a Sunday dress "of any colour."[21] The rural people of Conception Bay, like those of Ireland, saw the suit as "church clothes" rather than "business clothes," associated more with participation in public worship or rites of passage such as weddings than with commercial transactions. This, along with the fact that women were similarly dressed "in their Sunday best," suggests little influence of the male-commerce, female-religion divide.

While shrouds were used in Conception Bay, they were not the full burying garments of other jurisdictions. Rather, they were intricately cut pieces of fabric which were placed in the casket in such a way as to hang over both sides, and which were folded up over the corpse's face before the casket was sealed.[22] Similar shrouds have been described for Notre Dame Bay, on the north coast of Newfoundland.[23] As elements of a proper Christian burial, and as religiously significant textiles, in Conception Bay, these shrouds were associated with women as makers, rather than as wearers. Particular women had a special reputation for shroud making, and older people would select their shroud maker in advance.[24] Whether this choice was based on the maker's perceived piety, textile skills, or a combination of both is unknown. Rachel described the shroud-making method: "Using a pair of scissors she would cut a fancy design out of white cotton shirting material in less than an hour. It would be beautiful."[25] A more detailed description of shroud-cutting, reported from a maker, captures this art:

> Mrs Hettie Samsone has given me the following information. About two and a half yards of shirting was used, but only that part of the shirting material around the head and shoulders would

> be cut to create what was known as the shroud. First of all it would be scalloped (scallop shell shape) around the edge, which would eventually cover the face and chest. Secondly, it would be folded at each scallop join, and about every half an inch along the crease a half-inch diamond would be cut, thus forming a very beautiful pattern.[26]

For women makers, the quality of the finished shroud was a gesture of respect for the deceased but could also earn much praise from the living. According to Rachel, "when I dies, you got to make me shroud" were the words of admiration offered during Conception Bay wakes to the makers of these ritual textiles.[27]

Gender expectations and stereotypes around female beauty affected death rituals and could lead to informal agreements between women about the conduct of their laying out and wake. Minnie and Rachel recalled how some women were very concerned about their personal appearance and how they would look in their caskets. They would decide years in advance what clothes they wanted to be buried in and would sometimes buy special items to "put away" for this purpose, leaving instructions with younger female relatives about their wishes.[28] Minnie told how she and her mother-in-law "years before her death" were "up in her room one night talking about clothes she would wear when she was buried," with her mother-in-law "trying on this and trying on that" in order to figure out what would look best. "She even wanted her head to be tilted a certain way [in the casket]," Minnie reported, "and when she died … I carried out her every wish."[29] Such standards were not applied to men. Typical comments made during wakes for men, such as "b'y, he was some carpenter" or "there's no one could grow cabbage like him," were tied to labour. Comments at wakes for women were more likely to refer to the deceased's appearance, such as "she's some nice lookin', isn't she?" or "she looks like she's asleep."[30] This practice likewise appears in CEWA minute books, such as in the 31 March 1966 notation at Long Pond that late member Ruth Dawe "looked lovely" in her casket.

Preparing the Wake Room

While either men or women could wash and dress deceased persons, women always arranged a space in which to display the casket. This reflects the sexual division of family labour in which women were primarily responsible for housework and interior cleaning. While rural women often helped with outdoor farm work, men rarely helped with the housekeeping aspect of indoor work in return.[31] In Conception Bay, most bodies were waked in "the room" or "front room" of the house in which the deceased had lived. In rural Newfoundland, this parlour was distinctive from the "everyday" space of the kitchen: "Most residents refer to this space as 'the room' – a usage found in other regions as well. Rather than referring to it with a functional name (such as bedroom), simply calling it *the* room attests to it ritual importance."[32] The room was used mainly for special occasions and was "devoted to the stranger, to the outsider, to the visitor." In many households, it was "mostly ... done up for waking."[33] Using the room to wake a body showed respect for the deceased. It also set the corpse apart from the world of the living, which was centred on the kitchen, to a place somewhere between life and death.[34] In Conception Bay, when women reorganized the room for a wake, they not only rearranged furniture to make sure there was a place for the casket, but also ensured that it would lie in an east-west direction (head of the corpse to the west, feet to the east). While Rachel Fagan identified this as an Anglican practice which mirrored burial practices in Anglican cemeteries, where graves were likewise situated in an east-west direction, burials (and church architecture) reflected Christian ritual belief in worshippers facing east towards the holy city of Jerusalem during services and the need to ensure the deceased would face east when they were "raised from the dead" on "resurrection morn."[35] When there was no room for the casket in the middle of the room and it had to be placed to one side, women also made sure that the corpse's left hand would be the one nearest to the adjoining wall, although the significance of this is unknown.[36]

Along with arranging the wake room, women in Conception Bay followed the English tradition of covering mirrors and reflective objects, such as pictures in glass frames, in a house where someone had recently died.[37] Minnie Bussey described how "right away all mirrors and pictures were covered with a bit of white cloth. In them times houses had old-fashioned sideboards in the front room, full of dishes. This, too, would be covered with a white sheet." Women pulled down the blinds, as did those in neighbouring houses, with the wake-house blinds often staying down for nine days, a number associated also with vernacular healing practices and women lying in after childbirth. Neighbours' blinds would be raised after the funeral.[38] Women's covering of windows and mirrors in this way has been associated with "the Christian belief that the soul departs from the body at the time of death," and a popular belief that souls might get confused by reflections in shiny surfaces and objects and end up trapped in a house rather than making a free exit to the hereafter.[39] Keeping everything covered for the duration of the wake reflected a belief that the soul remained close to the body of the deceased and only departed after the funeral service and interment. While this was perhaps an earlier understanding of the ritual, by the mid-1900s such a belief was no longer pervasive in Anglican Conception Bay. When asked about the practice of covering mirrors, Rachel and Minnie linked it only with the emotional aspect of losing a loved one. Covering everything shiny was done "mainly to take the gay, happy feeling out of the house," they said, without reference to concerns about the free movement of souls.[40]

Besides laying out men's bodies, Conception Bay men contributed to wake preparation by building the casket, placing the body in the casket, and moving the casket into the wake room.[41] While "a bunch of men" did the lifting, building the casket was to an individual man what shroud-cutting was to a woman. This job was considered "a privilege," Rachel recalled, for which no man expected to be paid. Men also paid special attention to making this item attractive, as a gesture of respect for the deceased as well as a reflection of craft pride and the culture of seriousness which surrounded funeral ritual.[42] Caskets for the ordinary people of Conception Bay were similar to those described for rural working people in early twentieth-century England, "common wood covered with black cloth and black studs," rather than the brass-trimmed caskets of polished wood purchased by wealthy families.[43] Similar caskets, built by a male community member, were used in Notre Dame Bay.[44] The description of traditional Conception Bay caskets showed how their construction combined carpentry and textile skills, similar to the skills used in furniture making. The plain board box would be lined inside with white linen or cotton, while the outside was covered with "beautiful-designed soft wool material": grey for adults and white for children.[45] The work of making caskets and placing bodies in them provides evidence of blurred gender lines within the parish. While men built caskets in other jurisdictions, women took care of decoration and lining the interior with cloth. In Conception Bay, men completed all of these tasks. Likewise, while women elsewhere placed bodies in caskets, in Conception Bay men did all "lifting" related to burial ritual.[46]

Anglican Hybrid: Wakes and Viewing the Dead

Mostly associated with the Roman Catholic tradition, a wake was the practice of watching over the recently deceased, day and night, until the funeral service and burial.[47] This was the time in which community members, extended family, friends, and acquaintances could pay their respects to the deceased and their relations. This "old custom" was practised to "prevent body snatching by anatomists" (less of a concern in rural settings) and to address the popular fear of accidental live burial.[48] In the Irish tradition, women and older persons would be the first to attend a wake, with visitors usually touching, kissing, or praying over the body. The wake was a time when much food and drink would be consumed, with women of the household primarily responsible for its organization. While women prepared and drank tea at wakes, men mostly drank alcoholic beverages and there was a "general atmosphere of mirth and festivity." Along with telling stories and reminiscing about the deceased, there could be wake games and dances.[49] Standing in contrast to this Roman Catholic "celebration" was the more solemn Anglican practice of "viewing the dead": visiting a home where a corpse was laid out, admiring the body, and leaving. This was the Anglican working-class tradition in England, with wakes only occurring among Irish Roman Catholic immigrants living in cities such as Liverpool. For non-Catholics, the post-interment funeral tea was the primary occasion for friends and neighbours to gather, eat, drink, and remember the deceased.[50]

While wakes were part of Anglican death rituals in Conception Bay, the manner in which they were conducted showed the influence of viewing practices as well.[51] Rachel described how wakes began the moment a casket entered the home of the deceased, and that "you always saw three risin' suns" before it ended. Relatives of the deceased were expected to stay up all night and could be joined by other community members, although a widow was allowed to go to bed after midnight on the first night. All community members would come to pay their respects. In contrast to the Irish tradition, Anglican wakes in Conception Bay did not occur in the same room as the deceased was displayed. Most visitors and relatives gathered in the kitchen (with women sitting and men standing), and a close relative of the deceased took everyone in turn into the room to "view the dead." Rachel and Minnie recalled how most visitors touched the corpse's forehead with their hand ("to keep from having dreams about them") and that "you always knew if strangers were RC [Roman Catholic]" because they would kneel by the casket and say a prayer.[52] While Minnie and Rachel suggested only the people who planned to stay up all night at the wake brought food (tea, bread, jam, sugar, cheese, or a "boiler" of soup), Tom Dawe's mother described a more communal approach: "[She] told me [Tom] that some of the Protestant wakes had a little bit of food. Like, there'd be a cup of tea, and a bit of cake, and a bit of cheese. People provided that. She said that the minute they started preparing for the wake, neighbours would start bringing in a bit of food."[53] No one recalled drinking at Anglican wakes, but this did not mean alcohol was not consumed as part of the community's death rituals. Rachel and Minnie described how local men would dig the grave (a job that sometimes took up the full three days of the wake depending on the weather and the terrain) and that "this was where most of the drinking was done." A male relative of the deceased usually provided the alcohol, they recalled, but occasionally another man would bring it along.[54]

While Anglicans "didn't go for" drinking and dancing at wakes, as some reported seeing among Roman Catholics on the Southern Shore of the Avalon Peninsula, Minnie reported there were moments of levity, especially in the early hours of the morning:

> As the night wore on and the visitors thinned out, the sadness would lessen among the wakers. When everyone started to get tired, you'd find everything funny then. A cough would start people giggling and if a real queer stick was present he'd start makin' funny faces on purpose to get the women laughing. People belonging to the dead didn't like this and often spoke to those laughing. Half the time, meanwhile, they'd probably be laughin' themselves.[55]

Interestingly, given the CEWA ritual described below and the place hymn singing held in domestic religious practices, Minnie recalled how hymn singing was used to try to control the wake-house atmosphere and to re-establish a solemn tone: "Usually someone would start singing a hymn and all would join in and get serious again. Before the hymn was over, someone else would be up to his devilment. You'd laugh, make jokes, and tell funny stories at wakes but you didn't mean disrespect or harm. It was something to do to pass the time and keep awake."[56] At the same time, some of the "fun" Minnie recalled, especially that related to pipe smoking, was associated with more serious burial traditions. Pipe smoking was an important, although gendered, religious ritual at traditional Irish wakes. Men would smoke a pipe together, with women taking snuff, and while taking this tobacco everyone in turn would pray for the deceased.[57] While Minnie described pipe smoking at Foxtrap wakes, she interpreted it as "badness" rather than popular religious ritual: "Occasionally you'd get real badness, though ... a man would be smokin' his pipe and start passin' it around for everyone to take a puff, even the women ... Sometimes a real devil, on the sly of the relatives, would go in the front room and put the pipe to the corpse's mouth. Some would find this real funny while others figured you'd gone far enough. They'd start singing another hymn, then."[58] Despite Minnie's interpretation, the intention of those who started passing the pipe around may not have been primarily "badness," but to encourage ritual pipe-smoking in the Irish tradition, as described above, without distinguishing participants by gender. The intention could also have been to mock Irish Catholic wake traditions, an interpretation not outside the realm of possibility in a community with widespread participation in the Orange Order.

CEWA Ritual at Wakes

For women active in the CEWA, there was opportunity to pay tribute to deceased sisters by communal participation in funeral rituals, including conducting informal services of worship during wakes. One especially detailed account of a female-led wake ritual was recorded in March 1966 by Annie Greenslade, secretary of the Long Pond CEWA. The deceased was longtime member Ruth Dawe (born 1886) and Annie noted how CEWA members learned of Ruth's death and conducted a ceremony in her honour:

> The Worthy President notified all the sisters of her Passing, and for the sisters to meet in our classroom. Twenty of our sisters come along, from there we went to Sister Dawe's home for a few hours. She looked lovely and peaceful in her nice casket. The Worthy President said seeing we are all together, she gave each sister a bow of ribbon to place in her casket. Prayers were read

> by the Worthy President and all the Sisters joined in the singing of hymns.[59]

The hymns selected and the order in which they were sung reveal the women's understanding of their relationship with the divine, in life as well as in death. They opened with *Common Praise* 483, a call for spiritual blessing on faithful members of community: "O Holy Ghost, thy people bless who long to feel thy might / And fain would grow in holiness as children of the light." This was followed by 566, which expresses belief in communal Christian service, and hope in the face of hardship and grief: "Through the night of doubt and sorrow onward goes the pilgrim band / Singing songs of expectation, marching to the Promised Land." The next two selections, 769 and 614, demonstrate belief in a heaven where the spirits of the dead would be united with the divine, and the sisters' hope that "Sister Dawe" was entering this heavenly "light." The second of these shows how coastal living, on the edges of Conception Bay, could influence women's expression of Christian faith:

> O come to the merciful Saviour who calls you
> O come to the Lord who forgives and forgets
> Though dark be the fortune on earth that befalls you
> There's a bright home above, where the sun never sets.
>
> Where the Light forever shineth
> Where no storm ariseth more
> There the Saviour meets his loved one
> On the shore.

Finally, the women sang on behalf of their friend words she could no longer speak, Charlotte Elliot's classic 1841 hymn of Christian humility, dependence on God's mercy, and faith in the redeeming power of Christ's atonement: "Just as I am – without one plea / But that thy Blood was shed for me / And that thou bidd'st me come to thee / O Lamb of God, I come."[60] Annie concluded her account of this service: "The following Monday Sister Dawe was layed [*sic*] in her last resting place, a number of sisters attended her funeral. The Worthy President and Sisters sent wreaths to both Sister Dawe and Sister Tilley, and sympathy cards were sent to the bereaved relatives."

The bows of ribbon placed in Ruth's casket, like those put in Elizabeth Tilley's grave, reflect the ties between spirituality and textile production among the women who performed the ritual. While placing objects in caskets was a common lived religious practice, there was some difference between traditions. In Irish Roman Catholic practice, a variety of objects, including salt and/or tobacco, were placed in or around the corpse to protect the deceased from supernatural forces such as fairies. Other Roman Catholic families placed a prayer book next to the body, in the deceased's hands, or under their chin. Sometimes a rosary was woven between their fingers.[61] The placing of overtly religious objects can be seen as a gesture towards the devotional life of the deceased or of their family. Among Conception Bay Anglicans, objects placed in caskets tended not to be talismanic, as in the Irish case, but practical and personal, which suggests belief in resurrection of the body and a temporal and material idea of heaven where the deceased might live as they did on earth. Minnie and Rachel described how watches, rings, and eyeglasses, along with items to identify the deceased as a member of the Orange Order (pin and sash), could be placed in caskets. Rachel remembered putting her mother's false teeth and hairpin into the casket before it closed.[62] CEWA ribbons, placed in the context of clergy-led funeral rites or female-led wake ritual, publicly confirmed the deceased's religiosity and record of Christian service, as did prayer books.[63]

While placing items such as salt, tobacco, or bread in caskets was not part of the Conception Bay Anglican tradition that Rachel and Minnie described, it was for other Christians living in the area. Tom Dawe recalled his grandmother being "shocked" after she attended a (perhaps) Roman Catholic wake and saw something "she wasn't familiar with … somebody had put bread, a loaf of bread, into the coffin."[64] Bread's symbolic and cultural significance for Newfoundlanders included its use as protection "for body and soul" and for "those venturing out into liminal spaces" such as the woods or berry barrens. Bread in caskets may have been likewise thought to protect the deceased as they journeyed into the unknown regions between life and death, and symbolized comfort and protection not only because of its maternal and domestic associations, but also because of its religious connections to "the body of Christ" in sacramental ritual.[65] Similarly, while candles were commonly placed around the casket during a Roman Catholic wake, Minnie and Rachel stated that they were "never" used for Anglicans.[66]

Annie Greenslade's account of CEWA funeral ritual included reference to sending a memorial wreath on behalf of the association. A collection to help with burial costs or to purchase a wreath is one example of mutual aid among members of the working class seen in various religious traditions and practised by Conception Bay Anglican women through the last half of the twentieth century. At Seal Cove, this practice was so familiar and accepted that the women agreed in May 1943 "as we are closing for Summer recess ... that should one of our members happen to die a wreath should be sent her from the class without having to call a meeting for a decision."[67] "But we trust," branch secretary Phoebe Morgan was quick to add, "that all shall be spared Health and Strength to meet again in the fall." While funeral flowers were condemned as a "waste" by middle-class English reformers of lower-class practices, their beauty was something to admire in the midst of sorrow. Grieving survivors interpreted the note which usually accompanied a gift of flowers as a heartfelt message of condolence. Wreaths were a gesture of respect and, when sent to women, flowers stood as "a metaphor for the individual whose moral integrity remains intact" despite life's challenges. In rural settings, floral tributes often came from home gardens or nature.[68] This can be seen as evidence of rural women's understanding of the ties between the domestic and the spiritual, as well as their finding of spiritual meaning within natural landscapes.

Flowers have special significance in women's popular theology. The beauty of blossoms, especially for women who lived in challenging natural environments (such as along the coast of the North Atlantic), was symbolic of divine goodness, and their ability to perennially bloom despite winter's harshness represented women's strength and resilience in the face of patriarchal religious and social structures. Some women understood flowers as a means by which to come "closer to a true communion with God."[69] By the late 1950s, flowers had become a favourite tribute "to deceased sisters" of the CEWA. Through the 1960s, women purchased flowers in memory of late members each Easter, a time of rebirth and renewal, and used them to adorn the chancel and altar of All Saints, Foxtrap, and St Peter's in Upper Gullies.[70] At Seal Cove on 18 March 1964, for example, the women agreed "that we would give money for flowers for the altar as in past years in Memory of Departed Sisters of the CEWA who has passed on leaving us a good example of the work that they had done during their time with us."[71] At Long Pond on 4 April 1963, the women likewise agreed to pay "for flowers to be placed in Church for Easter Sunday in memory of departed Sisters," with secretary Myra Porter adding, "it was also agreed that we send flowers to elderly and sick Sisters of our class."[72] At Foxtrap, women ever-mindful of the material needs and physical well-being of their CEWA colleagues decided to send "three of our old sisters a tray of fruit" at Easter instead.[73]

Funerary Services and Processions

Women's participation in funeral services varies according to time and place, with class and religious identity combining with gender to influence social expectations and actual female practice. Historians have seen the influence of nineteenth-century middle-class notions of "true womanhood" in the idea that women were too emotionally fragile and physically delicate to attend funeral services (especially interments), although social expectations about women's supposed delicacy were put aside when it came to the duty of preparing corpses.[74] American women were more likely to participate in funerals and burials than their English middle- and upper-class counterparts, who were "actively discouraged" from attending such services, even those held upon the death of their own husbands or children.[75] Most funerals in nineteenth-century Montreal were "very masculine affair[s]," with few women in the cortege.[76] Among English working-class families, women's participation in funeral services was somewhat mixed, with some female mourners who insisted upon attending in the face of male discouragement while others accepted exclusion. Those who chose to stay home may have been more willing to comply with gender ideology, but they also may have been influenced by domestic roles and expectations, such as women staying home from burial services in order to prepare the funeral tea, an important post-burial ritual.[77]

The Australian experience suggests that women in that jurisdiction were likewise discouraged from attending funerals, especially if Anglican, Presbyterian, or Roman Catholic. In response, women developed a distinctive practice of holding their own female-only service of worship at home during the public service. In these private ceremonies, women would kneel together, with one reading the service as the male priest or lay reader would and the rest responding, followed by a period of silent prayer.[78] These private female services mirror somewhat the worship

Figure 6.1 Masonic ritual was a regular part of funeral practices in Conception Bay when the deceased person was a member of the men's Loyal Orange Association (LOA) or women's Loyal Orange Benevolent Association (LOBA). LOA Bands, such as the group from Hopewell Lodge pictured here, marched in the funeral procession from wake house to church, playing hymns along the way.

conducted at wakes by the executive and members of study area CEWA branches. In Australia, the stricture on women's participation in funerals had largely relaxed by the end of the nineteenth century.[79] Among the Anglicans of mid-twentieth-century Conception Bay, there was no tradition of women being excluded from funerals, including those of close relatives. In fact, there was an opposite social and religious expectation: "In cases where the person's been really sick, like the mother's been really grief-stricken, unless she passed out, unless she collapsed with nervous exhaustion, she was supposed to attend [the funeral]. All the relatives. It was the thing to do, you must be there."[80]

The role of the Orange Lodge, along with other voluntary associations, in Anglican funeral processions was well remembered in Conception Bay. As was the case in nineteenth-century Great Britain, Anglican church officials in twentieth-century Newfoundland tended to be tolerant of Orange ritual during burial services.[81] This tolerance came despite the order's link with anti-Catholicism, a sentiment which stood in contrast to the calls for Christian unity which began appearing regularly in *Diocesan Magazine* after the end of the Second

World War.[82] While Australian Masonic ritual, similar in form to the Orange ritual described for Conception Bay (regalia, honour guard, procession led by marching band, and special prayers), was condemned by some Roman Catholic and high Anglican priests as "un-Christian," clergy officiating at funerals in that colony largely accepted it by 1900. This may have been due to the popularity of Masonic societies among Australian working-class men, a colonial trend echoed in the Orange Lodge's popularity in Conception Bay.[83] Women's participation, and especially their recognition as full lodge members in funeral ritual, was a substantial Newfoundland distinction.

Minnie and Rachel recalled that many Conception Bay Anglicans were members of "the lodge," whether the men's Loyal Orange Association or the women's Loyal Orange Benevolent Association. This membership affected funeral ritual. On the day of the funeral, they recalled, the minister would arrive at the wake-house around 2:00 p.m., and by 2:30 p.m. the house and yard would be full of people waiting to participate in the cortege. If the deceased was a member of a society, be it the Loyal Orange Association, Loyal Orange Benevolent Association, Society of United Fishermen, or CEWA, fellow members would attend wearing their sashes or pins.[84] This was confirmed in the minute books of all local CEWA branches, where members usually agreed to attend a deceased sister's funeral en masse. This practice dated from at least 1920, when Long Pond branch secretary Lilly Greenslade noted branch president Susie Rendell's suggestion that "when a Sister departs this world a meeting should be called and arrange to walk in a Body to the Funeral," and the members "proposed second and carried to do so."[85] Similarly, in January 1929, members of the Seal Cove branch agreed "we should all pay our last respects to [our late sister Selina Dowden] by attending the funeral."[86] The Long Pond CEWA tribute to the late Emma Jane Kennedy, a founding member of the branch, captured this practice:

> It is with much regret that we record the death of one of our oldest members in the person of Emma Jane Kennedy ... Her funeral, which took place at All Saints' Church, Foxtrap, was largely attended, the Sisters of the CEWA, of which she was a devoted member, attending corporately. The Reverend George Elliott, rector of the parish, officiated. One of her favorite hymns – "O for a closer walk with God" – was sung at the graveside ... Our

> late Sister will be very greatly missed. She worked faithfully and unceasingly with untiring effort almost to the end, for the Church she loved. May her soul rest in peace and light perpetual shine upon her.[87]

Evidence of lived religiosity appears in personal requests for particular hymns or scripture passages to be sung or read at funeral services, works one can assume carried special spiritual meaning for the deceased or their family members.[88] As was the case for Emma, in Conception Bay the deceased's favourite hymn was "always" sung at their funeral service.[89]

As Minnie and Rachel described, the cortege from wake-house to church was led by two Orangemen, with the hearse likewise driven by a member of the order. This appeared to be the case regardless of the member's gender. For members of the Orange Order or the Society of United Fishermen, the society band attended and played a hymn in the yard to mark the start of the funeral. Pallbearers (men) walked alongside the casket, each with a hand placed on its lid. Then came the minister, the deceased's immediate family and more distant relatives, society members, and, when appropriate, the society band. The end of the procession was made up of people from the deceased's community and, if they were well-known and popular, neighbouring settlements. The procession made its way to the church with the society band playing hymns along the way. People living in houses on the funeral route kept their blinds down, and only raised them and joined the procession once the casket passed. After the church service, the procession made its way to the graveyard in similar fashion. After the interment, family members left the graveyard and returned to the wake-house. Women of the community would help prepare a meal and put the wake room back to its former appearance, while men stayed to help fill in the grave. The community then gathered for a post-funeral tea much like that Strange describes for working-class England. As Minnie and Rachel noted, this tea had a more jovial atmosphere than the wake, including men passing around rum.[90]

Restoring Order

Women's role in putting the wake room and house back in order after the funeral carried spiritual significance, as well as reflecting their responsibility for housework within the family labour system. In some

Irish communities, the woman who prepared the corpse for the wake was also responsible for putting the wake room back in its usual order once the casket was removed, a tradition associated with the idea of women being responsible not only for looking after the dead but also for removing the physical signs of sorrow from a grieving household.[91] Just as a group of women, rather than an individual, prepared a body in Conception Bay, they also worked together to clean the wake house. This task fell to women regardless of the deceased's gender. Rachel and Minnie remembered how groups of neighbouring women would clean the room where the person died, and that "everything washable was washed." If the person died of a contagious disease such as tuberculosis, which affected many people in Conception Bay as well as other parts of Newfoundland in the mid-twentieth century, the women would burn the mattress and bedclothes.[92] Tom Dawe recalled how "the whole house got a real scouring" the day after a funeral, with part of the work being to sort through the dead person's clothes and to give away anything the family did not want.[93]

While this work can be considered part of women's role in taking on and helping to alleviate the sorrow of others, one can also see in this tradition women's efforts to work out their own sorrow and to cope with loss. One woman wrote in 1920 of trying to "beat off her 'terrible depression'" with cleaning and other chores after her daughter's death.[94] By distributing the deceased's clothing in the community, women would also experience the spiritual benefits of participating in charity and mutual aid. If they were active CEWA members, as many were, this notion of serving Christ by clothing others would have been central to their spiritual worldview. The biblical figure of Dorcas, who was resurrected by virtue of her textile work and her generosity in distributing garments, was held up as a key religious role model by the Anglican women of Conception Bay.[95]

Conclusion

In a *Newfoundland Churchman* editorial titled "The Burial of the Dead," Abraham expressed concern in 1960 about the growing professionalization of mortuary and funeral services in Newfoundland, which he felt contributed to a more consumerist approach to what should be primarily a Christian service. Abraham feared that a commercialized funeral "industry" would displace some of the more admirable aspects of traditional Anglican rituals in the province, as well as weaken the Church's "right and duty to direct the details" of funerary rites: "Simplicity and naturalness should be the notes of Christian burial. We hope that it will never be considered unfitting for a man to be buried in a casket made by his neighbours: the ancient practice of covering the casket in church with a pall will discourage unseemly competition and is a sign of the equality of all men in God's sight."[96] Despite the move towards professional funeral services, in the mid-1900s the death of a member of a community within the study area remained a time for people to come together to show respect for the deceased and support for the grieving family in customary ways that reveal traditional, and often gendered, practices and beliefs.

Scholars have recognized women's key role in the rituals surrounding the end of life, just as they had in the childbirth rituals surrounding the beginning of life. The spiritual and the social interacted in a community's response to the loss of a member, with women especially negotiating the cultural space between those two worlds:

> Women's performance of the necessary rituals before, during and after the burial rites … includes a concern for the spiritual world and the ancestors as well as the society in general … The stability of the society and the cosmos is not only threatened during death but conversely, death is also a means by which it is possible to encapsulate and to grasp the dynamics that constitute both society and the cosmos.[97]

Existence of a cross-cultural female space between the temporal and the spiritual worlds suggests that inquiry into religious beliefs and practices of a particular society, and especially women's religiosity, must consider gender dynamics surrounding wakes, funerals, and burial rites. While in other jurisdictions women were responsible for washing and dressing corpses as well as preparing and restoring the wake room by virtue of such tasks being "indoor" work, in Conception Bay laying out corpses was work shared by men and women, based on the sex of the corpse, and done cooperatively. The housekeeping aspect of wake ritual, however, was considered women's sphere and required knowledge of specific rules for arranging the wake room, including belief that the casket should be oriented east to west. Women were responsible for making shrouds for the deceased, which in Conception Bay were not full burying garments but ornate, ceremonial textiles cut from white shirting. Men participated in death ritual by building and decorating caskets, lifting the deceased into them, and digging and filling in graves.

The Anglican practice of waking in Conception Bay was a hybrid of wake ritual associated with Roman Catholics and with viewing rituals practised by Anglicans in other jurisdictions. Descriptions of mid-twentieth-century wakes in the study area show the importance of hymn singing as a tribute to the deceased (practised by women of the CEWA) and as a way to control wake-house atmosphere. Committed Christian women's approach to funeral ritual is revealed in CEWA records, where hymns, bows of ribbon, and flowers were used as tributes to deceased members. While scholars associate flowers with women's popular theology elsewhere, the bows demonstrate the local connection between textiles and spirituality. As was typical practice in fraternal organizations, CEWA women attended funerals of late members en masse and walked in the cortege as a display of solidarity with, and respect for, the deceased. In Conception Bay, the Orange Order was remembered as playing an important processional role in Anglican funerals, a practice local clergy tolerated despite the criticism associated with Masonic participation in funerals. Exploring popular Anglican ritual surrounding wakes and funerals provides opportunity to consider the relationship between lived religious practice and what Abraham deemed "a truly Christian" conception of "death and the life to come," as well as the influence of gender ideology and the sexual division of household labour on Christian ritual. Popular Anglican understanding of "death and the life to come," especially the influence of domesticity and the interplay of popular and orthodox conceptions of the hereafter in local consolation and condolence practices are discussed in the next chapter.

CHAPTER SEVEN

"We Must Not Weep for a Sister Deceased": Women, Christian Consolation, and Imagining Eternity

But we must not weep for a Sister deceased
Our loss is her Infinite gain.
A soul out of prison released
And freed from her bodily chain

Phoebe Morgan, Secretary,
Seal Cove CEWA[1]

Many scholars have approached the history of death from a positivist, scientific perspective, and have focused on matters such as infectious disease and mortality rates without paying much attention to the "emotional and social responses to loss," including the place of religious belief in sustaining and comforting the bereaved.[2] While there have been calls for increased recognition of the place of faithfulness in the lives of historical agents as they dealt with death and loss, scholars' reliance on middle-class sources such as private diaries and letters generated within prominent families when exploring such topics means that grief and consolation seeking have sometimes come across as a largely bourgeois concern.[3] There have been some efforts to correct this, including the use of sources beyond diaries or journals in order to capture the experience of women of various social standings, as I have done here.[4]

In this chapter, I explore the religious responses to grief and loss as the ordinary Anglicans of Conception Bay expressed them, both in written messages of Christian condolence contained in CEWA minute books and in the epitaphs that appear on almost 500 local headstones erected between 1920 and 1970 in Anglican cemeteries at Upper Gullies and Foxtrap. While clergy and bishops of the Newfoundland Anglican church criticized popular expressions of consolation, analysis of CEWA women's writings reveals a more orthodox understanding of "eternal life" among ordinary female believers than male clergy assumed. CEWA members' response to a sister's death or bereavement provides valuable insight into how rural, working women understood this central tenet of Christian theology. By examining ritual practices and the written and spoken word, we can discover the vision(s) of heaven embraced by the activist Anglican women of Conception Bay and the types of Christian consolation they favoured. Published consolation literature, often consisting of poems written by Protestant clergymen and pious women, helped to shape local women's theological culture. Consolation literature, aimed especially at women readers, prescribed appropriate Christian responses to death and was increasingly popular in American newspapers through the nineteenth century.[5] In Newfoundland, consolation literature made its presence felt, especially in the context of the two world wars when many families lost members in overseas service.[6]

I conclude this chapter with an examination of popular consolation as expressed on grave markers. Epitaphs on headstones erected in the parish of Foxtrap and Hopewell during the mid-twentieth century can be categorized into five types based on the nature of the messages about loss and eternal life they contained. While the largest number were orthodox in terms of Christian language, imagery, and doctrine, others focused on the emotional impact of losing a loved one or expressed a domesticated vision of heaven. Further dominant themes included statements of the living's intention to remember the dead or inscriptions which portrayed death as a restful, peaceful release from earthly life. The types of headstone epitaphs which Conception Bay Anglicans preferred reveal much about popular Christianity, including ordinary believers' conception of eternal life and the meaning of resurrection, the nature of the deceased person's relationship with the living, the dead and the divine, and the relative importance of secular and religious responses to grief. Considering the content of epitaphs selected by women, as compared to those selected for women, reveals the gender dynamics of Christian condolence, including the extent to which the popular notion of a domesticated heaven, and the family unit as an eternal bond, had entered the religious world of Conception Bay.

Resurrection and the Promise of Eternal Life

Among the ordained clergy of the Newfoundland church, discussion of the meaning of Christ's resurrection and the Christian hope for resurrection and eternal life often took on a frustrated tone as they confronted what they considered an immeasurable gap between popular beliefs about the meaning of immortality and official church doctrine and teaching. The doctrine of the resurrection of the dead is central to Christianity, and for many believers it is closely tied to the resurrection of Christ as described in the New Testament and asserted in the creeds, though its meaning has varied over time and among traditions. In twentieth-century Newfoundland, there was a growing distinction between Anglicans who believed that the resurrection of the dead included a full restoration of the individual person (physically, mentally, and emotionally) and those who believed it to be more spiritual in nature. This latter understanding was largely based on St Paul's first letter to the Corinthians, which described a vision of eternal life which preserved the individual personality of the deceased within a new spiritual form, but not within the earthly body they had occupied before death.[7]

Within official Newfoundland Anglican discourse there were contradictory interpretations of this doctrine. The Right Reverend William White, writing in his capacity as Bishop of Newfoundland in 1930, assured readers of *Diocesan Magazine* that "the truth which Easter brings gives the assurance that Christ really has the power to raise both dead souls and dead bodies to life," yet his sermon delivered at the Anglican Cathedral on Easter Sunday 1934 focused on the Easter victory as a spiritual victory.[8] Believing in some sort of survival after death is not sufficient for Christians, White argued, especially since the New Testament only describes how *Jesus* (his emphasis) died and rose again. White explained that Christianity carried no general promise of physical resurrection, and condemned ordinary believers who focused on "frantically trying to revive a corpse" rather than on "spiritualizing the whole body so that it may no longer be subject to death."[9] Twenty years later, the Reverend E.P. Hiscock reflected likewise that "it is astonishing to find that there are still people who think that when we speak of the resurrection of the body we mean the actual material body laid to rest in the grave." He encouraged Newfoundland Anglicans to believe instead that "eternal life is not something away in the distant future. It is the new life which is ours by virtue of union with Christ; but whilst our mode of existence is a material body it cannot find its fullest expression."[10] Yet Easter messages continued to focus on the "resurrection of the body" (as did the creeds recited weekly at Anglican services), and each spring Newfoundland Anglicans were encouraged to turn their minds to thoughts of "the life beyond" and the "conquest of death by the King of Life."[11]

During the Second World War, the subject of "true" Christian consolation in the face of death and loss was taken up by new Anglican bishop the Right Reverend Philip Abraham, as well as by *Diocesan Magazine* editor (and future Bishop of Newfoundland) the Reverend John A. Meaden. Both men criticized popular responses to loss. Meaden called for increased celebration of All Souls' Day, suggesting that its neglect among Newfoundland Anglicans "has sometimes driven grief-stricken people to seek consolation in dangerous beliefs, especially in time of crisis like the present."[12] Abraham, newly enthroned as bishop in September 1942, took a more pointed approach and wrote in the spring of 1943 that bereaved Christians should "be prepared to put away easy short-cuts and smooth words, if [they] are to find the Truth. Only the Truth can help men and women, fathers, mothers, husbands and wives in their dire and sudden need" following a loved one's death. He provided as an example of the "easy way out" a verse popular in funeral notices of the time:

> I cannot say and I will not say
> That he is dead: he is just away.
> With a tender smile and a wave of the hand
> He has wandered into an unknown land.
> And left us dreaming how very fair
> It needs must be since he lingers there.

Abraham offered in contrast the words of "our greatest Christian poet, T.S. Eliot": "Though you forget the way to the Temple, There is One who remembers the way to your door: Life you may evade, but Death you shall not. You shall not deny the stranger." Grieving persons needed to face "the brutal fact of bodily destruction" and "the sudden break with earthly life" with courage, Abraham argued, rather than pursue "a doubtful and weak evasion of our destiny." With that being said, and after clearly advocating for one true Christian response to loss, he nevertheless left it up to the individual reader "to judge which poet in the end is going to be most help to those shocked and bereaved but desperately hoping for aid from their religion."[13]

Abraham's son, the Reverend Charles Abraham, took up this same cause during his own time as editor of the *Newfoundland Churchman*. In a 1960 editorial, "The Burial of the Dead," Charles (perhaps bothered by the tone and language of professional mortuary services, which he felt were displacing the church somewhat in assisting families with funeral planning) emphasized to readers that "when the committal says 'earth to earth, ashes to ashes,' that is exactly what it means and no device should be used in the interests of so-called 'peace of mind' that will even suggest that the natural process is being arrested. The Christian hope lies in the resurrection of the body, not in its preservation."[14] Despite the assumptions of ordained clergy, popular expressions of Christian consolation in Conception Bay, especially those written by and for women, reveal a range of responses to death, as well as varying conceptions of the doctrine of the resurrection of the body and the nature of eternal life. When approaching the writings and voices of these women, it is important to remember that ordinary believers, many of whom had access to basic educations only, often used words of consolation and expressions of condolence that secular readers might easily dismiss. Rather than passing judgments about artificial or formulaic content, it is important to understand that these words and expressions gave genuine comfort to people of a particular place and time, especially when written by someone who knew, and cared for, the deceased.[15]

Seeking Consolation: Female Voices and Actions

In the mid-1900s, women active in the CEWA responded immediately to news of the death of one of their own. On 8 May 1944, for example, the Seal Cove branch held an emergency meeting after word spread through the communities of Seal Cove and Indian Pond that Victoria (Rideout) Dawe, the twenty-five-year-old daughter-in-law of their association president Annie M. Dawe, had died.[16] Victoria was a dedicated CEWA member who joined the Long Pond branch in 1935 at age sixteen, prior to her marriage and move to Seal Cove.[17] While reported "very sick" in early April, by the middle of the month Annie could bring the encouraging news to the weekly meeting that that her daughter-in-law was "getting better." Despite the women's "hope and trust that [she] will be spared many years longer," Victoria died less than a month later, likely from tuberculosis, a disease that through the 1920s, 1930s, and

1940s was claiming other young women in the parish, including Laura Frances Morgan of Indian Pond and sisters Mabel and Virtue Roberts of Upper Gullies.[18]

The women's response to the news that Victoria had "passed from this life to the life eternal" was recorded by branch secretary Harriett Morgan, who described how members sought consolation through hymn singing and prayer. In many ways, this ritual was similar to the private female services which Australian Anglicans conducted as part of the preparation of a dead body.[19] It began, Harriett wrote, with the singing of "O Praise Our God Today," a hymn often used to open weekly meetings. After "the Prayers of the CEWA was read," first vice president of the branch Hilda Lear "said a little prayer to suit the occasion." No work was done, Harriett noted, nor were any minutes read. Instead, the women raised their voices in song again, this time choosing Charles Wesley's "Let saints on earth in concert sing / With those whose work is done / For all the servants of our King / In heaven and earth are one." The meeting closed with additional prayers and, given the wartime context, singing the national anthem. Knowing she would be reading these minutes aloud at the next meeting, Harriet included a short poem in her written account to inspire and console the sisters:

And thus I live in god at Peace
And die without a thought or fear
Content to take what god decrees
For through his Son my faith is clear
His grace Shall be in Death my Stay
And Peace Shall Bless my Dying Day.[20]

Victoria's death also affected the sisters of Long Pond branch. Two days after Seal Cove women met to honour and remember her, at a district branch meeting in Long Pond Annie Jefford acknowledged her passing and "sympathized with Seal Cove Branch on behalf of their dear sister, that was recently taken from their midst." Annie used the opportunity to remind the assembled women of their own mortality and reflected that "as we all know, it is only a matter of days when someone else will have to enter the same door … In the midst of life we are in death."[21]

Tributes written after CEWA members' deaths capture the religious voices of ordinary Anglican women, especially those who served as branch secretaries. These tributes were of two types. Most were written by association secretaries for internal use only: designed to be read aloud from the minute book to celebrate the deceased's life and to comfort and console her surviving sisters. Occasionally, as the diocesan council of the CEWA encouraged, branch secretaries sent a report of the year's work to *Diocesan Magazine* for publication. These could contain tributes to deceased sisters, but were written with a wider Anglican audience in mind. A good example appeared in the October 1943 issue of the *Diocesan*, in a report written by Seal Cove secretary Phoebe Morgan: "In May, 1942, we lost one of our older members, Sister Virtue Morgan, who was called to higher service. And in May of this year another of our Sisters was called to her Eternal Reward. Sister Enid Morgan, who was a young and energetic member; but 'in the midst of life we are in death.' May God help us to be faithful to our calling."[22] Virtue was Phoebe's grandmother-in-law, and a woman whose faith – and sanity – had been tested by tragic loss. Women of Seal Cove and Indian Pond would have been familiar with Virtue's story, and it affected their response to her death. During the First World War, two of Virtue's sons were killed in action within a month of each other, one on HMS *Vicknor* in January 1915 and the other on HMS *Clan McNaughton* in February. In 1920 she lost her husband, Joseph, in June, and her twenty-one-year-old daughter, Laura, in July. Between 1890 and 1904 Virtue had endured the deaths of three additional children.[23]

Children's deaths shaped women's theology. Even at a time when such loss was common, "each one of these deaths took an enormous emotional and psychic toll on the parents" and "no matter how many other children women had, they always remembered and mourned the ones they had lost too soon."[24] Christian women often experienced tension between "doubt and assurance, sorrow and hope" when they responded to the death of children. As they struggled to remain faithful yet sought to understand why God would allow such tragedies, women often turned to poetry as a way to express these conflicting emotions.[25] Virtue's experience demonstrates the emotional toll that losing children could take, with her response to the death of her sons described by granddaughter Reta (Morgan) Hill:

> John was only seventeen and Fred worked at Ayres and Son and [was] a school teacher … When the two men came and told her that her two sons were lost she flipped, she lost her mind. She ran

> away in the woods and before night my father and his brother and another man, I don't know who he was, and they went looking for her before dark. They found her down besides Billy's Brook … sitting in the bushes. They said "what are you doing here, Mother?" [She answered,] "I don't know, my child." Her mind was completely gone.

Yet Reta remembered Virtue as a person of enduring Christian faith in the face of loss, a faith that Reta admitted she sometimes found hard to understand:

> My grandmother had a nice grace I remember … now she lost two boys in the First World War and that was a tragedy. She had a nervous breakdown and I could never understand when I grew up later on that she could say this blessing, you know. And it goes like this: From Thy hand cometh every good / We thank Thee for our daily food / And with it Lord a blessing give / And to Thy glory may we live.

Reta also remembered a framed religious print displayed in her grandmother's front room that continues to have religious meaning for her: "It was the Lord's Prayer with pictures … I went to an auction one night in Maryland and if I didn't see one just like it. And I grabbed it … I haven't seen one since … I wouldn't part with it."

While great-granddaughter Eileen Morgan had few memories of Virtue beyond "a woman in a long skirt, arms rolled up in her apron, leaning on a fence and talking," Reta expressed clear and lasting affection: "I loved my grandmother. I chased her around like a little puppy dog all the time. I think it was because she loved me and maybe [she] was the only person I felt like I was comfortable with, you know. She was a darling." Seal Cove CEWA members carried similar affection for Virtue; she sometimes sang hymns for them during meetings, and they made a special effort to visit during her "lingering illness."[26] Consistent with women's use of poetry to express grief and Christian consolation, branch secretary Phoebe Morgan presented a poem to CEWA members in June 1942 upon the occasion of Virtue's death, just as Harriet Morgan would upon Victoria's death in 1944. Given the women's knowledge of Virtue's life story, the poem, which appears at the top of this chapter, combined hope for eternal life with thankfulness for the end of earthly hardships.[27]

The CEWA response to Enid (Dawe) Morgan's death just over a year after Virtue's showed a different expression of Christian consolation, one which emphasized the seeming distance between human desires and God's will. Phoebe wrote in October 1943: "It is fitting at this time that we pay tribute to the memory of one of our sisters, Sister Enid Morgan who was called to her Eternal reward since class closed for summer. She was a young and Energetic member and her presence will be greatly missed amongst us. But 'in the midst of life we are in Death,' and God's ways are not our way and it's hard for us to understand them now."[28] Enid was the daughter of long-time CEWA member Clara Dawe and her husband, Isaac.[29] She was only twenty-five at the time of her death, and Phoebe understood that that the loss of a young and dedicated church worker, from a church family, could test the faithfulness of some members. She again concluded her tribute with a poem, and this time emphasized humanity's imperfect understanding of God's will and heaven as a place to gain perfect knowledge of the divine: "Not now but in the Coming years / It may be in the Better Land / We'll reap the meaning of our tears / It's then, Oh then We'll understand."[30]

The deaths of younger CEWA members evoked the same tension between "doubt and assurance, sorrow and hope" as the deaths of children. The deaths of older members were less likely to provoke such a response. In April 1945, when "one of our oldest members in the person of Sister Patience Harvey" was "called to her eternal reward," secretary Harriet Morgan concluded philosophically that Patience had died "at the good old age of 81 years" and noted simply that "God's will must be done," a position that stood in contrast to the tribute she wrote, and the ritual she described, upon the death of young Victoria Dawe in 1944.[31]

Enid Morgan's death offers a point of comparison between lay women, ordained clergy, and clergy wives when it came to responding to the loss of a CEWA member. The Reverend Heber and Elizabeth Gosse were present at the meeting where Phoebe Morgan presented her tribute to Enid, and Phoebe carefully noted down the rector's response to Enid's death: "Though the Workmen die, still God's work must go on. And though we know that others may not be all they should be, still we as individuals must carry on our work and do our very best in the service of our Lord. God help us to be true and faithful to Our calling."[32] While Phoebe used his concluding sentiment in the tribute she prepared for publication in *Diocesan Magazine*, she chose to omit his thoughts about individual "workmen" which suggested he viewed CEWA members as primarily a source of labour for the church.[33] Elizabeth, in her capacity as president and chairperson of CEWA district branch meetings, responded to Enid's death by calling for "a few minutes silence in remembrance of her" and by extending sympathy to the women of Seal Cove branch.[34] Unlike her husband, she saw no need to comment on the infinite nature of church work or to draw negative comparisons between CEWA members and other parishioners. Instead, Enid's worth as an individual was recognized and honoured by her female colleagues.

Comforting the Bereaved: Condolence Letters

CEWA members sent letters of sympathy and condolence to bereaved sisters from their own branch and to the grieving families of their deceased branch members. They usually sent sympathy cards only to women in other CEWA branches who had lost a family member. In February 1937, for example, the Seal Cove CEWA sent a card to Amelia Coates, "Worthy President of the Upper Gullies branch," upon the death of her husband, Peter.[35] Seal Cove branch sent cards in 1942 and 1943 to Sister Elizabeth Tilley of Long Pond, "who a short while back lost her son Max," and to Sister Annie Greenslade, also of Long Pond, "who is bereaved by the death of her mother."[36] Sometimes a sympathy letter could be sent to a CEWA member elsewhere, such as that sent to "Mrs Fred Andrews" of St John's, a member of the Diocesan Council executive formerly resident in Conception Bay, who was "bereaved of her loving son" in March 1948.[37] Examples of consolation letters written by local women for local women were preserved on the back pages of Long Pond CEWA minute books, where they were carefully copied out as part of the association's records. Letters received from bereaved members could be preserved between the pages of bound minute books, as was the case for Seal Cove branch, which shows how highly the women respected the words and emotional content such letters contained and valued their relationships with each other.

"The craft of the consolation letter had risen to something of an art in New England in the mid-nineteenth century," one writer observes, "and it would persist for many decades."[38] Advice manuals on the writing of condolence letters were published at that time and specify, among other things, the use of black-bordered paper. Condolence-letter writing is often interpreted as evidence that middle-class people "embraced the cult of mourning and observed its practices" as a means to display "sincerity and gentility."[39] Historians' tendency to associate the condolence letter with upper- and middle-class writers likely reflects the nature of their sources, especially since collections of private documents (in which such letters are often located) are more likely to be produced, and preserved, when they originate from prominent families and individuals. Yet the evidence from Conception Bay reveals that such letters were also written by rural working women, women with often-rudimentary literacy skills, as a way to extend messages of sympathy to each other. Filled with the language of Christian condolence, these letters are important examples of ordinary women's religious voices and of closely held beliefs that did not always easily translate into the written word.

Condolence letters have been used to understand popular religiosity, especially the perceived change from heavily Christian content in the nineteenth century to more secular messages of sympathy by the early twentieth century. Before 1880, condolence letters "used a religious discourse drawn from familiar biblical passages, popular hymns, devotional texts and the prayer book" and stressed an orthodox Christian message about the soul's immortality and the deceased's union with God in heaven.[40] By the end of the nineteenth century, a new form of letter had begun to focus on the promise of "family reunion" in the hereafter and offer to the bereaved hope of seeing their loved ones again. This less orthodox and more domesticated vision of heaven became the primary form of consolation Christians offered to each other in the twentieth century. In addition, the use of secular condolence letters, most of which focused on the healing power of time, increased after 1900.[41] While letters written by women in mid-1900s Conception Bay reflect some of these patterns, they reveal additional information about female religiosity and popular Christian conceptions of heaven.

Members of the Long Pond CEWA wrote several condolence letters during the winter of 1942. Two responded to the deaths of branch president Elizabeth Tilley's brother, as well as her son, Max Greenslade, born in 1910 during her first marriage to John Greenslade.[42] Max was, in addition, member May Greenslade's husband. On 26 January 1942, first vice president Annie Jefford and secretary Lily Greenslade sat down to write letters of condolence to the bereaved women. They sent the first to Elizabeth: "My Dear President – We the sisters of the Long Pond Association wish to offer you and all the family our deepest Sympathy in the sudden passing of your Dear Son and Brother respectfully, Although in a way expecting it. It came has [*sic*] a shock. We must look to one above to sustain us in our hours of sorrow at all times and I am sure he will never fail us. So wear [*sic*] hoping we will all meet in Heaven where there is no parting." The next, addressed "Dear Sister May Greenslade," echoed, but did not duplicate, the first: "We ... wish to offer you our deep Sympathy in the loss you have sustained through the sudden passing of your Dear Husband. How true are the words 'In the midst of life We are in Death.' You know your loss is Heaven's gain. Yet we all find it hard to part with those we love so dear. Hoping that we will all meet in Heaven where there is no parting." While these letters express hope for heavenly reunion, the sentiment is more community focused ("we will all meet") than family centred. In addition, the women of mid-twentieth-century Conception Bay still favoured the use of religious discourse usually associated with mid-nineteenth-century letters. While they acknowledged the emotional toil of loss, they also expressed faith in a personal God who knew, and sympathized with, their personal situations.

A third condolence letter was sent to then-rector the Reverend Heber Gosse and rector's wife Elizabeth Gosse, honourary president of the Long Pond branch. This letter is interesting in that it was written in response to the news that their son, Frank Gosse, was missing in action in Europe, and not in response to news of his death. While the women of Seal Cove branch had discussed "sending Our Rector and Mrs Gosse a note of sympathy concerning their boy Frank who is reported missing in the War Zone," they concluded they should "not do this until further news is heard as he isn't officially declared dead as yet." Seal Cove women concluded their discussion of this matter with an expression of faith and hope: "We trust in God that it shall be brighter news that shall come next."[43] The women of Long Pond, however, went ahead with a condolence letter. Written by Annie Jefford, who had been elected president to replace the bereaved Elizabeth Tilley, and by Elsie Baird, new branch secretary, the letter took a middle ground that mixed Christian hope with presumption of death:

> We … wish to extend our deepest sympathy to you, for the sad news which you have received recently, on behalf of your Dear Son. We sincerely hope that in the near future you will receive some other message that will help to brighten up your hours of sorrow. And that "God in his own good time will restore unto his people the Blessings of peace." Hoping we will all meet in Heaven where there'll be no more Parting.[44]

In Seal Cove, a condolence letter was sent to branch president Annie Marie Dawe upon the death of her sixteen-year-old son Leonard Dawe in September 1939. Leonard died while the CEWA was on its annual summer recess, which usually stretched from the time vegetable gardens were planted in May until they were harvested in October. Despite the recess, CEWA members gathered and sent a note of condolence to the bereaved family. That October, Annie wrote to the Seal Cove CEWA on behalf of herself and her husband Isaac to thank them for this message of sympathy. Her letter captures the religious voice of a bereaved mother and depicted the consolation she sought for herself rather than what was offered by others: "We wish to thank you for your card of Sympathy to us in our recent bereavement in the death of our dear son Leonard which came to us so suddenly on Monday, Sept. 18th. When one is taken away so sudden it makes the sorrow harder to bear. Indeed life itself is very brief, Like the falling of a leaf. But we must not mourn as one without hope, for those who sleep in Him."[45] Secretary Lizzie Dawe read this letter aloud at the opening meeting for the CEWA year, in the presence of the Reverend Heber and Elizabeth Gosse.[46] Like those written by other CEWA women in Conception Bay, this letter acknowledges the emotional aspect of loss, yet Annie did not express hope of "meeting again" in heaven. Her consolation was a more orthodox Christian one: belief that her son, in death, had been united with God. Annie's beliefs were known, and perhaps shared, by her family. After her death in 1955, the epitaph her husband Isaac and their surviving children selected for her headstone borrowed the words of well-known Methodist hymnist Fanny Crosby to reflect their Christian understanding of her fate: "Safe in the arms of Jesus / Safe on his gentle breast."[47] A popular American Protestant hymn of the late 1800s which became especially associated with consolation of bereaved persons, "Safe in the Arms of Jesus" offered images of "safety and repose" and a "loving Christ" to believers who lived "in an era of cultural uncertainty and high mortality."[48]

Epitaphs: Gender and Christian Consolation

As material representations of burial practices within societies, cemetery landscapes and monuments, and especially headstone epitaphs and images, reveal the nature of grief, commemoration, and social relations.[49] This includes relations of gender, ethnicity, and class within particular communities.[50]

Choice of burial place can be an important indicator of family status, wealth, and respectability.[51] Growing differences in the size and complexity of monuments within communities over time can reflect increasing class consciousness.[52] Cemeteries that contain markers of a generally uniform size and style, like those in rural Conception Bay, were typical of communities with households of similar financial status and social standing.[53] This uniformity is visible in the Anglican cemeteries of Upper Gullies and Foxtrap. It is important to remember that regardless of the class status of those who purchased and raised them, cemetery markers would be of the best quality a family could afford, with inscriptions "carefully chosen."[54]

In terms of gender relations, the influence of separate spheres ideology can be seen when inscriptions on women's markers emphasize family while inscriptions on men's markers empathize work and social standing.[55] Similarly, the increased use of family plots in the nineteenth century reflected the growing influence of the "cult of domesticity": an ideology that placed central importance on the home and family and envisioned women as keepers of the domestic sphere. The growth in popularity of this ideology has been linked to the emergence of a domesticated vision of heaven among Christians. In this conception, heaven is not a place where the individual soul unites with God (the orthodox vision of heaven), but a place where earthly families reunite with each other for eternity.[56] As discussed below, this notion was embraced by some Conception Bay Anglicans, but not by all.

Epitaphs can enhance our understanding of women's social status within communities. Gender inequality is shown when, in the case of spouses with separate headstones, the men's are larger and the women's carry the inscription "wife of" with their husband's name.[57] This was not the case in headstones raised by Conception Bay Anglicans. Spouses' markers were of similar size and style and in some cases carried identical epitaphs. They were just as likely to carry the inscription "husband of" followed by a woman's name as they were to read "wife of" followed by a man's name. "In memory of a beloved husband" and "in memory of a beloved wife" likewise appeared in equal measure, suggesting a community with a less strict understanding of family hierarchies and patriarchal structures.

One study of late-nineteenth-century family and gender relations examines the popular "clasped-hand" motif on grave markers, a design popular within the Anglican cemeteries of Foxtrap and Upper Gullies. When used on headstones for married persons, the "dead" hand on the left was the gender of the deceased person (based on sleeve style) while the "living" hand on the right was portrayed the gender of the surviving spouse. On headstones for unmarried persons, the hand of the deceased clasped the hand of their same-gender parent, with daughters holding their mother's hand and sons holding their father's. In both instances, the motif demonstrates belief in the eternal nature of family relationships.[58] Despite the nineteenth-century middle-class construction of mothers as families' spiritual and religious caretakers, and arguments related to "patriarchal piety" as a defining aspect of Christian culture expressed in households, these motifs suggest a society in which both men and women were associated with their children's religious lives and an understanding among believers that eternal, spiritual connections could be made with fathers as well as with mothers.[59]

Headstones can also serve as material representations of lived Christianity, especially of beliefs related to the understanding of eternal life and the hope of resurrection, as well as popular conceptions of heaven. They provide insight into the social dimensions of Christian consolation by revealing what sentiments individuals at a particular place and time found comforting upon the loss of loved ones. Scholars have considered how headstone inscriptions "narrated a biography of the deceased, enabled relatives to reconstruct the family unit in stone and represented a metaphor for loss."[60] Yet, generally, scholars have not considered the religious content of headstone inscriptions as evidence of popular theology: how the sentiments expressed in epitaphs reflected patterns of spiritual belief as well as how social relations could shape Christian belief.

Surviving family members and friends often treated graves as sacred spaces, even in municipal cemeteries where the ground was not consecrated as it would have been in churchyard burial spaces. This can be seen partly in the content of inscriptions, which survivors selected to encourage "loftier reflections on spirituality" among those who read them.[61] Given this effort to create sacred space through choice of epitaph, the choice of words to be carved on headstones can also be understood to reflect the personal spiritual convictions of those who selected them.[62]

Headstones and inscriptions can show how those who selected markers and epitaphs understood social relations to extend beyond relationships people had with each other in life to include an eternity as shaped by a sense of relationship with the divine.[63] Epitaphs provide evidence of social relations that are understood by the living to continue beyond the grave; they represent how the living engaged with, and remained connected to, the dead.[64]

To understand popular religiosity with the parish of Foxtrap and Hopewell, I collected epitaphs which appear on headstones placed in the Anglican cemeteries of St Peter's and All Saints churches between 1920 and 1970 and considered their language for religious and secular content.[65] Religious epitaphs in this case contain Christian language and imagery; secular epitaphs do not contain religious content. Of the almost 500 headstones surveyed, nearly one hundred were secular in perspective, representing 21 per cent of all inscriptions. Almost 80 per cent of headstones carried Christian messages. I analyzed inscriptions for content and categorized them based on their dominant theme. In total, five recurring themes stood out: "lost love" (15.5 per cent), "orthodox Anglican" (29 per cent of total), "rest or peace attained" (20.5 per cent), "domesticated heaven" (19.5 per cent), and "remembrance" (15 per cent). As I discuss below, epitaphs that used remembrance language were mostly, although not exclusively, secular in tone.

LOST LOVE INSCRIPTIONS

Headstones epitaphs often contain language of "considerable affection and devotion," and this is likewise true of the Anglican cemeteries of Conception Bay.[66] Most headstones were raised "in loving memory of" followed by the name of the deceased, a kinship statement such as "son of" or "wife of," and the birth and death dates. Some headstones carried full epitaphs lamenting lost love, such as "It is hard to part with those we love / When love has bound the heart / It is harder yet to speak the words / We must forever part." Many lost love inscriptions contained no Christian language or imagery at all, which suggests that some members of the Anglican community felt little connection to religion and drew

Figure 7.1 Often studied for their representation of social relationships and identities, headstones and the epitaphs inscribed on them are also valuable for understanding patterns of spiritual belief among the people of particular communities.

no consolation from Christian doctrine when a loved one died. The following appeared in both Foxtrap and Upper Gullies, most notably selected by the husband of Lizzie Dawe, secretary of Seal Cove CEWA, who died unexpectedly in March 1931: "Stars are brightly shining / Upon a silent grave / In it lies a precious one / We loved but could not save."[67]

For the most part, lost love inscriptions in Conception Bay focused on the loss of domestic relationships and the disrupting effect on home life. One of the most popular lost love inscriptions, appearing on over a dozen markers in several variations, read: "A precious one from us is gone / A voice we loved is stilled / A place is vacant in our home / That never can be filled." Lost love inscriptions made up 15.5 per cent of epitaphs in the cemeteries surveyed and were used almost equally on headstones erected for women and men. Of this total, only a quarter carried a message of Christian consolation – typically statements of resignation to God's will and/or assertions of the deceased's place in heaven or union with the divine. Examples include "We shall miss her oh how sadly / None but aching hearts can tell / We have lost but heaven has gained her / God indeed does all things well" and "Jesus while our hearts are bleeding / Over the soul that thou hast won / May we at this hour of weeping / Calmly say thy will be done / Though cast down we're not forsaken / Though afflicted not alone / Thou didst give and thou hast taken / Blessed Lord, thy will be done." Other bereaved households sought the comfort of a caring and personal God:

A shadow rests upon our home
We miss his smiling face
Where'er we turn where'er we go
We see his vacant place
God is good he gives us strength
To bear our heavy loss
He is the only one who knows
How bitter is our loss.

ORTHODOX ANGLICAN EPITAPHS

While relatively few lost love epitaphs included the language of Christian consolation, a significant proportion of total headstones had exclusively religious inscriptions. Most of these were orthodox Christian messages about immortality, the union of the deceased's soul with God, and the hope of resurrection. Others reproduced Christian language and imagery from scripture, the *Book of Common Prayer*, and well-known hymns.[68] The single most popular epitaph among all surveyed was "Father in thy gracious keeping leave us now thy servant sleeping," which appeared on twenty separate headstones, fourteen of which were memorials to women. The selection of this epitaph mostly on headstones raised in memory of women speaks to a popular understanding of the connection between female religiosity and labour. Women's work, whether at home for the benefit of the family or in community for the benefit of neighbours, created a connection between them and the spiritual realm. Such an epitaph recognized women as workers, with death conceived of as both a "rest well earned" and a rite of passage into union with the divine.

Epitaphs that contained orthodox Anglican language and imagery represented, at 29 per cent, the most popular choice for headstone inscriptions. Of the 138 orthodox headstones identified, a majority (46 per cent) appeared on women's graves, which suggests an association between women, formal religion, and Christian faithfulness. Yet a significant proportion (33 per cent) appeared on men's graves, with the rest (21 per cent) used on headstones for children. The latter number is important, as it suggests that grieving parents were more likely to turn to the consoling promises of orthodox Christianity than to more popular notions of future reunion with their late children, inherent in the domesticated vision of heaven.

Among the nearly 500 headstones surveyed, sixty were erected in memory of children. Half of these bore language which was orthodox in tone. Epitaphs of the "we will meet again" and "domesticated heaven" variety came in a distant second, and appeared on only nine headstones raised by grieving parents. The remainder of headstones for children were of the "lives not lived" variety, preferred by working-class British families, along with the language of innocence, including symbols of flowers and lambs.[69] This pattern is consistent for the Anglican cemeteries of Conception Bay, represented in inscriptions such as "Budded on earth to bloom in heaven" and "He gathered the lambs in His arms." Many children's headstones were shaped like lambs. The language of angels was also common, as in this inscription from Foxtrap: "God needed one more angel child / To fill his heavenly band / So he bent with loving arms / And clasped our darling's hand."[70] Young children, especially babies, were popularly envisioned as angels in heaven after their deaths.[71]

For the most part, orthodox epitaphs were single sentences: "And as we have borne the image of the earthly we shall also bear the image of the heavenly" or "Make them to be numbered with the saints in glory everlasting" (selected for a husband and four children who died in infancy). Most were biblical: "The Lord is my shepherd" (from Psalm 23), "Her children rise up and call her blessed" (Proverbs 31:28), "I know that my redeemer liveth" (Job 19:20), and, from the Beatitudes, "Blessed are the pure in heart, for they shall see God." The succinct "Forever with the Lord," "Thy will be done," and "In God's holy keeping" each appeared numerous times. While an economical choice when one paid for inscriptions by the letter, the religious content of these epitaphs should not be downplayed. Bereaved families had the choice of cost-efficient secular epitaphs as well, such as the ubiquitous "Rest in Peace" or Bishop Abraham's despised "He is just away," a popular consolation discussed at the beginning of this chapter. Succinct religious messages from families, therefore, should be understood as expressions of faithfulness, even if household economics were part of the decision.

Not all orthodox inscriptions were brief: some took the form of the four-line rhyming verse, as did the majority of epitaphs across other themes I surveyed. One example includes the poem that Emma Anthony selected in 1930 for the grave marker of her husband Andrew: "Thy word is true / Thy will is just / To thee we leave him Lord in trust / Not left to lie like fallen tree / Not dead but living unto Thee." A second example was selected by Upper Gullies CEWA president Amelia Coates for her husband Peter in 1937: "Rest eternal grant him after weary fight / Shed on him the radiance of your heavenly light / Lead him onward, upward, to the Holy Place / Where the saints made perfect, gaze upon Thy face."

REST OR PEACE ATTAINED EPITAPHS

The second most popular inscription theme selected by Conception Bay Anglicans carried the language of rest and peace, a motif favoured as well by the British working classes.[72] These appeared equally on headstones raised for women and men, although there was some gender imbalance when it came to the type of rest the epitaphs envisioned. In her memoir, British activist Annie Kenney remembers how her working-class mother's Christianity, especially as she neared death, was predominantly characterized by a longing for rest: "The only thing she desired," Kenney recalls, "was a heaven where she could be at peace; release from a world full of struggle to make ends meet, a world full of anxiety and hard labour."[73]

This sentiment was echoed in 16.5 per cent of inscriptions surveyed at Foxtrap and Upper Gullies. Examples include "Rest in Peace" and its variations, such as "Rest in the Lord," "Resting in heavenly peace," and "Peace, Perfect Peace." Longer inscriptions engaged more fully with the notion of death as God's gift of rest to the faithful after the struggles of earthly life: "Asleep in Jesus blessed sleep / From which one never wakes to weep / A calm and undisturbed repose / Unbroken by the last of foes." The following appeared on multiple headstones, clearly a favourite tribute to women among Conception Bay Anglican families: "Sleep on dear mother thy work is done / Thy mortal cares are past / Jesus has come and borne thee home / To heavenly rest at last." While the language of "mother," "work," "Jesus," and "home" remained, occasionally the penultimate line was changed from "To heavenly rest at last" to "Beyond the stormy blast," a reflection perhaps on coastal Newfoundland weather. Interestingly, most local epitaphs that used the language of rest from "work," "toil," or "labours" were selected in memory of women, not men. This suggests recognition within families, as Arch Morgan stated in 1979, that "women worked the hardest" in Conception Bay households. It also recognizes the close ties between work and spirituality in women's lives.[74] In contrast, the majority of inscriptions that dealt with release after suffering, rather than labour, were raised in memory of men.[75]

DOMESTICATED HEAVEN EPITAPHS

A third category of headstone epitaph reflected "domestication of heaven" ideology, and envisioned the hereafter as a "homey, earthlike place" where families would be reunited for all eternity.[76] The idea of heaven as a place of domestic bliss, with the dead retaining their individual identity and earthly relationships, originated among nineteenth-century Evangelical Protestant and Nonconformist writers and hymnists.[77] The idea is especially associated with Wesleyan Methodism.[78] While the language of domesticity was used by both women and men, men were most likely to use "heaven as home" imagery to symbolize comfort or shelter while women used the imagery to critique family life. Rather than reproducing earthly domestic arrangements, the female vision of heaven was "a place of ultimate fulfillment and reconciliation, a place in which work, pain, suffering, and the storms of life will be eliminated."[79] The heaven thus imagined "does provide a haven in a heartless world," yet women writers recognized how "that heartless world often includes the home."[80] This same gendered response to domesticated heaven ideology may explain why CEWA women, as their condolence letters reveal, tended to envision a community-based rather than family-based hereafter.

For the most part, notions of "heaven as home" were received and expressed by lay members of the church before they were accepted by some (although not all) Anglican theologians.[81] As noted earlier, in Newfoundland, Anglican leadership resisted popular theologies of death well into the twentieth century. Inscriptions on Conception Bay headstones suggest that the family-oriented heaven was part of the Christian worldview of some ordinary Anglicans before priests accepted it, which points to the lasting influence of Methodism within the study area and/or the impact of popular condolence literature on local Christian thought. Along with gender considerations, belief in family reunion as the heart of the Christian promise of eternal life is an interesting example of the relationship between official and vernacular Anglicanism.

Closely related to "heaven as home" epitaphs are inscriptions that offer the Christian consolation of "celestial reunion" to bereaved families. While these were popular among the British working classes, less than 20 per cent of headstones surveyed at Foxtrap and Upper Gullies carried epitaphs of this type.[82] Scholarly work on the domesticated heaven often focuses on popular visions of mothers uniting with children and wives with husbands, yet in the Anglican cemeteries of Conception Bay expression of this hope appears equally on headstones memorializing women and men. Of the ninety-two markers that carried messages of Christian hope for family reunion in the hereafter, or which use the discourse of heaven as home, forty-two were for men and thirty-nine for women. (The remaining eleven were headstones for children.) Epitaphs that expressed hope of "meeting again" in heaven were more popular than those that explicitly described heaven as home, although some "we will meet again" inscriptions also referenced family relationships. For example, "Another link is broken in our household band / But a chain is forming in a better land," or "On that happy Easter morning / All the graves their dead restore / Father, sister, child and mother / Meet once more."

One especially popular epitaph for deceased women appeared on markers raised by the families of at least two long-time active CEWA members, Emma Jane Kennedy of Long Pond and Beliza Fagan of Foxtrap. It carried the language of flowers, especially associated with female consolation, as well as hope of family reunion: "Asleep in God's beautiful garden / Sheltered from sorrow and pain / Someday when life's journey is ended / We shall meet our dear Mother again." Other heavenly reunion epitaphs were more ambiguous in the type of reunion envisioned, such as "On that bright eternal shore / We shall meet to part no more." Along with epitaphs selected by families to explicitly express hope for heavenly reunion or a conception of heaven as home, many headstones read "We shall meet again" as part of an overall design distinct from the inscription, often coupled with motifs such as clasped hands, gates, flowers, or open Bibles, but did not otherwise have inscriptions with reunion themes.

REMEMBRANCE EPITAPHS

The final category of headstone inscription I identified in the Anglican cemeteries surveyed used the language of remembrance or memory only. Among the seventy headstones of this type, some of the most popular epitaphs were the simple "Ever remembered, ever loved" and "Gone but not forgotten." The inscription of this type most likely to be selected by families appeared thirteen times at Foxtrap and Upper Gullies, with minor variation in language: "You are gone but not forgotten / Never will your memory fade / Sweetest thoughts will always linger / Around the grave where you are laid." The majority of remembrance headstones were raised in the 1950s and 1960s, which suggests increased secularization in the general population. However, this trend should not be overstated. The vast majority of headstones used religious language and imagery, even after 1950. We can also understand the increased remembrance language on headstones as a popular response to the secular approach to consolation: that bereaved persons through the twentieth century were often encouraged to focus on the notion that time heals all wounds in order to recover from the loss of a loved one. In this context, the selection of epitaphs such as "She lives with us in memory and will forever more" can be read as a family's resistance to consolation which advocated forgetfulness as an antidote to grief and can stand as declarations of emotional constancy rather than religious disinterestedness.[83]

Conclusion

Exploring religious responses to grief and loss, and the types of consolation sought by the general Anglican population in comparison to that embraced by CEWA women demonstrates how gender could shape popular beliefs surrounding the Christian promises of eternal life and the

Christian hope for resurrection. Within the CEWA, women sought and brought comfort to each other through use of formal women-led rituals of prayer and hymn singing, rooted in official church practice, as well as through sharing poetry inspired by popular consolation literature, itself associated with women writers. The understanding of eternal life and the promise of resurrection reflected in CEWA writings and rituals was more orthodox than was presumed by male clergy of the time. In fact, the high percentage of orthodox epitaphs in local cemeteries suggest that Anglican Church leadership somewhat overstated the laity's inclination towards what Bishop Abraham deemed "the easy way out" when confronted with the loss of a loved one. Many ordinary Anglicans embraced ideas of spiritual rather than physical resurrection, especially CEWA women, and expressed an understanding of eternal life as a union of the individual soul "for all time" with the divine.

Gender relations influenced popular responses to death and shaped the expression of Christian consolation. Scholars have identified relationships (connections with others) as key influences upon women's religious expression, and in the CEWA branches of Conception Bay this is seen in responses to the death of association sisters.[84] While the loss of younger members provoked feelings of doubt balanced with faith, similar to that of women who lost children, the death of older members was easier to accept as God's will. Upon the death of a woman such as Virtue Morgan, who led a troubled yet faith-filled life, CEWA members expressed a hopeful thankfulness for her "release" from a "bodily chain" and the union of her soul with God.

While notions of heaven as a place of human reunion are evident in some CEWA writing, they differ from the idea of heaven as a place of family reunion (the domesticated heaven) which appeared on local headstones. CEWA women used language of community, not family, in their visions of heaven, and even bereaved mother Annie Dawe of Seal Cove found comfort in the idea of her son being united with God rather than in expressing hope of "meeting him again" in the hereafter. This is consistent with gender-shaped responses to domesticated heaven ideology among nineteenth century hymnists, in that male writers were more likely to embrace notions of "home as haven" than were female writers.[85]

Inscriptions on local headstones emphasized family relationships, with around 20 per cent of markers bearing epitaphs which envisioned a domesticated heaven. Lost love inscriptions were tied to family roles (mother, father, sister, brother) and mourned the disruption of home life, with heaven envisioned as a place where families (and individual's roles within those families) would be preserved for eternity. In this understanding of eternity, women were "locked in" to their gendered roles at the time of their deaths forever, be it mother, sister, wife, or daughter, with the same being true for men. Voices of Conception Bay women, as preserved within CEWA records, expressed a somewhat different hope for life after death: that Christian souls individually became one with God, with death as a release from earthly bonds and material concerns. This orthodox vision of heaven, reflected in use of scripture passages, excerpts from hymns and other religious language, and imagery in epitaphs, was evident in almost 30 per cent of headstones raised in local cemeteries between 1920 and 1970. Of the almost 500 markers surveyed, 80 per cent contained religious messages, which suggests that most Anglican families drew on Christian belief for consolation at times of bereavement and that despite increased secularization and institutionalized care for the dying through the twentieth century, spirituality remained important for family members confronted with death.

Conceiving the Christian hereafter as a place of rest and peace for deceased loved ones was also important to Conception Bay families. Central to British working-class religious thought, notions of heaven as a place of relief from labour were seen in over 20 per cent of local epitaphs, slightly above the number of domesticated heaven inscriptions. "Rest in peace" epitaphs had a gendered dimension in Conception Bay. Women's work in households informed their Christian beliefs and practices and helped to shape their spirituality and the religious lives of those around them. The family selection of epitaphs related to labour and toil especially for use on headstones erected for mothers and wives speaks to this tie between women's work and spirituality. Such epitaphs, which were meant not only to pay tribute to the dead but also to inspire and comfort the living, and which still stand in local cemeteries, speak to the social, cultural, and religious significance of women's work in the households of Conception Bay. In comparison, most epitaphs that used the language of suffering were raised for men, which reflects the empathy, and sympathy, of the women who cared for them in times of sickness. In the next chapter, I explore this theme, as well as how the local community, especially the community of women, expressed Christian belief through mutuality: caring for each other at times of physical, spiritual, and material need.

CHAPTER EIGHT

"Something Good Had Been Accomplished": Women, Cultures of Suffering, and Acts of Christian Mercy

Women's household work in mid-twentieth century Conception Bay involved caring for the sick, including those who were terminally ill. Performed in the home, this work was not only a valuable part of women's contribution to the family economy but also closely tied to their theological beliefs and religious practices; it had both "emotional and spiritual aspects."[1] How this particular aspect of Anglican women's household labour informed their theological culture, and how religious belief in turn influenced their treatment of the sick, is my focus in this chapter. I consider Christian cultures of suffering, including the belief among some theologians and church leaders that pain had the potential to enable the sufferer's redemption, bring them into closer communion with the divine, and, in cases of terminal illness, produce a "good death." For Methodists of outport Newfoundland, the idea of suffering or hardship as "a personal trial that opened the road to salvation" informed daily life and work and provided meaning in the face of tragedy.[2] Women's suffering, in particular, was important to some Christian thinkers.

Women can seek religious meaning within their suffering, whether experienced in the forms of sickness, hardships such as the loss of children, or patriarchal social systems and church structures. In some traditions, suffering was "an integral element" of being female, "a crucial experience on the road to salvation," and an "ideal to be achieved within women's lives."[3]

While the spiritual value of their own pain was part of official Newfoundland Anglican discourse, Conception Bay Anglican women sought to relieve and prevent the suffering of others. Like working-class

Christians in England, they preferred the idea of a caring and merciful God: a belief that carried with it a Christian duty to be similarly caring and merciful to others.[4] This response to suffering can be seen in the theological cultures of Newfoundland women post-cod-moratorium, the 1992 closure of the Northern cod fishery on which the island's economy had relied for hundreds of years.[5] "As human beings begin to become aware of the suffering of other human beings and all life in God's creation," one theologian wrote of these late twentieth-century Newfoundland women, they experience an "encounter with God that is grace … an experience of suffering that calls us toward the other."[6] The Christian beliefs of Methodist women included a concept that "works of mercy" were acts of faith, as taught by John Wesley. Rural women most often expressed this Christian benevolence in response to the needs of their neighbours.[7]

To understand cultures of suffering in Conception Bay, in this chapter I combine evidence from headstone surveys, CEWA minute books, MUN Folklore and Language Archives, and interviews with informants. To begin, I introduce women's traditional role in caring for the sick in Conception Bay, including physically, emotionally, and spiritually. Next, I discuss the culture of suffering in Christian thought and practice, and how ordinary Conception Bay women rejected notions of the redeeming value of pain in their treatment of dying persons. I consider women's practice of, and belief in, religiously invoked traditional healing methods, as well as how women active in the CEWA responded to diocesan leaders' expectation that they care for and support sick members as part of the association's mandate. While Long Pond women largely rejected this role, Seal Cove women developed and administered a system of benevolent care for each other that went beyond the church's official expectations. The different ways women cared for others in times of sickness indicates variety in female theological cultures, and how these cultures are shaped by particular settings. As I will discuss in chapter 9, women of Long Pond demonstrated a different (although still female-labour based) theological understanding of Christian benevolence which was centred on textile production rather than on caring for the sick.

Care as Women's Domestic Work

In mid-twentieth-century Conception Bay, care for the sick and/or dying was primarily women's responsibility and occurred within the home, consistent with traditional practices elsewhere in the Anglo-American world.[8] CEWA records reveal women's work in caring for sick family members. For several meetings in March 1931, Seal Cove branch secretary Lizzie Dawe was noted as "unable to attend owing to her mother being very ill."[9] In August 1947, Harriet Morgan apologized to her Seal Cove sisters for being absent from a special meeting "owing to ill health of my baby." In the mid-1960s, members of Long Pond CEWA welcomed back Annie Bishop "after an absence of ten years … due to her husband's lengthy illness."[10] Women who cared for the sick risked their own health, especially in cases of communicable disease. When Lizzie's mother Edith died in late March 1931, Seal Cove women agreed "to give our late sister [Edith's] … husband a little donation" and noted, using language borrowed from the *Book of Common Prayer*, that "it is our bound an [*sic*] duty to do so."[11] Shortly after, news came that Lizzie had died as well. "What man appoints god disappoints sometimes," the women noted, and as a gesture of respect "we have cancelled our [Easter] sale owing to [her] death."[12]

While wealthy households could hire nurses when extra help with a sick family member was needed, in the rural setting of Conception Bay female neighbours, friends, and family instead practised mutuality. As in British working-class neighbourhoods and rural communities, Conception Bay women helped families with domestic chores and provided direct physical care to the afflicted person, regardless of gender.[13] When a person was terminally ill, Rachel Fagan and Minnie Bussey recalled of 1930s Foxtrap, "for a week or more … groups of women would take turns staying up all night comforting the sick person and offering their help to him or her and the family concerned in whatever way they could."[14] Along with physical care, women attended to dying persons' spiritual needs.[15] Informant Marge (Saunders) Dawe described how in the 1940s "Aunt Selina" Andrews of Upper Gullies regularly visited a sick neighbour's house on Sunday afternoons to "read the Bible to the old woman," and brought her young grandson along to sit on the bed and listen, too. Reading scripture to the sick was also practised in working-class England, and ailing persons received great comfort from being read to by friends, especially when passages selected reminded them of their belief in God's love and the promise of eternal life.[16]

Women worked cooperatively to bring spiritual nurture and Christian comfort to dying persons and their families. On the evening of 10 November 1965, Annie E. Jefford, former president and long-time member of the Long Pond CEWA branch, was at home with her dying husband. This was a regular meeting night for Long Pond branch, and the women in attendance planned a special outing. In the words of branch secretary Selina Perrin:

> At this time the Worthy President [Marjorie Jefford], the 2nd Vice President [Dora Butler] and the Assistant Secretary [Irene Tilley] accompanied by Sisters Lizzie Greenslade, Lila Greenslade and Annie Dawe left the room and went to Sister Annie E. Jefford's home. The Worthy President read part of the [CEWA] prayers with her and the 2nd Vice President read the 25th Chapter of St Matthew. This is the Chapter read when we have a member join our Association. [Annie Jefford] told us she often repeats it to herself and wished us to have it read also the old hymn "Soldiers of Christ Arise." She also asked us to sing "O for a Closer Walk with God" for Mr Jefford as this is, she said, his favorite Hymn. He is blind and could not see us but he could hear us and we believe he must have realized we were there from the Association. Back again to our Association room where we enjoyed a nice cup of tea with light hearts, and a little bit sad, too, but we felt that something good had been accomplished.[17]

This example demonstrates how women-led CEWA ritual shaped the religious lives of its members and served as an outlet for their Christian beliefs and call to service. It demonstrates how caregivers benefitted religiously from spiritual work performed for others.[18] Hymns and hymn singing were part of local Anglicans' everyday devotional practices, and extended into CEWA ritual.[19] Singing at the bedside of dying persons was also practised by British Baptists and was tied to popular notions of the good death.[20] A similar belief appears to have been part of women's theological culture in Anglican Conception Bay.

Religious Cultures of Suffering

The religious culture surrounding Conception Bay women's work as caregivers to sick relatives, neighbours, and friends was informed by Christian thought on the redemptive power of "suffering" and notions of "good" and "bad" Christian deaths. In nineteenth-century Britain, Evangelical thinking informed low and high Anglican responses to death and grief, especially the idea of the good death "characterized by persistent faith, humility and submission to the will of God in the face of loss."[21] For Anglican theologians and lay leaders, good deaths required a long period of virtuous suffering, with plenty of time for self-examination and repentance. Bad deaths came suddenly, and robbed the deceased of the opportunity for spiritual growth or refinement in the fires of affliction.[22]

In American Roman Catholic popular literature written by priests, nuns, and prominent lay people, "pain was always the thoughtful prescription of the Divine Physician" and was understood as sacramental in helping to bring sufferers into the sacred presence of Jesus.[23] Robert Orsi identifies notions of good and bad deaths and a Christian culture of suffering within this tradition. In scholarship focused on the twentieth-century urban working-class Italian experience, Orsi engages especially with the prescriptive aspect of Christian ideologies related to sickness and death. "Catholics thrilled to describe the body in pain," Orsi observes, although suffering persons must never complain about this "chastisement and judgment," popularly believed to be linked to some "moral corruption" within them. He concludes: "Physical distress of all sorts, from conditions like cerebral palsy to the unexpected agonies of accidents and illness, was understood by American Catholics in the middle years of the last century as an individual's main opportunity for spiritual growth. Pain purged and disciplined the ego; stripping it of pride and self-love; it disclosed the emptiness of the world."[24] A key aspect of this religious culture was an understanding that the suffering and pain of afflicted persons served to spiritually benefit those around them. In what Orsi terms "a redistributive economy of distress," Catholics believed that God "sent pain to some people so that others might be edified, making the bodies of the sick conduits of communications and benefits from heaven to earth." Not only were "actual sick people … lost in this process," Orsi concludes, but it also led to the neglect of theological efforts to "account for [pain's] place in the universe, to respond to the spiritual and intellectual distress it might have occasioned."[25]

A culture of suffering, linked to the evangelical good death and associated especially with women, was part of the official Newfoundland Anglican worldview.[26] The obituary for rector's wife Frances Elizabeth (Bayley) Field, published in March 1931 in *Diocesan Magazine*, emphasized the spiritual benefits of her fifteen years of chronic illness, noting how "through suffering" she was "being gently moulded a fit vessel for the Master's Treasury."[27] "In quietness and confidence," the tribute continued, "she was able to acquire that strength of soul which is so often coupled with weakness of body."[28] Prescriptive notions of redemptive female suffering continued into the 1960s. The *Newfoundland Churchman* reported in 1964 that Eliza Greene of Fogo "will be long remembered for her Christian resignation to God's dealing with her. Her patience and courage throughout her illness is a shining example of a good Christian, who, having served God in her generation was not afraid when the end came."[29] In contrast, the 1968 death of Sabina Bridger of Twillingate was deemed "happy release" from suffering, with the writer emphasizing her belief in "the bright hope of a life beyond this veil [*sic*] of tears."[30] This suggested a religious culture in which an end to suffering, rather than suffering itself, defined the believer's relationship with God; instead of "refining" a believer, affliction created an opportunity for Christians to receive the blessing of God's intervening mercy. The good death was then one in which believers could perceive evidence of a gentle and loving divinity, a belief consistent with Conception Bay Anglicans' conception of, and sense of relationship with, Jesus as Good Shepherd.

Good Deaths and Bad Deaths

Belief in a caring and merciful God and, by extension, the need for Christians to show care and mercy to each other at times of hardship, characterized ordinary Anglican views of good and bad deaths. Some local traditions reflected evangelical notions of suffering as a sign of salvation, which suggests the lasting influence of Methodism within the study area. As Tom Dawe of Long Pond recalled:

> I heard the old women talk about it. That if a person died peacefully, that was a bad sign ... [T]hey used to say sometimes it was a good sign if the person is struggling in his or her death. They saw that as a sign that ... the devil and the angels, or powers of good and evil were struggling over the person. And then they'd say if the person died peacefully, it was usually a sign of the devil just lulling them into the sense of false security. But it never made sense to me.[31]

More common were traditions that demonstrated a preference for peaceful deaths and a desire to minimize the afflicted persons' suffering. Minnie (Butler) Bussey described how people in Foxtrap had a "staunch belief" that one should never disturb, or "raft," a dying person "no matter how uncomfortable they were."[32] Minnie did not link this practice with a struggle between good and evil, nor did she describe belief in the spiritual value of suffering. Her focus, instead, was on making the dying person as comfortable as possible. She recalled a story of how one dying woman's brother had noisily entered the bedroom where she lay, causing a terminal thirty-minute seizure. Minnie concluded, "she was rafted, you see, and stopped from dying a peaceful death."[33]

Insights into the local culture of suffering can be found on headstones erected in the Anglican cemeteries of Foxtrap and Upper Gullies. While some headstones carried epitaphs related to suffering, these were primarily verses which women selected in memory of their late husbands. For example: "You suffered much you murmured not / We watched you day by day / Until at last with broken hearts / We saw you pass away."[34] Patient tolerance of pain may have been associated especially with women by official commentators on Christian suffering, but for the ordinary Anglicans of Conception Bay it was neither a gendered virtue nor a passport to salvation. Instead, such epitaphs emphasized the domestic setting of care and a family's sorrow at losing a loved one. While "murmuring not" is consistent with the culture of suffering associated with evangelicals and American Catholicism, for widows such as Patience Tilley and Beliza Fagan suffering was no guarantee of eternal life or heavenly reunion: the verses conclude with the loved one's death and, importantly, the end of pain. Even the death of a child emphasized the end of pain as a sign of divine mercy: "God knew that she was suffering / When a cure they could not find / So he closed her little eyes / And whispered Peace be Thine."[35] Women's emotional sensitivity to the suffering of sick persons, especially of close family members, is likewise revealed in the selection of such epitaphs.[36]

Opposite the good death was the bad death. For evangelicals, a bad death was one in which the deceased was denied the opportunity to "repent of sin" and make peace with God before the end. The Anglican Church in Newfoundland encouraged daily self-reflection and penitence to accomplish this, with the Reverend Henry Peile reminding readers of *Diocesan Magazine* in 1933 that while Church of England rules did not make confession compulsory, it was "open to all."[37] Peile explained that there was nothing "morbid" in thinking about, and preparing for, one's own death, and concluded: "Happy indeed is the person who like Jesus can end his or her life with the two thoughts 'It is finished' and 'Father into Thy hands I command my spirit.' That will be a truly glorious and happy end to the story of our life."[38] Evidence from Conception Bay suggests that for most Anglicans, seeking services of a priest for the administration of deathbed sacraments was considered as much, or more, important for the deceased's spiritual welfare than their past record of personal preparation and penitence. This mirrors Roman Catholic practice in that adherents believed that "the final sacrament [was] so essential to the good Catholic death."[39] Rachel Fagan recalled of the 1930s and 1940s that when women caring for a terminally ill person realized that death was eminent they made sure "somebody rigged up the old horse" and went to bring the minister to perform last rites. Rachel noted how families were comforted, and grateful, if the priest came quickly and could "administer the last sacrament" before the person died.[40]

For a priest to not come when summoned to a sick bed would earn him lasting condemnation within the community. Reta (Morgan) Hill described the Reverend Henry Whitehouse, who was rector of the parish of Foxtrap and Hopewell between 1928 and 1936, making such refusals:

> He didn't make any impression. And he refused to visit. A man I know went to get him one night, about two o'clock in the night, his wife was sick or dying or something, I don't remember the details. But it was in the family and he refused to come. The man got angry and he threatened him. He said you are going to

> come anyway whether you want to or not. He didn't want to be disturbed. He wasn't much of a Christian was he? He refused to go where he was needed.

Marge (Saunders) Dawe also described the importance of last rites. She noted that while a rector such as the Reverend Henry Gosse could not visit families regularly due to the large geographic size of the parish, he always came, once called, to someone who was sick in order to "give the rites."[41] The personal responsibility some women felt about making sure loved ones had access to Holy Communion or Holy Unction was reflected in Marge's thoughts about the death of her first husband: "Dr Walsh told me to call the minister, but I couldn't accept that Ches was dying." Fifty years later, this inaction continued to cause her feelings of regret.[42]

Sudden deaths meant that the deceased had little or no time for spiritual self-examination or access to last rites. The possibility of sudden death was one reason the church encouraged its members to engage in ongoing preparation, and why evangelicals deemed such deaths to be bad deaths. For the people of Conception Bay, suddenness could make a loved one's death more difficult to bear emotionally, and headstone inscriptions demonstrated how important it was for survivors to create a permanent record that the deceased was "accidentally drowned," "accidentally killed," or "died in a tragic fire," yet they also tended to demonstrate standard messages of Christian consolation rather than reflection on the unexpectedness of the event. Epitaphs reflecting on suddenness were most often selected by a husband in memory of a wife, with the verse emphasizing the emotional impact on the living rather than the spiritual state of the deceased. Examples include: "Sad and sudden was the call / So sadly missed by one and all / Her memory is as near today / As in the hour she passed away," raised for Edith Searle in 1948, and "The call was sudden, the shock severe / To part with one we loved so dear" for Mary Fagan in 1969.[43]

Women and Religiously Invoked Healing

Most recent scholarship on the history of religious healing has considered the social and theological implications of the late nineteenth-century Protestant faith healing movement. There has been examination of the gendered aspects of faith healing in Canada, with primary focus on the urban, middle-class experience, and the place of women's bodies in the making of the movement. Work on faith healing among American Protestants similarly identifies faith healing leaders and adherents as largely the urban middle class, with emphasis on how participants' "enigmatic understanding of the relationship among personal volition, religious ritual, and divine supremacy" helped to construct an alternative Protestant culture of suffering. This culture allowed believers to "'completely reconstruct' their experiences of illness, pain and recovery" by "acting faith, engaging in healing rituals and resting in God."[44]

In contrast to the urban, middle-class faith-healing movement, women in Conception Bay experienced, and practised, "religiously invoked vernacular healing."[45] The work of Laurel Thatcher Ulrich, Marilyn Westercamp, and Marlene Epp, among others, establishes women (especially midwives) as practitioners of traditional medicine in North America, although in mid-1900s Conception Bay some men were identified as traditional healers as well.[46] Some Christian women gifted as healers considered their "knowledge and skills as divine gifts and assumed their medicines had spiritual powers."[47] Work on traditional healing in Newfoundland largely has offered secular perspectives.[48] "Charmers" in rural settings were said to offer "magical treatment … what was perceived by some people as a form of faith healing," but scholars have made little effort to understand the interaction between religious belief and vernacular healing in Newfoundland, or how vernacular healing can be understood as embodied religious practice that represents people's understanding of a direct, physical, and personal connection between humanity and the divine.[49]

When asked about "religious" cures or charms, Conception Bay women described the use of particular objects, gestures, and prayer to enable healing. Wedding rings were especially important objects, not only by virtue of being blessed by priests during services of matrimony, but also as symbols of respectable family status and domesticity.[50] Edna (Rideout) Warford remembered how her mother, Pearl Rideout of Long Pond (born 1905), used her wedding ring to invoke healing: "if you had a sty on your eye, Mom would always take off her wedding band and do the sign of the cross three times on my eye, on the sty. And, you wouldn't believe it, it always went away."[51] Enid (Porter) Haines described her grandmother, Fannie Porter of Foxtrap (born 1886), practising the same cure. Joyce (Andrews) Morgan recalled it applied to warts: "you would use your wedding ring and make a sign of the cross."[52] Making the sign of the cross was believed to enable healing independent of any object. Enid recalled: "My grandmother was the type if there was anything wrong no matter what she was always rubbing it and putting the sign of the cross and I still do the same today. I have a bad knee and I put the sign of the cross on that and say a prayer so often."[53] Men as well as women practised this cure. Marge described how "George Rideout on Kit's Turn" (born 1888 in Long Pond) would cure toothache by "putting the cross" and laying his hand against the sick person's jaw.

Other vernacular cures women described combined use of the cross with intercessory prayer. Emma recalled her grandmother Margaret Butler of Foxtrap (born 1866) "putting away ... boils. She had a little bag with something in it that you weren't allowed to see. She would have it done with the cross. You would put it on your neck for so many days and have prayers on it. And wait until it got better." Emma described the practice of using a vinegar plant to cure an abscessed tooth, as noted in other work on Newfoundland home medicine, but explained that prayer accompanied physical application of the dressing and her understanding that the cure was divine in nature: "Your teeth ... would swell up and they would have something ... in a vinegar jar, but I forget what they called it. That was put on your face in some kind of cotton. You would have to wait a certain time. So many days until the swelling went down. That was done by Jesus because they said all the prayers before."[54] Marjorie (Bullen) Morgan, known locally as a wart charmer, explained using wedding rings to "bless" a sty, meaning marking it with the sign of the cross, but added, "you always said the prayer for God to cure it ... there would always be some kind of little prayer said with it."

George Roberts of Upper Gullies (born 1916) described how the cross and prayer were used by Conception Bay healer James Moores, a Roman Catholic, and the air of solemnity Moores required of those who sought his services.[55] George remembered "Uncle Jimmy" charming a toothache:

> You'd kneel down in front of him. I don't know if he had a crucifix or what he had, but he'd put the sign of the cross on your jaw and you couldn't laugh and you couldn't tell him what you were down for. You'd go down [to his house] and he'd say kneel down there now my son, and you'd kneel down in front of him and take your cap off and he'd put the sign of the cross and he'd

> be muttering something, saying a prayer I suppose. By the time you got to Anthony's Road [about a five-minute walk west] the toothache would be gone.[56]

This formality may have been linked to Moores's status as a religious minority within the community, and a need to see an overt demonstration of respect through religious postures and gestures usually associated with services of worship. The requirement of solemnity and mystery likewise reflected the way religion influenced Moores's approach to healing.

Some women described traditional cures but were unwilling to associate them with religion. The work of Foxtrap healer Fannie (Butler) Porter was considered religious by Enid (Porter) Haines, but not by Mildred (Butler) Porter, Myra (Porter) Rideout, or Beulah (Porter) Morgan, who each described being cured by "Aunt Fan."[57] When asked about religious cures, Beulah, who was raised within a Pentecostal tradition with more official emphasis on faith healing than Anglicanism, was careful to separate religion from charms: "I don't know about religion, but where I grew up there was an old lady used to live just a little way away from me and her name was Aunt Fan. So if I had a sty on my eye she used to rub it with her wedding ring, over it, and it would go away." Faith healing was known to happen within the Pentecostal community where Beulah had worshipped prior to her marriage. Hugh Eason of Long Pond described how in the 1960s his wife had been "miraculously healed by faith" at the local Pentecostal church.[58] It was perhaps her experience of being taunted in childhood for her religious identity that led Beulah to distance herself from belief in religious cures.

Caring for the Sick: CEWA

The CEWA's official rules and regulations required members to support one another in times of sickness, especially through visitation. This reflected a gendered notion of caring for the sick as women's work, but also the sororal nature of the association. Among the offices the Reverend George Gardner prescribed in his original vision for the CEWA were "sick committees," whose members would report at weekly meetings the names of any sisters who were ill. Members of these committees were responsible for visiting sick members on behalf of other CEWA members. This structure was confirmed with the formation of the

Diocesan Council of the CEWA in 1926, a group of largely rectors' wives who would oversee the work of community and parish-based branches throughout Newfoundland and Labrador.[59]

While Diocesan leaders, women and men, directed women to form sick committees and provide sick reports as part of their responsibility as CEWA members, local practice demonstrates that ordinary women did not treat this aspect of their work as a simple duty or mere formality.[60] CEWA members, including those who were not members of sick committees, would visit with ill or elderly sisters and report on their health to the whole group. In April 1967, Annie Petten of the Kelligrews branch was visited by Mary Fagan, a member of the sick committee, but also by ordinary member Annie Haines, who reported that Petten's bad knee was getting better and she was "able to go about her work again."[61] Sick reports came from family members, as local CEWA branches often included kinship networks of mothers, daughters, sisters, aunts, and in-laws.[62] Reports reflect a variety of health issues: major, minor, temporary, and chronic. From Long Pond branch: "Sister Greenslade who was sick all the time ... getting a little better," "Sisters Carrie and Sarah Kennedy not very well," "Sister Gladys Greenslade still in hospital," "Sister Charlotte Ann Taylor fell and hurt herself," "Sister Jefford in bed through lameness," and, shortly after, "Sister Jefford on the road to recovery."[63] From the Kelligrews branch: "Sister Ada Taylor reported in Hospital," "Sister Annie Petten on the mend after a bout of pneumonia ... also has a bad knee," "Jessie Petten returned home from the Hospital feeling fairly well after her mishap by car," and "Sister Bertha Porter's memory was beginning to fail."[64] At Foxtrap, reports from 1960 included "Annie M. Batten very ill," "Selina Porter expected to enter hospital soon," and "Sister Caroline Butler had to have the doctor."[65] The determined and perhaps domestically overworked Martha Fagan, "who has been crippled in her legs for some time," was reported "still the same, getting around the kitchen by use of a chair."[66]

From the time women formed Long Pond CEWA in 1917, their weekly meetings included sick reports, yet they neither organized a sick committee nor developed a systematic program of visitation or relief.[67] In March 1920, secretary Lilly Greenslade described "a good many sisters sick," possibly with influenza. By June she could note "all sick reported getting better," with the exception of Fanny Eason, who had died.[68] Perhaps as a response to this epidemic of illness in the community, by the end of 1920 branch president Susan Rendell began to advise the women "that we should visit a Sister more when we hear they are sick," although members made no effort to organize a formal system.[69] In January 1940, branch president Lizzie Tilley made a second attempt to organize a sick committee and systematic visitation, but by the end of February her initiative had fizzled out.[70] It was Lizzie's own illness almost a decade later that triggered new efforts to organize a visiting and benefits group at Long Pond. On 10 March 1948, branch president Annie Jefford encouraged "some of the sisters" to visit with Lizzie, who had been reported sick. At the next weekly meeting, perhaps disappointed by their efforts, Annie again "tried to stress upon us all the duties and benefits of the CEWA towards sick sisters."[71]

Annie's interest in sick committee work may have been a response to the CEWA Diocesan Council's 1948 initiative to set up a special sick visiting committee in St John's "to visit sisters from outport branches while ill in [city] hospitals."[72] Yet she also had personal reasons for promoting the CEWA's duty to ill members. As noted in the Long Pond minute books, Annie suffered from "unfortunate health," which at times severely restricted her mobility.[73] In 1950, when she resigned as branch president, parish rector the Reverend Gordon Elliott commented "how surprising it was to him that she carried on so long," given her chronic health issues.[74] At a meeting in May 1950, while most members discussed the redecoration of the association room, Annie instead "spoke a few words referring to the sick committee of the District Branch, after which the Worthy President read the rules of the District Branch from the rule book."[75] The issue of setting up "an emergency fund for sick sisters" was addressed at the next meeting, and the women agreed "to put our tea money one side, once a month, for that purpose." This money would be used to buy fruit and "tins of juice" to bring to sick sisters at home or in hospital.[76]

It was only in the late 1950s and early 1960s, however, that regular visits to sick sisters, with gifts of flowers or fruit, were reported in the Long Pond minute books, and purchases such as get-well cards included in the accounts.[77] Such efforts were still not without controversy. In January 1963, one member "reported that the sick committees of other branches of the CEWA are operating in a different way" when it came to spending association funds and accounting for the expense in the annual report. This announcement triggered "a lengthy discussion" that ended with the agreement "that we wait and get advice on what to do regarding this matter."[78] Interestingly, the Long Pond sisters sought advice from their rector, who served as auditor of CEWA accounts, rather than from the Diocesan Council of the CEWA, and when unable to meet with him came up with a system of their own: "that we send $1.00 worth of fruit to any sister who has been sick for two weeks, once a year, and that [we] keep a record of the sick and what is paid out."[79]

Seal Cove women were more organized in their approach to visitation, and in the 1920s and 1930s exceeded CEWA expectations by providing financial support to each other at times of illness or bereavement. In 1928, Sister Louisa "Louie" Dowden suggested "giving our sick sister Sister Selina Dowden some little help out of our funds," to which the women agreed.[80] Similarly, "some little help out of our funds" was sent to Sister Emily Morgan, likely hospitalized with tuberculosis in St John's. In response, Emily sent a thank you letter to the association "telling us she was getting better and expected to be home soon." The women were "very sorry" to hear she relapsed during the following year, and agreed again to send her "$1.00 from our Benifit [*sic*] Fund."[81] Members believed that women who had been sick during the CEWA summer recess were still entitled to receive their sick benefit when meetings reconvened in the fall, and illnesses did not have to be long, or require hospitalization, for the benefit to be paid.[82] In March 1930, the women sent a dollar to Sister Edith Dawe, "who is sick," and two weeks later they "were all glad" to see Edith "so well improved in Health as to be able to be with us again."[83] Such expressions of happiness were typical when a sister returned to meetings after an absence through illness, whether long or short.

While organized under the Anglican Diocese of Newfoundland, local clergy were sometimes unaware of the extent to which Seal Cove CEWA operated as a mutual aid organization. Clergy underestimated the women's ongoing attention to the well-being, physically and financially, of their sisters. When branch president Susie Lear, first reported sick in April 1933, was unable to attend the annual meeting in November "owing to ill health," then rector the Reverend Henry Whitehouse took the opportunity to address the women on Christian compassion. As secretary Annie Dawe recorded: "[He] told us that it was his wish, as sister Susie Lear was ill, for the class to express their sympathy as a body and he believed her to be a good Christian woman and a good

Church worker, and he knew that she felt it hard to be laid aside that it was our duty as sisters of the CEWA to sympathize with her to the best of our ability."[84] The women of Seal Cove not only sympathized with the ailing Susie, but upon her recovery elected her their worthy president once more.[85]

How members expressed sympathetic feelings and support changed over time. After the 1940s, rather than providing cash, women offered gifts of food, usually fruit, to CEWA members reported sick. This reflects the greater availability of consumer goods. In 1947, for example, Seal Cove branch president Phoebe Morgan "thanked sisters for tin of fruit sent in to her" while she was sick.[86] The practice of visiting sick members and bringing them fruit continued into the 1960s.[87] The social aspect of these visits, as well as the gift, was appreciated by women isolated by age or illness. In May 1963, Ethel Lear returned to CEWA meetings after a month's absence, and "asked the President if she could speak to us for a little while." As Harriet Morgan recorded, Ethel "thanked us for the gift of fruit that we sent her during her time of illness. She said that she was thankful to receive the fruit but she was most pleased to receive the visit of one of our Sisters [Eileen Morgan] because she felt that in this one Sister's visit was a visit from all of us."[88]

Through the 1920s and 1930s, a program of communal CEWA visitation developed at Seal Cove alongside the paying of sick benefits, and eventually superseded it. This change coincided with the establishment of the commission government in 1934, and perhaps reflects the women's hope for increased medical services and relief programs under the new administration. It may also reflect limited access to cash money in difficult economic times. In December 1933, Sister Sarah Warford received the last one dollar sick benefit to be paid at Seal Cove.[89] Members were encouraged by their branch president to visit sick sisters more, and by the late 1930s a new practice had developed at Seal Cove that emphasized the spiritual and social, rather than financial, needs of sick members.[90] Now, the sisters regularly would hold CEWA meetings in the homes of sick or elderly members who could not get out to the association room, especially during the winter months. Between 1939 and 1940, such meetings were held "for the benefit of" Virtue Morgan, Belinda Anthony, Susie Lear, and Patience Harvey, all of whom were senior CEWA members and lived some distance from the usual meeting place at St Andrew's school.[91]

CEWA records indicate that women enjoyed these visits. Secretary Lizzie Dawe wrote in April 1940 that "Sister Harvey seemed to be delighted by our visit and invited us each and all to visit her again at some future date," and added that "we pray God that she shall be spared to us for several years yet."[92] Similarly, after a meeting at Ethel Morgan's house in May 1945, Harriet Morgan noted that "she was glad we came … and also wished we enjoyed it as much as she did. We trust that she will soon be able to come and join in our meetings … and fill her vacant chair."[93] The Long Pond CEWA only made one such visit during the same time period: to Betty Kennedy's home in February 1936.[94]

The language that CEWA secretaries used to express concern about sick members revealed theological differences between the women who held this office. Some, with belief in the power of intercession and of seeking the ear of God on behalf of sick members, demonstrated a Christianity informed by a sense of relationship with the divine. In April 1938, for example, Seal Cove branch president Susie Lear asked all sisters to visit ailing secretary Annie Dawe, with acting secretary Annie Morgan adding, "We earnestly pray if it be the Lords [*sic*] Will that she will be restored to health and strength again in his own good time and that she will soon be back with us again to carry on the good work."[95] Annie Dawe expressed similar beliefs in November 1938. Upon receiving news that rector's wife Elizabeth Gosse was sick, she noted: "we pray for the recovery of her health."[96] Long-time branch president Phoebe Morgan likewise expressed belief in intercessory prayer, as well as a taste for hymn singing, when she suggested that whenever a sister was sick the women should sing "the lovely hymn of 303 Holy Father in thy Mercy": "Holy Father, in thy mercy / Hear our earnest prayer; / Keep our loved ones, in their absence, / 'Neath thy care." Phoebe thought this "was a good idea for all of us to carry out at our meetings," but although hymn singing continued an important spiritual aspect of CEWA gatherings, the suggestion did not catch on.[97]

Seal Cove branch secretary Harriet Morgan, who held that office at various intervals through the 1940s, 1950s, and 1960s, tended to rely on providential mercy rather than on intercessory prayer. In December 1945, she wrote that Sister Priscilla Morgan was sick and that "we all trust if it is God's will that she will soon be well again."[98] Likewise in February 1946, with Priscilla still "not very well" and Sister Lizzie Dawe "not too good," Harriet wrote that "if it is God's will we hope that they will be spared to join with us again."[99] Other sick reports were met with similar comments, from her or sometimes from acting secretary Bertha Morgan: "it is our desire that they will soon be with us again in our meetings, God willing" or "we hope that by God's help they will soon be back with us."[100]

At Long Pond in the 1930s and 1940s, comments on sickness among CEWA members were rare, and when they did appear were somewhat secular in tone, offered hope for recovery without reference to God's help and focused more on a member resuming "her duties" than on a desire to regain her companionship.[101] While some secretaries did not invoke the name of God or mention prayer when writing about member's sickness, this should not be seen as evidence of general religious declension or religious disinterestedness, but of differences in religious culture and practice among individual women. When Irene Tilley (who grew up in Seal Cove) was branch secretary at Long Pond in the 1960s, she was always careful to offer "thanks to God" when no association members were reported sick.[102] Likewise, in 1963, Irene relayed a message from member Emma Jefford "that her nerves are still not good enough to undergo an operation and wished the Sisters to pray for her."[103]

CEWA members supported each other at times other than sickness. In 1929, Seal Cove women took up a collection to buy a wedding present for May Anthony, and later reported " a very nice letter from Sister May Rowe from Heart's Content thanking us for our gift … we are glad to hear she is well and happy in her new home."[104] For Christmas 1930, the women took a dollar from their funds to buy "some little thing in remembrance of our class to send to the sisters that are away."[105] As was seen among young women from the Maritimes, those of Newfoundland also travelled to the United States to seek employment.[106] At least two from Seal Cove, Lizzie Butler (then living in New York) and Dossie Dowden (Boston), were in contact with the CEWA during 1930, with Dossie sending along a donation of two dollars and receiving "a hearty clap … for her generosity" and Lizzie providing a "very nice letter."[107] Seal Cove members were sympathetic to women away from home, and decided on gifts of handkerchiefs and cards "to show we do not forget them."[108] "Tho' absent in body," wrote secretary Lizzie Dawe, "they are still with us in spirit." Similarly, while they did not provide a reason for her departure, at Long Pond in 1936 the "worthy president asked the class to get up a Surprise Party for Sister Louise Kennedy as she is going to leave us."[109] The women in turn organized a tea and "a nice present was also given her by the class as a little return for her good work." They bought this gift on credit, and practical-minded branch secretary Annie Bishop noted that "the cost of present being $1.45 amounting to 8 cents a member, 9 cents more owed on it."[110] Almost thirty years later, a similar party was held for departing Sister Joan Downton. In language that shows increased awareness of pride in female textile skills and how textile production could tie women together socially and spiritually, branch secretary Irene Tilley noted that Joan was given "a pair of pillow cases and a luncheon cloth both hand-done by members of the class" as a parting gift.[111]

Support in cash or kind was offered to CEWA sisters at times of loss or financial hardship. This could extend beyond the immediate membership to include the families of members and the broader community. In March 1965, Irene reported "how her and Sister [Lillian] Kennedy had cleaned the cupboards [of the association Room] and packed the old dishes in a box and should be given to some needy family." These items were equally distributed among three local families, and two weeks later Irene reported they were "thankful for the dishes we sent them."[112] The CEWA branch that appeared to give most direct support to sisters and families in financial need was Foxtrap, with expenditures that included "nourishment for Sister Susie Cable" (1941), "coal and nourishment for Sister Emma J. Christopher" (1942), and "$20.00 to Taylor Fire Sufferers" (1950). On 25 March 1960, Foxtrap branch president Lily Batten reported "loss by fire of the home of Sister Ida Porter" and the women immediately organized their response: "Sisters Fanny Porter, Marguerite Bussey and Ruby Delaney told of certain things she received, and of things that were needed. So [we agreed] that the class give her a pair of pillows. These are to be bought by Sister Abigail Rideout. It was also agreed that every sister bring something next meeting night to give her."[113] On 31 March, branch secretary Adella Jones reported that the two pillows were presented to Ida, and that "quiet [*sic*] a few sisters also gave her some needed articles. These were delivered to her home." In a remark that showed how community ties existed beyond the CEWA room, Jones noted that "the majority of sisters had contributed at an earlier date" and therefore did not bring donations to the meeting. Ida spoke at the 5 May CEWA meeting and "thanked all sisters who sent gifts when she was bereft of all her belongings."

At this same meeting a heated discussion arose over the amount of money the women would donate "to Sunday school for their literature." When one sister proposed one hundred dollars, "some said that $50.00 was enough and others $20.00." The decision was left until the next meeting, when they compromised on a thirty-dollar donation.[114] While the women could all agree immediately on helping a fellow member in need, concurrence on which church causes to support was not so clear cut. Foxtrap CEWA did not see support for the Christian education of children as a particularly female responsibility, consistent with family religious practice in which both parents contributed to the practice of domestic piety and their children's religious education. This contrasted with prescriptive notions, increasingly promoted by the Diocese of Newfoundland by 1960, that such issues were women's particular purview.[115]

Spending CEWA funds to support those in need could sometimes bring women into conflict with official church policy and procedures. At Seal Cove, women often sent donations to causes they believed to be worthy means of expressing Christian charity, although not directly connected with the church. In November 1929, for example, they agreed to send money to the disaster fund set up after a devastating tsunami hit the Burin peninsula on the south coast of the island.[116] In April 1943, with over $250 in the bank, Susie Lear suggested that the CEWA send a donation to the Twillingate Hospital Fund, a rebuilding fundraiser organized by the hospital board after fire destroyed Notre Dame Memorial on 27 February 1943.[117] Branch secretary Phoebe Morgan noted that "All Sisters readily agreed to this, but as we plan to hold our Easter tea on Monday night next it was thought wise to wait until proceeds were counted before sending it along as possibly we may be able to swell our donation a little more."[118] Unfortunately for the Twillingate Hospital Fund, the Reverend Heber Gosse happened to be at the next Seal Cove CEWA meeting and heard the women's plan to support this cause when the previous week's minutes were read aloud for approval. Phoebe recorded his comments: "Mr Gosse made it clear to us that new rules had been made concerning CEWA activities and we are strictly forbidden to send our money to anything other than church purposes. However, the Reverend Gentleman said he should like to see the Fund helped but it must be done outside CEWA which all now understand quite well. We thank him for enlightening us on this matter."[119] Phoebe's tone may have been politely deferential, but the CEWA branch she was a part of, and led for over thirty years as president, tended to run its affairs as the members saw fit, not as the church dictated.[120]

This extended to not keeping up with changes in CEWA rules instigated by the rectors' wives of the Diocesan Council, who in 1943 were likely responding to the number of church women putting energy and resources into patriotic work rather than their local parishes. Certainly at Long Pond, during the Second World War, much knitting for the Newfoundland Women's Patriotic Association was done during CEWA meetings.[121] While less of such knitting was done at Seal Cove, the women ended each meeting during the war years by singing the national anthem and organized complimentary socials for the benefit of local volunteers before they headed overseas. At the weekly meeting of 14 January 1941, for example, secretary Lizzie Dawe recorded that: "The Worthy President [Annie Dawe] read a note of thanks from Harold Spracklin on behalf of himself and Edgar Morgan, Abram Morgan and Lawrance [*sic*] Morgan for the free tea and dance which the Sisters gave them before they proceed overseas to do their part in his Majesties [*sic*] Services. We all wish them God Speed and a safe return."

Conclusion

In the mid-1900s, Conception Bay women were largely responsible for the care of sick and dying persons within their households and communities as part of their work within the family economy. Women did this labour cooperatively, and helped each other as needed in a spirit of mutuality typical of rural settings. Women-centred, spiritual, and emotional approaches to caring for sick family members could be undermined by development of a largely male culture of "scientific" medicine and institutional health care, and a "professional" approach which devalued this aspect of female domestic work.[122] Anglican women of mid-twentieth-century Conception Bay encountered increased access to physicians and hospitals, especially after Newfoundland's confederation with Canada, yet spiritual aspects of caring for the sick remained.[123]

The patriarchal authority associated with professional medicine mirrored that of institutional churches. Caring for others was part of Anglican women's lived Christianity, and their work patterns and practices reveal their theological understandings of the nature of God as well as their (and others') relationship with the divine. The resistance to men's authority (whether clerical or medical) which women demonstrated in other aspects of their theological culture may have likewise informed the spiritual culture around care.

Protestant and Catholic cultures have associated sickness and suffering with the afflicted persons' spiritual development. Suffering was thought to bring humans into the sacred presence of Jesus and to sanctify the sufferers, especially when they bore it without complaint. This was especially expected of women, a prescriptive gender construction which made its way into the official Anglican discourse in Newfoundland. Among ordinary believers in Conception Bay, however, men's suffering was more likely than women's to be immortalized in epitaphs. Moreover, the women who cared for sick persons did not see suffering as good. They believed instead that good deaths were peaceful and demonstrated God's benevolence and mercy. By being merciful themselves, whether by helping to make afflicted or elderly people more comfortable, providing them with human and spiritual companionship, or facilitating their access to last rites, women believed they were "doing good work" – work that reflected, and was consistent with, their Christian beliefs.

While the CEWA's official rules and regulations prescribed holding sick committees and visiting sick members, different branches reacted differently to this expectation. At Long Pond, women were reluctant to support sick members as part of their CEWA duties, and only came around to the idea, in a limited way, in the early 1960s. Yet, as their 1965 visit with former branch president Annie Jefford and her dying husband demonstrated, women of Long Pond could see the spiritual benefits, to themselves and others, of giving this kindness to those in need. At Seal Cove, the story was somewhat different: women had a longstanding tradition of providing financial, emotional, and spiritual support to other CEWA members and their families in times of need. This mutuality included a program of visitation to sick and elderly members. It is worth noting that the organizers of the 1965 Long Pond CEWA visit to Annie and Robert Jefford, namely Marjorie Jefford and Irene Tilley, both grew up in Seal Cove with female kin active in the Seal Cove branch and had been members while young girls, which may have shaped their perspective on sick visitation.

Women's response to others' sickness demonstrates different conceptions of the nature of God and their relationship with that God.

While some believed in intercessory prayer on behalf of sick persons, suggesting a sense of personal relationship with the divine, other women were more fatalistic, trusting "God's will" rather than actively seeking heavenly assistance. A sense of relationship with a caring and compassionate divinity informed vernacular healing practices. Women and men, Protestant and Catholic, were known as traditional healers within the local community, and some used religious language, objects, and gestures to affect cures. The use of prayer in conjunction with "charms," along with belief in the healing properties of "the cross," were especially noted by women, with one believing that such healing was "done by Jesus." This connection between religious belief and the practice of folk medicine suggests that in rural Newfoundland some traditional healing was understood as a variety of faith healing, in its association with Christian faithfulness or divine intervention, rather than with magical or generically supernatural processes.

In the next chapter, I pick up a thread that has woven through other aspects of women's theological culture discussed so far: women's use of textile production as a means to express their Christianity. Women made garments needed for church-based rites of passage, whether baptismal gowns and shawls or shrouds for the dead. They hooked mats as a way to observe Lent. CEWA members, especially, were familiar with the scriptural basis for believing textile making was a path to access salvation. They were reminded of the Biblical model of Dorcas (Tabitha) at weekly meetings, and read Christ's call to "cloth the naked" as way to serve him whenever a new member joined.[124] Textile production within the context of CEWA membership, including recognition of this work as sensory expression of Christian piety and a means of expressing a benevolent mutuality, is the focus of the next chapter.

CHAPTER NINE

Apron Christianity: Textile Production, Devotional Practice, and the Expression of Benevolent Mutuality

Church-based women's voluntary associations, in the experience of nineteenth- and early twentieth-century middle-class Protestant women, provided opportunities for empowerment, independence, and influence beyond what was formally available within largely patriarchal, institutional churches.[1] Scholars have found the antecedents of first-wave feminist activism in the way these organizations created a "respectable" stepping stone for women between the private and the public spheres. They have studied them as a source of companionship and mutual support for members, and recently have looked at the influence of class and race relations, ethnicity, and/or gender ideologies on their structures and activities. Works on moral and social reform movements, including poor relief efforts, demonstrate the influence of urban settings on Christian women's activism, but pay less attention to rural church women in association.[2] Many women's organizations were church based or "Christian," but scholars have sometimes neglected the religious motivations that underscored women's participation.[3] Similarly, studies of rural women's textile work have most often focused on household production for market and how their labour contributed to the family economy, or on how rural women translated their traditional weaving and needle-working skills into industrial wage employment at textile mills and garment factories.[4] Female textile production in Newfoundland and Labrador has been considered especially in light of women's reform organizations such as the mid-twentieth-century Jubilee Guilds, organized by largely urban upper- and middle-class women to "improve" the lives of rural, working women by teaching them domestic skills, including textile production for home use.[5] In contrast, the Co-operative Women's Guilds, a male-led Commission of Government initiative of the same era, encouraged women to produce goods for sale as a way to increase cash income in rural households.[6] The privileged urban women who led the Jubilee Guilds were more prescriptive in promoting female domesticity and middle-class gender expectations than were men of the Co-operative Women's Guilds.[7]

Rural reform, especially in health care, likewise motivated Lady Constance Harris to establish the Newfoundland Outport Nursing and Industrial Association in 1924, with the idea that sales from textiles handcrafted by outport women would pay the salaries of rural nurses and midwives. Like the textiles produced for external markets by northern Newfoundland and coastal Labrador women employed by the industrial department of the International Grenfell Association, the Newfoundland Outport Nursing and Industrial Association products were meant to please middle-class consumer tastes (largely British and American), and movement leaders brought in outside "experts" to teach rural women how to "properly" knit, sew, hook, and weave.[8] While markets for textiles from both associations were partially rooted in the arts and crafts movement, a widespread and influential "ideology of nostalgic aestheticism" that developed in the late nineteenth century in response to "the perceived ugliness and repetitiveness of industrialism," women producing hand-crafted textiles in the CEWA branches of Conception Bay seemed more concerned with the goods' usefulness and aesthetic appeal to other members than with marketability to middle-class outsiders.[9]

Focusing on evidence from CEWA minute books, in this chapter I consider how domestic textile skills were invested with religious meanings through women's CEWA involvement, as well as how different approaches to textile production shaped the nature of local branches and how women conceived their Christianity. Although designed by church officials to be a benevolent society (with some expectation of fundraising in the tradition of middle-class ladies' aids), the CEWA in Long Pond and Seal Cove was shaped by rural women's social and economic lives into an organization they found personally fulfilling and religiously meaningful.

At Long Pond, weekly records demonstrate how CEWA members primarily conceived of the association as a means of mutual aid, with members' "spiritual and temporal support" centred on textile production.

While they organized periodic fundraising events to support their church – usually soup suppers, teas, and dances, or else sales where the local community could purchase their hand-made goods – for the most part they concentrated on the communal production of goods for each other's use. Women pooled their financial resources and exchanged skills in what can be understood as "benevolent mutuality," in that women inspired by a charitable discourse drawn from Christian scripture (and common to other women's associations) acted cooperatively in relation to each other. They sold most textiles among themselves at little or no profit as a means to help each other run households affordably, with the association offering credit to members with limited access to cash. At Seal Cove, the approach to, and use of, textiles was somewhat different, but nevertheless reveals a women's community in which textiles, invested with spiritual and symbolic meaning, were used to mutual benefit.

North American women's experience of home sewing in the twentieth century was shaped by class, race, gender, ethnicity, and region. "Depending on the circumstances," women's textile production could be "a chore or a pleasure, a survival skill or a means of personal expression."[10] Women who had access to ready-made clothing and linens enjoyed home sewing chiefly as a creative process. The cultural significance of sewing grew as its household economic significance declined: a trend applicable to the increasingly prosperous, wage-earning families of post-1950 Conception Bay South.[11] This cultural significance could include theological culture, discovered through exploration of the spiritual aspects of creativity as well as women's textile production in religious settings.

Women who offered temporal support in the context of CEWA membership did so partly out of awareness of their mutual social and economic circumstances, and partly out of need for their actions to be seen as a manifestation of their Christianity. Such acts showcased their interpretation of Christian duty and benevolence, and transformed their domestic work of sewing, knitting, and needlework into acts of devotion and a gendered way to attain Christian salvation. Weekly CEWA meetings opened with prayer and scripture reading, with texts such as Matthew 25: 31–46 (Christ's call to clothe, feed, and care for "the least of those") and Acts 9: 36–42 (Dorcas redeemed through textile production) reminding women of the spiritual opportunity within mundane household labour.[12] Women's production of textiles and needlework bearing religious imagery, or intended for use in church settings, are

Figure 9.1 The making of needlework containing religious language and images can be understood as a sensory act of devotion, in which textile skills, sight, and touch brought women into a sense of relationship with the divine. The embroidered panel pictured above, featuring a well-known children's bedtime prayer, was made by Marjorie Morgan in Seal Cove circa 1958.

considered sensory acts of devotion that engaged their touch and sight and brought them into relationship with God.[13]

Textile production reveals the place of visual and sensory practice within the religious cultures of Conception Bay women. Women's production and use of household textiles in the context of participation in a women's church-based organization can be understood as just as much a sensory act of devotion as the making of an altar frontal for their local church building or a needlepoint image of Christ for their bedroom wall. The activities of women in the Long Pond and Seal Cove CEWA branches, when combined with the religious content of their weekly rituals, suggests a broader conception of devotional needlework that included everyday articles created within lay Christian contexts.

Among the most everyday of articles was the apron, uniform of the rural working woman and by far the most frequently produced (and consumed) textile among Long Pond and Seal Cove women. Feminist theologians recognize the link between women's creativity and spirituality: creativity is "a divine gift that affirms life" and religiously minded women often feel "in the process of creating ... there is something bigger going on that speaks of God."[14] In a Christian context, the production of aprons in bright cottons, often embroidered or trimmed with hand-crocheted lace, speaks to the integrated nature of women's community, creativity, labour, and faithfulness. To make and wear these garments is to practise female solidarity and mutual respect for each other's working lives, as well as to express Christian devotion and benevolence.

Textile Production in Association

In the middle decades of the 1900s, activist Anglican women of Long Pond focused their energies on textile production and textile sales, largely to each other. Weekly CEWA minute book entries of this branch, and others in Conception Bay, reveal detailed accounts of what kinds of fabrics and other needle-working materials were purchased by the association; the progress of cooperative projects; and the types of work women completed at meetings, whether knitting, hooking mats, cutting pattern pieces, quilting, or sewing. Secretaries carefully noted the materials women took to complete projects at home and the finished items returned. A typical mid-1900s minute book entry shows the focus on textiles:

> Sister Irene Tilley returned a tray cloth and runner worked. Sister Fannie Rideout returned three dresses made. Sister Eliza Jane Morgan returned a tea cloth worked. Sister Lucy Stanley took a child's dress to pay for. Sister Emma Jane Kennedy took a runner to pay for. Sister Pearl Rideout bought a tray cloth forty cents. Sister Fannie Rideout took two dresses to make. Sister Eliza Jane Morgan took a cloth to work. Sister Alice Kennedy took a piece to make a cushion. Sisters Lucy Stanley, Elsie Baird and Irene Tilley took home bags to make. Sister Frances Snow took a dress to make. There was no other business done.[15]

Mildred (Butler) Porter, a long-time Foxtrap CEWA member, described the combination of worship, work, and fellowship at weekly meetings: "I thought it was a wonderful thing. Wednesday night you went. You went in and you had your prayers and you had your reading of the Bible and then they read the minutes from the last meeting and then you ...

took your fancy work ... and settled in and time then to have a cup of tea and then go home." Mildred went on to add that, while the parish rector occasionally came to meetings, "the night he wasn't coming you could have a bit of fun."

At Seal Cove, the production of textiles at meetings (and increasingly at home after 1945) was a major aspect of women's activism. Minute book entries from the 1920s described how "an enjoyable time was spent sewing" or, after prayers and business was completed, "all settled down to a quiet night with work."[16] In January 1929, the women agreed to purchase a sewing machine to use during meetings and gave Gladys Butler twenty dollars to buy one for this purpose.[17] Through the 1930s and 1940s, women continued to jointly purchase material that they would cut and sew into various garments and household linens during meetings. Even when association funds were low, what little money they had was invested in fabric for sewing. In November 1930, for example, the buyer was given three dollars to buy material and returned thirty-seven cents change which branch secretary Lizzie Dawe noted "is all we have on hand at present."[18] Unlike the Long Pond branch, the Seal Cove branch did not produce textiles largely for ongoing sale within the association. While they sold some items this way, they preferred to work together to build up an inventory of goods to sell (including to each other) at the annual Christmas and Easter sales. In many ways, Seal Cove women were more strategic when it came to their textile production and distribution. They spent the meetings before sales pricing and arranging goods, including pressing linens to show them to their best advantage.[19] Profit-minded branch secretary Phoebe Morgan noted in March 1942 that some goods for their upcoming Easter sale could not be priced, as the treasurer was absent and "we had no bills" to determine how much the items had cost to produce.[20] Likewise, "considering increasing prices," the women agreed in the spring of 1942 to purchase "ten dollars' worth of goods for coming fall term" in order to minimize the effect of wartime inflation on their funds.[21] Despite these efforts, as was the case at Long Pond, Seal Cove made little money on textiles compared to food and social events such as "teas," "soup suppers," and, after 1960, catering and take-out turkey dinners.[22] The Seal Cove solution to low financial returns on textile work – ticket sales on cooperatively produced quilts and bedspreads, as well as the church's response to this initiative – is described below.

The types of textiles women produced, and the techniques they used, varied over time and shows a growing interest in decorative items produced through fancy work in contrast to plain sewing. This may be linked to increased exposure to decorative consumer goods, combined with increased prosperity in the 1940s and 1950s. Through the entire period, however, one aspect of textile work did not change: Aprons, whether of the everyday bibbed variety or the bibless tea apron worn for special occasions, were the single most popular item women made in the years between 1920 and 1950. Year after year, more of these garments were sewn, and sold, than any other item. In the winter of 1940, for example, Long Pond CEWA members made twenty-four aprons compared to eleven sets of pillowcases and two tablecloths. In 1950, they produced thirty-five aprons, but only seven sets of pillowcases and twelve tablecloths. For two consecutive meetings in late January and early February 1932, "the Sisters got to work and cut out some of the material into aprons," with the branch secretary noting of the 8 March 1932 meeting that ten of fifteen women present "took apron to bind."[23] In April 1923, members produced many aprons but only one "little dress"; likewise, they purchased a large number of aprons but only one handkerchief.[24] At Seal Cove, aprons were likewise prominent. During a January 1931 meeting, Lizzie Dawe reported, "Sister Nellie Morgan brought some very nice material to make aprons" and "the Worthy President said we were to get busy next week and make them."[25] By the 1930s, Seal Cove women were distinguishing "aprons" from "goods" when describing their textile production and sales, suggesting this garment had a special status.[26] Time not spent on communal projects such as quilts was dedicated to apron making, with few other types of textiles produced until the mid-1940s, when embroidered ("worked") cloths and pillowcases began to appear, along with knitted goods such as mitts ("cuffs"), gloves, and ankle socks ("vamps").[27] As members increasingly took sewing home from meetings, rather than completing it while together, in November 1946 they agreed to sell their sewing machine.[28] Yet they continued to make and sell aprons into the 1960s, with women at Seal Cove occasionally selling tickets among themselves "for an apron" at weekly meetings.[29]

During the 1920s, apart from aprons, Long Pond CEWA members mainly sewed clothing: blouses (some for boys), shirts, dresses (some "little"), overalls, petticoats, "pinnys" (pinafores), and bibs. They knitted goods such as socks and mitts. They made household linens, usually

Figures 9.2 and 9.3 Women engaged in various types of textile production, both at home and in the context of CEWA participation. For activist women of the CEWA, work such as sewing, knitting, crocheting, and quilting became understood as "good work" through connections with scripture (especially the Biblical example of Dorcas) and the way such work could be used to benefit other women within the community. Pictured in figure 9.2, Olive Taylor of Kelligrews crocheting; in figure 9.3, an example of "fancy work" that became a popular project among association women during the 1940s and 1950s.

"cloths" (tablecloths), handkerchiefs, and pillow cases. They sewed a few pincushions and produced a decorative cushion and a yoke, likely embellished. In the 1930s, the types of projects changed somewhat and the textile methods show the influence of commercially available patterns and notions. "Stamping" goods such as cloths, aprons, and pillowcases with images, especially of flowers and birds, using iron-on transfer patterns, and then "working" the images with embroidery became popular, with "working silks" a regular CEWA expenditure after 1932.[30] Members' output reflected the appeal of this technique, as worked items such as tray cloths, runners, and bureau scarves became part of their regular household linen production. Likewise, the use of ready-made binding for apron making became standard, with "cards" of binding purchased by association members and used to finish raw edges far more quickly than the traditional folding, pressing, and hemming.[31] The women purchased more "balls of wool" in the 1930s than in the 1920s, but knitted goods were not a CEWA priority, unless for a special cause such as the Church of England Orphanage in St John's (which occasionally issued a call for socks and mitts). An exception was during the Second World War, when many women used their weekly meeting time "knitting patriotic work" for the Newfoundland Women's Patriotic Association, which specialized in producing warm garments, especially socks, for troops overseas.[32]

During the 1930s and 1940s, the Long Pond CEWA produced clothing, whether pinafores, shirts, or dresses, for children only. This may have been the result of children's clothing being easier to fit, as well as increased availability of ready-made garments for adults.[33] However, many local women continued to sew their own clothing, especially dresses, well into the 1960s and 1970s.[34] In addition to children's clothes, the women created other "useful" household items and embellished linens: cup towels, laundry bags, shoe bags, pillowcases and cloths, runners, and bureau sets. The women continued to stamp and work linens, with some members adding a crocheted edge to the finished product.[35] Perhaps due to increased local prosperity, decorative cushions, not produced regularly since the 1910s, made a comeback in the 1940s, especially those made with wool. Analysis of work completed by members reveals that most women had the skills to produce a variety of textiles, but some individuals preferred, or excelled at, certain kinds of production. Annie Jefford, for example, was a talented embroiderer who between January and March 1940, at age forty-nine, turned out four pairs of pillowcases, two aprons, and two tea cloths, all worked. While winter was down time in terms of agricultural work, in 1935 Annie still had to care for a household of seven children and a husband.[36] Minute books reveal how women combined their skills to produce goods. In April 1940, for example, one woman brought in pillowcases made and stamped which other women then worked.[37]

The importance of textile production was reflected in Long Pond branch's association offices, which like other Conception Bay branches included buyers and cutters along with the president, vice president, secretary, treasurer, and assistant positions prescribed by CEWA rules. While lone women held executive offices, the volume of textile work in Long Pond branch often meant two buyers and three cutters were elected annually. Buyers were responsible for purchasing material for other association women to use, and were likely elected based on taste, thrift, knowledge of fabrics, and ability to estimate amounts needed for various projects. While buyers purchased some materials from local general stores, the ability to travel into St John's to shop on behalf of the group was important as well.[38] Buyers purchased a variety of goods for communal use. In the 1920s, these included gingham, lawn, "white dress goods," "cotton pieces," crochet cotton, lace, flannelette, shirting, "striped pieces," and crepe.[39] At times, buyers caught up in the purchase of attractive and useful fabrics to be "opened and admired" at meetings forgot necessities.[40] In November 1937, association women had to remind buyers of the "need to buy binding, sewing cotton and needles," as well as attractive materials, during their shopping trips.[41] The other textile officers, cutters, worked during meetings to turn lengths of fabric into the various pieces needed to assemble garments or household linens. They understood the impact of warp and weft on finished products, as well as how to minimize waste. At Long Pond, CEWA women valued a good cutter more than a good buyer, or at least considered cutting a special skill, just as it was considered skilled labour within industrial textile mills. Thirty-four different women were elected as cutters or buyers in Long Pond between 1920 and 1949, and while most buyers were only in office a year or two, cutters could hold longer tenures. Examples included Pearl Rideout (1933–7), Rachael Dawe (1932–6), Mary Bishop (1920–3), Lily Kennedy (1938–49), Emily Rideout (1932–9), and Eliza Jane Morgan (1933–40). All married to farmers, four of these six women were in their fifties while they served their terms. Pearl, elected at age twenty-eight, was less experienced but was clearly respected by the other members for the quality of her work.

Lengths of uncut material, once brought in by buyers, did not leave the association room. Women took only pre-cut pieces to sew at home and return upon completion. This reflects their understanding of association fabric and finished items as joint property, even when the woman who sewed and/or worked the project intended to purchase the end product herself. On 22 December 1937, for example, "Miss Trickett returned a pair of pillow cases worked, and sent to ask price of them as she wanted to buy them." On 2 February 1938, "Sister Annie Jefford returned apron and took it to pay for, 40 cents." On 15 January 1947, "Sister Irene Tilley returned a tea cloth worked. She also took the tea cloth back to pay for next meeting."[42] Despite clear pride in and attachment to the items they made, for the most part they sold them to each other, with secretaries tracking who bought what and if she paid cash or received credit.[43] In the latter case, secretaries noted the amount owed and issued occasional reminders about payment during meetings. Few goods, once taken by a member, were returned. The exception was children's clothing, as when "Sister Rachel Dawe returned a little dress that was too small" in April 1943.[44] Occasionally women would take clothing to try on before purchasing. In May 1943, Eliza Jane Morgan, a sixty-two-year-old widow, "took home three little dresses to pay for one next meeting if it fitted," but ended up paying for all three. Eliza likely gave these dresses as gifts to eight-year-old Doris Jefford and seven-year-old Laura Jefford, daughters in the household in which she lived.[45]

From the time of its organization, Long Pond CEWA sisters offered credit to each other.[46] Credit was important in the rural Newfoundland economy, used by families with little access to cash. It was especially important to fishing people, who received supplies from local merchants in anticipation of income from catches that did not always work out.[47] Within the CEWA, a list of women who "owed for work" appeared in 14 April 1920, along with a written statement that reflected a commitment to honesty in financial matters. Note the transition from third- to first-person voice in the secretary's entry: "Sister Emma Jane Kennedy took an apron Easter Tuesday from the trunk. Rachel Dawe, Edith Taylor and Carrie Kennedy was present when I took it and I paid 50 cents for it last meeting." Association secretaries regularly noted goods "took to pay for" and when the money was sent in, entries that intermingled with notes on cash buyers, taken material, and returned finished goods. Members attached little stigma to credit, which they offered to each other for tea and badges as well as for goods.[48] The women's nonjudgmental view can be seen in this sample entry: "The Worthy President paid $2.00 towards a quilt and owes $1.50 more. Sisters May Eason and Lavina Porter owes [*sic*] 5 cents each for tea. Sister Lily Greenslade paid 35 cents for small apron. Sisters Gladys and May Greenslade took an apron to pay at next meeting. Sister May Eason paid 40 cents for dress and pants. Sister Annie Jefford took a piece to bind the quilt she had worked."[49] While some women paid their bills promptly, others had balances outstanding for several months. Payments for credit purchases sometimes occurred outside regular meeting times. In May 1941, branch secretary Lily Greenslade noted that "Sister Lily Kennedy and the Worthy President promised to pay the treasurer what they owed has [*sic*] the meetings was going to close for the summer months."[50]

Textiles and Church Fundraising

Women in church-based associations were usually understood to produce textiles primarily to fundraise: they would stockpile a variety of handmade items, plain and fancy, and offer them for sale to the public at bazaars, usually in combination with a "tea meeting."[51] The Anglican women of St John's took this approach, and in city parishes such as St Thomas's and St Mary the Virgin, associations led by middle-class women and rectors' wives used sales of work to raise funds for a variety of church building projects.[52] Seal Cove CEWA members did the same, although with little profitability. For Long Pond CEWA members, however, sewing in association was not primarily about fundraising. In fact, fundraising had not been a priority for them since the association's foundation in 1917. Pressured by rector's wife Enid Colley to identify "what they were intending to work for" as a CEWA branch, the women at a 22 May 1917 meeting vaguely agreed that they "should work for the school if it should be repaired." In January 1918, Colley again visited the branch and spoke about fundraising. Besides encouraging support for church and school, she touched on the devastating Halifax Explosion of 6 December 1917, "how that we should try and collect some money to help them out a little," and the work of the Women's Patriotic

Association for Newfoundland troops overseas, "how we should try and do a little for them that are doing so much for us."[53] Despite this "touching address," women of the Long Pond CEWA chose not to raise funds for either of these causes, a reflection, perhaps, of their perception of the Newfoundland Women's Patriotic Association as a largely elite, St John's-centred organization.[54]

At the same time, while fundraising in the tradition of "ladies' aids" was not a priority of the Long Pond sewing class or the Long Pond CEWA, women could sometimes organize fundraising activities when a special need arose. As early as the summer of 1905, members hosted a church fundraiser Strawberry Festival and Tea where, along with the meal, they sold textiles they produced to raise funds towards a new parsonage after the old one was destroyed by fire.[55] Despite the women's primary object of supporting one another, and typical of the experience of women's church organizations in other jurisdictions, fundraising activities were singled out for praise by rector's wife Emily Caldwell and her husband upon his resignation from the parish in 1913. In a cosigned letter to the "dear Sisters" of Long Pond, the Caldwells acknowledged the association's "good work" in putting a carpet in the church and raising money towards a bell, but remained silent on the benefits of mutual aid.[56]

In Conception Bay, sales of handmade textiles did not make much money, at least not when women organized them in ways that male clergy found acceptable. Occasional public sales did not generate the same income that other activities did. At a Tea Meeting and Sale of Work held in February 1919, for example, branch treasurer Rachel Dawe noted the branch made just over fourteen dollars on goods, but almost fifty dollars on tea.[57] When the CEWA was called on to help raise money for a new church building in Foxtrap in the 1930s, the women relied on organizing and hosting social events, not on selling textiles. The Long Pond accounts for 1936, for example, show over one hundred dollars made on teas and hot suppers, but only $4.34 on goods sold at meetings.[58] In 1938, income from goods stood at $22.60; with $17.05 spent on material, this resulted in a small profit of $5.55. In contrast, two Soup Supper, Tea, and Dances brought in just over sixty dollars, with little expense beyond paying the fiddler. Income from textiles was so low that at times the women turned to social events to raise money to buy materials, as in November 1944 when they agreed to have a "tea and dance" in order "to get some money to pay our bills, and help carry on our work." They used the income from that social to buy fabric and wool.[59] In 1946, CEWA members spent over thirty dollars on "working material," but made only $15.45 income from "goods sold." As in years past, when Long Pond women wanted to raise money "for the build up and repairs of our church," they turned to the tea cup and fiddler rather than the needle and thread.

Long Pond CEWA members discovered they could make money from textiles by selling tickets on fancy work, especially on communally made projects such as quilts. Anglican Church leaders interpreted ticket sales as gambling, rather than a cooperative enterprise whereby every community member could contribute a small amount to a greater whole while sharing risk, and so found them unacceptable.[60] In November 1920, Long Pond women sold tickets on three cushions and "got $5.00 each for them," concluding from this success "to get some fancy work and put with the goods."[61] Occasional sales of tickets on fancy work continued into the early 1930s. In January 1933, faced with a bill for six dollars for flooring for the new All Saints Church building, which could not be paid "as there was not enough money on hand," the women decided to finish a quilt and raffle it on five-cent tickets.[62] With this expense met, in February 1933 "it was spoken of making a bed-spread out of the calico" and two weeks later "some of the members ... stamped the bed-spread for working" and the buyers were "asked to buy silks for next meeting." The women worked together to make the bedspread, along with a set of matching pillowcases, during meetings, and had finished the project by March 1933.[63] Yet the expected ticket sales on this project did not happen. Instead, it sat in the association trunk until March 1934, when President Lizzie Greenslade "took home the bedspread and pair of pillow cases with intention of selling it." She did this in the summer of 1934, perhaps at the diocesan CEWA meeting she attended at St John's in June, where delegates of various means, including those from relatively affluent city parishes, had gathered.[64]

While the secretary did not record a similar incident in Long Pond, the sale of tickets on a quilt made by the Seal Cove CEWA in 1930 was reprimanded by parish rector, and single man, the Reverend Henry Whitehouse. Seal Cove women raised over sixty dollars raffling a quilt they made communally during the winter of 1930, as much as they earned at their 1929 Christmas tea and sale, and double the income from the 1930 Easter sale.[65] The outcome of this success was recorded by Seal Cove secretary Lizzie Dawe, who wrote of the meeting following their "Quilt Party":

> We were surprised with a visit from the Reverend Mr Whitehouse and four men from the Church Building Committee. The Reverend Gentleman then told us the object of this visit was to get some money to help pay the expenses of the repairing of the church. Sixty dollars was handed over, for which they thank us very much. A paper was also read denouncing the sale of tickets on any goods for church purposes.[66]

It is worth noting that Lizzie added the "for which they thank us very much" after the fact. Amending the record to read that the men who invaded their meeting were at least grateful for the money they took may have been a way to preserve some level of dignity in the face of raw theological and patriarchal power. She further reworked the event for her annual report, composed just a month later, to state that the CEWA "gave" Whitehouse "sixty dollars for church purposes" in November.[67]

Whitehouse's moral outrage over ticket sales did not prevent him from adding the profits to the church accounts. A search of vestry minutes and other church records shows no mention of the issue of gambling, despite the fact that it was not just the selling of tickets that posed a moral problem, but the buying of them. Without the support of a largely Anglican community who clearly did not see tickets as immoral, the CEWA's project could not have succeeded. For the male, middle-class, English-born and -educated Whitehouse, this group of women, who had worked communally to turn "rags to riches" in a time of economic hardship, was responsible for the indiscretion. For the local men who had accompanied Whitehouse that night, notions of gender and deference to official power within the church clearly trumped community and class ties. Yet the Seal Cove women were not singled out for arbitrary treatment. Whitehouse's position was consistent with official Anglican policy in Newfoundland, and one suspects that Long Pond women either received a similar visit following their use of tickets to raise money from textiles, or else heard the news of what happened at Seal Cove through networks of kin and friendship.[68]

Quilting and Ticket Sales at Seal Cove

The Seal Cove quilt that provoked so much controversy began its life as a cooperative textile project which the women intended to complete during Lent. At the end of January 1930, branch secretary Lizzie Dawe noted that "the most attractive piece of work in our class is a quilt which our Worthy President [Susie Lear] intends getting done for our Easter sale."[69] By March they reported that "work on the Quilt is progressing very good" but either they did not meet the Easter deadline or the quilt did not sell.[70] At the first meeting of the fall session, 7 October 1930, Susie reported on the CEWA's Diocesan Council meetings she had attended in St John's over the summer. Along with instruction on running CEWA meetings ("she said we were to make use of our sign more often"), Susie may have picked up some new fundraising ideas from other delegates. "It was decided we would hold call cannon [*sic*] in the school on October 30th," Lizzie reported, "and dispose of our quilt by the sale of tickets."[71] Working on joint textile projects such as quilts or mats was part of Lenten observance for women of Long Pond and Foxtrap, both at home and in association. Such projects were rarely seen at other times of the year. At Seal Cove, however, cooperative projects were a regular part of CEWA activities. Through the 1940s these projects were largely quilts or bedspreads for which the women sold tickets. While this maximized income in return for materials and labour, as well as shared risk with the entire community and not just with association members, the practice suggested collective memory of the 1930 reprimand and a determination to preserve their autonomy in the face of clerical authority.

By the early 1940s, new tastes in interior decoration led Seal Cove women (like those of Long Pond) to produce stamped bedspreads as well as quilts. In January 1942, "after a little discussion," they "decided to buy a stamped bedspread and get it done for the Spring Sale." Since branch secretary Phoebe Morgan "said she was going to town," the women asked her to buy it, but Phoebe, perhaps due to cost and with an eye to profit, returned with transfers instead. Sister Priscilla Morgan "stamped out [the] bedspread" next meeting, and buyer Maria Seymour was asked to pick up "working silks and some shirting" for it. During the next couple of weekly meetings, the women were busy "working the quilt," with Priscilla completing the final stitches at the meeting of 3 March 1942.[72]

Aware of the need to produce a variety of goods for an increasingly consumption-minded population, the Seal Cove CEWA made a variety of different bed coverings in the 1940s to offer up on tickets. This work shows the range of their shared textile skills as well as their cooperative approach to fundraising.

Along with another stamped bedspread they made during the fall of 1942, in the winter of 1943 members decided "to start a scrap quilt to use up the cotton scraps now left over." Revealing of mid-1900s textile methods and the need for economy, Phoebe noted that the women were "asked to bring along a flour bag for this purpose."[73] Work on this quilt continued through February, and "Sister Olive Morgan" took "it home to finish" in early March.[74] In the fall of 1943, "it was decided by the class that a wool quilt be started to be sold on tickets." While all "the sisters were asked to bring a small bit of wool for this purpose," the quilt was made largely by Priscilla, who worked at it steadily through November and December.[75] A small number of women working on a wool quilt likely produced by knitting or crochet, rather than the whole group as was done for a patchwork quilt, reflects the women's awareness of the differences in each other's wool work. Variations in individual women's stitches meant blocks made after the same pattern could be significantly different in size and shape. This difference would not only make pieces difficult to join together but would mean a less attractive finished product. Despite this challenge, another wool quilt was made in the fall of 1944, with Priscilla, Hilda Lear, and Alma Dowden completing most of the work. Alma especially, as branch secretary Harriet Morgan noted, "worked away at the quilt till closing time" several nights in December. Although all the sisters donated some wool towards this project, they had to pay "sixty cents for feed sacks for the inside" in order to finish it.[76]

In the winter of 1944, work began on an appliquéd bedspread. On 16 February, Bessie Dowden and Harriet "cut out some flowers" and through February, March, and April "the Sisters worked away" at it, producing what Harriet declared "a lovely piece of work" in time for the Easter tea and sale.[77] Along with appliqué, the women made patchwork quilts, bringing along blocks completed at home in order to piece the top. In October 1945, the first blocks "for the quilt we intend doing for our Christmas sale" were brought in, with contributions following from Mamie Morgan (four blocks), Phoebe Morgan (four), Olive Morgan (two), Alice Young (one), Belinda Anthony (one), Hilda Lear (two), Annie Dawe (four), Violet Seymour (two), Ethel Dowden (two), Alma Dowden (two), and Harriet Morgan (two). On 4 December the members were "busy tearing the strips for the quilt" and on 18 December "Sister Alma Dowden and Sister Bertha [Morgan] worked at the quilt and finished joining it up. It was then decided that we would send the quilt along … to Sister Ethel Morgan to sew on the strips and finish." On 26 December Harriet happily reported that Ethel "brought along the quilt that was sent to her the Tuesday before to be finished for the sale and we all agreed that it was a Splendid Piece of Work."[78] While the women worked on a patchwork quilt sporadically through 1946 and 1947, they decided to focus on completing a wool rug for the 1946 Christmas sale and next, in the winter of 1947, once more took on a "stamped" bedspread for Easter. They "disposed of" each of these items using tickets, and by the mid-1940s occasionally raffled purchased items such as glassware as well.[79]

In the late nineteenth and early twentieth centuries, cooperative quilting was a leading means by which activist women used needlework skills to raise money for church purposes. Like other group projects which offered opportunity to work and chat together, quilting was an activity many women enjoyed despite critical voices who suggested the monetary return on the time it took did not make it worth the effort.[80] While the social nature of the work made quilting appealing to church women, the language of weekly CEWA ritual suggests that for members it could also have a spiritual aspect, whereby sewing was transformed into a devotional activity by the religious context in which it was performed. This contrasted with the views of some Canadian male clergy, who as part of their efforts to reform women's church work in the 1960s suggested that women's voluntary association activities such as quilting "hinder[ed] the personal encounter with Christ" rather than enhanced it.[81] The women of Seal Cove demonstrated a commitment to quilting not seen at Long Pond, suggesting the activity had special meaning for them. This meaning was rooted not just in the communal nature of the work, in women bringing shared skills and materials together for the common good, but in the way that raffling quilts served as a symbol of feminine resistance to male power and the women's determination to live a Christianity conceived of on their own moral terms. Raffling aprons at meetings further demonstrated how this sense of resistance was gendered and helped to strengthen the bonds of women's community at Seal Cove.

Conclusion

In the early 1960s, the Anglican Diocese of Newfoundland started to reorganize women's church associations based on the vision of rector's wives and other middle-class women of St John's.[82] This was consistent with efforts led by male clergy within the Canadian Anglican church to reform the work of women's associations. Part of this exercise in Newfoundland and Labrador was transforming the CEWA into the Anglican Church Women's Association (ACWA), a process that included discontinuance of passwords and the balloting in of new members. Within the ACWA model, membership in local branches was to be controlled by the parish clergy rather than by the lay female members. Mary (Petten) Porter described one woman's anger at the top-down reorganization of the CEWA into the ACWA: "One lady she was really old and they just changed ... she wasn't satisfied with it and she stayed away from the meetings for three meetings ... she wasn't coming back anymore, but anyway she did [and] when she came she brought aprons." This woman's use of the apron as a way to demonstrate her desire to return to the community of Christian women with whom she had worked and worshipped for many years speaks to the importance of textiles, and the apron especially, as a common bond between rural women. This woman clearly understood a gift of aprons, rather than pillowslips, tablecloths, or knitted socks, as the best way to express her social and spiritual need for membership within the association, despite her rejection of the church's organizational changes. The symbolic importance of the apron continued even as Conception Bay South transitioned from a family-based economy to a wage-based economy with increased opportunities for women to work outside the home. In a project that combined old roles with new skills, in 1967 Long Pond Worthy President Dora Butler "asked each Sister to make a small apron and put a verse in the pocket and send it to their friends, for a donation ... Sister Myra Porter typed the verses and they were given to the Sisters."[83] Typing was an option for vocational training at the newly opened Trades School in Seal Cove, where program offerings were designed to provide office skills to younger women seeking paid employment, or else to enhance women's domestic ability and physical appearance.[84]

Rural women of Conception Bay understood and expressed Christian benevolence through mutual aid. Only once in the seventy years of surviving Long Pond records did women use a textile they had made to "clothe the poor" of the community. On 29 April 1920, "the Sisters sent an overall pinny to a little orphan child Eason … for the sisters to pay for it between themselves." Instead, the Biblical example of Dorcas and the answering of Christ's teaching to "do unto the least of them" were met through cooperative textile production and consumption. CEWA sisters pooled their financial resources to buy fabric, treated it as joint property, exchanged textile skills, and offered credit to each other when needed. By doing so, they believed they were doing work that was "for the good and welfare of the class," or, as they most often put it: "good work." Not "church work" or "association work" but good work, the goodness of which they believed transcended earthly institutions, and through which they, as rural women together using everyday household skills and demonstrating mutual support, could build a relationship with God and attain salvation. Women in the Seal Cove CEWA did not use goods to "clothe the poor" either, beyond knitting mittens to send to the Church of England Orphanage in St John's in 1930 and 1934.[85] They practised mutual aid by offering each other financial, emotional, and spiritual support in times of need, and this communal instinct likewise informed their textile work. While different than the approach at Long Pond, cooperative textile production at Seal Cove created female bonds of community and confirmed a shared vision of lived Christianity that sometimes stood in opposition to the official church.

The example of the Long Pond CEWA demonstrates how for some women active in church-based associations, textile production was not simply a matter of denominational fundraising, or of using skills central to their participation in the household economy in a public way, to benefit the infrastructure of the institutional church. Women of Conception Bay, like others in rural Newfoundland, produced knitted and sewn goods for their families, but they were also active in outdoor work, whether curing fish, tending gardens, or making hay. At both Long Pond and Seal Cove, wintertime was textile time: CEWA production of goods peaked in February and March each year, corresponding with Lent when Christians are expected to prepare themselves spiritually for the great festival of Easter. Women filled cold days and long nights with warm wool on needles, colourful fabrics, and bright working silks, an experience enhanced when gathered with other women for sociability and conversation. "All the Sisters worked and chatted around the fire side," Long Pond secretary Elsie Baird wrote of a December evening in 1944, "and a very enjoyable evening was spent."[86] Women demonstrated craft pride in their work, whether purchasing material that would be admired by their peers or bringing in finished articles for other women to see and, ultimately, use within their own households. Outside the influence of reforming textile "experts" associated with groups such as the Newfoundland Outport Nursing and Industrial Association and the industrial department of the International Grenfell Association, CEWA women in Long Pond and Seal Cove cultivated their own aesthetic rather than one designed to please middle-class American or British consumers.

Yet social needs and craft pride does not entirely explain why, week after week, busy rural women left the CEWA meeting room with individual textile projects in hand, whether pieces for a child's dress, a square of white shirting together with a handful of working silks for a tea cloth, or, more likely, the makings of an apron that one of their association sisters would eventually wear as she went about her daily work in kitchen, garden, and yard. Given the Christian character of the CEWA, the decision to participate in communal textile production can be understood as an act of benevolence and religious devotion. At Long Pond, shared textile work was a way for women to help each other materially and spiritually. At Seal Cove, it enabled them to financially support their local church, while simultaneously facilitating their resistance to clerical authority. Textile production provided individual women opportunity to exercise the "divine gift" of creativity: "a vital spiritual force … wherein [creators] participate with God" to produce objects of beauty and, through a sense of relationship with some mysterious, transcendent and transformational power, "break through to eternity."[87] Inspired by the rituals of worship that opened and closed their meetings, CEWA members understood that producing household linens and clothing could bring each and every one of their sisters into a beneficial relationship with each other and with the divine, a relationship recalled and confirmed each morning as the women of Conception Bay donned their association-made aprons and, in preparation for the day's labour, tied the strings of friendship and faith.

CHAPTER TEN

"Do You Mean Catering?": Food, Fellowship, and the Domestication of Anglican Church Women

In the spring of 1965, the Reverend David Genge, fresh from a term as curate in the elite urban parish of St Thomas's in St John's, met with the presidents of the CEWA branches of Foxtrap and Hopewell to discuss a fundraising idea he thought would interest local women.[1] This was the compilation of a community cookbook, or "charity cookbook," a project popular among activist church women and other women's voluntary groups elsewhere in mid-1900s North America.[2] Community cookbooks provide insight into gender and class consciousness, as the recipes within often reflect a woman's desire to project a middle-class identity, especially to other women. Participation in such projects demonstrated a feminine consciousness that accepted prescribed ideas of "the importance of women's domestic role, and her power within the home as nurturer." There was a moral instruction aspect as well, especially in the way women authors used such cookbooks to model their embrace of domesticity and to suggest that other women do the same.[3]

For the Anglican women of the south side of Conception Bay, Genge's suggestion was not particularly appealing, pious, or practical. After a May 1965 meeting at Long Pond where, in the words of branch secretary Selina Perrin, the new rector "spoke about making up Coock Boocks [*sic*] to sell during the Summer," Genge called a meeting of all branch CEWA presidents to discuss the project.[4] Subsequent special CEWA meetings were held independently in mid-June, and local women largely rejected their rector's proposal. At Seal Cove, women declined to create what they considered a useless and unnecessary end product. "There were other ways of making money for the church than by making cookbooks and selling them," branch secretary Eileen Morgan recorded, "because everyone in the Parish had a cookbook already so this project was dropped right away as far as our members were concerned."[5] For these women, one cookbook only was deemed necessary to feed a household. Long Pond women were equally decisive, with their criticism centred on expenses, workload, and the idea of an outside "expert" supervising their efforts. Selina Perrin did not mince words:

> The Worthy President [Marjorie Jefford] informed us that this meeting was called for the purpose of discussing a Coock Boock … that a lady from the mainland was to come hear [*sic*] and help with it and her expencess [*sic*] were to be paid which would cost around $400.00. So after earing [*sic*] what work would be envalved [*sic*] in it none of the Sisters were willing to do anything about it. So the Worthy President were to go to Reverend Genge and tell him. Which she did. And all the other Presidents did the likewise so all of the Branches turned it down.[6]

Despite Selina's assertion, Kelligrews women were initially divided. At their 11 June 1965 meeting, branch secretary Phoebe Butler noted there was "nothing settled on" regarding "the possibilities of composing a cook book," suggesting some members were open to the idea.[7] Interestingly, St Alban's ACWA, as the branch was later known, eventually produced *Home Cooking Secrets of Kelligrews*.[8] This cookbook included submissions from women throughout the parish (including Seal Cove but not Long Pond) and demonstrated the characteristics of post-1950s baking. Such "modern" recipes used convenience foods, such as Jell-O, Dream Whip, and marshmallows, as well as "exotic" ingredients, such as pineapple or walnuts.[9] The main dishes in *Home Cooking Secrets of Kelligrews* showcased women's desire to project middle-class domesticity, including access to consumer goods.[10] Recipes called for canned foods such as mushrooms, tomatoes, and cream soups, and many featured ground beef. No recipes called for game meats, and of the three recipes for cod, only one, "Fish and Brewis with Potato," could be deemed traditional in ingredients and method.[11] Just as this cookbook revealed how some Newfoundland Anglican women of the mid-1970s "saw themselves and projected their values," the rejection of this project in 1965 reveals CEWA values, including resistance to clerical authority and rejection of middle-class gender roles and expectations.[12] Food practices can represent social conflict and contest, signify difference, and demonstrate the exercise of power. Scholars recognize how "food traditions evolve in social and cultural contexts that are shaped by economic conditions," as well as by relations of class, gender, race, and ethnicity.[13]

Connections between religion, food, and domesticity can be seen in the Roman Catholic Church's encouragement of mid-twentieth century women to engage daily with its liturgy. One aspect of this movement was the publication of cookbooks designed to help the "ordinary housewife" become mindful of the church year, especially the cycle of feasts and fasts. Titles such as *The Feast Day Cookbook* and *Cookbook for Fridays and Lent* were designed to aid devotional practices within the home, centred on family meals, just as the family rosary campaign of the 1950s centred on home prayer.[14] A volume like *Cooking for Christ: The Liturgical Year in the Kitchen* assumed that women were domestic, responsible for maintaining family piety, and found religious meaning in household tasks. As *Cooking for Christ* author Florence S. Berger writes, "If I am to carry Christ home with me from the altar, I am afraid he will have to come to the kitchen because much of my time is spent there."[15]

In this chapter, I explore the relationship between food and religion among Conception Bay Anglicans, and especially how women used food production to express their faithfulness. I bring together material from informant interviews, the MUN Folklore and Language Archive, and CEWA minute books. Traditional food ways in the parish reflected women's notion of cooking as work, performed primarily to feed families and households with thrift and efficiency, rather than as a way to demonstrate commitment to domesticity. Most Conception Bay women of the mid-1900s were not concerned about producing "dainty" dishes designed to tempt middle-class palates, but sought instead to satisfy appetites sharpened by manual labour and to offer some variety in the daily menu despite limited access to ingredients. In the context of weekly CEWA teas, this included satisfying their own appetites. Food traditions marked the Christian calendar for families, whether abstaining at Lent and Holy Week or feasting at Christmas and Easter. Women's domestic religious practice included "blessing" bread as they made it, as many Anglican women recalled and practised.

Women contributed their food production skills to community celebrations of religious festivals, using these "times" to raise money for church purposes. In the 1930s and 1940s, women organized times on their own terms, and sometimes against clerical wishes, as they did in their other fundraising efforts.[16] Women's cooking and baking "for the church" inspired their daughters to become active Anglicans. Other women used domestic skills as a means to gain acceptance in the church community. Using food for fundraising and fellowship was part of local CEWA practice from the 1920s, but by the mid-1960s increased financial pressure from church leadership led Anglican women to provide large-scale food service as part and parcel of their active participation in church life. It is not surprising that former CEWA member Eileen Morgan, when asked about religious practices surrounding food, replied, "Do you mean catering?" The idea that activist women could best serve the church through food service helped to shape Anglican women's gender and class consciousness, and may explain why a women's community which rejected making cookbooks in 1965 was willing to embrace the project less than a decade later.

Traditional Food Practices

For women in mid-twentieth-century Conception Bay, domestic food production followed a predictable, weekly round, remembered by Mildred (Butler) Porter and Myra (Porter) Rideout. Mildred recalled "the menu for the week" as "Sunday dinner; Monday was leftovers. Tuesday was cooked dinner again. Wednesday was fish. Thursday was cooked dinner again and Friday was fish. Saturday was soup." Daughter Myra agreed, and noted how families accepted the predictability of meals: "Wednesday and Friday were fish days. Tuesday and Thursdays was corn beef and cabbage. Saturday was a kind of a free day. Sometimes you had soup and some days maybe boiled beans. But you always seemed to be [having] the one thing. You didn't wonder and you didn't growl or anything. You just knew what you were having." Selina Porter of Long Pond outlined this same pattern.[17] Several women made connections between eating fish on Fridays and religious observance. Enid (Porter) Haines, for example, noted that "although we weren't Catholic there was always fish on Friday."[18]

Selina described how the daily meal schedule was tied to family labour patterns.[19] Excepting Sundays, daily meals started with eight o'clock breakfast, served after early morning farm chores were complete, followed by a ten o'clock "lunch or mug-up" for "the working men."[20] Selina described how "all hands would be home for dinner," the main meal of the day, at 12:30 p.m. Supper was served at six o'clock after chores were done. She noted how "men or anyone working hard" would have a "fourer" between dinner and supper.[21] At bedtime, children had milk and "a bun," while adults drank tea.[22] Meals reflected local ingredients available through subsistence farming, fishing, and hunting, as well as rural working people's taste for "plain fare." The diet was similar to that described for mainland Nova Scotia, although in coastal Conception Bay people tended to eat more fish.[23] Extensive use of leftovers for suppers and snacks suggested economic circumstances in which nothing could be wasted. Selina's characterization of March as "the long and hungry month," when supplies would run low and some Conception Bay men would try to earn extra cash in the spring seal hunt, likewise reflected hardship.[24]

When asked about religious practices around food, most women recalled grace before meals.[25] Others recalled particular rituals of their mothers. Sandra (Taylor) Tilley described a ceremony her mother Olive (Rideout) Taylor practised on "Christmas Eve in the afternoon":

> My older brothers would be out ... putting Christmas lights on the Christmas tree and I remember mom would be ... making Christmas pudding and I distinctly remember her saying go tell the boys to come in ... [and] before it was put in the pudding mould ... everyone in the family stirred the Christmas pudding ... You were supposed to stir the Christmas pudding and think of something, I don't know if it was a memory or a blessing, thanksgiving or what. But everyone took a turn stirring the Christmas pudding before it was baked.

A more widespread practice was women's ritual of blessing bread as they made it, a ritual that has been associated specifically with Pentecostalism in northern Newfoundland. For "fundamentalist apostolic women" in that region, "the three humps [of a homemade loaf] stand for the Christian trinity," yet women from other Christian traditions did not describe this belief.[26]

In Conception Bay, women did not associate three-part loaves of bread with the Trinity, yet widely described blessing bread.[27] "Whenever mom made bread," Sandra recalled, "of course it would be sign the bread with the cross."[28] Enid noted how her grandmother "just made the sign," and never spoke any words aloud (such as invoking the Trinity, "In the name of the Father and the Son and the Holy Spirit," as male clergy would do in formal worship). Marjorie (Bullen) Morgan explained the process: "You would get it all kneaded and ready and turn it over and put smooth side up and you would put the sign of the cross on it and bless it." Women noted that they learned this ritual in the home from mothers and grandmothers, and some added, "I still do it today."

Bread has cultural significance in Newfoundland, including gendered and religious meanings. Making bread, a family food staple, was central to women's household labour.[29] "If bread fuelled men's work," Diane Tye observes, "it structured women's," as "the demands of bread-making filled women's days."[30] While other household tasks filled up the time between mixing and kneading the dough, setting it to rise, "punching down" and shaping it into loaves, putting it in pans, setting it to rise once more, baking it, and setting it to cool, the entire process required many hours of women's labour and was recalled by one woman as "the hardest kind of work."[31] Girls were taught to make bread at a young age.[32] In terms of domestic Christian practices, making bread and eating certain kinds of bread were especially associated with Good Friday. In some Newfoundland communities, bread made on Good Fridays was considered magical or thought to carry healing powers and women who baked on Good Friday were thought to be blessed, but in Conception Bay eating raisin bread (without butter) was the only tradition noted.[33] Just as traditional patterns of meals and food preparation protected women's Sabbath, the absence of traditions that encouraged women to labour at bread making on Good Friday protected Anglican women's observance of an especially holy day within the Christian calendar.

CEWA: The "Usual Cup of Tea"

The phenomenon of women serving the "usual cup of tea" at association meetings is associated with female community building, but it was also a way to display gender and class consciousness.[34] The variety and quality of food offered at women's church groups in the Maritimes changed in the 1950s and became far more elaborate (and sweet) than that offered in earlier decades.[35] Domestic ideology which envisioned women as skilled cooks and gracious hostesses elevated the amount of labour which they were expected to invest in cooking and baking. Women involved with church groups in the mid-1900s felt pressured by the social expectations surrounding tea, and feared that other women would negatively judge their hostess and culinary skills.[36] Some North American women's groups, aware of difference in economic means between members or of wastefulness, were strict about keeping refreshments at meetings "light" or "simple." With rules such as "two kinds of cake and one or two kinds of fruit and radishes, cheese, etc." or "*five* different kinds of foods" only, the potential for cups of tea to serve as displays of wealth, culinary prowess, manners, and feminine "daintiness" remained.[37]

At Seal Cove in the late 1920s and early 1930s, the weekly cup of tea appeared to be literal: a hot beverage prepared, "passed around," and drunk while the sisters worked at textile projects, rather than a tea with baked goods or other foods prepared in advance and served once the business of the meeting was finished.[38] No food with tea may have been a function of economic hardship, which even affected food-based fundraising efforts. In April 1933, Seal Cove branch discussed cancelling their regular Easter sale "because there was some of the sisters could not provide much for the tea."[39] Even when the rector visited, tea was offered but not food. Such was the case on 28 November 1933, when the Reverend Whitehouse encouraged the women to "continue on the good work" even though "he knew it was hard in this time of depression" and expressed hope that "God would make prosperity to flow among us in the end."[40]

Despite financial hardship, Seal Cove women understood tea as a gesture of hospitality and friendship. In February 1934 members made tea "most especially for our visiting sisters from Upper Gullies," and in May 1934 they prepared "a cup of tea … in honour of our older members."[41] Other beverages besides tea could be served at meetings, such as cocoa on a cold March evening.[42] Occasionally, "some of the members provided soup," which they either made during the meeting or cooked at home and brought in. In March 1930, the "long and hungry month," branch secretary Lizzie Dawe noted that "all the sisters are very thankful to Sister Gladys Butler for the nice boiler of soup she brought along which was thoroughly enjoyed by all."[43] Tea could also serve as a point of good-humoured fellowship, as when Lizzie observed in the 25 March 1930 sick report that "Sister Louie Dowden," known to "entertain the members by some of her funny pranks," was "not feeling very well owing to not having a cup of tea."[44]

During the 1930s, Long Pond CEWA served tea at meetings only during Lent, with every member taking a turn and charging ten cents per cup to raise money towards their self-denial offering.[45] Given the hard economic times, no one was willing to volunteer for a second turn, nor did anyone crave an extra opportunity to show off her hostess skills.[46] As economic depression deepened in 1933, Long Pond CEWA dropped the price of tea to five cents, but even then secretary Annie Bishop noted weekly how many members "owes for tea" as cups were offered on credit.[47] Serving tea at Long Pond was considered first and foremost a matter of fundraising, as Annie summarized in March 1934: "Tea was served again in the usual way by Sisters Susie Richards, Pearl Rideout, Lily Greenslade and Lizzie J. Greenslade and raised the sum of 55 cents making a total of $3.05 made on 5 cent teas. This finishes our teas at meetings for this year."[48] On occasion, members offered a communal "free tea," such as for the 1935 annual meeting when "all members were asked to bring something along," and for the closing meeting of May 1937 to which the Reverend Heber and Elizabeth Gosse were invited.[49]

Starting in the late 1930s, Long Pond CEWA no longer limited tea to Lent, but for the most part women continued to only take one turn each per year and used it primarily to raise funds.[50] Cups of tea remained available on credit. In November 1938, the forgetful "Miss Trickett" was reminded that she "owes 35 cents for seven cups of tea which she had got from the class," a bill she promptly paid at the next meeting.[51] As economic prosperity increased during the 1940s, the price of tea returned to ten cents per cup.[52] There was also increased attention to the quality of "eatables" members presented, suggesting a growing awareness of middle-class domestic expectations. On 4 December 1946, for example, branch secretary Irene Tilley reported "a beautiful cup of tea and all the nice things that go with it."[53] Yet the focus remained on tea as fundraiser. "A beautiful cup of tea ... always goes to make up a pleasant evening," Irene noted in January 1947, "when the grand sum of $2.40 was realized."[54]

Food was served at CEWA meetings to satisfy household-labour-sharpened appetites. During the 1930s and 1940s, members at both Seal Cove and Long Pond sometimes brought in pots of soup to share, indicating women with a traditional taste for "food" rather than a modern taste for "sweet stuff" such as cookies and cakes.[55] Ingredients for soup were locally available, and were mostly produced in households or gathered from the sea or land rather than purchased. Root vegetables came from gardens; broth was flavoured with the tail or shinbone of a recently butchered cow, or with game such as rabbit or seabird.[56] Women in Conception Bay were not ashamed of their appetites, as North American gender constructions of the mid-1900s would encourage them to be.[57] On 14 February 1940 at Long Pond, although no lunch was planned, "all the Sisters got hungry for a cup of tea and Sisters Gladys Greenslade and Alice Kennedy went and provided material with all the Sisters to chip in." Likewise, bills for "wax and pie" were submitted to the Long Pond treasurer after a group of women cleaned the association room in April 1957.[58] When the next cleaning session was planned eighteen months later, the women were prepared for the appetites that followed manual labour. As described by secretary Lilla Greenslade:

> The Sisters of the CEWA met on December 3 in the class-room about 7 pm and gave the room a "clean up." Some of the sisters dusting, others scrubbing and doing the dishes. In about an hour all the work was done and the room arranged for our meeting … A supper was now served by three of the sisters who gave us a wonderful treat. Sister Dora Butler made the apple pies which were delicious and Sister Vera Baird and Sister Lena Perrin made two boilers of soup which was also delicious and thoroughly enjoyed by all present. Sister Baird brought the real cream for the pies, which was good. We had a very happy meeting.[59]

When the parish rector was present, women sometimes changed the language used to report on teas and focused on quality and presentation rather than on appetite. In 1942 and 1943, for example, Long Pond secretary Elsie Baird used phrases such as "heartily enjoyed by all" or "very much enjoyed by all" to describe tea served among the sisters but switched to "delightful" and "delicious" for tea served to clergy.[60] This distinction was not noted at Seal Cove.

Food prepared and served in association could reflect domestic religious practices and family celebrations. On 9 February 1937 in Seal Cove, Harriet Morgan and Sarah Dowden "fried pancakes and prepared a nice cup of tea" for the women at their Shrove Tuesday meeting.[61] Syrup (locally known as "swanky" and served as a festive drink at Christmas, especially to mummers) was served at the Seal Cove CEWA meeting of 27 December 1929.[62] Association women prepared meals for each other in order to show appreciation for leadership, to celebrate special times, to boost each other's spirits, and, sometimes, to resist clerical authority. At Seal Cove in November 1930, women chastised by their rector for selling tickets on a quilt organized for their next meeting "a very nice hot supper of pork and cabbage" to celebrate two members' birthdays.[63] In May 1957, Long Pond women held a turkey supper to honour six members receiving their forty-year CEWA pins.[64] By the 1960s, when association women no longer organized and hosted community times at Christmas, some CEWA branches held their own celebrations. With "a turkey and cook[ed] vegetables" plus "exchange of gifts," these parties reflected growing Christmas consumerism, although some communal aspects persisted.[65] In 1965, for example, Long Pond women agreed to buy the turkey "out of our tea money," with "each Sister to bring along vegetables ... salt beef [or] pies." In addition, "all Sisters" were to provide "a gift at a cost of $1.00 for the Christmas tree."[66]

For CEWA women, teas were not always about making and displaying home-baked goods. Even the food provided for a community social could be store bought, especially in the 1940s and 1950s. This was particularly true for bread.[67] Home-made bread was a point of pride for some Newfoundland women, both for the way it demonstrated self-sufficiency and for its alleged superiority to commercially produced loaves.[68] However, for women of Conception Bay, publicly displaying bread-making skill was not part of church fundraising, and store-bought food appeared regularly at weekly meetings after the Second World War. On 23 December 1947 at Seal Cove, "a cup of tea and some biscuits were passed along to the sisters." At Long Pond, women enjoyed "tea and cakes" at a March 1945 meeting, with ready-made treats becoming more common in the 1950s.[69] Yet as local church women embraced new consumer goods and convenience foods, the expectation of commitment to domesticity, especially in preparing and serving meals, increased among Anglican Church leaders.

Food and Church Fundraising

Tea meetings and socials were the major form of church fundraising for the activist Anglican women of Conception Bay. This work included preparing and serving food, setting up tables, clearing and washing dishes, and recruiting entertainment. While some scholars conclude that the fellowship associated with organizing and running church socials made it worthwhile to women who were "used to hard work in their homes," and that "putting on church suppers was a practical way for the Marthas to feel that they were serving their Lord and their church," others recognize that women found church suppers exhausting and offered them out of financial necessity, not choice.[70] In Conception Bay, Anglican women's food service demonstrated fellowship and devotional service, but also rivalry with other CEWA branches and a desire to publicly display female domestic skills, something they were less interested in exhibiting within the walls of association rooms. Selina (Dawe) Porter described how women went "all out" to supply foods for church-sponsored garden parties and soup suppers. They prepared boilers of soup at home, usually "rice soup with salt meat" (considered economical), and brought them to the lodge, hall, or school where the event was being held.[71] These meals gave women opportunity to display culinary skills, with Selina noting that there was often competition "to get a bowl of so-and-so's soup 'cause she could make the best."[72] This competition suggested that diners helped themselves to food, buffet style, rather than sitting at tables and being served. Eliza (Delaney) Taylor of Foxtrap (born 1928) described the cookies, cakes, and tea offered at Christmas dances, noting that women sometimes served "pea soup with dumplings, oxtail soup, [and] vegetable soup with rice" as well.[73]

Edna (Roberts) Haines remembered the work for the annual St Peter's garden party. She described women bringing their own dishes and silverware from home to set the tables, and noted that "the Queen of England could sit to it" when they were done. They spent days baking and cooking in preparation for the event. Edna described how each CEWA branch and the societies (such as the Loyal Orange Association or Society for United Fisherman) would "have their own table," with which each competed.[74] The amount of money they raised depended on how many customers opted to eat at a particular table, and Edna recalled having to keep an eye out for people trying to move "lovely cakes," especially, from one table to another. She described women serving food and steadily washing dishes at the garden party, using water men brought from nearby Lawrence Pond that was heated on a fire lit in the church yard for that purpose. While her mother labored with the women, she noted of her father, a church warden and "well up" in the Orange Lodge, "he was in the beer tent always." Seal Cove CEWA women were busy before, and during, this event, traditionally held on Regatta Day.[75] On 27 July 1964, they held a special meeting to "wash the dishes and pack them away to be taken to Upper Gullies for use at the Garden Party." In addition, "all sisters were asked to bring along Cakes, Cookies and Salads."

At Foxtrap and Long Pond, food service at the St George's day celebration was organized like the Upper Gullies Garden Party, with community-based CEWA branches competing for customers based on culinary skill and "the nicest table." As Myra (Porter) Rideout described: "St George's Day … you would go out to your supper … Foxtrap had their table, Long Pond had theirs. Greeleytown, small as they were, they had theirs. Kelligrews had theirs. So when you went in that was a big thing … you looked at each table, well now, this is what you liked so that was the table you sat to. Everyone was in competition, so you would get the most money." As was the case in Upper Gullies, moving food "from one table to the other" was prohibited. According to Myra, community loyalty was not important ("You didn't think of that when you were thinking about your belly") but family loyalty was: "Some probably didn't know [about the different tables], weren't in the Association … Only the ones in the ACW knew, or if you had children – now you go over there and sit to that table because that's mom's table." She also described some association women "encouraging" people to sit at their branch's table by campaigning at the entrance doors.

The Upper Gullies garden party and the Foxtrap St George's Day celebration were church-sponsored events, organized by clergy and male laity with women expected to take a supportive, "helpmeet" role. In contrast, the CEWA-initiated and -led soup supper, tea, and dance can be considered a point of women's resistance to patriarchal church structures. Church socials organized by women could serve as "a subtle challenge to ministerial control" in that they brought "secular" activities within the "sacred" sphere of church life.[76] In Anglican Conception Bay, women's challenge to clerical authority was often not at all subtle, as they organized socials featuring drinking, dancing, gambling, and card playing in direct conflict with the ideals of Christian morality promoted by ordained clergy. At Seal Cove, two primary CEWA fund-raising events were the Christmas tea and sale and the Easter tea and sale. While called a "tea and sale," bringing to mind quiet afternoons with linens, china, and middle-class women in hats and gloves, these teas were often rowdy community events, traditionally known as "times" in Newfoundland, which sometimes featured a concert but always (up until the late 1940s) included a dance.[77] CEWA women hired and paid fiddlers for their socials, which were enjoyed by association members as well as by patrons.[78] When asked about her CEWA memories, Eileen Morgan described "getting ready for a time. Soup supper and a dance and leffin' her go ... Take the pot belly stove out of the way and get the dance goin'. Yummies on the table, soup. That is where we made a lot of money for our church." These were similar to community dances held in Northeastern Ontario, where a "country dance" featured a single fiddle player and town events featured a local dance band or "orchestra."[79]

Women questioned about religious practices around food described foods prepared for consumption at times of Christian festival and feasting, especially Christmas. Edna (Roberts) Haines described making cookies and "dark cake and light cake" for Christmas.[80] Selina (Dawe) Porter described how "a day or two before Christmas," women would "bak[e] bread, lots of sweet bread, cakes and buns and stuff like that." Turkey was considered a "town" tradition, and local families would "try to have something extra, lamb or meat or fresh pork" instead.[81] Eliza (Delaney) Taylor likewise recalled no turkey dinner, but preparing extra "sweet" foods, including special desserts, such as stewed dried prunes or apples with custard, caramel pudding (similar to the toffee pudding of English tradition), cake, syrup, and homemade molasses and peppermint candies.[82]

Women's domestic practice of baking richer, sweeter goods to mark Christmas festivities extended into the socials they organized as church fundraisers. Hugh Eason of Long Pond (born 1913) described how women would lay "cakes, biscuits, jelly and stuff like that" on tables for Christmas dances, with "all hands sitting to the table, one big table, just the same as up there," pointing to a print of *The Last Supper* hanging in his living room.[83] Food was placed on tables ahead of time and covered up, Hugh recalled, with supper offered about half way through the dance, which often went on until daylight. All ages attended, and while men drank and smoked, women did not.[84] Selina likewise noted that women did not drink at dances, although they were responsible for making the wine, if not the homebrew, served.[85] Hugh described fights at dances ("of course the Orangemen would come and drive you out" when that happened) and how there was always a game of cards being played on the side by those who did not want to dance but enjoyed the festive atmosphere and music. While most community residents attended these events, Hugh noted how "high status people" would not, as they were "too rough for them."[86] Mollie (Nugent) Penney described Christmas times at the Orange or Society of United Fisherman halls as "dance all night and come home daylight" affairs, noting typical food was "cold meat and cold plate" rather than the soup offered at most dances.[87] Important for the workload of women who provided food service, at most Conception Bay times people helped themselves. In contrast to the midnight supper Hugh described, Selina (Dawe) Porter and Heber Peach recalled times as "supper first, dance after."[88] Either way, since most work was completed in advance, women were free to socialize rather than serving or being invisible in the kitchen throughout.

Easter was another time of Christian festival when women activists organized community socials for the financial benefit of the church and the entertainment of themselves and their neighbours. In 1934, Seal Cove CEWA members held their Easter tea in the Orange Hall at Upper Gullies, and noted "the floor of the schoolroom was too bad for the young people to dance on." The extent of community celebrations that year can be seen in the women's comment that "there was so many entertainments for [Easter] week we would have to postpone ours."[89] Seal Cove women were unwilling to sacrifice the dance and, despite delay, the social at Upper Gullies proved a financial success and the women made almost thirty dollars in profit compared to the less than ten dollars made at the Christmas time.[90]

Anglican women's fundraising efforts sometimes brought them into direct conflict with local clergy. The 1930 soup supper and quilt party affair, in which rector the Reverend Henry Whitehouse chastised Seal Cove CEWA women after they sold tickets on a quilt they made communally, resulted in a brief abstention from ticket sales, but by the 1940s this method of fundraising was back in regular use, both in meetings (where women sold tickets among themselves on small items such as tea towels) and at community socials.[91] By 1951, the Seal Cove CEWA also fundraised with card games where players competed for prizes.[92] These card games, sometimes held in a series, replaced the community dance, which had declined in popularity. Like dances, games of 120s (nicknamed "growl") could turn rowdy, with Reginald and Marjorie Morgan recalling tension over misplayed hands, "cross plays," and people leaving "in a huff" after losing a game or "going in the hole." Like the times of previous decades, card game nights featured a cup of tea or soup, with a January 1965 minute book entry noting how "eight women volunteered to prepare food for our next card game."[93] Despite the "gambling" it involved, competitive card-playing was never singled out for clerical sanction in the same way bingo or ticket sales were.

The Foxtrap CEWA account book for the years 1938 through 1967 demonstrates the types of fundraising events members favoured, as well as events that proved to be most financially successful. For the most part, through the 1940s Anglican women of Foxtrap organized socials identified as "Card Party," "Supper, Tea and Dance," "Tea, Dance and Sale," "Tea, Dance and Bingo," or "Supper, Dance, and Bingo." After 1950, the CEWA dance largely disappeared, replaced with "Tea and Sale" or "Tea and Goods." Fundraising with teas and soup suppers remained important in the 1950s, but by 1959 and through the 1960s there were new food-centred events: "Turkey Supper," "Card Game and Bean Supper," and "Turkey Dinner." While the card party remained a headline event after 1950, bingo did not. For the most part, bingo became a way to fundraise during weekly meetings, a practice the women continued even when parish clergy condemned it. In May 1961, the Foxtrap CEWA received a surprise visit, which branch secretary Della Jones described: "[The] meeting then closed with prayers, after which bingo was played. Just as the game was started Rev and Mrs Genge arrived." Della recorded how Genge "addressed us" on a variety of topics, including an update on new furniture ordered for All Saints Church and an inquiry into how much they were willing to pay towards it. He requested that they serve "tea, sandwiches and cookies" at an upcoming parish meeting, and then outlined "his view concerning bingo, [that it] is alright as an entertainment but not as raising funds." After this, the Genges left, but "returned later, when tea was being served." Della ended her description of the evening's events with words that captured Foxtrap women's resistance to clerical authority: "About ten games of bingo played. Realized from this $17.50."[94]

CEWA: Catering and the Age of Turkey Teas

Whether preparing and serving meals for large gatherings or assembling hundreds of take-out turkey teas, fundraising efforts centred on large-scale food production engaged domestic skills in a more "respectable" way than did CEWA-led events of the 1920s and 1930s. By replacing times, catering reimagined women's place within the church and community.

Organized by CEWA members, soup suppers were relatively simple meals that left women time to dance and play cards. But catering focused on food preparation and presentation. Rather than being full participants in social functions, church women became staff: cooks and dishwashers invisible in the kitchen and waiters run off their feet to provide a pleasant social experience for guests at tables that they had arranged and set with their own cutlery in local banquet halls or school gymnasiums.

The degree to which women accepted this new fundraising method reflects the degree to which they internalized gender expectations of the 1950s and 1960s, as well as the increased financial demands they faced. In January 1960, Mark Genge informed Foxtrap CEWA that he expected help paying for $700 worth of Sunday school equipment and $300 in church vestments that he had ordered. He also "hoped the CEWA would consider buying a carpet to go inside the High Altar Rail." Along with extra financial responsibilities came additional reporting requirements, including a demand that association books be "properly audited."[95] In February 1961, the rector presented the four CEWA branches with a $1,300 bill for choir stalls "expected to be paid by the spring."[96] In 1962, Seal Cove spent over $330 putting electric light fixtures in St Peter's Church; in 1963 Kelligrews put $200 towards reredos to adorn the back of the altar at All Saints.[97] In October 1967, Long Pond women were "notified ... that $1300.00 would complete the church floor" and that the rector "would like for the CEWA to raise money to finish it."[98]

Expecting women in church-based voluntary associations to dedicate most of their time and energy to fundraising for institutional needs was a middle-class phenomenon common in the urban Anglican parishes of St John's.[99] It was also a long-standing expectation that the Anglican Church of Canada had of women's associations.[100] In Conception Bay, CEWA women contributed money towards church and school expenses, yet fundraising was only a small part of a larger whole centred on worship, fellowship, and mutual aid. Supporting each other, whether emotionally, spiritually, or financially, was just as important as meeting financial obligations imposed by male church leaders. Starting in the 1960s, however, as their rural community transitioned to a modern, wage-based economy complete with consumer goods and male breadwinners, Anglican women of Conception Bay were faced with an old, yet new to them, vision of Christian womanhood: domesticated helpmeet.

Figure 10.1 Members of the Upper Gullies branch of the Anglican Church Women's Association (formerly CEWA). When this picture was taken in 1963, activist women in the study area were starting to face increased financial demands from institutional Anglican leadership, as well as middle-class gender and domestic expectations, as part of a general effort to "improve" and "modernize" the Newfoundland church.

Gendered expectations that association women should cater to church functions and community events began to increase after the Second World War. On 16 April 1947 at Long Pond, branch president Annie Jefford informed the sisters that, "as it is in aid of the church," they were "expected ... [to] serve teas" for the Orangemen on St George's Day, although in previous years the CEWA had donated items rather than labour to this event. In December 1950, president Lilla Greenslade informed her branch that they were "to help provide tea for the visiting choir after service in Foxtrap School, as asked so by the Rector."[101] The notion of activist Anglican women as food service providers for public events grew among other community volunteer groups, although largely those with ties to the local Anglican churches. In the fall of 1955, for example, Long Pond CEWA received letters from both the Agricultural Fair committee and the Regional High School committee asking the members to provide and serve food at upcoming events.[102]

A request from their new rector in February 1960 launched Long Pond CEWA's first discussion of "having Turkey Teas" as a fundraiser. For the most part, members were not keen, and branch secretary Alma French noted that "the idea was given up" and the women decided instead to hold a Valentine party, with "invitations to Seal Cove, Upper Gullies, Kelligrews and Foxtrap branches inviting all Sisters to attend."[103] While women of Long Pond branch "were to provide the eats" for this social, they clearly preferred the idea of a fun get-together with their CEWA sisters to the work of preparing and assembling cold-plate suppers for community delivery. Yet in October of that year, under pressure from church leadership, they finally agreed to give this new fundraising method a try and accepted the enormous task of producing 300 take-out turkey teas. Minute book entries revealed the level of work and amount of donated food required: 150 pounds of turkey ordered, ten women to cook it at home; all members "to bring one package of tomatoes and one head of lettuce" as well as "cookies, rolls, salads." Turkey and tomatoes had to be sliced, lettuce cleaned, and each meal assembled on a paper plate, covered with another, and tied into a plastic bag. "All sisters," branch president Irene Tilley requested, were to "try to come along to help."[104] The result was association income higher than any the women had seen before. A 21 January 1959 social was deemed "a great success" when "from this party we added [$27.50] to our funds." The turkey teas of November 1960 made, as Alma noted, a "very satisfying" profit of $256.99.[105]

At Seal Cove, the story was similar, and the first takeout turkey tea appeared in the CEWA account book in 1960. Again, the income from these meals was remarkable. In October 1962, Seal Cove branch made over $400 on a turkey supper for which women not only provided the "salads and cookies" but also "took part in going around and selling" in advance.[106] The amount of work involved meant that Seal Cove members did not plan another take-out dinner until 1965, although in February 1964 they did "help" with a turkey dinner "put off in the Orange Hall" in Upper Gullies.[107] While scholars have not explored the preparation and service of these meals in terms of Newfoundland women's work or spirituality, they have discussed how community suppers changed after confederation with Canada. Traditionally a hot supper using local meats and vegetables, in the 1950s a common meal was more likely to be cold plates made with store-bought ingredients such as processed meats, bottled salad dressing, lettuce, and tomatoes. Dishes prepared for cold plates on the Northern Peninsula were "home-made but rarely of home-grown vegetables."[108] In Conception Bay, while this might have applied to lettuce and tomato, local potato and cabbage was most likely used in salads and coleslaw.

Along with producing take-out teas, by the mid-1960s church women were fundraising with catered turkey dinners to community events. On 13 January 1965, Kelligrews CEWA members discussed this type of work for the first time. Branch secretary Ida Tilley wrote:

> The Worthy President [Hazel Morgan] informed the class of a turkey supper we were asked to serve to the Kelligrews Kiwanis on Monday, January 18th and said they would pay us $1.25 per plate. As all sisters present agreed to this it was decided to buy 60 lbs of turkey, 12 head of lettuce, 12 packages of tomatoes and one bottle of pickles. Turkeys to be baked by Worthy President Sister Hazel Morgan, Sister Susan Richards and Sister Emmie Haines.[109]

When asked by the Queen Elizabeth Regional High School student council "to cater at their banquet" in June 1966, the women readily agreed, and branch secretary Barbara Butler noted that "it was thought by all that this would be a sure way of making some money."[110]

Long Pond was the last CEWA branch to accept this new approach to parish fundraising, and finally agreed to "cater to the Grade 11 Students" at their 1967 graduation banquet. This was a cold turkey supper, and the women charged "$1.25 with fruit" per plate, or "$1.00 without."[111] It is worth noting that most Conception Bay CEWA branches' first catering experience was the local high school graduation, which shows the influence of Newfoundland's denominational educational system and the ties it built between church and school, as well as the impact of domestic and family ties, since most of the graduates would have been CEWA members' children or grandchildren. The improved education system that followed confederation with Canada was considered a sign of progress among local women and held the promise of a brighter economic future for the next generation. It was a benefit of the "new" Newfoundland with which few would argue. Encouraging and celebrating the educational accomplishments of local young people was worth the aching feet that came with catering contracts and is another example of the caring impulse that motivated women's Christian activism.

Food as Religious Experience and Expression

For CEWA women, food service was largely about fundraising, and they distinguished serving tea at meetings from catering meals to outside groups. This was captured by Myra (Porter) Rideout, who described 1960s meetings: "You had your prayers and when they would be having general business you would be doing the crocheting, you know. You have your cup of tea and your bit of fun, laugh and joke and tidy away … To make money, we used to cater. Take all the dishes and go to Topsail … [a] full-time job." For Myra, the amount of labour and the financial focus of catering made it distinct from other CEWA activities. Eileen Morgan likewise identified the connection between food service and fundraising: "We catered for years for the church. Making a bit of money. I think we hit every place from [Seal Cove] to Topsail except the Canadian Legion – they had their own caterers. But every other place on this shore and we did it over and over and over. The Kiwanis and the Lions Club and weddings and whatever was going on." Eileen remembered a time when the "fifteen of us … were asked by a member of the Kiwanis to get ready a dinner for 300 people, which was a lot … The man in charge got a bunch of Girl Guides to run up to the tables and we put her off without a hitch." Young girls as well as women, it seemed, were considered well-suited to food service. This presumption, coupled with notions of the connections between domestic work and female religious practice, informed Genge's organization of a regular monthly breakfast at the rectory for altar boys and male servers in 1963. In an address to the newly formed All Saints Altar Guild, the rector described how "a speaker is usually present [for the meal] and the theme of the addresses is 'What it means to be a Christian' in his profession. Girls from the High School serve the breakfast. It is hoped they will be thus encouraged to become interested in church work."[112] Christian men pursuing careers while women did domestic work in service to them, both at home and in the church, had become the official Anglican model of gender and family relations.

While CEWA activists primarily associated food production and service with fundraising, the work could inspire other women to get involved with church life, especially daughters who observed their mothers cooking and baking "for the church" within the domestic setting. When a woman performed what was otherwise routine household labour for a Christian purpose, she indicated to other members of the household the importance of religion in her own life and in the life of the community. This was particularly communicated when mothers prepared especially nice foods in the family home and forbid family members to consume them. Cynthia (Scott) Dawe recalled: "When I was growing up I could always see my mother involved in the church and then the ACW and baking and cooking and all that and I think that influenced my growing up and what I wanted to do. That was what I saw. Cookies and cakes coming out of the house and you don't eat that that is for the church. I pretty much seen a lot of that." Edna (Rideout) Warford had similar memories of her mother Pearl (Scott) Rideout, who was well respected in the Long Pond branch for her textile work yet whose daughter primarily recalled her church work in terms of baked goods.

Even Anglican women who were not active in association life would bring their household food production skills into service for the church. Pat (Morgan) Woolgar recalled how her mother Marion (Tilley) Morgan "didn't go to any of the meetings, she was something like me. I don't go either," but: "We have always been involved in the food part of it … if there is a salad or turkey or whatever anybody wanted at the church, just call and we were always there eager and happy to do it … I always provided food and cooked pots for dinner and cooked hams and things like that when they were doing cold plates. My mom did that before me too." Likewise, Marge (Saunders) Dawe described how she would help with food for the annual garden party at Upper Gullies but was not active in church life beyond that. Shared female kitchen skills could provide a bridge to Anglican Church involvement, even for women from different religious traditions. Doris (Nagle) Bishop described how dish washing helped her fit into the local women's community despite her Roman Catholic background: "I remember when I came up here first … I wasn't … part of it at the time … whatever they were doing, a social or something, and I used to often laugh and say to myself, well if I can't do anything else I can wash dishes. Where I was from outside sort of thing. That is how I started [in the CEWA], washing dishes."

Conclusion

In mid-1900s Conception Bay, women were engaged in outdoor work as much as indoor work as a result of their participation in the family economy. Time was spent in the kitchen, but women did not embrace domestic food production in the way that middle-class ideology might have expected of them. Day to day, food was treated as nourishment for working families rather than as a means for women to display their culinary accomplishments and social status. Sundays and festivals such as Christmas were the exceptions, as women expressed their religious beliefs and observed religious festivals through the production of special foods, especially sweet baked goods. For CEWA women, the connection between food production and Christian festival translated into hosting Christmas and Easter times as church fundraisers in the decades before 1950. Combining feasting, dancing, drinking, and card playing, times could be rowdy events in contrast to middle-class ideals of Christian morality promoted by Anglican clergy. Unlike church women in other jurisdictions, CEWA members did not treat their weekly teas as a time to display bourgeois notions of women's daintiness and domesticity. Instead, they used them to raise funds, to honour and support each other, and to satisfy appetites whetted by manual labour.

The connections between food and women's religious practice as expressed through involvement in church-based organizations began to change in the 1950s, as Newfoundland, like the rest of Atlantic Canada, began to change socially and economically. Increased access to consumer goods altered the kinds of meals women prepared for church fundraising, while a wage-based economy that presumed male breadwinners and female homemakers influenced how church and community leaders, including women, understood women's social and religious roles. Church leaders' increasing demand for financial contributions, coupled with CEWA members' growing awareness of domestic gender expectations, meant that women's place within the local Anglican community became defined by their ability to offer domestic cooking and cleaning skills on a large scale to the benefit of the institutional church.

Consistent with middle-class constructions of women as pious mothers and homemakers, church cookbooks often included prayers or religious poetry to link family food preparation with Christian instruction.[113] Yet such inclusions were not part of the parish of Foxtrap and Hopewell's *Home Cooking Secrets of Kelligrews.* Instead, this cookbook reflects what had become the connection between food and Christian service for activist Anglican women of Conception Bay by the early 1970s: back pages filled with instructions for "Supper Quantity Cooking," including "Ham Supper for 225," "Turkey Dinner for 250," and "Baked Beans for 100." While domestic religious practices associated with food, such as blessing bread, eating salt fish on Good Friday, cooking Sunday dinner, or baking light and dark fruitcakes at Christmas, continued in many families after 1960, increasingly for Anglican women food production was linked to religion primarily through the official church and its financial needs, as well as the making and sharing of tea and food with each other, rather than through taking responsibility for bringing "Christ into the kitchen" of the family home.

CONCLUSION

"Christianity Conceived": Women's Theological Cultures of Anglican Conception Bay

Reflecting on the connections between work and religion for the women of Conception Bay, my thoughts return to the Lodge kitchen at Upper Gullies over forty years ago. Women of what had become the ACWA were busy preparing a cold plate supper, their best cakes and pies waiting on long tables for the eager appetites of garden party goers from the St Peter's church community. Although a child, I knew most of the faces, and many of the names and voices, of the women who worked together on that long-ago summer day. Their voices told me stories. As I participated in their church work, on that day and others, I began to realize that their labour told a story, too: it had meaning that transcended its physical tasks. Many years later, sitting together and engaged in the conversations which informed this book, I came to realize how much these women want their stories told. They want to share their experiences and ideas to help others understand what it meant to be a Christian woman within a particular tradition at a particular place and time. They want their voices to matter; they want their stories to be remembered.

Their stories, whether in interviews with the living or in words written by those long dead, together tell how rural women could practise Christianity through their labour. Work "for the church," whether cooking, cleaning, knitting, sewing, or caring for others, was imbued with spiritual and theological significance. This significance extended to daily work completed in the household, where Christian belief and practice informed lived religious practices surrounding childbirth, mortuary services, food preparation, and home medicine. In an era when

Anglican women, especially rural Anglican women, had little access to formal church leadership roles, work was a primary way for them to express their understanding of, and maintain a relationship with, God. The ties between labour and faithfulness were profound: work not only expressed belief, but shaped belief. Women's household work in the family economy was a lens through which they filtered, reflected, and remade Christianity. In doing so, they created a theological culture characterized by a feminist consciousness of resistance to patriarchal authority, the practice of mutuality, and the negotiation of gender divisions in their daily lives.[1] While they identified as Anglicans, the lived Christian practices of Conception Bay women demonstrate that they did not passively accept clerical authority or the teachings, doctrines, and dogma of their church.

In their understanding of what it meant to be Christian, the women of mid-1900s Conception Bay avoided the gendered stereotypes prescribed by church leaders. The lived religion of Anglican households was not characterized by the naturally pious mother responsible for the spiritual life of her family, especially the religious upbringing of children; neither did it uniformly display a tradition of patriarchal piety in which earthly male authority was informed, and strengthened, by virtue of its association with the authority of "God the Father." The dynamics of the family economy, in which women's labour was as valuable as men's to household survival, informed instead relationships of shared spiritual authority. Mothers and fathers shared responsibility for family religious life, and both participated in (and led) household rituals and engaged in personal devotional practices such as private prayer and hymn singing. Family observation of Sunday and other holy days centred on food practices and rest from household work, and lived rituals such as men taking children to church or cooking the special Sunday dinner show an effort to protect the Sabbath for women as well as for men.

In the 1950s and 1960s, as material prosperity increased, Sabbath observance in many families extended to wearing special Sunday clothes and taking a Sunday drive, usually to buy ice cream. Restrictions on children's Sunday play decreased as these material signs of observance increased, yet men continued to cook Sunday dinner or take children to church. Enforced as well as practised by both parents, self-denial during Lent included no games (especially not cards). Certain foods, such as sugar, were commonly given up for the season, while holy days were marked with boiled salt fish, bread without butter, and dumplings with molasses.

Women's spiritual choices informed family stability. In Conception Bay, this became apparent as mixed marriages or acts of conversion brought about household disruption or restoration. Patterns of religious experimentation within Anglican households suggest that where women went religiously, men and children followed. For some women, the need for family stability meant religious change was about preserving earthly relationships rather than seeking personal spiritual fulfillment. Women could act with intolerance towards female relations when conversion or religious difference disrupted households and communities. Yet Conception Bay Anglicans accepted women's public ministry within local Salvationist and Pentecostal congregations, which suggests a theological culture tolerant of female religious authority and open to resistance against patriarchal church structures. The expression of religious intolerance for Pentecostals in gendered terms, including sexualized gossip and cautionary tales about compromised reproductive capacity, shows, when combined with efforts to control conversions within households, a local population who felt women's primary responsibility should be to their families (and the reproduction thereof) rather than to their personal spirituality.

Women's work around childbirth included beliefs and practices which located sacred presence in female bodies. Midwives' work brought them special spiritual status, with other women showing appreciation for their care in religious, emotional, and financial terms. At a time of high infant mortality, practising midwifery could shape a woman's spiritual life. Church registers indicate midwives' concern for the souls of children they delivered and, with the compliance of local clergy, most made sure sickly and even stillborn infants were baptized. Popular practices around baptism sometimes conflicted with official Anglican views, as did local beliefs associated with churching, considered a ceremony of thanksgiving by the official church. Conception Bay women described how unchurched women were prohibited from preparing food, going outside, or taking communion, indicating popular belief that a woman's purity was compromised by pregnancy and childbirth. Female kin enforced such prohibitions, and in Newfoundland churching remained popular through the twentieth century despite its decline in many other jurisdictions. Female-enforced limitations on a new mother getting her hands wet or going outdoors indicate a women's community mindful of her need for rest and recovery after delivery. It shows a theological culture where religion became a means to protect each other from the most physically demanding aspects of household labour when necessary, including laundry, bread making, and agricultural work.

As they did for times of childbirth, Conception Bay Anglicans developed ceremonies and customs which coexisted alongside formal Christian ritual for times of death and grieving. Women's work included arranging domestic spaces to display the casket and restoring order after the wake. While in many jurisdictions women traditionally prepared and laid out the bodies of deceased persons, in Conception Bay men could conduct this spiritually charged ritual as well. Women participated in public death and burial rituals surrounding wakes, funeral processions, and church services. In the context of CEWA participation, women organized and led commemoration ceremonies for their deceased sisters, which illustrates the place of procession, prayer, and hymn singing in their lived religiosity. Such ceremonies show Anglican women acting publicly as spiritual leaders, capable of conducting services of worship although then-barred from ordination.

The female theological culture of Conception Bay included a more orthodox understanding of eternal life among ordinary female believers than male clergy assumed. Activist Anglican women conceived of heaven primarily as reunion of the soul individually with the divine, and while they acknowledged the emotional aspects of loss, they largely rejected a domesticated heaven in which families (and the gendered roles they contained) were preserved for all eternity. CEWA women tended to envision a community-based rather than family-based hereafter, reflecting rural mutuality and a gendered response to eternity also seen among female hymnists.

Cemetery landscape within the parish, especially similarity in the language and type of headstones raised by families for men and women, suggests a community with a less strict patriarchal understanding of gender relations within families, as well as a place where most households were of equal social standing economically. Conception Bay Anglicans expressed a sense of death as release from the cares and worries of earthly life, with most epitaphs celebrating escape from earthly labour selected by families in remembrance of women. This reflects the diversity and quantity of women's household work in rural settings, as well as the connection between work and women's identity. Linked to women's work as caregivers, especially to the terminally ill, headstone epitaphs celebrating the end of earthly suffering were particularly associated with men and were likely selected by the widows who had cared for them during times of sickness. CEWA women called each other "sister" and cared for each other like family. While finding it easier to accept the deaths of older members as "God's will," they responded to the deaths of younger members with the same mix of sorrow and hope that characterized the theology of bereaved mothers.

A culture of shared spiritual authority within households informed women's resistance to patriarchal, clerical authority in church life, especially when working together in the CEWA's sisterhood. Many Anglican women rejected authoritarian notions of God, preferring conceptions of the Almighty (including the figure of Jesus) that included an ethic of care and mercy, and a sense of a personal relationship between humanity and the divine. Relationships with religious role models, both female and male, were built on demonstrated personal piety and Christian service rather than on gender, authority, or kinship. Women likewise preferred pastoral images, such as Jesus as Good Shepherd, in the religious art they displayed in their homes, and rejected muscular Christian, authoritative images and those which emphasized social hierarchies. Rejection of such masculine imagery can be understood as resistance to male authority. Beyond the home and within local CEWA branches, much of this resistance centred on fundraising efforts, especially activist women's use of methods deemed immoral by middle-class male clergy.

Women's work in caring for the sick was informed by their Christian beliefs and practices. Female commitment to the emotional and spiritual aspects of caregiving stood in contrast to emerging scientific, male medical authority. While a "culture of suffering" centred on belief that pain and hardship redeemed those Christians (especially women) who bore it without complaint was part of official Anglican discourse, the female theological culture of Conception Bay preferred peaceful deaths, believed to indicate God's mercy and divine concern for the well-being of all believers. For female caregivers, facilitating a good death included relieving suffering and providing access to last rites. Women's theological culture included translating belief in God's mercy to showing mercy to others, which they practised in the domestic setting as well as in the context of a church-based voluntary association. CEWA members supported each other in times of hardship and considered their efforts to relieve suffering as good work and a lived demonstration of Christian belief. Women's use of prayer and the cross in vernacular healing practices indicated a Christianity informed by a personal relationship with the divine: that one could seek the ear of God on behalf of others and know that God would respond. But while some CEWA women followed this theology, others demonstrated passive reliance on providential mercy.

The activities of the Seal Cove CEWA indicate integration of Christian benevolence and rural mutuality. Members paid sick benefits and engaged in communal visitation to their sick or elderly sisters that exceeded prescribed association expectations. They fed each other through the financial hardships of the 1930s and believed in a cooperative and shared-risk approach to fundraising, best illustrated in their ticket sales on quilts. This activity, condemned by the church, serves as an example of Seal Cove women's resistance to male clerical authority. In Long Pond, CEWA women demonstrated benevolent mutuality through cooperative textile production for the benefit of other members, which they understood to be a way to meet their Christian duty to "do unto others" while engaging in a women-specific path to redemption. While they show variety in female theological cultures and how these cultures can be shaped by very particular social settings, the activities of Seal Cove and Long Pond CEWA women demonstrate an impulse to care for "each other" rather than "the other" and the centrality of a women's community in religious practice.

Textile production by CEWA members was a sensory act of religious devotion. The items they produced, such as embroidered pillowslips, table cloths, and aprons, were sacred by virtue not of the product but of the process in which the women engaged. Participating in weekly Christian ritual, including prayers and scripture reading, informed an understanding that making these items, mostly to be used by their association sisters, was a Christian act, and not because of their use in church fundraising. Food and socials, not sewing and embroidery work, were the primary money-makers for CEWA branches. Handmade textiles had little monetary value. Like much of women's work textile production was devalued compared to the work of men, yet women's theological culture imbued it with spiritual meaning, including a means of building a personal sense of relationship with God. Along with work made in association, women of Conception Bay produced other textiles with religious connotations. These included shrouds for the dead, christening gowns and shawls for baptisms, and mats hooked "in place of cards" as part of Lenten observance.

The example of the Anglican south side of Conception Bay presents an alternative vision of the importance of women's work: that it was valuable not only economically and socially, but also spiritually and emotionally. Religious belief informed women's understanding of the value of their labour, and elevated mundane tasks such as food preparation, textile production, and caring for others into devotional acts. Women found the "extraordinary in the ordinary" as they contributed to the household economy and served church and community. This spiritual valuing of female labour, a central aspect of local women's theological culture, contrasted patriarchal worldviews which diminished women's work and especially domestic work.[2]

This culture began to change in the 1960s, as local women became more receptive to gender ideology and accepting of patriarchal authority as their economic power within households was displaced by wage-based, largely male, breadwinning. Middle-class notions of feminized religion and female domesticity, with their accompanying prescribed roles for women within churches and families, gained popularity in official Newfoundland Anglican discourse during the mid-twentieth century.[3] These prescriptions included notions of women as caretakers of morality, naturally pious, and inseparable from the social expectation of marriage and motherhood. The idea of separate spheres that informed these gender roles and expectations also suggested to women that they should be primarily interested in the domestic: homemaking, cooking, and caring for children.

Ideological prescriptions are not always lived by ordinary women, including church women who are sometimes popularly portrayed as most receptive to conservative hegemonic visions of home and family. Although food service was a regular part of CEWA fundraising, members rejected middle-class gender expectations around female domesticity. At mid-century, Conception Bay women prepared daily meals following a common and predictable pattern, with attention to thrift, local ingredients, and satisfying appetites – including their own. Conception Bay women's resistance to domesticity was apparent in 1965, when a rector's suggestion that the CEWA raise funds by producing a community cookbook was met with disdain. This had changed by the early 1970s, reflecting new social and economic circumstances as well as a more general cultural change in post-confederation Newfoundland.

While local women rejected domesticity, their theological culture was shaped by the domestic: the division of household labour and the negotiation of familial relationships. Shared female-male religious authority and acts of personal piety in families contributed to a female theological culture which was essentially feminist in character. Women may not have engaged in formal activism aimed at the recognition of their political and social rights, but their working and religious lives, so closely intertwined, nevertheless demonstrate a "feminist consciousness." Embrace of Christianity did not necessarily negate women's belief in their own social, economic, and political equality with men; religiosity and feminism did not always stand in binary opposition, even among rural Christians. For the Anglican women of mid-twentieth-century Conception Bay, Christian belief was not synonymous with passive acceptance of male authority or deference to patriarchal church structures. Neither did it manifest in a commitment to living the gendered stereotype of the "Christian woman," which can be seen as a largely middle-class construction of female faithfulness.

Visions of a "new" Newfoundland and Labrador informed post-1949 government policy and programming, which was largely focused on "modernizing" the province from a rural to an industrial social and economic way of life. Premier Joseph R. Smallwood's famous declaration of his intent to "drag" Newfoundland "kicking and screaming into the twentieth century" captures the post-confederation atmosphere of cultural "improvement" and industrial development.[4] The expansion of educational opportunities for Newfoundlanders was part of this mandate, including a new government-operated vocational school at Seal Cove offering three streams of home economics, a sign that the science of household management, with its middle-class expectations of female domesticity, had officially arrived in Conception Bay. At the same time, 1960s Anglican Church leaders worked to promote prescriptive notions of motherhood, especially ideas that women were the keepers of family piety and the parent primarily responsible for children's religious education.

Scholars have interpreted "feminized religion" and prescribed gender roles for women within church and family as stepping stones to feminist consciousness, which may have been true for middle- and upper-class women. Yet the example of Conception Bay shows that in some circumstances these concepts can negatively affect a culture of lived feminism for working and rural women. Middle-class Anglican women of St John's, many of them rector's wives, may have gained increased power and autonomy through creation of a women-led Diocesan Committee on Women's Work, but their vision of women's place within a modern Newfoundland church, a vision which included the CEWA's dissolution, undermined a sisterhood with clear feminist consciousness. The autonomy of activist women in the parish of Foxtrap and Hopewell, and their culture of resistance to clerical efforts to infringe on that autonomy – so pronounced through the 1930s, 1940s, and most of the 1950s – seemed to decline in the 1960s as local church leaders pushed for church buildings and vestments to please a middle-class aesthetic. Women's autonomy was challenged with clerical efforts to make local church administration more bureaucratic (including male oversight of all parish organizations and activities) and questioned by the diocese's new emphasis on youth ministries and family-oriented church life.

In the case of Anglican Conception Bay, promotion (and acceptance) of ideology that linked women, religion, motherhood, and home worked to undermine, rather than enhance, ordinary women's social status and autonomy: a status rooted in local communities' social and economic circumstances. As a rural family-based economy transitioned to a wage-based economy through the 1950s and 1960s, with attendant increased prosperity, growing consumerism, and suburbanization, Anglican women became increasingly deferential to clerical authority and likely to accept and internalize middle-class standards of domesticity. With the launch of Altar Guilds and pressure to finance the refurbishment of interiors at St Peter's and All Saints, the Anglican women of Conception Bay were presented with new roles as "church housekeepers" and "community caterers." Many women, seeing their place and power in the family economy slipping away, accepted this new vision of womanhood and began to construct a new theological culture.

The emergence of a wage-based economy led some women to find a new sense of identity within domestic ideology. They continued to resist some clerical authority, but were more willing to defer when becoming domestic (especially catering church suppers and putting out cold plates) significantly enhanced their ability to contribute financially to the well-being of the church. Scholars have demonstrated how women in other jurisdictions exercised informal power and autonomy in churches as a result of financial contributions within church-based voluntary associations. The case of the Conception Bay CEWA shows how women's need to seek financial empowerment within a church setting could be tied to the transition from a family- to a wage-based economy. As women experienced declining economic power and devaluing labour within households, they sought a renewed sense of the financial value of their work through church-based activism.

The story of lived religion among Anglican women in Conception Bay confirms theologian Teresa Berger's assertion that "wherever women's lives and liturgy touch each other, a distinct way of living the faith materializes."[5] Listening to the voices of women, and to the stories of their work in households and communities, reveals the gender-specific ways in which religious belief and practice could be made meaningful in a particular place and time.[6] Women found a sense of sacred presence and turned their thoughts to the nature of God and their relationship with the almighty in many places: kitchen table, church pew, garden, association meeting, cemetery, and birthing room. They found communion in daily tasks: sewing, knitting, cooking, caring for others, and putting houses in order. Women's work in mid-1900s Conception Bay was necessary for family survival; it was constant and, as Arch Morgan noted, "they worked harder than the men." This labour was mundane, yet women created something profound within it: a means by which to practise their Christianity and a lens through which to conceive what it meant to be a Christian woman.

A final story of women in association, told to me by a professional church worker once employed by the parish of Foxtrap, ends this account. I met with her to borrow a book and, as we chatted, she told me of one rector's efforts in the 1980s to make women of the various ACW branches (Long Pond, Foxtrap, Kelligrews) have a joint "sale of work" instead of separate ones. "He met with all of them," she related, "and told them how it was going to be. Then he found out that the crowd down in Long Pond was after holding back pillow slips. They had tablecloths and other goods kept in their trunk and planned to hold their own sale. He went straight down and asked them what did they think they were doing?" As I listened to her indignant voice, her conviction that the rector was right, I knew exactly what the women of Long Pond were doing: resisting authority.

The same impulse was expressed by women, most of them in their seventies, eighties, and nineties, who invited me into their homes to talk about what it meant to be a Christian woman in Conception Bay during the mid-twentieth century. This is not surprising for women whose history included leading the Battle of Foxtrap in 1880 and wrecking a Department of Highways truck in the 1930s. Despite changes in their church and communities and households, despite the increased acceptance of domestic ideology, and regardless of dissolution of the CEWA – or perhaps because of these factors – the theological culture of activist Anglican women still includes a need to assert autonomy in the face of authority. It is still informed by connections between religious practice and the work of women's hands. While more invisible in association records subject to review by clergy in a way CEWA records never were, this theological culture still resonates with sisterhood; it still pushes back at patriarchal efforts to control the nature, and the expression, of women's faithfulness.

Appendix

Informants, with Date and Place of Interview(s)

Informant's name	*Interview date*	*Interview location*	*Recorded?*
Doris (Nagle) Bishop	2 Sept. 2011	Long Pond, CBS	Yes
Cynthia (Scott) Dawe	15 Aug. 2011	Upper Gullies, CBS	Yes
Judy (Rideout) Dawe	28 Sept. 2011	Long Pond, CBS	Yes
Marge (Saunders) Dawe	21 Sept. 2011	Upper Gullies, CBS	No
Edna (Roberts) Haines	12 Sept. 2011	Kelligrews, CBS	No
Enid (Porter) Haines	23 Aug. 2011	Foxtrap, CBS	Yes
Reta (Morgan) Hill	29 Aug. 2011	Seal Cove, CBS	Yes
Joan (Petten) Jefford	10 Aug. 2011 12 Sept. 2011	Kelligrews, CBS Kelligrews, CBS	Yes Yes
Beulah (Porter) Morgan	1 Sept. 2011	Seal Cove, CBS	Yes
Eileen Morgan	9 Aug. 2011	Seal Cove, CBS	Yes
Joyce (Andrews) Morgan	20 Sept. 2011	Seal Cove, CBS	Yes
Marjorie (Bullen) Morgan	15 Aug. 2011	Seal Cove, CBS	Yes
Mary (Petten) Porter	23 Aug. 2011	Foxtrap, CBS	Yes
Mildred (Butler) Porter	6 Sept. 2011	Kelligrews, CBS	Yes
Myra (Porter) Rideout	6 Sept. 2011	Kelligrews, CBS	Yes
Prudence (Morgan) Rideout	28 Sept. 2011	Long Pond, CBS	Yes
Sandra (Taylor) Tilley	13 Oct. 2011	St John's	Yes
Edna (Rideout) Warford	17 Aug. 2011	Upper Gullies, CBS	Yes
Emma (Petten) Warford	8 Sept. 2011	Seal Cove, CBS	Yes
Violet Warford	19 Aug. 2011	Upper Gullies, CBS	Yes
Pat (Morgan) Woolgar	17 Aug. 2011	Kelligrews, CBS	Yes
Name Withheld by Request	19 Aug. 2011	Upper Gullies, CBS	Yes

Notes

Preface

1 Sue Morgan and Jacqueline deVries, eds., *Women, Gender and Religious Cultures in Britain, 1800–1940* (New York: Routledge, 2010), 24, 11–12.

2 Françoise Noël, *Family and Community Life in Northeastern Ontario: The Interwar Years* (Montreal: McGill-Queen's University Press, 2009), 12.

3 Frank A. Abbott, *The Body or the Soul? Religion and Culture in a Quebec Parish, 1736–1901* (Montreal: McGill-Queen's University Press, 2016), xx.

4 Calvin Hollett, *Beating against the Wind: Popular Opposition to Bishop Field and Tractarianism in Newfoundland and Labrador* (Montreal: McGill-Queen's University Press, 2016), 5.

5 The impact of mainland North American and European (especially British and Irish) articles in church publications on local theological cultures is an interesting area for further study.

6 Current members of what are now the St Peter's and All Saints Anglican Church Women graciously allowed me unrestricted access to these records.

7 This analysis was facilitated by summary data for Conception Bay South from the 1921, 1935, and 1945 Census of Newfoundland prepared by the Newfoundland and Labrador Statistics Agency as part of the Canadian Century Research Infrastructure project.

8 Susanna Morrill, "Women," in Philip Goff, ed., *The Blackwell Companion to Religion in America* (Malden, MA: Blackwell, 2010), 378. For discussion of oral history methodology, see Steven High, "Sharing Authority: An Introduction," *Journal of Canadian Studies* 43, 1 (2009): 13.

9 Exploration of challenges around use of oral history methodology, especially work on the history of memory, is a growing area of scholarship relevant to future work on twentieth-century lived religion.

10 This important facility preserves recorded interviews and other fieldwork completed by undergraduate students in Newfoundland since the 1960s and has proved invaluable in recovering the voices of long-dead Conception Bay residents.

11 Three of the women interviewed were relatives of mine: Marjorie (Bullen) Morgan, Eileen Morgan, and Reta (Morgan Hill). This represents 13.5 per cent of total informants. Only one interview accessed through the MUN Folklore and Language Archive was a relation: Arch Morgan of Seal Cove.

12 Diane Tye, *Baking as Biography: A Life Story in Recipes* (Montreal: McGill-Queen's University Press, 2010), 40–1.

13 Morrill, "Women," 376.

14 "Editors' Introduction," in Mona Gleason, Adele Perry, and Tamara Myers, eds., *Rethinking Canada: The Promise of Women's History*, 6th ed. (New York: Oxford University Press, 2011), 58. The lack of research in this area is reflected in the three-volume *Encyclopedia of Women and Religion in North America* in 2006, edited by Rosemary Radford Ruether and Rosemary Skinner Keller, which despite its title and some excellent contributions on the Canadian experience is overwhelmingly American in content. Exceptions to the largely middle-class focus include Marta Danylewycz, *Taking the Veil: An Alternative to Marriage, Motherhood, and Spinsterhood in Quebec, 1840–1920* (Toronto: McClelland & Stewart, 1987); and Heidi E. MacDonald, "The Sisters of St Martha and Prince Edward Island Social Institutions, 1916–1982" (PhD thesis, University of New Brunswick, 2000).

15 See Lynne Marks, "The Knights of Labor and the Salvation Army: Religion and Working-Class Culture in Ontario, 1882–90," *Labour/Le Travail* 28 (1991): 89–127; and Elizabeth Muir, *Petticoats in the Pulpit: The Story of Early Nineteenth Century Methodist Women Preachers in Upper Canada* (Toronto: Trinity House, 1991).

16 Examples include Nancy Christie, ed., *Households of Faith: Family, Gender, and Community in Canada, 1760–1969* (Montreal: McGill-Queen's University Press, 2001); Marlene Epp, *World Without Men: Mennonite Refugees of the Second World War* (Toronto: University of Toronto Press, 2000); and Marguerite Van Die, *Religion, Family and*

Community in Victorian Canada: The Colbys of Carrollcroft (Montreal: McGill-Queen's University Press, 2005). Willeen Keough, "The 'Old Hag' Revisits St Brigid: Irish Newfoundland Women and Spirituality on the Southern Avalon," in Gleason, Perry, and Myers, *Rethinking Canada*, 6th ed., 59.

17 Ann Braude, "Faith, Feminism, and History," in Catherine A. Brekus, ed., *The Religious History of American Women: Reimagining the Past* (Chapel Hill: University of North Carolina Press, 2007), 237.

18 Jacqueline deVries, "More than Paradoxes to Offer: Feminism, History and Religious Cultures," in Morgan and deVries, *Women, Gender and Religious Cultures*, 194.

19 One leading North American example is the Woman's Christian Temperance Union, whose members used the expectation that women were responsible for safeguarding the private sphere of home and family to justify women's involvement in a public crusade against alcohol use. Johnson, "Gender," in Goff, *Blackwell Companion to Religion in America*, 150.

20 Examples include Sharon Ann Cook, *"Through Sunshine and Shadow": The Woman's Christian Temperance Union, Evangelicalism and Reform in Ontario, 1874–1930* (Montreal: McGill-Queen's University Press, 1995); Gagan, *A Sensitive Independence*; and Muir, *Petticoats in the Pulpit*.

21 Definition of feminism is taken from Ruth M. Mann, "Invisibilizing Violence against Women," in Les Samuelson and Wayne Antony, eds., *Power and Resistance: Critical Thinking about Canadian Social Issues*, 5th ed. (Halifax: Fernwood, 2012), 65. Canadian studies of "feminist consciousness" and "grassroots feminism" among rural women include Mona Halpern, *And on That Farm He Had a Wife: Ontario Farm Women and Feminism, 1900–1970* (Montreal: McGill-Queen's University Press, 2001), especially 4–7, 12–16; Gail Cuthbert Brandt and Naomi Black, "'Il en faut un peu': Farm Women and Feminism in Quebec and France since 1945," *Journal of the Canadian Historical Association* 1 (1990): 73–96; and Veronica Strong-Boag, "Pulling in Double Harness or Hauling a Double Load: Women, Work and Feminism on the Canadian Prairie," *Journal of Canadian Studies* 21 (1986): 32–52. For a discussion of mutuality and the negotiation of gender within rural households and communities, see Grey Osterud, *Putting the Barn before the House: Women and Family Farming in Early Twentieth-Century New York* (Ithaca: Cornell University Press, 2012), 109–11. Marilyn Porter

and Barbara Neis, among others, consider gender relations within the fishing households and coastal communities of Newfoundland and Labrador, more fully discussed in chapter 2 in this volume.

22 Keough, "The 'Old Hag' Revisits St Brigid," 377–8, 384.

23 Morgan and deVries, *Women, Gender and Religious Cultures*, 2–3.

24 For Newfoundland examples, see Calvin Hollett, *Shouting, Embracing, and Dancing with Ecstasy: The Growth of Methodism in Newfoundland, 1774–1874* (Montreal: McGill-Queen's University Press, 2010); and Hollett, *Beating against the Wind*.

25 Marks, "Challenging Binaries," 109. Recent excellent examples include Janis Thiessen, *Not Talking Union: An Oral History of North American Mennonites and Labour* (Montreal: McGill-Queen's University Press, 2016); and Hillary Kaell, ed., *Everyday Sacred: Religion in Contemporary Quebec* (Montreal: McGill-Queen's University Press, 2017).

26 Callahan, "Class and Labor," in Goff, *Blackwell Companion to Religion in America*, 76. Robert Anthony Orsi, *The Madonna of 115th Street: Faith and Community in Italian Harlem, 1880–1950* (New Haven: Yale University Press, 1985), xv, 219–20; and Davis, "Family," in Goff, *Blackwell Companion to Religion in America*, 124. Robert Orsi, *Thank You St Jude: Women's Devotion to the Patron Saint of Hopeless Causes* (New Haven: Yale University Press, 1998).

27 Robert Orsi, *Between Heaven and Earth: The Religious Worlds People Make and the Scholars Who Study Them* (Princeton: Princeton University Press, 2004).

28 See David Morgan, *Visual Piety: A History and Theory of Popular Religious Images* (Berkeley: University of California Press, 1998); and David Morgan, *Protestants and Pictures: Religion, Visual Culture, and the Age of American Mass Production* (New York: Oxford University Press, 1999). For sensory piety, see Sally M. Promey and Shira Brisman, "Sensory Cultures: Material and Visual Religion Reconsidered," in Goff, *Blackwell Companion to Religion in America*, 188, 191.

29 Julie Melnyk, "Women, Writing and the Creation of Theological Cultures," in Morgan and deVries, *Women, Gender and Religious Cultures*, 49.

30 Colleen McDannell, "Scrambling the Sacred and the Profane," in Gordon Lynch and Jolyon Mitchell with Anna Strhan, eds., *Religion, Media and Culture: A Reader* (New York: Routledge, 2012), 135; Julie-Marie Strange, *Death, Grief and Poverty in Britain, 1870–1914*

(Cambridge: Cambridge University Press, 2005), 102; Jenny Butler, "Symbolic and Social Roles of Women in Death Ritual in Traditional Irish Society," in Evy Johanne Håland, ed., *Women, Pain and Death: Rituals and Everyday Life on the Margins of Europe and Beyond* (Newcastle-upon-Tyne: Cambridge Scholars Publishing, 2008), 120; and Sarah Parsons, "The 'Wonders in the Deep' and the 'Mighty Tempest of the Sea': Nature, Providence and English Seafarers' Piety, c. 1580–1640," in Peter Clarke and Tony Claydon, eds., *God's Bounty? The Churches and the Natural World. Papers Read at the 2008 Summer Meeting and the 2009 Winter Meeting of the Ecclesiastical History Society* (Rochester, NY: Ecclesiastical History Society by Boydell Press, 2010), 203, 194–5. Parsons ties religious belief to the nature of seafarers' work, concludes that labouring at sea "gave rise to subtle differences between seafarers and land dwellers" when it came to belief in supernatural influences or the "hand of Providence," and goes on to link patterns of disbelief to changes in individual mariners' experience and confidence. As was the case for Anglican women of Conception Bay, Parsons demonstrates how the character of daily labour and the nature of the workplace were instrumental to ordinary Christians' religious beliefs and practices.

31 Strange, *Death, Grief and Poverty*, 103.

Chapter One

1 While not an institutional study, the time frame was determined partly by formation of the Church of England Women's Association (CEWA) branch at Long Pond in 1917, the earliest in the parish for which there are extant records, and the diocesan-wide dissolution of the CEWA in 1969. The existence of CEWA records for this period helped focus the study on the five decades between 1920 and 1970, as did the availability of living memory among the local Anglican population. This time frame was determined by socioeconomic changes within the study area, especially the transition from a family- to a wage-based economy, and the transformation of the area from a largely agricultural setting, made up of small settlements, to an incorporated, and increasingly suburban, municipality in 1971. The CEWA was succeeded by the Anglican Church Women's Association, as recommended by the Diocesan Committee on Women's Work in 1968. See "Detailed Plans Revealed for One Women's

Organization," *Newfoundland Churchman* (Nov. 1968), 5; and "Welcome ACWA," *Newfoundland Churchman* (Oct. 1969), 1.

2 Elsa Hochwald and Janet Smith, *Conception Bay South Past and Present: A History of Conception Bay South* (Conception Bay South: Conception Bay South Heritage Society, 1988), 22.

3 Sean T. Cadigan, *Newfoundland and Labrador: A History* (Toronto: University of Toronto Press, 2009), 206–8; and Sean T. Cadigan, "Battle Harbour in Transition: Merchants, Fishermen, and the State in the Struggle for Relief in a Labrador Community during the 1930s," *Labour/Le Travail* 26 (Fall 1990): 142.

4 Brenda Rowsell, "An Old Man's Reflection: Mr Archibald Morgan [of Seal Cove, Conception Bay]," Memorial University Folklore and Language Archives [hereafter MUNFLA] 79–99, 5.

5 Anthony Grant Morgan, "The Oral Narratives of Clarence Morgan Sr," MUNFLA 84–019.

6 Cadigan, *Newfoundland and Labrador*, 199, 238–9.

7 *Census of Newfoundland*, 1921, 1935, 1945.

8 For a study of farming in and around St John's, see Hilda Chaulk Murray, *Cows Don't Know It's Sunday: Agricultural Life in St John's* (St John's: ISER Books, 2002).

9 Kurt Korneski, "Railways and Rebellion: The 'Battle of Foxtrap' Reconsidered," *Newfoundland and Labrador Studies* 28, 1 (Spring 2013): 99.

10 Darren Chubbs, "A Recollection of Times Gone by, Good and Bad, by Elizabeth Taylor and George Lear," MUNFLA 86–051, 8; Edwina Shea, "Towards an Ethnography of Times… The Community of Kelligrews," MUNFLA 84–134. Shea's informant was Mollie Nugent Penney. For discussion of Conception Bay South as an excursion destination and site of summer homes for wealthy residents of St John's, see Craig Westcott, *The Kelligrews Soiree* (Conception Bay South: The Town, 2010), 5–8.

11 For overview of farming in the study area, see Craig Westcott, *A Place to Grow: Agricultural History of Conception Bay South* (Conception Bay South: The Town, 2010), 11–17, 27–30.

12 Westcott, *A Place to Grow*, 30. For this trend elsewhere in North America, see Osterud, *Putting the Barn before the House*, 7, 9.

13 Morgan, "Oral Narratives," MUNFLA 84–019. Morgan likewise recalled local farmers in winter bringing "loads of potatoes" across the frozen

waters of Conception Bay to Bell Island, where iron ore mines operated 1895–1966. See Gail Weir, *The Miners of Wabana: The Story of the Iron Ore Miners of Bell Island*, 2nd ed. (St John's: Breakwater Books, 2006).

14 David Joseph Tilley, "The Role of Tradition in the Personal History of Ron Walsh, Kelligrews, Newfoundland," MUNFLA 86–040, 10, 30.

15 Rowsell, "An Old Man's Reflection," MUNFLA 79–99, 7–8; and Reginald Morgan, informal interview with the author, 3 Feb. 2014.

16 Construction work at Argentia began in January 1941, with "hundreds of Newfoundlanders" hired. Robert G. Joergensen, *Newfoundland Gallentry in Action: The History of the Argentia Naval Facility* (St John's: Jespersen, 1993), 6.

17 Morgan added that once families gave up their cattle, lack of access to manure meant they could no longer grow vegetables even if they wanted to.

18 Topsail resident Phebe Florence Miller (1889–1979) described in her poem "The Market Carts" farmers travelling from Conception Bay South into St John's to sell meat, fish, vegetables, and dairy products. See Florence Miller, *In Caribou Land* (Toronto: Ryerson Press, 1929), 58. For a study of Miller, see Vicki Sara Hallett, "Mistress of the Blue Castle: Phebe Florence Miller and Her Writing Life in Newfoundland" (PhD thesis, York University, 2009).

19 Glenda M. Cooper, "Towards and Ethnography of Times… in the Community of Long Pond, [Conception Bay]," MUNFLA 85–131.

20 Morgan, "Oral Narratives," MUNFLA 84–019. My grandfather, Arch Morgan (1904–88), told also of "the women who tipped over the highways truck" in Kelligrews. He himself gained access to relief work in 1932 by standing in the middle of the highway in Seal Cove to "block the way" of the "superintendent of highways" car and demanding help. See Rowsell, "An Old Man's Reflection," MUNFLA 79–99, 4.

21 While the primary confrontation was at Fox Trap Bridge, residents of Kelligrews and Upper Gullies also protested against railway surveying across their agricultural land. See Craig Westcott, *The Battle of Fox Trap* (Conception Bay South: The Town, 2010), 22–6. Westcott described Roman Catholic residents of Holyrood, Harbour Main, and Conception Harbour as pro-railway, following the lead of a local priest. While the Reverend Edward Colley, then Anglican rector at Foxtrap, was able to briefly calm protesters, he could not prevent "a crowd of

over 600" gathering several days later to confront the surveyors and the eleven police officers brought in to protect them.

22 James Hiller, "The Railway and Local Politics in Newfoundland, 1870–1901," in James Hiller and Peter Neary, eds., *Newfoundland in the Nineteenth and Twentieth Centuries: Essays in Interpretation* (Toronto: University of Toronto Press, 1980), 130.

23 Korneski, "Railways and Rebellion," 97.

24 "Foxtrap," *Encyclopedia of Newfoundland and Labrador* [hereafter ENL], vol. 2 (St John's: Joseph R. Smallwood Heritage Foundation, 1988), 368. As Rusty Bittermann notes, "in locales where women 'worked shoulder to shoulder with men' they also 'marched shoulder to shoulder with men' in defense of their households and communities." See Bittermann, "Women and the Escheat Movement: The Politics of Everyday Life on Prince Edward Island," in Janet Guildford and Suzanne Morton, eds., *Separate Spheres: Women's Worlds in the 19th-Century Maritimes* (Fredericton: Acadiensis Press, 1994), 37.

25 Marilyn Porter, "She Was Skipper of the Shore Crew: Notes on the History of the Sexual Division of Labour in Newfoundland," in Carmelita McGrath, Barbara Neis, and Marilyn Porter, eds., *Their Lives and Times: Women in Newfoundland and Labrador: A Collage* (St John's: Killick, 1995), 35; Barbara Neis, "From 'Shipped Girls' to 'Brides of the State': The Transition from Familial to Social Patriarchy in the Newfoundland Fishing Industry," *Canadian Journal of Regional Science* 16, 2 (1993): 185–202. Other discussions of the sexual division of labour and its impact on gender relations in rural Newfoundland society can be found in the work of Hilda Chaulk Murray, *More than Fifty Percent: Woman's Life in a Newfoundland Outport, 1900–1950* (St John's: Breakwater, 1979); Ingrid Botting, "Understanding Domestic Service through Oral History and the Census: The Case of Grand Falls, Newfoundland," *Resources for Feminist Research* 28 (2000): 99–113; and Wileen Keough, *The Slender Thread: Irish Women on the Southern Avalon, 1750–1860* (New York: Columbia University Press, 2006). For women's responsibility for clothing, see Marilyn Färdig Whiteley, *Canadian Methodist Women, 1766–1925: Marys, Marthas, Mothers in Israel* (Waterloo: Wilfrid Laurier University Press for Canadian Corporation for Studies in Religion, 2005), 72. For a recent study of women's farm labour, see Osterud, *Putting the Barn before the House*.

26 In April 1937, the women of Seal Cove likewise "decided to close our meetings ... as the busy season was come." Anglican Diocese of Eastern

Newfoundland and Labrador, All Saint's Parish, Conception Bay South, Long Pond CEWA *Minute Book*, 29 Apr. 1942; and Anglican Diocese of Eastern Newfoundland and Labrador, St Peter's Parish, Conception Bay South, Seal Cove CEWA *Minute Book*, 2 May 1934, 27 Apr. 1937. The next meeting at Seal Cove was held on 6 Nov. 1934, post-harvest. At Long Pond, CEWA meetings resumed on 4 Nov. 1942. Hereafter, CEWA minute books held at these parishes will be cited in the format [branch name] CEWA, *Minute Book*, [date], as appropriate.

27 Foxtrap CEWA, *Minute Book*, 12 May 1960.

28 The MUNFLA holdings include two separate interviews with a Selina Porter of Long Pond. While they contain some conflicting demographic information, I suspect these interviews may be with the same woman, as the 1945 census lists only one Selina Porter (born 1898). However, without confirmation, I opted to treat these interviews separately.

29 Sharon Selina Porter, "Mrs Selina Porter: Traditional Foodways of Conception Bay South, Newfoundland," MUNFLA 81–219, 2, 16.

30 Rowsell, "An Old Man's Reflection," MUNFLA 79–99, 12.

31 Phoebe (Dawe) Morgan's activism is discussed in chapters 8 and 9 in this volume.

32 Karen Louise Jefford, "The Role of Tradition in the Personal Life History of Elizabeth Petten, Housewife," MUNFLA 81–554.

33 William James Reid, "Calendar Customs: In the Community of Foxtrap, East Coast of Newfoundland, Conception Bay, during the 1920s and early 1930s," MUNFLA 73–99D, 66–8.

34 Under the denominational education system, churches "owned and operated" separate schools in which most students, teachers, and administrators were members of a particular religious tradition. For an overview, see Don Downer and Jody Bull, "Newfoundland's Denominational Education System: Stages of Development, the Constitution and Legislative Changes," a paper presented at the Annual Conference of the Canadian Association for Studies in Educational Administration, Brock University, June 1996.

35 Jefford, "Role of Tradition," MUNFLA 81–554.

36 Judy Cooper, "School Days: A Personal View," MUNFLA 78–171. While the Lord's Prayer was said in unison by the class, Eddy went on to recall how she "would never, never start my day" without saying a special prayer she learned from "her teacher at home" in Bay de Verde, adding "there was never a day in all my days teaching that I would start my day's work without saying that prayer."

37 Ralph L. Andrews, *Post-Confederation Developments in Newfoundland Education, 1949–75* (St John's: Harry Cuff Publications, 1985), 173; "Education History Made in Conception Bay," *Newfoundland Churchman* (Oct. 1959), 15. In 1964, Roman Catholic priest Father Francis Jackman (Parish of Topsail) reported that seventeen Roman Catholic children, mostly from Kelligrews, were attending classes at Queen Elizabeth Regional High. In response, Holy Spirit School in Manuels phased in grades 9 through 11 in the 1970s. Father Francis Jackman, RC *Students Enrolled in Anglican Schools, Foxtrap Area, 1963–64*, report dated 12 May 1964; Archbishop Patrick J. Skinner, St John's, to Reverend Francis J. Jackman, Topsail, 30 May 1964, Archives of the Roman Catholic Archdiocese of St John's, "Topsail Parish, 1960–64," files 400.42.3 and 400.42.6, Newfoundland and Labrador, Department of Education, *Directory of Schools* (St John's: The Dept., 1974–5, 1976–7, 1977–8.)

38 Andrews, *Post-Confederation Developments*, 345. Initial vocational subjects at Seal Cove were mechanics, woodworking, electronics, drafting, agricultural science, typing, shorthand, beauty culture, and three streams of home economics (cooking and catering, home management, and sewing and crafts).

39 *Census of Newfoundland*, 1945, summary table provided to author by Newfoundland Statistics Agency. The agency likewise provided the author with Microsoft Excel files containing 1921, 1935, and 1945 census data for Conception Bay South.

40 In 1945, the percentages of Anglicans in each community were as follows: Foxtrap 99 per cent, Greeleytown 96.5 per cent, Hopewell 91.5 per cent, Indian Pond 100 per cent, Kelligrews 67.5 per cent, Lance Cove 66.5 per cent, Long Pond 75.5 per cent, Middle Bight 97.5 per cent , Peachytown 96 per cent , Riverdale 39 per cent, Seal Cove 81.5 per cent, and Upper Gullies 92 per cent. *Census of Newfoundland*, 1945.

41 Ibid.

42 See Cecil J. Houston and William J. Smyth, *The Sash Canada Wore: A Historical Geography of the Orange Order in Canada* (Toronto: University of Toronto Press, 1980).

43 A "from the bottom up" approach to studying Orangeism in Newfoundland and Labrador, including exploration of material culture in lodges and locally held documentary records, coupled with oral history methodology, would help us better understand this organization.

44 Hollett, *Beating against the Wind*, 4–5. Hollett provides an excellent synopsis of Field's episcopate and promotion of Tractarian spirituality in his opening chapters of this work.

45 Lorraine Moores, *They Were Pioneers: Of the Town of Conception Bay South: A Legacy of Five Generations of Ancestors* (Conception Bay South: the author, 2004), 41, 43.

46 Women's Sewing Class, Long Pond, *Minute Book, 1905–1916*, 16 Mar. 1905.

47 Ibid., 9, 16 Mar. 1905; 5, 18 May 1905.

48 Ibid., 23 Mar. 1905.

49 Ibid., 18 May 1905.

50 Analysis of demographic profiles and social dynamics within voluntary associations is an important area of research and would require use of data from membership rolls. Given lack of consistent records of participation for local CEWA branches, such analysis was not completed as part of this study.

51 Pauline Bradbrook, "A Brief Account of the Work of the CEWA in Newfoundland," *Journal of Canadian Church History Society* 28 (1986): 93–4. While responsible for the particular features of the CEWA, the Reverend Gardner should not be considered the fountainhead of Anglican women's work in Newfoundland. During the nineteenth century, women in many parishes and missions formed church-based associations, as they did elsewhere in the Anglo-American world.

52 Long Pond CEWA, *Minute Book*, 27 Apr. 1917.

53 Ibid., 4, 8, 15 May 1917.

54 While the term "sister" can be linked to the mutual benefit society origins of the CEWA, as conceived by Gardner, women themselves used the term for members they considered to be their social equals and with whom they shared a common identity and experience. Members such as school teachers were called "Miss" rather than "Sister," while rector's wives were usually identified as "Mrs."

55 Greenslade was fifty-six years old, living with her husband, sixty-seven-year-old farmer Matthew Greenslade, and their eighteen-year-old daughter,Rosetta Jane. Lillian was born in the town of Harbour Grace, on the north side of Conception Bay, but moved to the largely agricultural community of Long Pond at the time of her marriage. She raised five children, born between 1900 and 1919, and while only Rosetta Jane remained at home in 1937, by 1945 both twenty-six-year-

old Rosetta and thirty-two-year-old Nellie, each a single woman, were living with their parents.

Note that there were two women with similar names active in the Long Pond CEWA. Lillian (Lily) Greenslade (born 1886) was elected president of the branch in 1917 and remembered as "a lifelong and faithful member" upon her death in 1951. Long Pond CEWA, *Minute Book*, 4 May 1917, 24 Oct. 1951. Lilla Greenslade (born 1908) became an active member starting in the late 1940s.

56 *Census of Newfoundland*, 1921, 1935, 1945; and "District of Harbor Main-Bell Island," *Newfoundland Directory, 1936* (St John's: Newfoundland Directories, 1936), 27.

57 Julie Melnyk, "Women, Writing and the Creation of Theological Cultures," in Morgan and deVries, *Women, Gender and Religious Cultures*, 44.

58 A complete list of informants, with date and place of interview with the author, appears in the appendix.

59 This password remained in use until discontinued by order of Anglican Bishop John Meaden in the early 1960s as part of a reorganization of women's work within the Diocese of Newfoundland. "Dorcas" was used until 1930, when Seal Cove CEWA noted "our password was altered, but means the same." Seal Cove CEWA, *Minute Book*, 7 Oct. 1930. Passwords reflected a sense of the CEWA as secret society, and while prescribed by the Reverend Gardner (who also founded the men-only mutual benefit Society of United Fisherman), women's continued use of this ritual demonstrated their interest in preserving an adult women's space as part of CEWA participation. "Gardner, Rev. George," in ENL, vol. 2, 476–7.

60 While Marilyn Färdig Whiteley focused on the Methodist experience, Sharon Cook identified similar distinctions within Anglican women's organizations. See Whiteley, *Marys, Marthas*; and Sharon Anne Cook, "Women in the Anglican Church of Canada," in Rosemary Skinner Keller and Rosemary Radford Ruether, eds., *Encyclopedia of Women and Religion in North America* [hereafter EWRNA] (Bloomington: Indiana University Press, 2006), 279–85.

61 Whiteley, *Marys, Marthas*, 101–2. The nature of urban women's church-based activities could be affected by the social character of particular congregations and neighbourhoods, a topic explored within my own work as well as in Michael Gauvreau, "Factories and Foreigners: Church Life in Working-Class Neighbourhoods in Hamilton and Montreal, 1890–1930," in Gauvreau and Hubert, *Churches and Social Order*, 225–73.

See also Bonnie Morgan, "Activist Anglicans and Rectors' Wives: The Impact of Class and Gender on Women's Church Work in St John's," in Linda Cullum and Marilyn Porter, eds., *Creating This Place: Women, Family and Class in St John's, 1900–1950* (Montreal: McGill-Queen's University Press, 2014), 25–46.

62 Whiteley, *Marys, Marthas*, 101–2. In a recent essay on the Dorcas Society of St John's, Newfoundland, Suzanne Sexty recognizes the Biblical origins of the society's name, and how it inspired the society's "clothe the poor" mandate, yet she does not recognize religiosity as a motivation for the prosperous urban women who were active members. Suzanne Sexty, "Dorcas Society: The Fruit of Her Hands," *Newfoundland Quarterly* 105 (2013): 34–8.

63 "Confirmation," *Diocesan Magazine* [hereafter DM] (July 1930), 248.

64 Ibid.

65 See, for example, "Queen's College," DM (Dec. 1951), 333; and "Foxtrap Parish," *Newfoundland Churchman* [hereafter NC] (Jan. 1962), 9.

66 The Reverend Mark Genge was rector of Foxtrap and Hopewell from 1959 to 1964, and was succeeded by his brother, the Reverend David Genge, who served from 1964 to 1970. *All Saints' Anglican Church, Foxtrap, Newfoundland 50th Anniversary 1931–1981* (Kelligrews: Kelligrews Printers, 1981), n.p. Examination of local congregations' response to institutional efforts to standardize parish structures and lines of authority within different traditions is an interesting area for further study.

67 "Avalon Deanery Notes," NC (Mar. 1959), 2; and "Foxtrap," NC (Apr. 1963), 12.

68 "Preaching Mission at Foxtrap," NC (Feb. 1963), 2; "Parish Life Conference at Foxtrap," NC (Mar. 1965), 2.

69 "Parish Life Conference at Foxtrap," NC (Mar. 1965), 2.

70 "Address of the Right Reverend Philip Selwyn Abraham, DD, Lord Bishop of Newfoundland…," DM (July 1945), 235; "The Position of Deaconess," DM (Jan. 1947), 47; and "Correspondence," DM (May 1945), 187.

71 "Diocesan Board of Women's Work," DM (Jan. 1951), 20.

72 "Diocesan Board of Women's Work," DM (Apr. 1958), 124.

73 Cook, "Women in the Anglican Church of Canada," *EWRNA*, 279–85.

74 Ibid., 282. Little Helpers was a branch of Women's Auxiliary work operating in the Canadian church since the late 1800s but only introduced to Newfoundland in the 1950s.

75 Another example of the growing Anglican emphasis on motherhood and domesticity was the Home Makers' Group organized in 1965 by nine middle-class women in St John's to "work with families" on "best foods," "best budgeting," "new and better cooking methods," "sewing projects," and "health matters." Lauded by the *Newfoundland Churchman* as an example of "real Christian concern," members of this group targeted "people receiv[ing] welfare payments" with whom, the anonymous writer added, they were "very glad to mix." "Homemakers Group Concerned with People," NC (Feb. 1965), 7.

76 Charles Abraham, "Editorial," NC (Feb. 1962), 4. The Mother's Union was a branch of Anglican Church work established in England in 1876 based on the notion that mothers, as family leaders in "purity" and "holiness," were primarily responsible for children's spiritual education. Along with accepting this gendered role, women active in the Anglican Mothers' Union were expected to uphold the "sanctity of marriage" and to actively recruit other women to become Union members. Cook, "Women in the Anglican Church of Canada," in *EWRNA*, 282.

77 "Little Helpers and Family Concerns," NC (Apr. 1965), 8.

78 "A Life to Give: Women in the Service of the Church," NC (May 1960), 1, 13.

79 "'The First Three Years,' reprinted from *The Magnificat*, Church of St Mary the Virgin, St John's," NC (Apr. 1969), 9. In the 1970s, the Reverend Joyce Payne became one of the first women ordained as a priest in the Diocese of Newfoundland.

80 Altar Guild of All Saints Church, Foxtrap, CB, *Minute Book [1959–65]*, 27 Oct. 1959.

81 "Editorial: Altar Guilds," NC (Jan. 1961), 4; and Joan B. Howes, "God's Housekeeper's," NC (Jan. 1969), 10.

82 Joan B. Howes's poem, "God's Housekeepers," NC (Jan. 1969), 10, spoke to the spiritual benefits of polishing silver and "keeping linen fair."

Chapter Two

1 Lynne Marks, "A Fragment of Heaven on Earth? Religion, Gender, and Family in Turn-of-the-Century Canadian Church Periodicals," *Journal of Family History* 26, 2 (2001): 251.

2 Whiteley, *Marys, Marthas*, 70.

3 Margaret Lamberts Bendroth, *Growing up Protestant: Parents, Children,*

and Mainline Churches (New Brunswick, NJ: Rutgers University Press, 2002), 4–5, 51–2.

4 Whiteley, *Marys, Marthas*, 69–70. Whiteley describes family worship in late nineteenth- and early twentieth-century Methodist households, and notes how "it was part of a patriarchal tradition that the prayers be led by the male head of household" with children in attendance.

5 Marks, "A Fragment of Heaven on Earth?," 261.

6 A photograph of Grenfell in seafarers' clothing, legs astride, holding a ship's wheel bearing the motto "Jesus Saith Follow Me" is a classic example of muscular Christian imagery. Ronald Rompkey, *Grenfell of Labrador: A Biography* (Toronto: University of Toronto Press, 1991), 76.

7 Tina Block, "'Families That Pray Together, Stay Together': Religion, Gender and Family in Postwar Victoria, British Columbia," BC *Studies* 145 (2005): 51.

8 Christie, *Households of Faith*, 1, 4, 377.

9 J.I. Little, "The Fireside Kingdom: A Mid-Nineteenth-Century Anglican Perspective on Marriage and Parenthood," in Christie, *Households of Faith*, 77–102.

10 Sarah E. Johnson, "Gender," in Goff, *Blackwell Companion to Religion in America*, 149.

11 Marks, "A Fragment of Heaven on Earth?," 256.

12 Ibid., 262.

13 Block, "Families That Pray Together," 53.

14 Ibid., 45, 51, 54. Pentecostal leaders were more concerned about maintaining the family altar of male-led, formal prayer rituals than United Church leadership. In either case, such prescriptions were unlikely to be lived within ordinary families where women (especially in United Church families) often took the lead in children's religious education and development.

15 Rick Ostrander, "Practice of Prayer in a Modern Age: Liberals, Fundamentalists, and Prayer in the Early Twentieth Century," in Laurie F. Maffly-Kipp, Leigh E. Schmidt, and Mark Valeri, eds., *Practicing Protestants: Histories of Christian Life in America, 1630–1965* (Baltimore: Johns Hopkins University Press, 2006), 179–80.

16 Block, "Families That Pray Together," 41. In the mid-nineteenth century, leadership of the Newfoundland Anglican Church moved theologically from more personal, Evangelical perspectives to an emphasis on liturgy-centred, high church (Tractarian) worship. Despite this official

"shift away from Evangelicalism … it was never totally extinguished" in Newfoundland Anglican practice. See Heather Rose Russell, "Evangelicalism in the Anglican Church in Nineteenth-Century Newfoundland" (MA thesis, Memorial University, 2005), ii, 163–4. For personal religiosity and Newfoundland Methodism see Hollett, *Shouting, Embracing, and Dancing with Ecstasy.*

17 Block, "Families That Pray Together," 45.

18 Alec Ryrie argues that while the household was an important place of sacred presence for Protestants in early modern Britain (including use of religious decoration) and church leaders prescribed the use of family devotions, most people "did not pray very much outside of church" beyond bedtime prayers and grace before meals. Alec Ryrie, *Being Protestant in Reformation Britain* (Oxford: Oxford University Press, 2013), 363, 365, 381.

19 For discussion of the grace learned by Hill and Rideout (both born 1914) from their Indian Pond and Seal Cove grandmothers, see chapter 4 in this volume.

20 Block, "Families That Pray Together," 43. No family prayer beyond grace was reported only by Gordon and Beulah (Porter) Morgan, and Cynthia (Scott) Dawe.

21 Ibid., 42.

22 Analysis of children's religiosity, including the influence of gender and the location of adult spirituality in children's bodies (associated especially with the work of Robert Orsi), is a subject for further study.

23 Bendroth, *Growing up Protestant*, 51. Described by Bendroth as a "quaintly patriarchal image," "The Cotter's Saturday Night" depicted a rural Scottish household, with family members gathered "in reverential silence" while the "priest-like father" reads aloud from the Bible.

24 Russell, "Evangelicalism in the Anglican Church," 164, 167.

25 Whiteley, *Marys, Marthas*, 70.

26 Sally M. Promey, "Hearts and Stones: Material Transformations and the Stuff of Christian Practice in the United States," in Catherine A. Brekus and W. Clark Gilpin, eds., *American Christianities: A History of Dominance and Diversity* (Chapel Hill: University of North Carolina Press, 2011), 205.

27 Donald M. MacRaild, *Faith, Fraternity and Fighting: The Orange Order and Irish Migrants in Northern England, c. 1850–1920* (Liverpool: Liverpool University Press, 2005), 25. MacRaild argues that the Orange Order encouraged "Bible Christianity" among members, who were

to "honour and diligently study the Holy Scriptures and make them the rule of his faith and practice." The open Bible motif appeared commonly on Anglican headstones erected in the study area during the first half of twentieth century, although whether primarily for deceased LOA or LOBA members, rather than Anglicans generally, is a matter for further study.

28 Sandra (Taylor) Tilley recalled as well how the Bible was kept in the living room of her childhood home.

29 One of the primary criticisms leveled at the Roman Catholic church by Protestant groups such as the Orange Order was the idea that "Catholics were discouraged from reading the Bible, relying instead on priestly interpretation." MacRaild, *Faith, Fraternity and Fighting*, 25.

30 Isabel Rivers and David L. Wykes, "Introduction," in Isabel Rivers and David L. Wykes, eds., *Dissenting Praise: Religious Dissent and the Hymn in England and Wales* (Oxford: Oxford University Press, 2011), 1–2.

31 Follow up interview, 3 Feb. 2012.

32 Informal interview with author, 3 Feb. 2012.

33 See chapters 7, 8, and 9 in this volume for use of hymns by CEWA women.

34 See Morgan, *Protestants and Pictures*. Morgan's work was groundbreaking in countering the dominant narrative of visual practice and iconography as primarily Catholic phenomena. See also Colleen McDannell, *Material Christianity: Religion and Popular Culture in America* (New Haven: Yale, 1995).

35 For discussion of Sallman's *Head of Christ* in devotional practices of American Protestants, see Morgan, *Visual Piety*, 4, 32–3, 40, 56–7, 156–67.

36 Promey, "Heart and Stones," 196.

37 Ibid., 183.

38 Morgan, *Protestants and Pictures*, 171–2. Marks notes editorials in Canadian church periodicals which encouraged men to be more "willing" to accept the public display of religious images and objects in their homes. Marks, "A Fragment of Heaven on Earth?," 262.

39 Promey, "Heart and Stones," 207.

40 For gender and Christian symbolism of flowers, see Morrill, *White Roses on the Floor of Heaven*, 4–5, 70, 110.

41 Promey, "Heart and Stones," 207.

42 As an adult living in the United States, Reta purchased a copy of this print at an auction in Maryland and continues to display it in her home.

43 Upon moving to a senior's residence, Edna recalled that she gave other pictures in her home, including images of guardian angels and a tree of life, to her daughter.

44 Mentioned by informants Pat (Morgan) Woolgar, Reta (Morgan) Hill, Beulah (Porter) Morgan, among others.

45 David Morgan, *The Sacred Gaze: Religious Visual Culture in Theory and Practice* (Berkeley: University of California Press, 2005), 155–6; Morgan, *Visual Piety*, 118.

46 For social and cultural impact of the American military presence in Newfoundland, see Stephen High, ed., *Occupied St John's: A Social History of a City at War, 1939–1945* (Montreal: McGill-Queen's University Press, 2010).

47 Morgan, *Sacred Gaze*, 164–5.

48 Ibid., 97, 115. Whether or not "Christ Our Pilot" images were more popular in areas of Newfoundland with economies based in fishing and seafaring is a matter for further study.

49 Sally M. Promey, "Taste Cultures: The Visual Practice of Liberal Protestantism, 1940–1965," in Maffly-Kipp, Schmidt, and Valeri, *Practicing Protestants*, 263.

50 Ibid., 261.

51 Ibid., 263.

52 Ibid., 288–9. Quotation attributed to John Dixon.

53 Morgan, *Protestants and Pictures*, 274–5.

54 Morgan, *Visual Piety*, 21.

55 For ongoing spiritual significance of agricultural imagery for rural Anglicans, see Richard T. France, "Sheep and Goats: Pastoral Imagery in the Bible and Today," in Leslie J. Francis and Mandy Robbins, eds., *Rural Life and Rural Church: Theological and Empirical Perspectives* (Bristol, CT: Equinox, 2012), 34.

56 Morgan, *Visual Piety*, 24.

57 See ibid., 39, for an image of Sallman's *Christ in Gethsemene*.

58 Ibid., 78, 82–3.

59 Ibid., 90, 88.

60 Osterud, *Putting the Barn before the House*, 13, 19, 211.

61 See chapters 9, 10, and 11 in this volume.

62 Robert Orsi explores sacred presence and the relationship between his grandmother and Saint Gemma Galgani, whose picture she kept at her bedside, in *Between Heaven and Earth*, ch. 4.

63 Promey, "Hearts and Stones," 208.

64 Ibid., 207–8.

65 Joan (Petten) Jefford also named her father, although sister Mary (Petten) Porter found inspiration in the CEWA, noting that "all our leaders were older people, older than we were" and naming especially the rector's wife Elizabeth Gosse, who "worshipped us … and she was sweet."

Chapter Three

1 Block, "Families That Pray Together," 46.

2 Marge (Saunders) Dawe, Pat (Morgan) Woolgar, Judy (Rideout) Dawe, Cynthia (Scott) Dawe, and Enid (Porter) Haines all described Sunday in a similar way: no work, church, Sunday school, dinner.

3 L. Lynda Harling Stalker, "She Seeketh Wool: Newfoundland Women's Use of Handknitting," in Linda Cullum, Carmelita McGrath, and Marilyn Porter, eds., *Weather's Edge: Women in Newfoundland and Labrador, A Compendium* (St John's: Killick Press, 2006), 209. Stalker opens her essay by noting the phrase "she seeketh wool" is taken from Proverbs 31.13, but does not explore connections between knitting and church work.

4 Danielle Pearl Rideout, "The Crocheting Tradition in Conception Bay," MUNFLA 81–500, 8–9.

5 For discussion of religious life of Virtue (Bishop) Morgan, see chapter 6 in this volume.

6 The grace is: "From thy hand comes all good / We thank thee for our daily food / But with it Lord thy blessing give / And to thy glory may we live." Reta (Morgan) Hill also recalled this as her grandmother's special grace, which suggests it was in common usage at Seal Cove and Indian Pond during the late nineteenth and early twentieth centuries.

7 Bendroth, *Growing up Protestant*, 51.

8 G.M. Story, W.J. Kirwin, and J.D.A. Widdowson, eds., *Dictionary of Newfoundland English* (Toronto: University of Toronto Press, 1982), 482. Hereafter DNE.

9 For discussion of Anglican attendance at Salvation Army services, see chapter 5 in this volume.

10 Marks, "Fragment of Heaven on Earth?," 256; and Bendroth, *Growing up Protestant*, 101–4.

11 Block, "Families That Pray Together," 12; and Bendroth, *Growing up Protestant*, 101–5.

12 Claudette Kennedy of Seal Cove described in 1991 how she was going to cut her brother's hair one Sunday and was warned by her father that on the Sabbath, "he who cuts hair or horn will wish that he was never born." MUNFLA Folklore Survey Cards 91–372, 2.

13 MUNFLA Folklore Survey Cards, 91–372, 2. The popularity of the folk song "The Old Sunday Dinner" by the Martin Family is an example of the continuing importance of this tradition in Newfoundland. Diane Tye, "Bread for the Road: Intersections of Food and Culture in Newfoundland and Labrador," *Newfoundland and Labrador Studies* 26, 2 (2011): 189. Among Tye's sources is Alexandra States, "Sunday Dinner Is Alive and Well: An Analysis of the Evolution of Sunday Dinner in a Single Household," paper submitted for Folklore 1000, Nov. 2009.

14 Teresa Berger, *Fragments of Real Presence*, 9. Sunday would have been even less of a "day of rest" for domestic servants within those households, although in St John's some domestics would have Sunday afternoon as their "personal time." See Linda Cullum, "Below Stairs: Domestic Service in Twentieth-Century St John's," in Cullum and Porter, *Creating This Place*, 101.

15 Sharon Selina Porter, "Mrs Selina Porter: Traditional Foodways of Conception Bay South, Newfoundland," MUNFLA 81–219, 7.

16 Ibid., 6–7.

17 For link between cold plates and consumer goods, see John T. Omohundro, *Rough Food: The Seasons of Subsistence in Northern Newfoundland* (St John's: ISER Books, 1994), 197.

18 Diane Tye, *Baking as Biography*, 6, 72. For her discussion of "satisfaction" of appetite associated with eating sweet foods, see 87.

19 For Methodist Effie (Morrey) Morgan's experience of female Anglican bigotry, see chapter 5 in this volume.

20 For history of radio in Newfoundland and Labrador, see Jeff A. Webb, *The Voice of Newfoundland: A Social History of the Broadcasting Corporation of Newfoundland, 1939–1949* (Toronto: University of Toronto Press, 2008).

21 This is personal impression, based on my father, Reginald Morgan, who listened to services broadcasted on VOWR from Wesley United Church in St John's while he cooked our Sunday meal. See also Judith Klassen, "'I Am VOWR': Living Radio in Newfoundland," *Newfoundland Studies* 22, 1 (2007): 205–26.

22 "The Bishop's Monthly Letter," DM (Feb. 1925), 45–7.
23 "The Bishop's Letter," DM (Mar. 1936), 83.
24 "Editorial Notes," DM (Feb. 1944), 41. Commentary on "minute regulations" may have been a reference to Roman Catholic "Regulations for Lent," which appeared in the St John's newspapers and were distributed by the archdiocese of St John's annually on Quinquagesima Sunday. Despite this official effort to distinguish Anglican and Roman Catholic practices, the language and expectations surrounding Lenten observance appear to be similar in both traditions. See "Pastoral Letter of His Grace the Archbishop of St John's," *Daily News* (5 Feb. 1940).
25 "The Bishop's Monthly Letter," DM (Feb. 1927), 45.
26 "Notes from the Editor," DM (Feb. 1929), 48. See also "Notes from the Editor," DM (Mar. 1943), 88; "The Bishop's Monthly Letter," DM (Feb. 1929), 46–8; and "Notes from the Editor," DM (Feb. 1931), 47.
27 "The Bishop's Monthly Letter," DM (Mar. 1937), 75. In Conception Bay, CEWA women were asked to pay for these booklets, which were distributed by the clergy to all parish households.
28 "Outline Special Prayer [for Good Friday]," DM (Mar. 1934), 86; and "Meditations: Specially for Good Friday," DM (Mar. 1936), 107.
29 "Notes from the Editor," DM (Feb. 1937), 46; "Editorial Notes," DM (Feb. 1944), 41; "Editorial," DM (Mar. 1955), 59–60; and "The Bishop's Lenten Pastoral Letter," NC (Feb. 1961), 2.
30 "Notes from the Editor," DM (Mar. 1938), 74; and (Feb. 1940), 38.
31 "Notes from the Editor," DM (Feb. 1941), 37. For "moral panic" in wartime St John's, including the association of rural women especially with promiscuity, concerns about venereal disease, and increased "illegitimate" births, see Stephen High, "Rethinking the Friendly Invasion," in High, *Occupied St John's*, 179–82.
32 "Editorial Notes: The Keeping of Lent," DM (Mar. 1944), 72.
33 "The Bishop's Letter," DM (Apr. 1953), 99.
34 Vernon Staley, "Fasting," NC (Mar. 1960), 10; and "What to 'Give up' in Lent," NC (Feb. 1961), 1. This piece also advised Anglicans to give up complaining, criticizing others, harsh speech, hatred, worry, and fear.
35 "The Bishop's Lenten Pastoral Letter," NC (Feb. 1961), 2.
36 Porter, "Mrs Selina Porter," MUNFLA 81–219, 13.
37 Reid, "Calendar Customs: Foxtrap," MUNFLA 73–99D, 43. "Dough b'ys and lassy" was a meal of boiled dumplings (made with flour, baking powder, water, and salt) served with molasses.

38 Ibid., 14; *Census* 1945.

39 Most informants, including Doris (Nagle) Bishop, Edna (Rideout) Warford, Mildred (Butler) Porter, and Emma (Petten) Warford, recalled attending church on Wednesday or Friday nights during Lent. Enid (Porter) Haines and Judy (Rideout) Dawe described parading from school to church for special Lenten services.

40 Joyce (Andrews) Morgan, Edna (Rideout) Warford, Mary (Petten) Porter, and Marjorie (Bullen) Morgan.

41 Marjorie (Bullen) Morgan, E.N.

42 Described by Prudence (Morgan) Rideout, Marjorie (Bullen) Morgan, Cynthia (Scott) Dawe, Myra (Porter) Rideout, Mildred (Butler) Porter, Enid (Porter) Haines, Joan (Petten) Jefford, and Mary (Petten) Porter.

43 The place of card games in community recreational life, especially as a fundraising activity, has been noted by Françoise Noël for mid-1900s Northeastern Ontario. Noël, *Family and Community Life*, 188–90.

44 Reid, "Calendar Customs: Foxtrap," MUNFLA 73–99D, 44.

45 Long Pond CEWA, *Minute Book*, 16, 23 Feb. 1938; 3, 9, 30 Mar. 1938; 2, 22 Mar. 1939.

46 Seal Cove CEWA, *Minute Book*, 16, 21 Mar. 1939.

47 Seal Cove CEWA, *Minute Book*, 26 Dec. 1939, 2 Apr. 1940, 12 Nov. 1940, 11 Mar. 1941.

48 The connection between textile work and devotional practices is more fully discussed in chapter 10 in this volume.

49 Long Pond CEWA, *Minute Book*, 23 Mar. 1921, 6 Apr. 1921.

50 Long Pond CEWA, *Minute Book*, 27 Feb. 1923.

51 See chapter 10 for a further discussion of the Long Pond CEWA's teas during Lent.

52 Throughout 1930, 1934, 1938, and 1939, Seal Cove branch had tea during meetings. See examples in Seal Cove CEWA, *Minute Book*, 21 Feb. 1939, 6 Mar. 1939, 4 Apr. 1939. This pattern was also seen in 1945 and 1946.

53 For discussion of this practice of benevolent mutuality in Association at Seal Cove, see chapter 9 in this volume.

54 Reid, "Calendar Customs: Foxtrap," MUNFLA 73–99D, 44, 77.

55 The work of Dufferin Sutherland considered woods work in twentieth-century Newfoundland. See "The Men Went to Work by the Stars and Returned by Them: The Experience of Work in the Newfoundland Woods during the 1930s," *Newfoundland Studies* 7, 2 (Fall 1991): 143–72; and "Newfoundland Loggers Respond to the Great Depression,"

Labour/Le Travail 29 (Spring 1992): 83–115. For a first-hand account of woods work, including Sunday observance in the logging camps, see John Kitchen, *By the Sweat of My Brow: The Life of a Newfoundland Logger* (St John's: J. Kitchen, 2005), 44–7.

56 Marion Bowman, "Vernacular Religion and Nature: The 'Bible of the Folk' Tradition in Newfoundland," *Folklore* 114 (2003): 288–9, 292–3.

57 Practice noted by Joan (Petten) Jefford, Beulah (Porter) Morgan, Marjorie (Bullen) Morgan, Myra (Porter) Rideout, and Mildred (Butler) Porter.

58 As Charles Bussey stated, "You'd have the fingers beat off ya by your mother or father if you dared go towards the cupboard where the butter was at. You'd have to make do with jam or molasses on your bread." Reid, "Calendar Customs: Foxtrap," MUNFLA 73–99D, 44–5.

59 Porter, "Mrs Selina Porter," MUNFLA 81–219, 13.

60 A description of Kennedy's CEWA service appeared in "Long Pond, CB," DM (Dec. 1948), 370.

61 This meal described by Violet Warford, Joan (Petten) Jefford, Mary (Petten) Porter, Enid (Porter) Haines, Myra (Porter) Rideout, Gordon Morgan, and Mildred (Butler) Porter. Haines noted that her mother "still does this for us now" in 2011.

62 Porter, "Mrs Selina Porter," MUNFLA 81–219, 13.

63 Meal described by Marge (Saunders) Dawe, Marjorie (Bullen) Morgan, Edna (Rideout) Warford, Enid (Porter) Haines, and Sandra (Taylor) Tilley.

64 Reid, "Calendar Customs: Foxtrap," MUNFLA 73–99D, 45. Fish on Good Friday (but not specifically salt fish) was described Doris (Nagle) Bishop, Myra (Porter) Rideout, and Mildred (Butler) Porter.

65 Good Friday "fish and raisin bread" was recalled by Sandra (Taylor) Tilley, who noted this was also her family's Christmas Eve supper before going to evening service.

66 Reid, "Calendar Customs: Foxtrap," MUNFLA 73–99D, 45.

67 Quotation from Joyce (Andrews) Morgan; family staying for full three hours described by Cynthia (Scott) Dawe, Emma (Petten) Warford, Enid (Porter) Haines, Prudence (Morgan) Rideout, Judy (Rideout) Dawe, Myra (Porter) Rideout, and Edna (Rideout) Warford. See also Reid, "Calendar Customs: Foxtrap," MUNFLA 73–99D, 45.

68 Gosse was the rector of the Parish of Foxtrap and Hopewell from 1936 to 1947. *All Saints' Anglican Church, Foxtrap, Newfoundland 50th Anniversary 1931–1981* (Kelligrews: Kelligrews Printers, 1981), n.p.

69 Comparisons by Beulah (Porter) Morgan, Gordon Morgan, Cynthia (Scott) Dawe, Pat (Morgan) Woolgar, and Joan (Petten) Jefford.

70 Joan (Petten) Jefford also described how "Father had cattle" so some work would have to be done in the barn on Good Friday.

71 "Making splits" was cutting kindling to light wood stoves. See DNE, 511.

Chapter Four

1 Deidre Meintel, "Where There Is No Conversion: Spiritualists and Personal Religious Change," *Anthropologica* 49, 1 (2007): 149–50. Seminal studies of women and conversion include Eileen Barker, *The Making of a Moonie: Choice or Brainwashing?* (Oxford: Basil Blackwell, 1984); and Lynn Davidman, *Tradition in a Rootless World: Women Turn to Orthodox Judaism* (Berkeley: University of California Press, 1991).

2 Midori Yamaguchi, "The Religious Rebellion of a Clergyman's Daughter," *Women's History Review* 16, 1 (2007): 642–3, 656.

3 Ibid., 648.

4 For institutional focus of Newfoundland historiography of religion, see Hollett, *Shouting, Embracing, and Dancing with Ecstasy*, 3–7. Examples of the sectarian narrative can be found in John E. FitzGerald, "'British Union,' the Orange Order and Newfoundland's Confederation with Canada," in David A. Wilson, ed., *The Orange Order in Canada* (Dublin: Four Courts Press, 2007), 146–69; David Dawe, *Riots and Religion in Newfoundland: The Clash between Protestants and Catholics in the Early Settlement of Newfoundland* (St John's: Flanker Press, 2011); Patrick O'Flaherty, *Old Newfoundland: A History to 1843* (St John's: Long Beach Press, 1999); Patrick O'Flaherty, *Lost Country: The Rise and Fall of Newfoundland 1843–1943* (St John's: Long Beach Press, 2005); and Patrick O'Flaherty, *Leaving the Past Behind: Newfoundland History from 1934* (St John's: Long Beach Press, 2011).

5 Intolerance likely affected relationships between men, especially in relation to participation in associations such as the Orange Order. While informants related incidents of conflict between Anglican and Roman Catholic men especially in relation to Orange parades, there was also evidence of cooperation, such as when the Foxtrap LOA Band played in the annual St Patrick's Day parade at Holyrood, a largely Roman Catholic community located at the head of Conception Bay.

6 "The Bishop's Monthly Letter," DM (Apr. 1926), 127. While the Bishop's overt emphasis in this letter was preservation of loyal Anglicans, scholars have recognized the Girls' Friendly Society for its gendered mandate to protect female purity by attempting to control young women's morality and sexuality. See Cullum, "Below Stairs," in Cullum and Porter, *Creating This Place*, 105.

7 "The Bishop's Monthly Letter," DM (May 1930), 166.

8 "Bishop's Address to Synod," DM (July 1936), 228.

9 "A Charge [to Synod]," DM (July 1938), 206.

10 "The Bishop's Lenten Pastoral Letter," DM (Feb. 1947), 51–2; "The Church in an Age of Crisis," DM (Oct. 1948), 293; and "Prayers for the Reunion of Christendom," NC (May 1962), 1.

11 See "The Bishop's Charge," DM (July–Aug. 1957), 2; "The Bishop's Charge," NC (July 1963), 2; and Kelligrews CEWA, *Minute Book*, 24 Jan. 1968. For Ecumenical movement in Anglican Church of Canada, see Alan Lauffer Hayes, *Anglicans in Canada: Controversies and Identity in Historical Perspective* (Urbana: University of Illinois Press, 2004).

12 Hiller, "Railway and Local Politics," in Hiller and Neary, *Newfoundland in the Nineteenth and Twentieth Centuries*, 132–3. Hiller discusses the sectarian Harbour Grace Affray, in which four Orangemen and one Roman Catholic were killed over railway politics, and this too may have shaped Jefford's family narrative of Protestant access to construction work. For a more recent study, see Willeen G. Keough, "Contested Terrains: Ethnic and Gendered Spaces in the Harbour Grace Affray," *Canadian Historical Review* 90, 1 (2009): 29–70. Keough suggests "communal, gender inclusive" social relations were historically specific to the Irish Roman Catholic population of Newfoundland, in contrast to the culture of male domination among English Protestants.

13 Institutional churches' opposition to mixed marriages was seen elsewhere. Bettina Bradbury notes in her study of nineteenth-century Montreal that "marriages that transgressed the boundaries of religion were not taken lightly," with Roman Catholic clergy especially discouraging marriages with Protestants. Anti-Catholic sentiments among Protestants, especially those of British ethnicity, likewise contributed to a pattern of largely endogamous marriages despite growing diversity within the city's population. Bettina Bradbury, *Wife to Widow: Lives, Laws, and Politics in Nineteenth-Century Montreal* (Vancouver: University of British Columbia Press, 2011), 37–8.

14 "Your Own Problems," DM (Nov. 1949), 317.

15 "Christian Marriage," NC (June 1960), 4.

16 This was evident with other traditions. In the Methodist household of Alexander and Mabel Tilley of Kelligrews, for example, Alexander's mother Louisa (Winsor) Tilley, originally of Green Bay, Trinity Bay, identified as Salvation Army. Her brother John, who also lived in the Tilley residence, identified as Methodist.

17 *Census of Newfoundland*, 1935.

18 There were four households in Kelligrews (including the Roman Catholic and United Church marriage) and one in Seal Cove.

19 The Reverend F.J. Jackman, P.P., Parish of Topsail, to Most Reverend P.J. Skinner, Archbishop of St John's, 22 May 1963, Archives of the Roman Catholic Archdiocese of St John's, Topsail Parish, 1960–64, file 400.42.3.

20 A sole exception was the family of Alexander and Irene Batten of Foxtrap, where Irene reported Pentecostal and the rest of the family reported Anglican. There were two similar cases in the 1945 *Census*, with women reported Salvation Army or Pentecostal and the rest of their families Anglican.

21 Bendroth, *Growing up Protestant*, 21.

22 Keough, *The Slender Thread*, 198.

23 Newfoundland Presbyterians and Congregationalists rejected union with the much larger Methodist Conference, and therefore Newfoundland Methodists only joined in the formation of the United Church of Canada in 1925. See David G. Pitt, "United Church of Canada," ENL, vol. 5, 460.

24 John Vaters of Seal Cove, the one person in the study area who continued to identify as Methodist in 1935, was an active member of St Peter's Anglican Church in Upper Gullies and was married to the equally activist Anglican Ethel. His older brother Mark and Mark's wife Elsie were activist Anglicans as well. The aforementioned family of Alexander and Mabel Tilley had likewise switched from Methodist to Anglican by 1935.

25 Hollett, *Shouting, Embracing, and Dancing with Ecstasy*, 112.

26 Ibid., 113–4, 123.

27 Roger Wayne Coady, "Customs and Stories Connected with Death, as told by Mr Tom Dawe," MUNFLA 82–294, 29–30.

28 *Census of Newfoundland*, 1921, 1935, 1945.

29 Keough, *The Slender Thread*, 174–5, 179. For gossip as a means of social and religious control in Protestant settings, see Lynne Marks, "Railing, Tattling, and General Rumour: Gossip, Gender and Church Regulation in Upper Canada," *Canadian Historical Review* 81, 3 (2000): 380–402.

30 By 1945, there were 22,571 Salvationists in Newfoundland. "Salvation Army," ENL, vol. 5, 74–6.

31 These families included seniors John and Elizabeth Eason and their two adult children, forty-year-old widow Selina Porter and her three children, Eli and Belinda Bishop and their two children, Noah and Elizabeth Pottle and their three children, James and Selina Porter and their four children, and Walter and Abigail Dawe and their two children.

32 These included seventy-two-year-old Abraham Dawe and seventy-year-old Louisa Tilley, who each resided in an adult child's household. Fifty-three-year-old Selina Hayes was Salvationist, while her husband and child were Anglicans. Similarly, twenty-two-year-old William Stanley and nineteen-year-old Eliza Stanley were converts to the Salvation Army while their widowed mother Mary Ann remained Anglican.

33 Morgan, "Oral Narratives," MUNFLA 84–019. According to Morgan, these services, complete with the music of tambourines and kettle drums, could go on until 10:00 p.m. He described how Pentecostals "took over" the Salvationists of Seal Cove, yet census data suggests that most people who converted to Pentecostalism in Seal Cove were previously Anglican.

34 Otto Tucker, "Salvation Army," ENL, vol. 5, 75.

35 See chapter 2 in this volume for a more robust discussion of CEWA rules and rituals.

36 For joyful singing as embodied practice, see Anthea Butler, "Observing the Lives of the Saints Sanctification as Practice in the Church of God in Christ," in Maffly-Kipp, Schmidt, and Valeri, *Practicing Protestants*, 171.

37 Long Pond CEWA, *Minute Book*, 9 Mar. 1921.

38 Ibid., 16 Mar. 1921.

39 Ibid., 23 Mar. 1921; 6, 20, 27 Apr. 1921; Renee Dowden, "Home Remedies [from Long Pond, Manuels]," MUNFLA 88–098, 9. For Eunice Perrin and her family, membership in the Salvation Army came later. Eunice and her husband Richard were recorded as Anglican in the 1921 and 1935 *Census*, but Salvationist in 1945 when he was seventy-five years of age and she was sixty-seven.

40 Conversely, informant Marge (Saunders) Dawe recalled in 2011 that her family was "always Anglican," yet 1935 and 1945 census takers recorded their religious identity as "Salvation Army."
41 Described by Doris (Nagle) Bishop, Joan (Petten) Jefford, Mildred (Butler) Porter, and Myra (Porter) Rideout.
42 Valerie Brace, "Towards and Ethnography of 'Times': Newfoundland Party Traditions, Past and Present, Community of Long Pond, Manuels, Conception Bay South," MUNFLA 86–314, 28–9.
43 Catherine Gidney, "The Dredger's Daughter: Courtship and Marriage in the Baptist Community of Welland, Ontario, 1934–1944," *Labour/LeTravail* 54 (Fall 2004): 121–3, 129.
44 Jefford, "Role of Tradition," MUNFLA 81–554.
45 "The Salvation Army," DM (Sept. 1944), 245. The chief doctrinal criticisms were omitting "the Sacraments of the Gospel – Baptism and the Holy Communion – and the Apostolic Ministry." The Salvation Army was respected by the English Church, so much so that a possible union between them was considered in the 1880s. Yamaguchi, "Religious Rebellion," 646, 650.
46 Burton Janes, *The History of the Pentecostal Assemblies of Newfoundland* (St John's: Pentecostal Assemblies of Newfoundland, 1996), 208.
47 Brenda Hattie-Longmire, "'Sit Down, Brother!': Alice B. Garrigus and the Pentecostal Assemblies of Newfoundland" (MA thesis, Mount St Vincent University, 2001), 72–3.
48 Janes, *History of the Pentecostal Assemblies*, 208.
49 Irene Tilley was the daughter of Moses and Belinda Anthony of Seal Cove. Raised in a committed Anglican family, she had a long and active CEWA career.
50 Janes, *History of the Pentecostal Assemblies*, 209.
51 Long Pond CEWA, *Minute Book*, 10 Dec. 1958. Another Long Pond family, that of William and Annie Porter, was likewise formerly Anglican, but their experiment with Pentecostalism ended with a collective move to the Salvation Army by 1945.
52 Janes, *History of the Pentecostal Assemblies*, 209.
53 Maud Evans Whitt began to attend Bethesda Mission in 1919, at age twelve. Hattie-Longmire, "Sit Down, Brother!," 74–5.
54 Butler, "Observing the Lives of the Saints," 159, 165, 171.
55 Seal Cove CEWA, *Minute Book*, 11 Apr. 1933. For discussion of CEWA tea and sale events as community dance parties, known locally as "times," see chapter 11 in this volume.

56 Ibid., 14 Nov. 1933.

57 Ibid., 25 Apr. 1933, 28 Nov. 1933, 5 Dec 1933.

58 Hattie-Longmire, "Sit Down, Brother!," 43. After the 1960s, Anglicans who had Pentecostal experience and preferred praise services to traditional Anglican worship were associated with the "charismatic renewal movement," and most retained their connection to the church rather than opting to join Pentecostal congregations. See David A. Reed, "Denominational Charismatics – Where Have They All Gone? An Anglican Case Study," in Michael Wilkinson, ed., *Canadian Pentecostalism: Transition and Transformation* (Montreal: McGill-Queen's University Press, 2009), 197–9, 201.

59 While the latter family remained Pentecostal, by 1945 the former gave their religious affiliation as "Christian Association" instead.

60 Seal Cove CEWA, *Minute Book*, 29 Mar. 1943.

61 Janes, *History of the Pentecostal Assemblies*, 209.

62 Robert Anthony married Anne Morgan, who brought her mother into the household, while Joseph Morgan married Mary C. Dawe, a widow with two sons.

63 Wanda Petten, informal interview with author, 30 Aug. 2011.

64 Yamaguchi, "Religious Rebellion," 647.

65 Elaine J. Lawless, *Handmaidens of the Lord: Pentecostal Women Preachers and Traditional Religion* (Philadelphia: University of Pennsylvania Press, 1988); and Hattie-Longmire, "Sit Down, Brother!," 25. Linda Ambrose's recent work on gender and Pentecostalism is valuable. See, for example, "Gender History in Newfoundland Pentecostalism: Alice Belle Garrigus and Beyond," *PentecoStudies: An Interdisciplinary Journal for Research on the Pentecostal and Charismatic Movements* 15, 2 (2016): 172–99.

66 Hattie-Longmire, "Sit Down, Brother!," 18–20.

67 Lynne Marks, "The Knights of Labor and the Salvation Army: Religion and Working-Class Culture in Ontario, 1882–90," *Labour/Le Travail* 28 (1991): 97.

68 Ibid., 9–11, 16.

69 Robert Orsi explores the use of children's bodies as a vehicle for the expression of adult spirituality in relation to twentieth century American Roman Catholicism. See Orsi, "Material Children: Making God's Presence Real for Catholic Boys and Girls and for the Adults in Relation to Them," in *Between Heaven and Earth*, 77–8.

70 Hattie-Longmire, "Sit Down, Brother!," 16. As Butler states of the African American Holiness movement: "the body, normally rigidly

controlled, became uncontrolled," as worshippers met their ultimate goal of having "the Holy Spirit flow through their bodies." Butler, "Observing the Lives of the Saints," in Maffly-Kipp, Schmidt, and Valeri, *Practicing Protestants*, 159, 168–9.

71 Hattie-Longmire, "Sit Down, Brother!," 10.

72 Reginald Morgan, informal interview with the author, 20 Apr. 2012.

73 C. Fifield, "The Church and the Sects," NC (Feb. 1961), 8.

74 Originating in sectarian tensions of the mid-nineteenth century and confirmed in the 1949 Terms of Union with Canada, Newfoundland's denominational school system meant different religious traditions received government funding in order to "own and operate" separate schools. While discontinuance was recommended in 1964, Pentecostal, Roman Catholic, and, after 1969, integrated (largely Anglican, United Church, and Salvationist) schools operated independently until 1997, when a provincial referendum ended the denominational system. Cadigan, *Newfoundland and Labrador: A History*, 285; and "Schools," ENL, vol. 5, 102, 105–6.

75 Described by Reta (Morgan) Hill, Mildred (Butler) Porter, Joan (Petten) Jefford, Doris (Nagle) Bishop, Judy (Rideout) Dawe, and Beulah (Porter) Morgan.

Chapter Five

1 Religious belief contributes to ideological constructions of the body, including popular understanding of "adored and despised" physiognomies. See R. Marie Griffith, *Born Again Bodies: Flesh and Spirit in American Christianity* (Berkeley: University of California Press), xi, 10. The relationship between religion and the body can be seen in the history of ascetic practices, where "rituals of purification and self-denial" were "aimed at subjugating the flesh or achieving identification with the suffering, crucified Christ" as well as in Christian traditions, both Protestant and Catholic, which view material abundance and self-indulgence as antithetical to spiritual growth and righteousness. See Griffith, *Born Again Bodies*, 4. For Canadian work on "the distinction between the morally inferior body and the transcendent soul" as interpreted in the lived religious practices of Roman Catholics see Abbott, *The Body or the Soul?*, xix.

2 Orsi, *Between Heaven and Earth*, 73–4.

3 Ibid., 75. Orsi has identified among twentieth-century American Roman Catholics a religious culture in which the bodies of children and of people with disabilities were considered particularly conducive to the creation of sacred presence. See *Between Heaven and Earth*, chs. 1 and 3.
4 Christopher G. White, "Health," in Goff, *Blackwell Companion to Religion in America*, 163.
5 Opp, *The Lord for the Body*, 205.
6 Ibid.
7 This has been especially considered by Rosemary Radford Ruether. For discussion of Ruether's theology in relation to lived religion in Newfoundland see Brewer, "Mending Our Nets," 156–7.
8 Ibid.
9 Marlene Epp, "Catching Babies and Delivering the Dead: Midwives and Undertakers in Mennonite Settlement Communities," in Myra Rutherdale, ed., *Caregiving on the Periphery: Historical Perspectives on Nursing and Midwifery in Canada* (Montreal: McGill-Queen's University Press, 2010), 76.
10 See, for example, Natalie Knödel, "Reconsidering an Obsolete Rite: The Churching of Women and Feminist Liturgical Theology," *Feminist Theology* 14 (1997): 106–25; and Brigitte Enzner-Probst, "Waiting for Delivery: Counseling Pregnant Women as an Issue for the Church," *International Journal of Practical Theology* 8 (2004): 185–201.
11 Epp, "Catching Babies," 76–7.
12 See chapter 7 in this volume.
13 Linda Pauline Warford, "Reminiscences of a Midwife of Upper Gullies in Conception Bay South," MUNFLA 77–247, 5, 7.
14 Name in census is Elizabeth Eva Morgan. "Valley Abe" was a nickname based on the location of their home in the valley area of Seal Cove. This distinguished him from Emily Morgan's husband Abraham, "Abe Kearney," who lived on Kearney's Turn in Seal Cove.
15 Reta (Morgan) Hill, post-interview telephone call to author. The other child born that day was Mildred Morgan, daughter of Henry Dawe and Emma (Effern) Morgan. Laurel Thatcher Ulrich, *A Midwife's Tale: The Life of Martha Ballard, Based on Her Diary, 1785–1812* (New York: Vintage Books, 1990).
16 Seal Cove CEWA, *Minute Book*, 25 Feb. 1929.
17 Ibid., 19 Mar. 1929.

18 Ibid., 26 Mar. 1929.
19 Ibid., 13 Mar. 1934, 11 Apr. 1944.
20 Ibid., 9 Apr. 1946.
21 Ibid., 28 Jan. 1947.
22 Ibid., 2 Dec. 1947.
23 Long Pond CEWA, *Minute Book*, 14 Oct. 1953.
24 Studies of midwifery in Newfoundland and Labrador include Janet Elizabeth McNaughton, "The Role of the Newfoundland Midwife in Traditional Health Care, 1900–1970" (PhD thesis, Memorial University, 1990); Cecilia Benoit, *Midwives in Passage: The Modernisation of Maternity Care* (St John's: ISER, 1991); Victoria Sparkes Belbin, "Midwifery and Rural Newfoundland Health Care 1920–1950: A Case Study of Myra Bennett, Nurse Midwife" (honours dissertation, Memorial University, 1996); Wendy Mitchinson, *Giving Birth in Canada, 1900–1950* (Toronto: University of Toronto Press, 2002); and Esther Slaney Brown, *Labours of Love: Midwives of Newfoundland and Labrador* (St John's: DRC Publishing, 2007).
25 Diocese of Newfoundland, Parish of Foxtrap and Hopewell, *Register of Baptisms* [1934–47].
26 Warford, "Reminiscences of a Midwife," MUNFLA 77–247, 1, 3; Renee Dowden, "Home Remedies [from Long Pond, Manuels]," MUNFLA 88–098.
27 For midwives' work (and status) as community healers in rural Canada, see Epp, "Catching Babies," 68.
28 Dowden, "Home Remedies," MUNFLA 88–098.
29 Warford, "Reminiscences of a Midwife," MUNFLA 77–247, 3.
30 Elizabeth L'Estrange, *Holy Motherhood: Gender, Dynasty and Visual Culture in the Later Middle Ages* (New York: Manchester University Press, 2008), 77.
31 Ibid., 78.
32 Ibid., 79.
33 Diocese of Newfoundland, Parish of Foxtrap and Hopewell, *Burial Register* [1915–44]; and Parish of Foxtrap, *Burial Register* [1944–]. In the decade 1920–9, 80 of 262 burials were for infants (30.5 per cent). In 1930–9 the ratio was 87 of 248 (35 per cent). In 1940–9 it was 87 of 260 (33.5 per cent). In 1950–9 it dropped to 32 of 168 (19 per cent), and in 1960–9 it was 38 of 197 (19 per cent).
34 On 22 November 1938 at Seal Cove, for example, "Sister Eve Morgan suggested that we should all go and visit Sister Phoebe Morgan as she

has been sick and unable to attend." (Phoebe had delivered a baby boy on 16 November.)

35 Epp, "Catching Babies," 63, 68.

36 Dowden, "Home Remedies," MUNFLA 88–098.

37 Mildred (Butler) Porter and Beulah (Porter) Morgan.

38 Warford, "Reminiscences of a Midwife," MUNFLA 77–247, 1, 3

39 Margaret Houlbrooke, *Rite out of Time: A Study of the Churching of Women and Its Survival in the Twentieth Century* (Donington: Shaun Tyas, 2012), 111. Nine days was common for Irish confinements. Eileen M. Murphy, "Children's Burial Grounds in Ireland (*Cillíní*) and Parental Emotions towards Infant Death," *International Journal of Historical Archaeology* 15 (2011): 424.

40 Donna E. Ray, "A View from the Churchwife's Pew: The Development of Rites around Childbirth in the Anglican Communion," *Anglican & Episcopal History* 69, 4 (2000): 445.

41 See chapters 7 and 9 in this volume for discussion of the significance of "nine" in vernacular healing practices.

42 John K. Crellin, *Home Medicine: The Newfoundland Experience* (Montreal: McGill-Queen's University Press, 1994), 109–10.

43 Sandra Morgan, "[Interview with Henry Angus Morgan of Seal Cove, Conception Bay]," MUNFLA 72–116. In 1945, Rachael Hennessey, born 1881, was a widow living alone at Kelligrews.

44 Raymond Tilley, born 1915, was the son of Robert H. and Lavinia Tilley of Kelligrews.

45 William James Reid, "Death: In the Anglican Tradition during the 1935–40 period in the Community of Foxtrap, East Coast of Newfoundland," MUNFLA 73–99A, 78.

46 This practice of not taking the baby out until it was baptized was likewise described by Marge (Saunders) Dawe and Joyce (Andrews) Morgan.

47 An Outport Priest, "The Church's Doctrine of Holy Baptism," DM (Apr. 1931), 133.

48 "Correspondence," DM (Nov. 1947), 357.

49 Ibid.

50 Julie-Marie Strange, *Death, Grief and Poverty in Britain, 1870–1914* (Cambridge: Cambridge University Press, 2005), 106. Within Roman Catholicism, the idea of Limbo (a place outside heaven, yet without suffering) evolved partly in response to theological concerns about the spiritual destiny of unbaptized infants. See Murphy, "Children's Burial Grounds," 410.

51 Murphy, "Children's Burial Grounds," 418–25.
52 Coady, "Customs and Stories Connected with Death," MUNFLA 82–294, 101.
53 "A Christian's Birthday," DM (June 1944), 201.
54 [C.J. Abraham], "Editorial," NC (Feb. 1962), 4.
55 For examples, see NC (Feb. 1962), 15; and NC (June 1962), 7.
56 Jefford, "Role of Tradition," MUNFLA 81–554. Noël notes in her study of northeastern Ontario that family baptismal celebrations were more common within the Greek and Italian communities than among Anglophone Protestant and French Canadian households. Noël, *Family and Community Life*, 84.
57 For discussion of devotional textile making, see chapter 9 in this volume.
58 Noël, *Family and Community Life*, 83–4.
59 Informal interview with Joyce (Barnes) Howe, 25 Sept. 2011, in which she described a blanket made by her mother-in-law Olga Barnes and used by all grandchildren at their baptisms.
60 Jefford, "Role of Tradition," MUNFLA 81–554.
61 During the ceremony of baptism, godmothers promised to "pray for" the child and, on her or his behalf, "acknowledge the duty to keep God's holy will and commandments" as well as to "walk steadfastly in the Way of Christ." General Synod of the Anglican Church of Canada, *The Book of Common Prayer 1962 Canada* (Cambridge: Cambridge University Press, 1962), 525–7. Warford, "Reminiscences of a Midwife," MUNFLA 77–247, 9.
62 David Cressy, "Purification, Thanksgiving and the Churching of Women in Post-Reformation England," *Past & Present* 141 (1993): 114, 143.
63 Arguments that churching was valued by sixteenth- and seventeenth-century English women as a women-centred ritual of thanksgiving appear in the work of Cressy and Ray. Tait likewise explores early modern women-centred cultures surrounding childbirth in Ireland in "Safely Delivered: Childbirth, Wet-Nursing, Gossip-Feasts and Churching in Ireland, c. 1530–1690s," *Irish Economic & Social History* 30 (2003): 1–23.
64 Enzner-Probst, "Waiting for Delivery," 187.
65 Knödel, "Reconsidering an Obsolete Rite," 106–7; and Enzner-Probst, "Waiting for Delivery," 187–8.
66 Attention to churching within the Orthodox Eastern tradition is increasing. See Kathryn Wehr, "Understanding Ritual Purity and Sin in the Churching of Women: From Ontological to Pedagogical to

Eschatological," *St Vladimir's Theological Quarterly* 55, 1 (2011): 85–105; and Matthew J. Streett, "What to Do with the Baby? The Historical Development of the Rite of Churching," *St Vladimir's Theological Quarterly* 56, 1 (2012): 51–71.

67 Examples include Susan Karant-Nunn, *The Reformation of Ritual: An Interpretation of Early Modern Germany* (London: Routledge, 1997); Paula M. Rieder, *On the Purification of Women: Churching in Northern France, 1100–1500* (New York: Palgrave, 2006); and L'Estrange, *Holy Motherhood*, 77, 94–5.

68 Paula M. Rieder, "Insecure Borders: Symbols of Clerical Privilege and Gender Ambiguity in the Liturgy of Churching," in Anne L. McClanan and Karen Rosoff Encarnación, eds., *The Material Culture of Sex, Procreation, and Marriage in Premodern Europe* (New York: Palgrave, 2002), 93, 95, 108.

69 David Cressy, *Birth, Marriage, and Death: Ritual, Religion, and the Life-Cycle in Tudor and Stuart England* (Oxford University Press, 1997), 201

70 Ray, "A View from the Churchwife's Pew," 449, 458–9.

71 Cressy, "Purification, Thanksgiving and the Churching of Women," 111.

72 Despite limited sources, Rieder considers the meaning of churching for late-medieval women participants in *On the Purification of Women*.

73 Ray, "A View from the Churchwife's Pew," 467. Perceived unpopularity of the rite may explain why the *Oxford History of Christian Worship* includes no discussion of churching practices beyond giving it as an example of an "occasional office" within the seventeenth-century church. See *Oxford History of Christian Worship*, 513.

74 Houlbrooke, *Rite out of Time*, 65–6.

75 Ibid., 101–24.

76 Cressy, "Purification, Thanksgiving, and the Churching of Women," 106–46; Sarah C. Williams, "Urban Popular Religion and the Rites of Passage," in Hugh McLeod, ed., *European Religion in the Age of Great Cities, 1830–1930* (London: Routledge, 1995), 216–36; Ray, "A View from the Churchwife's Pew," 444–61; and Becky R. Lee, "Men's Recollections of a Women's Rite: Medieval English Men's Recollections Regarding the Rite of the Purification of Women after Childbirth," *Gender & History* 14, 2 (2002): 224–41. Lee identifies regional differences in English churching traditions and discusses popular practices (especially feasting) primarily in relation to negotiation of social status by families. Lee, "Men's Recollections," 227, 234.

77 Houlbrooke, *Rite out of Time*, 8, 10, 13.

78 Ibid.

79 Ray, "A View from the Churchwife's Pew," 454–5. Ray notes how High Church Anglican clerics such as John Donne viewed churching as primarily an act of purification rather than thanksgiving, believing that "only the churching rite, performed by a priest, could bring a clean thing out of filthiness." While Puritans rejected churching, she argues this should be considered more of a political gesture against clerical authority than against ideas of women being "polluted" by conception and childbirth.

80 Houlbrooke, *Rite out of Time*, 6–7.

81 W.J. Armitage, *The Story of the Canadian Revision of the Prayer Book* (Toronto: McClelland and Stewart, 1922), 291. Armitage notes that while the service is "based upon the Old Testament rite of Purification. It is not, however, intended to be a ceremonial suggesting the removal of any defilement through child-birth … Its sole note is that of thanksgiving."

82 "The Bishop's Monthly Letter," DM (Mar. 1926), 86–7.

83 Churching was described by Doris (Nagle) Bishop, Prudence (Morgan) Rideout, Judy (Rideout) Dawe, Mildred (Butler) Porter, Myra (Porter) Rideout, and Sandra (Taylor) Tilley.

84 Ray, "A View from the Childwife's Pew," 446, 448, 450.

85 Keith Thomas, *Religion and the Decline of Magic: Studies in Popular Beliefs in 16th and 17th Century England* (New York: Oxford University Press, 1997 [1971]), 39, 60.

86 Ray, "A View from the Childwife's Pew," 459.

87 Quoted in ibid., 461.

88 Armitage, *Story of the Canadian Revision of the Prayer Book*, 291. Churching's association with rest from agricultural work for women in rural societies was suggested by Paul Marshall in *Prayer Book Parallels: The Public Services of the Church Arranged for Comparative Study* (New York: The Church Hymnal Corporation, 1989), 51.

89 For social status of immigrants to Canada from the British Isles, see Rebecca J. Mancuso, "Three Thousand Families: English Canada's Colonizing Vision and British Family Settlement, 1919–39," *Journal of Canadian Studies* 45, 3 (2011): 5–33; and Franca Iacovetta, Michael Quinlan, and Ian Radforth, "Immigration and Labour: Australia and Canada Compared," *Labour/Le Travail* 38 (1996): 90–115.

90 Pointing to the example of Foucault's analytical use of religious and confessional discourses, she concludes that "analyses that depict religion as antithetical to sexuality ... misunderstand their interdependence as modes of truth-telling and self-making." Sue Morgan, "'The Word Made Flesh': Women, Religion and Sexual Cultures," in Morgan and DeVries, *Women, Gender and Religious Cultures*, 159.
91 Ibid., 161ff, 159.
92 Ibid., 159.
93 Houlbrooke, *Rite out of Time*, 106, 109, 111, 114, 117.
94 Ibid., 105, 113.
95 Epp, "Catching Babies," 78.

Chapter Six

1 Charles Abraham, "The Burial of the Dead," NC (Feb. 1960), 4.
2 Alan Swedlund, *Shadows in the Valley: A Cultural History of Illness, Death, and Loss in New England, 1840–1916* (Amherst: University of Massachusetts Press, 2010), 1–2.
3 Bradbury, *Wife to Widow*, 218.
4 The sexual division of labour in rural Newfoundland households is more fully discussed in chapter 2 in this volume.
5 Strange, *Death, Grief and Poverty*, 100–2.
6 Swedlund, *Shadows in the Valley*, 171–2; and Strange, *Death, Grief and Poverty*, 72–5, 83.
7 Hickey's Funeral Home, "Our Heritage," http://www.hickeysfuneralhome.ca/our_heritage.html; and Mary G. Veitch, *Come Ashore to Holyrood: A Folk History of Holyrood, Newfoundland* (St John's: Creative, 1989), 103. For changing funeral practices elsewhere, see Gillian Poulter, "What's Traditional about 'the Traditional Funeral'? Funeral Rituals and the Evolution of the Funeral Industry in Nova Scotia," *Journal of the Canadian Historical Association* 22, 1 (2011): 133–59.
8 Long Pond CEWA, *Minute Book*, 31 Mar. 1966.
9 Devotional textile production within the CEWA is discussed in chapter 9 in this volume.
10 Bradbury, *Wife to Widow*, 218.
11 Butler, "Symbolic and Social Roles of Women in Death Ritual," in Håland, *Women, Pain and Death*, 109–10. Butler describes a taboo on relatives handling the dead. While informants from Conception Bay

do not discuss it in terms of prohibition, they did say that relatives gave directions only and let neighbouring men and women take care of preparation for the funeral and wake. Reid, "Death: In the Anglican Tradition," MUNFLA 72–99A, 81.

12 Strange, *Death, Grief and Poverty*, pp. 83, 72, 74. Female relatives, female neighbours, or midwives laying out the deceased was noted as well for Montreal. See Bradbury, *Wife to Widow*, 218. Marlene Epp notes participation of midwives in death rituals, including laying out bodies, and argues the close connection between life and death at childbirth gave midwives special spiritual status in Mennonite communities. See Epp, "Catching Babies," 71–3.

13 Strange, *Death, Grief and Poverty*, 75.

14 Pat Jalland, *Australian Ways of Death: A Social and Cultural History, 1840–1918* (Oxford: Oxford University Press, 2002), 129.

15 Eva Åhrén, *Death, Modernity, and the Body: Sweden 1870–1940*, trans. Daniel W. Olson (Rochester: University of Rochester Press, 2009), 81; and Reid, "Death: In the Anglican Tradition," 81. Epp describes how women were primarily responsible for laying out bodies in Mennonite communities, although sometimes men were asked to prepare male bodies. Epp, "Catching Babies," 71–3.

16 Coady, "Customs and Stories Connected with Death," MUNFLA 82–294, 32–3.

17 Marjorie Morgan, informal interview with author, 15 Jan. 2012.

18 Strange, *Death, Grief and Poverty*, 66.

19 Butler, "Symbolic and Social Roles of Women," 110–11.

20 Swedlund, *Shadows in the Valley*, 177.

21 Reid, "Death: In the Anglican Tradition," 84.

22 Ibid., 82.

23 Aubrey M. Tizzard, *On Sloping Ground: Reminiscences of Outport Life in Notre Dame Bay, Newfoundland* (St John's: Breakwater, 1984), 95.

24 Reid, "Death: In the Anglican Tradition," 82.

25 Ibid.

26 Tizzard, *On Sloping Ground*, 223n33.

27 Reid, "Death: In the Anglican Tradition," 82.

28 Ibid.

29 Ibid.

30 Ibid., 88.

31 Osterud, *Putting the Barn before the House*, 129.

32 Gerald L. Pocius, *A Place to Belong: Community Order and Everyday Space in Calvert, Newfoundland* (Athens; Montreal: University of Georgia Press; McGill-Queen's University Press, 1991), 238.
33 Ibid.
34 Butler, "Symbolic and Social Roles of Women," 113.
35 Reid, "Death: In the Anglican Tradition," 104.
36 Ibid., 84.
37 Butler, "Symbolic and Social Roles of Women," 113.
38 Reid, "Death: In the Anglican Tradition," 83.
39 Butler, "Symbolic and Social Roles of Women," 113.
40 Reid, "Death: In the Anglican Tradition," 83.
41 Ibid., 83.
42 Ibid., 85. Age or occupation did not determine a man's casket-making reputation. By the 1940s and 1950s, transportation worker Eddie Jim Delaney (born 1922) was considered one of the best and most committed casket-makers in Foxtrap. Minnie Bussey described how "many a time I heard the hammerin' late in the night over at Eddie Jim's when he was makin' a casket."
43 Strange, *Death, Grief, and Poverty*, 117.
44 Tizzard, *On Sloping Ground*, 95.
45 Reid, "Death: In the Anglican Tradition," Coady, "Customs and Stories Connected with Death," 59–60. By the mid-twentieth century, commercially produced handles and breast plates were available at local general stores such as J.J. Butler's and would be used by casket makers.
46 Epp, "Catching Babies," 73.
47 Butler, "Symbolic and Social Roles of Women," 111–12.
48 Bradbury, *Wife to Widow*, 218.
49 Butler, "Symbolic and Social Roles of Women," 111–12.
50 Strange, *Death, Grief and Poverty*, 81–3, 87, 127–9.
51 Coady, "Customs and Stories Connected with Death," 48–50.
52 Reid, "Death: In the Anglican Tradition," 87.
53 Coady, "Customs and Stories Connected with Death," 41–2.
54 Reid, "Death: In the Anglican Tradition," 91.
55 Coady, "Customs and Stories Connected with Death," 41–2, 55.
56 Reid, "Death: In the Anglican Tradition," 89.
57 Butler, "Symbolic and Social Roles of Women," 112.
58 Reid, "Death: In the Anglican Tradition," 89.
59 Long Pond CEWA, *Minute Book*, 31 Mar. 1966.

60 Ironically, Elliot wrote this in response to her feelings of inadequacy as an "invalid" who was unable to serve the church as other women did: labouring at fundraising events such teas and bazaars. Susan VanZanten Gallagher, "Domesticity in American Hymns, 1820–1870," in Mark A. Noll and Edith L. Blumhofer, eds., *Sing Them Over to Me Again: Hymns and Hymnbooks in America* (Tuscaloosa: University of Alabama Press, 2006), 246.
61 Butler, "Symbolic and Social Roles of Women," 111.
62 Reid, "Death: In the Anglican Tradition," 93.
63 Ibid., 82, 93.
64 Coady, "Customs and Stories Connected with Death," 63.
65 Tye, "Bread for the Road," 187.
66 Butler, "Symbolic and Social Roles of Women," 111; and Reid, "Death: In the Anglican Tradition," 88.
67 Seal Cove CEWA, *Minute Book*, 6 May 1943.
68 Strange, *Death, Grief and Poverty*, 125–6.
69 Morrill, *White Roses on the Floor of Heaven*, 4–5, 70, 110.
70 Examples include Seal Cove CEWA, *Minute Book*, 9 Dec. 1947, 10 Apr. 1962, 22 Apr. 1963, 18 Mar. 1964; Foxtrap CEWA, *Account Book*, 27 Mar. 1958, 14 Apr. 1959, 1960 passim for funeral flowers, 1961 and 1962 for Easter flowers; Foxtrap CEWA, *Minute Book*, Annual Report 1959, 7 Apr. 1960. The St Peter's ACW continued to give Easter flowers in memory of late members as of 2013.
71 Seal Cove CEWA, *Minute Book*, 18 Mar. 1964.
72 Long Pond CEWA, *Minute Book*, 4 Apr. 1963.
73 Foxtrap CEWA, *Minute Book*, 7 Apr. 1966.
74 Jalland, *Australian Ways of Death*, 129.
75 Swedlund, *Shadows in the Valley*, 171.
76 Bradbury, *Wife to Widow*, 226.
77 Strange, *Death, Grief and Poverty*, 123–4.
78 Jalland, *Australian Ways of Death*, 82, 130.
79 Ibid., 82.
80 Coady, "Customs and Stories Connected with Death," 71.
81 Strange, *Death, Grief and Poverty*, 171.
82 See, for example, "The Bishop's Lenten Pastoral Letter," DM (Feb. 1947), 51–2; "Archbishops' Statement on the Assumption," DM (Oct. 1950), 258; "The Bishop's Charge," DM (Jul.–Aug. 1957), 2; and "The Bishop's Charge," NC (Jul. 1963), 2. The latter piece included discussion of the

Ecumenical Movement, an effort "to create understanding among Christians of all denominations, and this does not exclude our Roman Catholic brethren."

83 Jalland, *Australian Ways of Death*, 124–5.

84 Reid, "Death: In the Anglican Tradition," 92; and Coady, "Customs and Stories Connected with Death," 72. The Society of United Fishermen, like the CEWA, was initially organized by the Reverend George Gardner as a mutual benefit society. Processional culture informed its activity, and an annual parade on New Year's Day featuring the society's brass band occurred in most Newfoundland communities with its lodges. L.L. Hodder, *Brief History of the Society of United Fishermen, 1873–1973* (n.p.: n.d.), 4–5.

85 Long Pond CEWA, *Minute Book*, 8 Dec. 1920.

86 Seal Cove CEWA, *Minute Book*, 22 Jan. 1929.

87 "Long Pond, CB," DM (Dec. 1948), 370.

88 Strange, *Death, Grief and Poverty*, 104.

89 Reid, "Death: In the Anglican Tradition," 95.

90 Ibid., 95–9.

91 Butler, "Symbolic and Social Roles of Women," 113–14, 118.

92 Reid, "Death: In the Anglican Tradition," 99. For a history of the pervasiveness of this disease in Newfoundland see Edgar House, *Light at Last: Triumph over Tuberculosis, 1900–2005* (St John's: Lung Association of Newfoundland and Labrador, 2005).

93 Coady, "Customs and Stories Connected with Death," 67.

94 Jalland, *Australian Ways of Death*, 148.

95 The story of Dorcas, or Tabitha, is found in Acts 9: 36–42.

96 NC (Feb. 1960), 4. At same time, increasing advertisements for funeral services and monuments appeared in the *Newfoundland Churchman*. An advertisement for Muir's Marble Works, "A Memorial Is a Prayer in Stone," NC (Apr. 1959), 9, is one example.

97 Håland, "Introduction," in Håland, *Women, Pain and Death*, 2.

Chapter Seven

1 *Minute Book*, 17 Jun. 1942.

2 Swedlund, *Shadows in the Valley*, 4–5, 52, 167. Bettina Bradbury's recent work on Montreal demonstrates increased attention to the social context of death and the impact of social relations on women's

experience of widowhood, yet "emotional responses," including female grief and consolation, "would require different sources and different sensibilities" than she engaged with in her study. See Bradbury, *Wife to Widow*, 206.

3 Swedlund, *Shadows in the Valley*, 52.

4 In *Death in the Victorian Family*, published in 1996, Pat Jalland draws broad conclusions about grief and mourning practices while relying almost exclusively on elite sources. In her more recent work on the Australian experience, Jalland considers the impact of class as well as gender on death rituals and consolation practices, and broadens her evidence to include that produced by people of varying social backgrounds. See Strange, *Death, Grief and Poverty*, 8; Jalland, *Australian Ways of Death*, 139, 142; and Bradbury, *Wife to Widow*, 4, 19, 206.

5 Swedlund, *Shadows in the Valley*, 186–7.

6 Examples include Ena Constance Barrett, "It Must Not Be Again"; and Evan Whiteway, "Sonnet to Newfoundland's Dead," printed together in *Veteran Magazine* 10, 2 (Dec. 1934), 101. For a study of Conception Bay South poet Phebe Florence Miller's wartime poetry, which helped "preserve" Newfoundlander's "humanity in an inhumane time," see Vicki S. Hallett, "Verses in the Darkness: A Newfoundland Poet Responds to the First World War," in Sarah Glassford and Amy Shaw, eds., *A Sisterhood of Suffering and Service: Women and Girls of Canada and Newfoundland During the First World War* (Toronto: University of British Columbia Press, 2012), 246–69. For public response to First World War casualties, especially those of Beaumont Hamel, see Sean Cadigan, *Death on Two Fronts: National Tragedies and the Fate of Democracy in Newfoundland, 1914–34* (Toronto: Penguin Group, 2013), 134–5.

7 "Resurrection of Christ" and "Resurrection of the Dead," in *Oxford Dictionary of the Christian Church*, 2nd ed. (Oxford: Oxford University Press, 1993), 1177–9.

8 "The Bishop's Monthly Letter," DM (Mar. 1930), 86.

9 "The Easter Victory: A Sermon by the Right Reverend William White, Bishop of Newfoundland, preached at the Cathedral of St John the Baptist on Easter Sunday," DM (Apr. 1934), 102.

10 "Editorial," DM (Apr. 1955), 94.

11 The Rev. B.S. Murray, "The Latch of Life," DM (Apr. 1949), 116; and "Notes from the Editor," DM (Apr. 1950), 96.

12 "Notes from the Editor," DM (Nov. 1942), 332.

13 "The Bishop's Monthly Letter," DM (Apr. 1943), 116–18.

14 NC (Feb. 1960), 4.

15 Jalland, *Australian Ways of Death*, 149.

16 Victoria Beatrice Rideout, the daughter of George and Emily Rideout of Foxtrap, moved to Seal Cove after her marriage to Albert Dawe. *Census* 1935.

17 Long Pond CEWA, *Minute Book*, 23 Jan. 1935.

18 Seal Cove CEWA, *Minute Book*, 4, 11 Apr. 1944. Laura Morgan died in 1921 at age nineteen, Mabel Roberts in 1940 at age twenty-six, and Isabel Roberts in 1946 at age twenty-three. St Peter's Cemetery, Upper Gullies, survey completed 29 Nov. 2011.

19 Jalland, *Australian Ways of Death*, 129.

20 Seal Cove CEWA, *Minute Book*, 8 May 1944.

21 Long Pond CEWA, *Minute Book*, 10 May 1944.

22 "The Diocesan Council, CEWA," DM (Oct. 1943), 321.

23 Cemetery survey, St Peter's Anglican, Upper Gullies, completed 29 Nov. 2011.

24 Morrill, *White Roses on the Floor of Heaven*, 149.

25 Ibid., 149–50, 157.

26 See Seal Cove CEWA, *Minute Book*, 6, 13 Mar. 1934, 2 May 1934, 4 Apr. 1939, 17 Jun. 1942.

27 Ibid., 17 Jun. 1942.

28 Ibid., 12 Oct. 1943.

29 *Census* 1935. Seal Cove CEWA, *Minute Book*, 12 Oct. 1943: "Sister Clara Dawe thanked the class for cards of sympathy and kindness shown her on the death of her Dear daughter during Summer recess."

30 Seal Cove CEWA, *Minute Book*, 12 Oct. 1943.

31 Ibid., 17 Apr. 1945.

32 Ibid., 12 Oct. 1943.

33 "The Diocesan Council, CEWA," DM (Oct. 1943), 321.

34 District Branch meeting described in Seal Cove CEWA, *Minute Book*, 1 May 1944.

35 Seal Cove CEWA, *Minute Book*, 16 Feb. 1937; and *Census* 1935.

36 Seal Cove CEWA, *Minute Book*, 28 Jan. 1942, 26 Jan. 1943.

37 Long Pond CEWA, *Minute Book*, 31 Mar. 1948. Selina Andrews of 29 Henry Street, St John's, age eighty-three, was buried in Upper Gullies on 27 Apr. 1960. Diocese of Newfoundland, *Register of Burials in the Parish of Foxtrap and Hopewell, 1899–1980*.

38 Swedlund, *Shadows in the Valley*, 185.
39 Ibid.
40 Jalland, *Australian Ways of Death*, 149, 151–2.
41 Ibid., 151–2, 159–60.
42 *Census* 1921, 1935, 1945. Elizabeth's second marriage was to Clarence Tilley.
43 Seal Cove CEWA, *Minute Book*, 17 Mar. 1942.
44 Long Pond CEWA, *Minute Book [1941–46]*.
45 Mr and Mrs Isaac Dawe to CEWA Seal Cove, Officers and Members, 30 Oct. 1939. Letter folded in Seal Cove CEWA, *Minute Book [1936–39]*.
46 Seal Cove CEWA, *Minute Book*, 31 Oct. 1939.
47 Headstone erected in memory of "Annie Marie, beloved wife of Isaac F. Dawe," who died in 1955 at age sixty-three. The inscription reads: "Erected by her husband and family." St Peter's Cemetery, Conception Bay South, survey completed 29 Nov. 2011. It is worth noting that Annie and Isaac Dawe's daughter Marjorie, who married Thomas Jefford of Long Pond, was likewise a CEWA member. Elected president of Long Pond branch for several years in the 1960s, Marjorie's leadership in women's religious ritual is described in chapter 9.
48 Edith L. Blumhofer, "Fanny Crosby, William Doane, and the Making of Gospel Hymns in the Late Nineteenth Century," in Noll and Blumhofer, *Sing Them Over Again to Me*, 156, 162.
49 Swedlund, *Shadows in the Valley*, 177.
50 For cemetery landscapes that reflect social relationships between people of differing ethnic identities and provide evidence of resistance to assimilation, see Lukasz Albanski and John C. Lehr, "Identity Integration and Assimilation Recorded in Manitoba's Polish and Ukrainian Cemeteries," *Great Plains Research* 22 (2012): 3–14. See also recent work by Laurie Stanley-Blackwell on the Nova Scotia experience, including "Romancing the Stone: Female Figural Monuments in Late Nineteenth-Century Nova Scotian Cemeteries" (with Brenda Appleby), *Markers: Annual Journal of the Association for Gravestone Studies 2014*, vol. 24 (2014): 16–53.
51 Bradbury, *Wife to Widow*, 220–1.
52 *Ibid.*, 179.
53 Swedlund, *Shadows in the Valley*, 179.
54 Ibid., 98; Jalland, *Australian Ways of Death*, 144.
55 Joy M. Giguere, "Virtuous Women, Useful Men, and Lovely Children:

Epitaph Language and the Construction of Gender and Social Status in Cumberland County, Maine, 1720–1820," *Markers* 24 (2007): 1–23. Gender and family relationships are also revealed in cemetery landscapes. See Roben Campbell, "The Harvard Shaker Cemetery," *American Communal Societies Quarterly* 5 (2011): 179–203.

56 Swedlund, *Shadows in the Valley*, 179, 186. For overview of changing Christian conceptions of heaven over time, see Colleen McDannell and Bernhard Lang, *Heaven: A History*, 2nd ed. (New Haven: Yale University Press, 2001).

57 Ibid., 179.

58 Gary S. Foster and Lisa New Freeland, "Hand in Hand Til Death Doth Part: A Historical Assessment of the Clasped-Hand Motif in Rural Illinois," *Journal of the Illinois State Historical Society* 100 (2007): 128–46.

59 Examination of these patterns on Conception Bay headstones is a matter for further study. A preliminary survey of the motif in the Anglican cemetery at Upper Gullies suggests that in the study area both male and female unmarried persons were likely to be shown holding a father's hand.

60 Strange, *Death, Grief and Poverty*, 163.

61 Ibid., 163, 165–6.

62 Ibid., 167–8. The extent of her engagement with the religious aspect of grave markers was a brief discussion of the influence of different Christian traditions on the appearance and content of headstones, following late-nineteenth-century English commentary on the plainness of Nonconformist markers, the sentiment, symbolism, and heavy inscription of Anglican monuments and the use of crucifix imagery and calls for intercessory prayer on Roman Catholic stones.

63 Swedlund, *Shadows in the Valley*, 168.

64 Ibid., 35–6, 206n35. Iconography of headstones, and its cultural significance, is well-studied in the American literature, including considerable work on the New England region.

65 Cemetery surveys completed by author, 20 Jul. 2011 (All Saint's Cemetery #3, Foxtrap), 14–16 Nov. 2011 (All Saint's Cemetery #2, Foxtrap), 23, 29 Nov. 2011 (St Peter's Cemetery, Upper Gullies).

66 Swedlund, *Shadows in the Valley*, 179.

67 Seal Cove CEWA members were saddened by the death of fun-loving Lizzie Dawe, with acting secretary Emily Morgan noting in relation to the news that "what man appoints God disappoints sometimes" and

that their planned Easter tea and sale had been postponed "owing to the death of our late sister." Seal Cove CEWA, *Minute Book*, 31 Mar. 1931.

68 Christian consolation was common in the epitaphs identified in nineteenth-century American and British cemeteries. See Swedlund, *Shadows in the Valley*, 98; and Strange, *Death, Grief and Poverty*, 165.

69 Strange, *Death, Grief and Poverty*, 173.

70 Headstones dated 1929 and 1953, for female children.

71 Jalland, *Australian Ways of Death*, 152.

72 Strange, *Death, Grief and Poverty*, 52.

73 Ibid.

74 Rowsell, "An Old Man's Reflection," MUNFLA 79-99, 26.

75 See chapter 9 in this volume for discussion of men and Christian cultures of suffering.

76 Swedlund, *Shadows in the Valley*, 186.

77 Jalland, *Australian Ways of Death*, 157–8.

78 Ibid., 157.

79 Gallagher, "Domesticity in American Hymns," in Noll and Blumhofer, *Sing Them Over Again to Me*, 246.

80 Ibid., 244.

81 Jalland, *Australian Ways of Death*, 157–8.

82 Strange, *Death, Grief and Poverty*, 169.

83 Emily K. Abel has recently questioned the dichotomy of sacred/secular in family responses to the death (and dying) of loved ones, identifying a combination of "orthodox" Christian and alternative spiritual approaches to death among Americans of the late nineteenth and early-to-mid twentieth centuries. See Emily K. Abel, *The Inevitable Hour: A History of Caring for Dying Patients in America* (Baltimore: Johns Hopkins University Press, 2013), ch. 8.

84 Ann Belford Ulanov, "The Psychology of Women's Religious Experience," in Rosemary Skinner Keller and Rosemary Radford Ruether, eds., *EWRNA* (Bloomington: Indiana University Press, 2006), 64.

85 Gallagher, "Domesticity in American Hymns," in Noll and Blumhofer, *Sing Them Over Again to Me*, 235–52.

Chapter Eight

1 Emily K. Abel, *Hearts of Wisdom: American Women Caring for Kin* (Cambridge, MA: Harvard University Press, 2000), 1, 3, 8. In *The*

Inevitable Hour (2013), Abel likewise examines the persistence of spirituality among family caregivers of the twentieth century, even when providing that care within "secular," institutional settings. In this way, religion becomes a way to resist "scientific" (and often male) medical authority.

2 Cadigan, *Death on Two Fronts*, 20. See Sandra Beardsall, "Methodist Religious Practices in Outport Newfoundland" (PhD dissertation, University of Victoria and University of Toronto, 1996).

3 Morrill, *White Roses on the Floor of Heaven*, 12, 141.

4 Strange, *Death, Grief and Poverty*, 52.

5 Cadigan, *Newfoundland and Labrador: A History*, 280.

6 Brewer, "Mending Our Nets," 168.

7 Whiteley, *Marys, Marthas*, 101.

8 Jalland, *Australian Ways of Death*, 129; and Abel, *Hearts of Wisdom*, 2.

9 Seal Cove CEWA, *Minute Book*, 17, 24 Mar. 1931.

10 Long Pond CEWA, *Minute Book*, 14 Mar. 1963. The return of "Sister Mamie Morgan … who has not been able to attend because her husband has been sick" was in Seal Cove CEWA, *Minute Book*, 25 Nov. 1964.

11 Seal Cove CEWA, *Minute Book*, 31 Mar. 1931. "It is very meet, right and our bounden duty, that we should at all times, and in all places, give thanks onto thee, O Lord" is part of the Prayer of Thanksgiving and Consecration and spoken by the priest during Holy Communion.

12 Ibid.

13 Strange, *Death, Grief and Poverty*, 45.

14 Reid, "Death: In the Anglican Tradition," MUNFLA 73–99A, 78.

15 Abel, *Hearts of Wisdom*, 52–3.

16 Strange, *Death, Grief and Poverty*, 51.

17 Long Pond CEWA, *Minute Book*, 10 Nov. 1965. Robert R. Jefford died three weeks later.

18 Abel, *Hearts of Wisdom*, 53.

19 See chapters 3 and 8 in this volume for the importance of hymn singing in popular religious practices.

20 Ken R. Manley, "John Rippon and Baptist Hymnody," in Isabel Rivers and David L. Wykes, eds., *Dissenting Praise: Religious Dissent and the Hymn in England and Wales* (New York: Oxford University Press, 2011), 120–2.

21 Strange, *Death, Grief and Poverty*, 9.

22 Ibid.

23 Orsi, *Between Heaven and Earth*, 21–2.
24 Ibid., 22, 23, 21.
25 Ibid., 29.
26 "Notes from the Editor: The Sanctification of Pain," DM (Mar. 1940), 70.
27 "Obituary: Frances Elizabeth Field," DM (Mar. 1931), 96. Field was the daughter of the Reverend Augustus and Elizabeth (Pittman) Bayley and was married to the Reverend Canon George H. Field. She was sister-in-law to then-bishop of Newfoundland, the Right Reverend William White.
28 Ibid.
29 "In Memoriam: Eliza Amanda Greene," NC (Dec. 1964), 10. Likewise, "crippled" Mary Jackson of Cavendish "never murmured but offered her suffering to God." "Obituaries," NC (Mar. 1960), 4.
30 "Obituary: Sabina Rose Bridger," NC (Jan. 1968), 2.
31 Coady, "Customs and Stories Connected with Death," 30–1.
32 Reid, "Death: In the Anglican Tradition," 78. To "raft" was to "disturb or irritate" a person. DNE, 402.
33 Reid, "Death: In the Anglican Tradition," 78.
34 Erected "in memory of James Tilley, beloved husband of Patience Tilley" who died at age forty-nine in 1922. A similar verse was raised "in memory of John Frederick Fagan, beloved husband of Beliza Fagan" who died at age sixty-nine in 1955.
35 Raised for Linda Louise Peach, age two.
36 Abel, *Hearts of Wisdom*, 55.
37 H.G.P. [Henry George Peile], "A Meditation," DM (Oct. 1933), 351.
38 Ibid.
39 Bradbury, *Wife to Widow*, 178. *Book of Common Prayer* services for "Ministry to the Sick" included a range of options for priest and people in situations of serious or terminal illness. These moved in a continuum from prayers appropriate for clerical visitation to forms for hearing confession and granting absolution, administering communion, laying on of hands, and anointing with oil (Holy Unction).
40 Reid, "Death: In the Anglican Tradition," 79.
41 Tom Dawe likewise confirmed how "the priest or the clergyman would have been there for the last rites" at Long Pond deathbeds. Coady, "Customs and Stories Connected with Death," 29–30.
42 Chesley Andrews died of a heart attack at age forty in 1962 leaving her with three small children.

43 Headstone erected in memory of Edith Flora Searle, wife of Samuel Searle, who died in 1948 at age thirty-four; Headstone "erected by her husband" in memory of Mary Emma, beloved wife of Allan Fagan, who died in 1969 at age sixty-eight.

44 Heather D. Curtis, "Acting Faith: Practices of Religious Healing in Late-Nineteenth-Century Protestantism," in Maffly-Kipp, Schmidt, and Valeri, *Practicing Protestants*, 139, 157.

45 Orsi, *Between Heaven and Earth*, 214n69, 39–40.

46 Ulrich, *A Midwife's Tale*; Laurel Thatcher Ulrich, *Good Wives: Image and Reality in the Lives of Women in Northern New England, 1650–1750* (New York: Vintage Books, 1980); and Marilyn J. Westerkamp, *Women and Religion in Early America, 1600–1850: The Puritan and Evangelical Traditions* (New York: Routledge, 1999).

47 Abel, *Hearts of Wisdom*, 4.

48 Crellin, *Home Medicine;* and Barbara Rieti, *Making Witches: Newfoundland Traditions of Spells and Counterspells* (Montreal: McGill-Queen's University Press, 2008).

49 Crellin, *Home Medicine*, 109 for quotation.

50 Crellin, *Home Medicine*, 145. Crellin described how a wedding ring's blessed status was often mentioned by Newfoundlanders when describing its curative powers. Being made of gold was considered important for some, as was the need for the ring to belong to a mother or widow.

51 Edna described practising this charm herself "with the girls," adding that it always worked.

52 While Crellin reported other gestures associated with traditional healing using wedding rings, the Conception Bay women informants mentioned making the sign of the cross only, possibly due to the use of the phrase "religious cure" in the question posed.

53 "Nothing more than just the cross" was mentioned as a cure by Joan (Petten) Jefford.

54 Crellin, *Home Medicine*, 236.

55 "Uncle Jimmy" was a Roman Catholic, born in Harbour Main, a settlement at the head of Conception Bay, in 1849. In 1921 he and wife Margaret, a native of Kelligrews born in 1852, were living together at Riverdale, a settlement just east of Robert's home in Upper Gullies.

56 Wade Dawe, "Stories from George Roberts [of Upper Gullies]," MUNFLA 88–045.

57 Fannie Porter was Mildred's paternal aunt, and sister of local "half doctor" William Butler. Myra (Porter) Rideout noted how a "Mrs Perrin" in Long Pond healed her son of warts (likely midwife Eunice "Aunt Nicie" Perrin) and how local healers used different methods. One remedy for warts involved knots in yarn; this is interesting given connections between religion and textile work, and Myra stressed the wool "has got to be home spun" for the cure to work.

58 Brace, "Towards an Ethnography of Times," MUNFLA 86–314, 6–7; For faith healing among Newfoundland Pentecostals see Crellin, *Home Medicine*, 55.

59 "CEWA Diocesan Council," DM (Nov. 1930), 434–5; E.M. Tulk, "CEWA," DM (July 1938), 224; "The Diocesan Council, CEWA," DM (Jul. 1945), 280–1; E.M.T., "The Diocesan Council CEWA," DM (Jul.-Aug. 1949), 215–6; C.F. Hunt, "Biennial Meeting Diocesan Council CEWA," DM (Jan. 1954), 16–7; "Full of Good Works: 8000 CEWA Sisters in 200 Branches," NC (Apr. 1960), 1; and "CEWA's Progress Reviewed at Largely Attended Meeting," NC (Aug. 1963), 3.

60 In her work on Myra (Grimsley) Bennett, Linda Kealey identifies how the "working-class moral code of helping others," combined with an interest in social outreach associated with Anglican missionary activities, led Bennett towards a career in nursing. Seal Cove CEWA likewise combined helping impulse with church-based expectations. Linda Kealey, "On the Edge of Empire: The Working Life of Myra (Grimsley) Bennett," in Rutherdale, *Caregiving on the Periphery*, 92–3.

61 Kelligrews CEWA, *Minute Book*, 26 Apr. 1967, 3 May 1967.

62 In April 1944 at Seal Cove, for example, Ethel Morgan reported on the health of niece-in-law Phoebe Morgan, while Annie Dawe provided an update on daughter-in-law Victoria. Seal Cove CEWA, *Minute Book*, 11 Apr. 1944.

63 Long Pond CEWA, *Minute Book*, 19 Jul. 1922, 8 Apr. 1931, 11 Nov. 1942, 20 Jan. 1960, 18 Nov. 1943, 5 Mar. 1946.

64 Kelligrews CEWA, *Minute Book*, 14 Apr. 1966, 19 Apr. 1967, 23 Oct. 1968, 1 Nov. 1967; and *Census* 1945.

65 Foxtrap CEWA, *Minute Book*, 14 Jan. 1960, 8 Dec. 1960.

66 Ibid., 17 Nov. 1960, 8 Dec. 1960.

67 Long Pond Sewing Circle, *Minute Book*, 15 Jan. 1918.

68 Long Pond CEWA, *Minute Book*, 18 Mar. 1920, 24 Mar. 1920, 14 Apr. 1920, 11 May 1920, 2 Jun. 1920. No cause of Eason's death recorded; possibly Spanish Influenza.

69 Long Pond CEWA, *Minute Book*, 8 Dec. 1920.
70 Ibid., 17 Jan. 1940; visits on 21, 28 Feb. 1940.
71 Ibid., 17 Mar. 1948.
72 Ibid., 7 Jan. 1948.
73 Long Pond CEWA, *Minute Book*, 1 Feb. 1950.
74 Ibid.
75 Ibid., 3 May 1950.
76 Ibid., 10 May 1950; 1, 19 Nov. 1950; 20 May 1952; 1 Apr. 1953.
77 Ibid., 19, 26 Mar. 1958; 26 Nov. 1958; 4, 14 Jan. 1959; 4 Feb. 1959; 16 Jan. 1963; 24 Jan. 1964.
78 Ibid., 23 Jan. 1963.
79 Ibid., 6 Feb. 1963. Suggested by Irene Tilley and seconded by Mattie Jefford.
80 Selina Dowden may have been Louie Dowden's mother-in-law, at that time an eighty-year-old widowed head of household and, as the CEWA branch secretary noted, "the oldest member in our class." Seal Cove CEWA, *Minute Book*, 18 Dec. 1928, 22 Jan. 1929.
81 Ibid., 11 Dec. 1928, 8 Jan. 1929, 7 Oct. 1930.
82 In 1929, the women of Seal Cove agreed to send a dollar each to Nellie Morgan and Alice Anthony "who were in the hospital this summer." Seal Cove CEWA, *Minute Book*, 19 Nov. 1929.
83 Ibid., 4, 18 Mar. 1930; 3 May 1931.
84 Seal Cove CEWA, *Minute Book*, 28 Nov. 1933.
85 Ibid., 19 Jan. 1937.
86 Ibid., 11 Mar. 1947.
87 Ibid., 22 Apr. 1963.
88 Seal Cove CEWA, *Minute Book*, 21 May 1963.
89 Ibid., 12 Dec. 1933.
90 Ibid., 12 Mar. 1929, 25 Mar. 1930, 30 Jan. 1934.
91 Ibid., 6 Mar. 1939, 4 Apr. 1939, 26 Feb. 1940, 9 Apr. 1940.
92 Ibid., 9 Apr. 1940. Harvey's death at age eighty-one was noted in the 17 Apr. 1945 minutes.
93 Seal Cove CEWA, *Minute Book*, 6 Mar. 1945.
94 In March 1933, Betty Kennedy was reported sick, and when she attended a meeting after an almost two-year absence (during which no visits were held), "the President with the members gave her a hearty welcome." Kennedy remained ill, however, and on 12 February 1936, a CEWA meeting was held at her house. This was the only organized visit, despite the fact that Kennedy was reported sick for sometime

afterwards. Long Pond CEWA, *Minute Book*, 12 Mar. 1933, 23 Jan. 1935, 1 Apr. 1936, 25 Nov. 1936.

95 Seal Cove CEWA, *Minute Book*, 5 Apr. 1938.

96 Ibid., 14 Nov. 1938.

97 Seal Cove CEWA, *Minute Book*, 22 Jan. 1964.

98 Ibid., 12 Dec. 1945.

99 Ibid., 26 Feb. 1946.

100 Ibid., 5, 19 Nov. 1946.

101 Long Pond CEWA, *Minute Book*, 30 Mar. 1937. Secretary Annie Bishop wrote that Winnie Dawe "has entered the Sanitorium for treatment, it is our sincere hope that she will soon be restored to her usual health and be able to resume her duties again." As similar sentiment was expressed by the Long Pond president Annie Jefford on 21 January 1948 upon hearing that long-time treasurer Emma Jane Kennedy was "very sick."

102 See examples in Long Pond CEWA, *Minute Book*, 15 Apr. 1964, 6 May 1964.

103 Ibid., 7 Mar. 1963.

104 Seal Cove CEWA, *Minute Book*, 26 Nov. 1929, 27 Dec. 1929.

105 Ibid., 16 Dec. 1930.

106 Betsy Beattie, *Obligation and Opportunity: Single Maritime Women in Boston, 1870–1930* (Montreal: McGill-Queen's University Press, 2000).

107 Seal Cove CEWA, *Minute Book*, 11 Mar. 1930, 29 Dec. 1930. Dorothy "Dossie" Dowden was born in 1905, and Lizzie Butler in 1904, making them in their mid-twenties when they travelled to America for work. Interestingly, Lizzie and her family are listed as Salvation Army in the 1921 *Census*.

108 Seal Cove CEWA, *Minute Book*, 23 Dec. 1930.

109 Long Pond CEWA, *Minute Book*, 16 Dec. 1936. Louise Kennedy (born 1916) was twenty years old at the time.

110 Ibid., 16 Dec. 1936. On use of credit at Long Pond, see chapter 10 in this volume.

111 Ibid., 15 May 1963.

112 Long Pond CEWA, *Minute Book*, 18 Mar. 1965, 1 Apr. 1965.

113 Foxtrap CEWA, *Minute Book*, 25 Mar. 1960.

114 Ibid., 5 May 1960.

115 Likewise, the rector's request for an annual "donation of at least $20.00 from each branch towards Sunday School expenses" was proposed, but

failed to pass at Long Pond in 1961. Long Pond CEWA, *Minute Book*, 10 May 1961.

116 Seal Cove CEWA, *Minute Book*, 26 Nov. 1929. The tidal wave of 18 November 1929 affected 10,000 people living on the Burin Peninsula. Waves destroyed homes, fishing premises, and gear at an estimated cost of one million dollars. Twenty-seven people were killed. The South Coast Disaster Committee raised almost $257,000 in relief money and in-kind gifts. Over $87,000 of this total came from areas of Newfoundland outside St John's, of which the Seal Cove CEWA donation would have been a part. See Maura Hanrahan, *Tsunami: The Newfoundland Tidal Wave Disaster* (St John's: Flanker, 2004), 7, 224–5.

117 Gary L. Saunders, *Doctor Olds of Twillingate: Portrait of an American Surgeon in Newfoundland* (St John's: Breakwater, 1994), 144, 147.

118 Seal Cove CEWA, *Minute Book*, 27 Apr. 1943.

119 Seal Cove CEWA, *Minute Book*, 6 May 1943.

120 See chapters 10 and 11 in this volume for discussion of women's resistance to clerical authority at Seal Cove.

121 For a discussion of Newfoundland women and patriotic work during the Second World War, see Jennifer Flight, "'We Are All in the Front Line This Time': The Patriotic Association of the Women of Newfoundland during the Second World War" (MA report, Memorial University, 2007). Long Pond CEWA meetings where "sisters was knitting patriotic work" or "knitting for the W.P.A." included 12, 19, 30 Nov. 1941; 11 Dec. 1941; 21 Jan. 1942; 25 Mar. 1942; 1, 15 Apr. 1942; 13 Jan. 1943; 7 Apr. 1943; 10, 18 Nov. 1943; 9 Feb. 1944; 1 Nov. 1944.

122 Abel, *Hearts of Wisdom*, 119.

123 Patricia O'Brien, "Medicine," ENL, vol. 3, 499.

124 See chapter 1 in this volume.

Chapter Nine

1 For a Newfoundland example, see Bradbrook, "A Brief Account of the Work of the CEWA," 92–105, in which she strives to make women's contribution to the Anglican Church in Newfoundland visible and to find evidence of women's public, secular influence through church work.

2 In Canada, Linda Ambrose, Monda Halpern, and Margaret Kechnie on the Women's Institutes explore female organization and the

rural reform movement. While engaging questions of rural women's feminism, these works do not focus on the impact of religion on women's activities or worldview. See Linda Ambrose, *Women's Institutes in Canada: The First One Hundred Years, 1897–1997* (Ottawa: Federated Women's Institutes of Canada, 2000); Halpern, *And on That Farm He Had a Wife*; and Margaret Kechnie, *Organizing Rural Women: The Federated Women's Institutes of Ontario, 1897–1919* (Montreal: McGill-Queen's University Press, 2003).

3 Recent work by Clare Midgley has recovered the importance of Christianity in motivating and shaping the work of British female reformers. See "Women, Religion and Reform," in Morgan and deVries, *Women, Gender, and Religious Cultures*, 138–40.

4 For Atlantic Canadian studies of rural women's textile production, see Judith Rygiel, "Thread in Her Hands, Cash in Her Pockets: Women and Domestic Textile Production in 19th-century New Brunswick," *Acadiensis* 30 (2001): 56–70; Béatrice Craig and Judith Rygiel, "Femmes, marchés et production textile au Nouveau-Brunswick au cours du XIXe siècle," *Histoire & Mesure* 15, 1–2 (2000): 83–111; and Cynthia Wallace-Casey, "Providential Openings: The Women Weavers of Nineteenth-Century Queens County, New Brunswick," *Material History Review* 46 (1997): 29–44. Chad Montrie's work on the development of spiritual and theological perspectives on nature among women of rural backgrounds employed in industrial textile mills is unusual in its consideration of religious themes. See "'I Think Less of the Factory than of my Native Dell': Labor, Nature, and the Lowell 'Mill Girls,'" *Environmental History* 9, 2 (2004): 275–95.

5 Linda Cullum, "'A Woman's Place': The Work of Two Women's Voluntary Organizations in Newfoundland, 1934–41," in Carmelita McGrath, Barbara Neis, and Marilyn Porter, eds., *Their Lives and Times: Women in Newfoundland and Labrador: A Collage* (St John's: Killick, 1995), 94–5. In 1935 a Jubilee Guild branch was established at Upper Gullies. Ibid., 99.

6 Ibid., 103.

7 Ibid., 108. The Newfoundland Outport Nursing and Industrial Association was similarly organized and led by upper- and middle-class women of St John's. Ibid., 91.

8 Patricia O'Brien, "Nursing and Industrial Association, Newfoundland Outport (NONIA)," ENL, vol. 4, 136; and Ronald Rompkey, ed., *Jessie*

Luther at the Grenfell Mission (Montreal: McGill-Queen's University Press, 2001), xxxi–xxxii.

9 Rompkey, *Jessie Luther*, xxvi.

10 Sarah A. Gordon, *Make It Yourself: Home Sewing, Gender, and Culture, 1890–1930* (New York: Columbia University Press, 2007), x.

11 Ibid., 125–6, 129.

12 See chapter 2 in this volume for a more complete description of religious ritual in the CEWA.

13 Promey and Brisman, "Sensory Cultures," in Goff, *The Blackwell Companion to Religion in America*, 197–8.

14 Karen Buckenham, "Creativity and Spirituality: Two Threads of the Same Cloth," *Religion & Theology* 18 (2011): 56, 59.

15 Long Pond CEWA, *Minute Book*, 27 Mar. 1946.

16 Seal Cove CEWA, *Minute Book*, 18 Dec. 1928, 12 Feb. 1929.

17 Ibid., 8 Jan. 1929, 10 Dec. 1929.

18 Ibid., 18 Nov. 1930.

19 Seal Cove CEWA, *Minute Book*, 29 Dec. 1930, 3 Apr. 1934, 29 Dec. 1942, 11 Apr. 1944, 1 Apr. 1947.

20 Ibid., 4 Mar. 1942.

21 Ibid., 14 Apr. 1942.

22 For example, at the 1929 Christmas tea and sale, "tea and dance" made double the revenue of "goods and candy." Seal Cove CEWA, *Minute Book*, 9 Jan. 1934. For post-1960 food service, see chapter 10 in this volume.

23 Long Pond CEWA, *Minute Book*, 27 Jan. 1932, 9 Feb. 1932, 8 Mar. 1932.

24 Ibid., 18, 26 Apr. 1923.

25 Seal Cove CEWA, *Minute Book*, 13 Jan. 1931. Cutting and sewing aprons occupied the women for the following month and culminated in a tea and apron sale on 16 February 1931.

26 Ibid., 3, 10 Apr. 1934.

27 Seal Cove CEWA, *Minute Book*, 2 Jan. 1940, 11 Mar. 1941, 16 Feb. 1942, 24 Nov. 1942, 9 Feb. 1943, 24 Nov. 1943, 16 Feb 1944. For pillowcases and cloths, see 21 Nov. 1944, 20 Feb. 1945, 3 May 1962, 4 Feb. 1963. Purchases of wool noted 20 Nov. 1945, 19 Mar. 1946, 9 Dec. 1947, 4 Nov. 1963.

28 Seal Cove CEWA, *Minute Book*, 5 Nov. 1946. Women sold the machine for ten dollars.

29 Ibid., 3 May 1962, 4 Feb. 1963, 14 May 1963, 11 Nov. 63, 29 Jan 1964, 7 Oct. 1964.

30 Long Pond CEWA, *Minute Book*, 11 Mar. 1931, 7, 11 Oct. 1931, 9 Feb. 1932, 8 Mar. 1932.

31 Ibid., 8 Mar. 1932.

32 In 1934 and 1935, despite difficult economic times, Long Pond CEWA women donated twenty-five pairs of mitts and eight pairs of socks to the Church of England Orphanage in St John's, see *Minute Book* entries of 21 Feb. 1934; 28 Feb. 1935. Meetings where "sisters was knitting patriotic work" or "knitting for the W.P.A. [Newfoundland Women's Patriotic Association]" included 12, 19, 30 Nov. 1941; 11 Dec. 1941; 21 Jan. 1942; 25 Mar. 1942; 1, 15 Apr. 1942; 13 Jan. 1943; 7 Apr. 1943; 10, 18 Nov. 1943; 9 Feb. 1944; 1 Nov. 1944. For a discussion of Newfoundland women and patriotic work, see Flight, "We Are All in the Front Line This Time."

33 Gordon, *Make It Yourself*, 125–6.

34 This is partly personal observation, based on activities of my female kin. During the 1970s, the vocational school at Seal Cove offered home sewing night classes, demonstrating the continuing popularity of sewing clothing at home within the study area. Furthermore, Gordon notes the links between home sewing, women's creativity, and ethnic identity in *Make It Yourself*, 129. The continued importance of home sewing for Newfoundland women through the twentieth century is a topic for further study.

35 See Long Pond CEWA, *Minute Book*, 26 Mar. 1941: "Sister Alice Kennedy returned cloth she had put lace on. Sister Eliza Jane Morgan returned pillow cases she had worked. Sister Lenie Perrin returned a cloth."

36 *Census of Newfoundland*, 1935, 1945.

37 Long Pond CEWA, *Minute Book*, 24 Apr. 1940.

38 Ibid., 14 Oct. 1931.

39 Ibid., 6 Jun. 1923, 5 Dec. 1923, 23 Jan. 1924, 2 Apr. 1924, 29 Apr. 1925.

40 Ibid., 2 Feb. 1943, 9 Feb. 1944, 29 Mar. 1944, 30 Mar. 1949.

41 Ibid., 24 Nov. 1937.

42 Association secretaries' use of "Miss" or "Sister" reflected women's understanding of differing social status: "Miss" indicated a school teacher and "Sister" everyone else.

43 Long Pond CEWA, *Minute Book*, 16 Dec. 1931; 27 Jan. 1932; 8 Mar. 1932; 21 Feb. 1934; 28 Feb. 1935; 4 Dec. 1935; 22 Jan. 1936; 19 Feb. 1936; 4, 18, 25 Mar. 1936; 6 May 1936; 16 Apr. 1937; 24 Nov. 1937; 16 Feb. 1938; 24 Apr. 1940.

44 Ibid., 28 Apr. 1943.

45 Ibid., 5, 12 May 1943; and *Census of Newfoundland*, 1945.

46 Credit sales were mentioned occasionally at Seal Cove, such as on 5 December 1933 when Gladys Butler "sent along ninety cents for a dress she owed for," but do not seem to have been practised to the extent they were at Long Pond. The Seal Cove branch could be a creditor: on 17 December 1929 the women paid branch president Susie Lear the five dollars she "loaned us to buy material for our class."

47 Cadigan, *Newfoundland and Labrador*, 169, 176. For women as creditors in a rural setting, see Charles F. Heller Jr and John T. Houdek, "Women Lenders as Sources of Land Credit in Nineteenth-Century Michigan," *Journal of Interdisciplinary History* 35 (2004): 37–67.

48 Long Pond CEWA, *Minute Book*, 2 Dec. 1919 noted that "a number of sisters owes for badges," referring to the CEWA insignia members wore. Women sold ten-cent teas to each other during Lent, and the total taken in at meetings always showed a shortfall, such as on 4 March 1931, when sixteen attended but only $1.30 was taken in for tea. The price was put down to five cents in 1933, but credit was still available. On 22 March 1933, five women paid for their tea, "leaving six more to pay at next meeting." On 15 December 1937 there was a note that a "couple of sisters owe for tea"; and on 9 November 1938: "Miss Trickett owes 35 cents for seven cups of tea which she had got from the class."

49 Ibid., 2 May 1941.

50 Ibid., 9 May 1941.

51 Whiteley, *Marys, Marthas*, 104.

52 Morgan, "Activist Anglicans and Rectors' Wives," in Cullum and Porter, *Creating this Place*, 37–8, 41–2.

53 Long Pond CEWA, *Minute Book*, 22 Jan. 1918.

54 For discussion of the Women's Patriotic Association, see Gail Denise Warren, "Voluntarism and Patriotism: Newfoundland Women's War Work during the First World War" (MA report, Memorial University, 2005). For the Halifax Explosion, see John Reid, *Nova Scotia: A Pocket History* (Halifax: Fernwood, 2009), 121.

55 Long Pond Women's Sewing Class, *Minute Book*, 2 Aug. 1905, 5 Oct. 1905.

56 E.K.H. Caldwell and Emily Caldwell to Long Pond Sewing Class, October 1913. The letter was preserved as a loose item in Long Pond Women's Sewing Class, *Minute Book [1905–1916]*.

57 Long Pond CEWA, *Minute Book*, 28 Jan. 1919, 4 Feb. 1919.

58 Ibid., 13 Jan. 1937.

59 Ibid., 1 Nov. 1944.

60 For local condemnation of gambling by Anglican Church leadership, see H.S.H., "Our Play – Who Pays for It?" DM (Aug. 1930), 292; and Leslie Pike, "Notes from the Editor," DM (Oct. 1930), 393, in which he wrote of "the appalling length to which the gambling craze has gone in this country." In 1946, future bishop John Meaden, then-editor of *Diocesan Magazine*, reminded readers of the 1924 Synod of Newfoundland resolution against church fundraising using ticket sales, and suggested this applied to bingo and other "games of chance" (including grab-bags for children). "Notes from the Editor," DM (Jul.–Aug. 1946), 218–22.

61 Long Pond CEWA, *Minute Book*, 24 Nov. 1920.

62 Ibid., 25 Jan. 1933; 1, 8 Feb. 1933.

63 Ibid., 8, 22 Feb. 1933; 2 Mar. 1933.

64 Long Pond CEWA, *Minute Book*, 22 Mar. 1934, 8 Nov. 1934. For description of this meeting, see E.M. Tulk, "The Diocesan Council of the CEWA," DM (July 1934), 208. Bringing a piece of textile work into St John's to sell would have been part of some local women's household economic experience, as Selina (Dawe) Porter of Long Pond noted in a 1984 interview. See Cooper, "Towards and Ethnography of Times," MUNFLA 85–131.

65 Seal Cove CEWA, *Minute Book*, 7 Jan. 1930, 6 May 1930, 7 Oct. 1930, 4 Nov. 1930.

66 Seal Cove CEWA, *Minute Book*, 4 Nov. 1930. The Reverend Henry V. Whitehouse was an English cleric who came to Newfoundland in 1901 and served eight parishes and missions before he returned to England in 1936.

67 Ibid., 2 Dec. 1930.

68 Women revived ticket sales at Long Pond at the end of the 1940s and at Seal Cove somewhat earlier. At Long Pond, see tickets on cushions and bedspread in minute book entry of 12 March 1947; on tea cloth and bedspread, 21 January 1948.

69 Seal Cove CEWA, *Minute Book*, 21 Jan. 1930.

70 Ibid., 4 Mar. 1930

71 "Call cannon" was likely the meal "colcannon": "a mixture or hash of various vegetables, and sometimes meat, eaten on Hallowe'en" and especially associated with Newfoundlanders of Irish heritage. In

nineteenth-century St John's, Hallowe'en was known as "Colcannon night." DNE, 108.

72 Seal Cove CEWA, *Minute Book*, 28 Jan. 1942; 4, 16 Feb. 1942; 3 Mar. 1942.

73 Ibid., 19 Nov. 1942; 1, 15 Dec. 1942; 19 Jan. 1943.

74 Ibid., 2, 9, 16, 23 Feb. 1943; 2 Mar. 1943.

75 Seal Cove CEWA, *Minute Book*, 2, 24, 30 Nov. 1943; 14 Dec. 1943.

76 Ibid., 7, 21 Nov. 1944; 5, 12, 20 Dec. 1944.

77 Ibid., 16, 22, 29 Feb. 1944; 7, 14 Mar. 1944; 4, 11 Apr. 1944.

78 Seal Cove CEWA, *Minute Book*, 30 Oct. 1945; 6, 13, 20 Nov. 1945; 4, 12, 18, 26 Dec. 1945.

79 Ibid., 29 Mar. 1943, 27 Mar. 1945.

80 Whiteley, *Marys, Marthas*, 110.

81 Ruth Taylor and Lucy Bolton, "W.A. Sets out on New Paths," *Canadian Churchman* (Nov. 1964), 13. Included with this article was a photo of women working at a quilt frame, captioned: "Quilting is one of the traditional activities of the W.A. which may be scrutinized during its period of transition."

82 For Diocesan-level leadership of reorganization efforts, see "The Executive Committee of the Women's Auxiliary," NC (Sept. 1961), 5. See also "Welcome A.C.W.A.: Inaugural Meeting Marks New Era of Women's Work in the Diocese," NC (Oct. 1969), 1.

83 Long Pond AWCA, *Minute Book*, 23 Feb. 1967; 9, 16 Mar. 1967; 11, 25 Oct. 1967; 6 Dec. 1967.

84 Initial vocational subjects at Seal Cove were: mechanics, woodworking, electronics, drafting, agricultural science, typing, shorthand, beauty culture, and three streams of home economics (cooking and catering, home management, and sewing and crafts). Andrews, *Post-Confederation Developments*, 345.

85 Seal Cove CEWA, *Minute Book*, 23 Dec. 1930, 2 May 1934.

86 Long Pond CEWA, *Minute Book*, 13 Dec. 1944.

87 Buckenham, "Creativity and Spirituality," 59.

Chapter Ten

1 *All Saints' Anglican Church, Foxtrap*, n.p. For class character and gender dynamics of St Thomas's, see Morgan, "Activist Anglicans and Rector's Wives," in Cullum and Porter, *Creating This Place*, 25–45.

2 Tye, *Baking as Biography*, 32–4. Women submitted recipes to be compiled, printed, bound, and sold as cookbooks (mainly locally, and

to other women) to make money. An Atlantic Canadian example, recently studied by Diane Tye, is *Tested Sweet Recipes,* produced by a United Church women's association in Parrsboro, Nova Scotia, around 1959. Tye, *Baking as Biography*, 110.

3 Tye, *Baking as Biography*, 120, 34.

4 Long Pond CEWA, *Minute Book*, 5 May 1965, 14 Jun. 1965.

5 Seal Cove CEWA, *Minute Book*, 12 Jun. 1965.

6 Long Pond CEWA, *Minute Book*, 14 Jun. 1965.

7 Kelligrews CEWA, *Minute Book*, 11 Jun. 1965.

8 This undated cookbook has been assigned the date of 1970 by cataloguers at the Centre for Newfoundland Studies, Memorial University of Newfoundland. Having read St Alban's ACWA minutes up to and including 1970, and seeing no mention of the cookbook project, I suspect a later production date. Full inquiry into the production and contents of *Home Cooking Secrets of Kelligrews* is a planned future research project.

9 Tye, *Baking as Biography*, 119, 126; and *Home Cooking Secrets*, 17–42.

10 Tye, *Baking as Biography*, 120, 126.

11 *Home Cooking Secrets*, 9–15, 44–6. The other cod recipes were "Fish in Batter" and "Dressed Cod Fillets."

12 Anne Bower cited by Tye, *Baking as Biography*, 111.

13 Franca Iacovetta and Valerie J. Korinek, "Jell-O Salads, One-Stop Shopping, and Maria the Homemaker: The Gender Politics of Food," in Marlene Epp, Franca Iacovetta, and Frances Swyripa, eds., *Sisters or Strangers: Immigrant, Ethnic and Racialized Women in Canadian History* (Toronto: University of Toronto Press, 2004), 190.

14 For more information on this campaign, see Richard Gribble, "Patrick Peyton, C.S.C., and the International Rosary Crusade, 1948–1959," *U.S. Catholic Historian* 33, 4 (Fall 2015), 53–78.

15 Berger, *Fragments of Real Presence*, 9–10.

16 See chapter 9 in this volume.

17 Porter, "Mrs Selina Porter," MUNFLA 81–219. Selina's interview included information on supper practices and on how foods for "pot day" (corned beef and cabbage), "fish day," "meat day," and "pea soup day" would be prepared.

18 Along with Enid (Porter) Haines, fish on Friday as "religious practice around food" noted by Edna (Rideout) Warford, Gordon Morgan, and Beulah (Porter) Morgan (raised Pentecostal).

19 Porter, "Mrs Selina Porter," 5.

20 Selina's recollection of Sunday meals is described in chapter 4 in this volume.

21 This was similar to the morning "mug up" of tea, bread, or bun (biscuit), eaten with a bit of leftover fish.

22 Porter, "Mrs Selina Porter," 2, 5, 7–8. Clarence Morgan of Upper Gullies (born 1917) described a typical breakfast as "gallon of eggs, ham you cured yourself, home-made bread." Morgan, "Oral Narratives," MUNFLA 84–019.

23 Omohundro, *Rough Food*, 182–5.

24 Porter, "Mrs Selina Porter," 2, 5, 7–8. For March as hungry month, see Murray, *More than Fifty Percent*, 120. For participation in the spring seal hunt, see Rodney Charles Dowden, "The Adventures of a Conception Bayman at the Annual Newfoundland Seal Hunt during the Early 20th Century," MUNFLA 83–259. This was an interview with Will Dowden, born 26 September 1902. His spouse, Bessie Dowden, was an active member of Seal Cove CEWA. So was Will's mother, Louisa "Louie" (Hynes) Dowden, who was born at Indian Islands on the northeast coast of Newfoundland, and moved to Seal Cove after her marriage to Eli Dowden. Dowden, "Adventures of a Conception Bayman," MUNFLA 83–259.

25 See chapter 2 in this volume for discussion of grace before meals as an everyday family prayer ritual.

26 Omohundro, *Rough Food*, 221. For Anglican presence in the area, see ibid., 30, 196.

27 This included women who grew up on the south and west coasts of the island.

28 Described by Mary (Petten) Porter, Enid (Porter) Haines, Marjorie (Bullen) Morgan, and Pat (Morgan) Woolgar.

29 Tye, "Bread for the Road," 176.

30 Ibid., 180.

31 Ibid., 181–2. For a description of traditional bread making, see Murray, *More than Fifty Percent*, 120–2.

32 Murray, *More than Fifty Percent*, 122. Informant Marjorie (Bullen) Morgan (born 1938) recalled making bread when she was too small to reach the kitchen table and placing the mixing bowl on the seat of a kitchen chair instead.

33 Tye, "Bread for the Road," 177–8.

34 Tye, *Baking as Biography*, 130–2. For language of "usual cup of tea," Long Pond CEWA, *Minute Book*, 12 Oct. 1938, 9 Nov. 1938, 15 Feb. 1939.

35 Tye, *Baking as Biography*, 130–2.
36 Ibid., 131.
37 Whiteley, *Marys, Marthas*, 108; and Tye, *Baking as Biography*, 130.
38 Seal Cove CEWA, *Minute Book*, 19, 25 Feb. 1929; 4, 12 Mar. 1929; 10 Dec. 1929; 4 Feb. 1930; 15 Apr. 1930; 20, 27 Jan. 1931; 14 Nov. 1933; 13 Mar. 1934.
39 Ibid., 11 Apr. 1933.
40 Ibid., 28 Nov. 1933.
41 Ibid., 6 Feb. 1934, 2 May 1934.
42 Ibid., 4 Mar. 1930.
43 Ibid., 16, 29 Apr. 1929; 18 Mar. 1930.
44 Ibid., 10 Dec. 1929, 25 Mar. 1930.
45 This five-dollar payment was expected to be made to the parish in cash, prescribed by the CEWA's diocesan council. On 27 January 1932 branch secretary Lily Greenslade noted that the serving of tea would start at the next meeting, with every member expected to take a turn providing food.
46 When few members attended the meeting of 16 March 1932 (Easter Day was 27 March), Lily Greenslade recorded a conundrum: "all the sisters that was to the meeting had their turn serving teas so it was undecided who would serve … next meeting."
47 Long Pond CEWA, *Minute Book*, 22, 29 Mar. 1933; 5 Apr. 1933.
48 Ibid., 7 Mar. 1934.
49 Ibid., 16, 23 Jan. 1935; 5, 11 May 1937; 26 Apr. 1939.
50 Ibid., 12 Oct. 1938, 9 Nov. 1938, 15 Feb. 1939.
51 Ibid., 9, 16 Nov. 1938.
52 Ibid., 23 Jan. 1943.
53 Ibid., 4 Dec. 1946. There was a similar report for 11 Dec. 1946.
54 Ibid., 29 Jan 1947; other examples on 26 Oct. 1949, 29 Nov. 1950, 9 May 1951, 27 Feb. 1952.
55 Tye, *Baking as Biography*, 6, 74; Seal Cove CEWA, *Minute Book*, 3 Mar. 1937, 6 Mar. 1939, 4 Apr. 1939, 4 Feb. 1942, 22 Dec. 1943, 6 Mar. 1945; and Long Pond CEWA, *Minute Book*, 29 Nov. 1939.
56 Porter, "Mrs Selina Porter," 8, 14–15.
57 For construction of the ideal thin female body type in the twentieth century, see Marianne Parsons, "Fat Phobia and the Politics of Gender," in Les Samuelson and Wayne Antony, eds., *Power and Resistance: Critical Thinking about Canadian Social Issues*, 5th ed. (Halifax: Fernwood, 2012), 199–201.

58 Long Pond CEWA, *Minute Book*, 24 Apr. 1957.

59 Long Pond CEWA, *Minute Book*, 3 Dec. 1958. The Baird's kept cattle, so likely Vera scalded the "real cream" herself.

60 Long Pond CEWA, *Minute Book*, 11 Feb. 1942, 6 May 1942, 4 Nov. 1942, 29 Jan. 1943, 3 Feb. 1943.

61 Seal Cove CEWA, *Minute Book*, 21 Feb. 1939; see Lizzie Dawe and Ethel Lear doing the same.

62 Pam Taylor, "Past Traditions of Christmas [in Foxtrap]," MUNFLA 91–440, 22.

63 Seal Cove CEWA, *Minute Book*, 18 Nov. 1930.

64 Long Pond CEWA, *Minute Book*, 9 May 1957. The forty-year members were Elizabeth Greenslade, Elizabeth Tilley, Harriet May Petten, Elfreda Greenslade, Sarah Kennedy, and Caroline Kennedy.

65 See Noël, *Family and Community Life*, 69, for growing Christmas consumerism in mid-1900s rural Ontario.

66 Long Pond CEWA, *Minute Book*, 18 Dec. 1963; 1, 22 Dec. 1965.

67 At Seal Cove, "twelve tins of meat" were bought for the 1942 Christmas tea and "a dozen loaves of bread" purchased for the 1943 Easter sale. Seal Cove CEWA, *Minute Book*, 4 Jan. 1943, 16 Mar. 1943; bread bought for Christmas tea, 2 Jan. 1945. In November 1942, the women of Long Pond bought "loaves" and canned "corned meat" for a tea and bingo fundraiser. Similarly, when asked for help towards the parish's St George's Day tea in 1946, the sisters agreed to buy and donate "one dozen loaves of bread and half-dozen tins of fruit." Long Pond CEWA, *Minute Book*, 18 Nov. 1942, 9 Dec. 1942, 17 Apr. 1946.

68 Omohundro, *Rough Food*, 220–1.

69 Long Pond CEWA, *Minute Book*, 7 Mar. 1945. On 8 April 1952, "some of the Sisters … went to the shop and got some food, after which they prepared and served a lovely cup of tea." Likewise, on 19 November 1952, "as no one provided for a cup of tea a collection was now taken and Sisters Olive Jefford and Selina Perrin bought some food." On 8 October 1958, "our Worthy President asked two sisters … to go to the store and get something for a lunch" while "other sisters filled the kettles," and again on 15 October two members "did the shopping for our lunch" while two others "cleared up."

70 Whiteley, *Marys, Marthas*, 109, 112–13.

71 The place of the soup supper in rural Newfoundland community life is reflected in such literary and musical works as Ray Guy, *That Far*

Greater Bay (St John's: Flanker Press, 2011 [1977]); and Anita Best, "The Soup Supper in Clattice Harbour," on *Crosshanded*, produced by Pamela Morgan (Topsail, NL: Amber Music, 1997).

72 Porter, "Mrs Selina Porter," 11, 14–15.

73 Taylor, "Past Traditions of Christmas [in Fox Trap]," 18.

74 Marge (Saunders) Dawe described how Orange wives "worked like dogs" and men "took all the credit." The expectation among male members of the Orange Order that their wives would prepare and serve food at Orange socials was noted in other jurisdictions. See MacRaild, *Faith, Fraternity and Fighting*, 99.

75 "Considered the oldest continuing sports event in North America, the annual St John's Regatta is traditionally held the first Wednesday in August on Quidi Vidi Lake." ENL, vol. 4, 549. St Peter's Church usually held its annual Garden Party on Regatta Day, a civic holiday in St John's, in hopes of attracting visitors from the city who travelled to the area on special holiday excursion trains.

76 Marks, *Revivals and Roller Rinks*, 78–9.

77 Omohundro defined "times" in northern Newfoundland as "music and food parties," and this description held true for Conception Bay. While women's roles in organizing times and using them as church fundraisers was not recognized in his work, women's leadership and participation, from a social if not religious perspective, has been described by Hilda Chaulk Murray in her work on Elliston, Trinity Bay. Omohundro, *Rough Food*, 196; and Murray, *More than Fifty Percent*, 142–3.

78 Seal Cove CEWA, *Minute Book*: Christmas tea and sale, 28, 31 Dec. 1928; 27, 30 Dec. 1929; "Getting up a concert," 31 Dec. 1930; hiring fiddlers, 25 Nov. 1930, 23 Dec. 1930, 26 Dec. 1938, 10 Jan. 1939, 22 Dec 1943, 2 Jan. 1945, 7 Jan. 1947. Easter tea and sale: 2 Apr. 1929, 15 Apr. 1930, 6 Apr. 1937, 2 Apr. 1940, 8 Apr 1941, 24 Mar. 1942. Fiddler hired for Easter sale: 17 Apr. 1945, 30 Apr. 1946.

79 Noël, *Family and Community Life*, 191–2. CEWA minute books suggest some hiring of local bands, such as "Ray Tilley's group" in the late 1950s to replace the "fiddler" of the 1920s to 1940s.

80 This referred to varieties of rich fruit cake traditionally offered to visitors in Conception Bay homes during the Christmas season. Eating fruitcake, along with rum or "swanky" (syrup), especially associated with the mummering tradition, is described for Conception Bay South in Taylor, "Past Traditions of Christmas," 22; and Reid, "Calendar Customs [in Foxtrap]," MUNFLA 73–99D, 22.

81 Porter, "Mrs Selina Porter," 11–12. Porter noted how killing an animal at Christmas and "go around and sell 'em door to door" was a common practice.

82 Taylor, "Past Traditions at Christmas," 9–12. She describes a typical Christmas dinner as salt meat, cabbage, turnip, carrot, parsnip, bottled beets, and potatoes, with a large dumpling (duff) cooked on top of the salt meat and cabbage, served with a roasted chicken "fattened up over the summer." Françoise Noël also describes special foods at Christmas, with working-class Italian family celebrations involving salt fish and sweet foods. Noël, *Family and Community Life in Northeastern Ontario*, 69.

83 Brace, "Towards an Ethnography of 'Times': Long Pond," MUNFLA 86–314, 22.

84 Ibid.

85 Ibid., 20–4; Glenda Cooper, "Towards an Ethnography of Times: Newfoundland Party Traditions, Past and Present, in the Community of Long Pond, Conception Bay," MUNFLA 85–131.

86 Brace, "Towards an Ethnography of 'Times': Long Pond," 20–4; and Reid, "Calendar Customs [in Foxtrap]," 30.

87 Edwina Shea, "Towards an Ethnography of Times: Newfoundland Party Traditions, Past and Present, the Community of Kelligrews, Conception Bay," MUNFLA 84–134.

88 Cooper, "Towards an Ethnography of Times," MUNFLA 85–131; and Taylor, "Past Traditions of Christmas [in Fox Trap]," 22.

89 Seal Cove CEWA, *Minute Book*, 10 Apr. 1934.

90 Ibid., 18 Apr. 1934.

91 Conflict between women and clergy over ticket sales on textiles is discussed in chapter 10 in this volume.

92 During 1940s, ticket sales were a regular part of Seal Cove CEWA teas. By the 1960s, the women ran regular card games, but see the first mention of this fundraising method in 1951. Seal Cove CEWA, *Account Book*. For card games, Seal Cove CEWA, *Minute Book*, 18 Feb. 1963, 17 Sept. 1963, 16 Oct. 1963, 17 Dec. 1964.

93 Seal Cove CEWA, *Minute Book*, 27 Jan. 1965.

94 Foxtrap CEWA, *Minute Book*, 4 May 1961. Bingo continued to be played at meetings; see examples on 11 May 1961 and 5 Oct. 1961. On 12 October 1961, the rector visited Foxtrap CEWA to ask the women to sew junior choir gowns, bringing with him fabric and patterns. As soon as he left, they played bingo.

95 Foxtrap CEWA, *Minute Book*, 14 Jan. 1960.

96 Ibid., 15 Feb. 1961. Anticipating more expenses, Foxtrap branch secretary Adella Jones noted: "The pulpit and Altar are already ordered."

97 Kelligrews CEWA/ACW, *Account Book and Roll Book, [1963–81]*; Foxtrap CEWA, *Minute Book*, 11 Jan. 1962, see total cost was $900; Foxtrap CEWA, *Account Book*, see donation of forty dollars to rectory drapes in 1963, and the same given by Seal Cove branch (21 Jan. 1963). Long Pond CEWA, *Minute Book*, 10 Feb. 1965, see $120 towards new rectory.

98 Long Pond CEWA, *Minute Book*, 4 Oct. 1967.

99 Morgan, "Activist Anglicans and Rectors' Wives," in Cullum and Porter, *Creating This Place*, 37–8, 4–12.

100 Cook, "Women in the Anglican Church of Canada," in *EWRNA*, 279–80.

101 Long Pond CEWA, *Minute Book*, 6 Dec. 1950.

102 Long Pond CEWA, *Minute Book*, 12 Oct. 1955, 23 Nov. 1955.

103 Ibid., 10 Feb. 1960.

104 Ibid., 9 Nov. 1960, 19 Apr. 1961.

105 Long Pond CEWA, *Minute Book*, 28 Jan. 1959, 17 Nov. 1960. The branch made over $200 on take out teas in 1963. Ibid., 29 Nov. 1963.

106 Seal Cove CEWA, *Minute Book*, 1, 22 Oct. 1962; Seal Cove CEWA, *Account Book [1948–69]*.

107 Seal Cove CEWA, *Minute Book*, 29 Jan. 1964; Seal Cove CEWA, *Account Book [1948–69]*.

108 Omohundro, *Rough Food*, 196–7.

109 Kelligrews CEWA, *Minute Book*, 13, 20 Jan. 1965. On 29 January 1965, Tilley reported on "the new venture" of "catering for the Kiwanis Charter Night," and noted how it was "apparently quite successful." They took on this again in 1968. Ibid., 10, 17 Jan. 1968.

110 Kelligrews CEWA, *Minute Book*, 11 May 1966, 29 June 1966. In other years, the Foxtrap CEWA catered the high school graduation. See Foxtrap CEWA, *Minute Book*, "Annual Report Jan–Dec 1965," 13 Jan. 1966.

111 Long Pond CEWA, *Minute Book*, 12 June 1967, 29 Nov 1967. While turkey was paid for from class funds, as in Kelligrews, "sisters were asked to bring along cookies, salads, etc." In addition, each woman was asked to donate one dollar towards the purchase of fruit, tea, sugar, milk, "and other things" needed for the evening. Income was $184.50.

112 Altar Guild of All Saints' Church, Foxtrap, CB, *Minute Book [1959–65]*, 8 Nov. 1963. The Altar Guild established by the Reverend Mark Genge likewise promoted domestic skills as key to the maintenance and expression of women's spirituality. As "housekeepers of the church,"

Altar Guild members were responsible for cleaning the chancel and nave carpets, laundering church linens, and "setting the Lord's table" prior to Sunday services. Providing and arranging church flowers were important parts of Altar Guild work, as was fundraising. Like the CEWA, in 1960 women of Foxtrap Altar Guild were introduced to the take-out turkey dinner, putting out over 300 meals in February of that year, and to catering for outside groups. In May 1960, the women served dinner to one hundred guests at a Health Education and Rehabilitation Institute meeting held in the Regional High School. Ibid., 12 Feb. 1960, 13 May 1960.

113 Tye, *Baking as Biography*, 140.

Conclusion

1 deVries, "More than Paradoxes to Offer," in Morgan and deVries, *Women, Gender and Religious*, 188–9.

2 Judith Young, "'Monthly' Nurses, 'Sick' Nurses, and Midwives: Working-Class Caregivers in Toronto, 1830–91," in Rutherdale, *Caregiving on the Periphery*, 52.

3 There appeared to be less concern about congregations becoming women-dominated in local discourse, a trend often associated with "feminization of religion."

4 For post-confederation social, cultural, and economic change, see Miriam Wright, *A Fishery for Modern Times: The State and the Industrialization of the Newfoundland Fishery, 1934–1968* (Don Mills: Oxford University Press, 2001); Cadigan, *Newfoundland and Labrador, A History*, 241; and Robert Mellin, *Newfoundland Modern: Architecture in the Smallwood Years, 1949–1972* (Montreal: McGill-Queen's University Press, 2011).

5 Teresa Berger, *Fragments of Real Presence: Liturgical Traditions in the Hands of Women* (New York: Crossroad Publishing, 2005), 2, 4. Berger's understanding of liturgy includes "a wealth of popular devotions" practised by women, a perspective which informed this research.

6 Teresa Berger, "Feminist Ritual Practice," in Mary McClintock Fulkerson and Sheila Briggs, eds., *The Oxford Handbook of Feminist Theology* (New York: Oxford University Press, 2012), 542.

Index